The War Diary of
Johanna Brandt

By the same author:

A decisive clash? A short history of Black protest politics in South Africa, 1875–1976. 1988.

Discover the Voortrekker Monument. 2001.

The War reporter. The Anglo-Boer War through the eyes of the Burghers. 2004.

The War Diary of

Johanna Brandt

Aan my liewe sus Hester
— met hartlike dank vir
jare se ondersteuning,
aanmoediging en liefde
van jou kleinboet
Jackie Grobler
24-2-2008

Edited by Jackie Grobler

Protea Book House
Pretoria
2007

© 2007 Jackie Grobler
First edition, first impression in 2007 by Protea Book House
PO Box 35110, Menlopark, 0102
1067 Burnett Street, Hatfield, Pretoria
8 Minni Street, Clydesdale, Pretoria
protea@intekom.co.za
www.proteaboekhuis.co.za
Editor: Karen Horn
Cover design: Discover Design & Photography, Pretoria
Cover image: Surgeon Major W. Beevor from *With the Central Column in South Africa. From Belmont to Komatipoort 1899–1901.*
Set in Baskerville Old Face on 11 pt by Discover Design & Photography, Pretoria
Printed and bound by Interpak Books, Pietermaritzburg

ISBN 978-1-86919-164-1

Protea Book House: We make history.

Johanna in 1898

Contents

Biographical review

Johanna van Warmelo was born on 18 November 1876 in Heidelberg, a small town in the southeast of the South African Republic – today in the Gauteng Province in South Africa. She was the fourth child of Nicolaas Jacobus van Warmelo and his second wife, Maria Magdalena Elizabeth Maré. The family into which she was born had a major impact on her life. Both her parents were well educated, which ensured an atmosphere in her home that stimulated her sharp intelligence. Her father came from the Netherlands and this ensured a link between Johanna and that European country that significantly influenced her activities and her outlook on life, which was certainly not insular but mirrored a global worldview. Her mother came from a family of leading *Afrikaner* pioneers of the South African Republic, which firmly established a positive attitude toward *Afrikaner* traditions and patriotism in Johanna. Both her parents were good musicians – her father being an able pianist and lover of classical music and her mother a church organist. She inherited their musical talent and often writes in her diary about singing and playing classical music on the piano.[1]

The Reverend N.J. van Warmelo

Johanna's father, Nicolaas Jacobus van Warmelo, was born in Gouda in the Netherlands on 8 September 1835. He grew up in a parsonage, as his father was a minister in the Dutch Reformed Church. Indeed, van Warmelo's father himself descended from a long line of theologians. Nicolaas van Warmelo enrolled as a student in theology at the University of Leiden in 1853. Even though his teachers were reputed to be radical in their theological views, he turned out to be an orthodox student, rather conservative in his

[1]   F.G.M. du Toit, Brandt, Johanna, in *DSAB IV*, p 55; M.E. van der Merwe, *Johanna Brandt en die kritieke jare in Transvaal, 1899–1908* (Unpublished MA dissertation, University of Pretoria, Pretoria, 1989), p 1; A.D. Pont, *Nicolaas Jacobus van Warmelo 1835–1892*, p 34.

theological standpoints. After completing his studies in 1858, he was accepted as a minister in the Dutch Reformed Church. However, due to an over-supply of ministers in the Netherlands at that time, he failed to find a congregation. Under the influence of one of his former teachers, Dr J.W.G. van Oordt, who had also been a teacher in South Africa, Van Warmelo eventually decided to attempt to find a congregation in the Cape Colony. Consequently, he travelled to Cape Town in 1862. However, due to the anti-Dutch sentiments of leading members of the Scottish-dominated synod of the Cape Dutch Reformed Church, his acceptance as a minister of the Dutch Reformed Church of the Cape Colony was held back. Since he was eager to start working in a congregation as soon as possible, he accepted an invitation to become the minister of the Soutpansberg congregation of the Dutch Reformed Church in the

Mrs Maria van Warmelo

South African Republic.[2] That church was known in Dutch as the *Nederduitsch Hervormde Kerk* and was not officially recognised by the Cape Colony's Dutch Reformed Church.

Before proceeding from Cape Town to the Soutpansberg, which is situated in the present Limpopo Province of South Africa, Van Warmelo returned briefly to the Netherlands where he married Josina van Vollenhoven early in 1864. She then accompanied him to Schoemansdal, the biggest settlement of the Transvaal Boers in the Soutpansberg district. Van Warmelo was finally ordained as Minister

---

2   A.D. Pont, Van Warmelo, Nicolaas Jacobus, in *DSAB* I, pp 840–841; A.D. Pont, *Nicolaas Jacobus van Warmelo 1835–1892*, pp 5–49.

of the *Hervormde* Church soon after their arrival. Not long afterwards, early in 1865, his young wife passed away.[3]

Van Warmelo subsequently married 17-year-old Maria Magdalena Elizabeth Maré in 1867. She came from a prominent family. Her father, Dietlof Siegfried Maré, had served for many years as the *landdrost* (magistrate) of the Soutpansberg district. Dietlof's parents were themselves prominent people. His father was Paulus Maré, who was a leading citizen of Graaff-Reinet and later of Uitenhage in the eastern part of the Cape Colony, and who was married to Johanna Magdalena Pretorius, a cousin of the famous Voortrekker leader Andries Pretorius. Paulus Maré was 70 years old when he joined in the Great Trek in 1838 with his family. Dietlof was their youngest son. He married Johanna Elizabeth Kruger (after whom Johanna van Warmelo was probably named according to the Boer tradition to name children after their grandparents) in 1848 and settled in Schoemansdal in 1862 with his family. He established himself as an ivory trader.[4]

Maria was Dietlof and Johanna Maré's eldest daughter. Before her parents moved to Schoemansdal, she had received some formal education in Pietermaritzburg in Natal. The atmosphere in that town was English, and so was her education. That helps to explain why as an adult she did most of her writing in English. However, the spoken language

Dietlof Siegfried Maré

[3] A.D. Pont, Van Warmelo, Nicolaas Jacobus, in *DSAB* I, pp 840–841.
[4] R.T.J. Lombard, Maré, Dietlof Siegfried, in *DSAB* II, p 446; B. Roberts, *Those Bloody Women. Three Heroines of the Boer War*, p 101.

in their house was Dutch. One of Maria Maré's brothers was the first missionary who came from the Transvaal, T.J.A. Maré, and another was Paul Maré. Nicolaas van Warmelo and his wife Maria had five sons, of who three lived to become adults, and are often mentioned in the diary, namely Dietlof Siegfried, Willem and Frederik (Fritz), as well as two daughters, namely Christiana Deliana (called Line in the diary) and then Johanna.[5]

Mrs van Warmelo (sitting in the middle) with her five children in about 1904. From the left Willem, Johanna, Fritz, Deliana and Dietlof

As a result of pressure from the Venda, a black community with whom the Boers regularly clashed, the Boers abandoned the village of Schoemansdal in mid-1867, only a few months after Nicolaas van Warmelo's marriage with Maria Maré. The Van Warmelo's temporarily settled in Marabastad, a village some 130 kilometres south of Schoemansdal, but in 1868 moved further south to Heidelberg, where Van Warmelo became the minister of the local *Hervormde* congregation,[6] and where his

---

5   A.D. Pont, Van Warmelo, Nicolaas Jacobus, in *DSAB* I, pp 840–841; R.T.J. Lombard, Maré, Dietlof Siegfried, in *DSAB* II, p 446; R.T.J. Lombard, Maré, Tobias Johannes Albertus, in *DSAB* III, p 581; M.E. van der Merwe, *Johanna Brandt*, p 7.

6   A.D. Pont, Van Warmelo, Nicolaas Jacobus, in *DSAB* I, pp 840–841.

family stayed for the next 25 years. He himself baptised Johanna on 17 December in Heidelberg, when she was one month and one day old.[7]

Van Warmelo became a staunch Boer patriot and in 1877, when the British annexed the South African Republic, he refused to accept the new dispensation. He attended the people's meetings of the Boers who passively resisted the occupation and was the only minister present at Paardekraal in December 1880, when the Boers decided to unilaterally re-establish their Republic. The so-called First Boer War followed, and Heidelberg became the temporary capital of the South African Republic for the duration of the war.[8] Johanna was four years old at that time – too young to know what the conflict was about, but her father's patriotism certainly inspired her, since she herself became an equally staunch Boer patriot when she reached adulthood.

Van Warmelo played a leading role in attempts to unite the *Hervormde* Church and the Dutch Reformed Church of the Cape, which had from the mid-1860s established a number of congregations in the South African Republic. A united church was eventually established in 1885, but the fragile unity was soon shattered and bitterly contested court battles over the property of congregations followed. The conflict over church unity unfortunately for Van Warmelo ran much deeper than mere wrangling over property – even within his own family his wife did not agree with his stance. She remained loyal to the *Hervormde* Church and refused to participate in Holy Communion in the United Church, she also arranged for Johanna and her sister to be confirmed in the *Hervormde* church. It is probable that the failure of his endeavours to bring about church unity shattered Van Warmelo's self-image since his health failed and he died at the age of 56 in Heidelberg on 21 April 1892.[9] Johanna was 15 years old at that time, and her father's death was a major loss to her.

---

7   Archives of the *Hervormde Kerk van Afrika*, Pretoria (NHKA), G7 3/1/2, Doopregister, *Nederduitsch Hervormde Gemeente* Heidelberg.

8   J.E.H. Grobler, *Die Eerste Vryheidsoorlog 1880–1881, 'n militêr-historiese benadering* (Unpublished D Phil thesis, University of Pretoria, Pretoria, 1980), p 27.

9   R. van der Merwe, *Johanna Brandt*, pp 4–5; A.D. Pont, Van Warmelo, Nicolaas Jacobus, in *DSAB* I, pp 840–841; B. du Toit, *Die verhaal van Johanna Brandt*, p 22.

Johanna, 12 years old

Johanna had received some education from an impoverished English nobleman, a Mr Ayliff, in Heidelberg, before going to Cape Town where she attended the Good Hope Seminary for Young Ladies.[10] After her father's death she did not return to Cape Town, but stayed with her mother. Dietlof and Willem were at that time studying in Holland and Fritz was attending school in Cape Town. Deliana was living in Sunnyside in Pretoria with her husband, Henry Cloete, who was a practising lawyer and came from a distinguished Cape Afrikaner family. Mrs Maria van Warmelo and Johanna initially stayed in the parsonage in Heidelberg, but in July 1893 moved to their farm in the Heidelberg district and in 1895 to Pretoria. The emotional ties between Johanna and her mother became very strong – almost unnaturally so – in these years. It was probably during this time that she attended the Doornfontein College in Johannesburg.[11] An im-

10   B. du Toit, *Die verhaal van Johanna Brandt,* pp 18–19.
11   M.E. van der Merwe, *Johanna Brandt,* pp 8–10.

portant aspect of her formal school education was that the medium of education was in all cases English. The result was that she gained a good command of the English language, and preferred to write in English, which was also the language of her diary. As she had no formal training in Dutch, she was not comfortable with writing in Dutch. Afrikaans was not yet well enough developed as a written language to suit her taste.

In Pretoria the Van Warmelo ladies settled on an estate known as Harmony (*Harmonie* in Dutch). It was 4,23 hectares in size and situated adjacent to the suburb Sunnyside and about two kilometres south east of the city centre, bordered by the Apies River in the west. The Apies was usually a quiet brook, but could and often did turn into a raging torrent after heavy rain. Harmony originally formed part of the farm Elandspoort, on which Pretoria was laid out in 1855. Mrs van Warmelo bought the property with money from her late husband's estate. Previous owners had planted large numbers of fruit trees on this property. There was a sturdy, although not luxurious, house on Harmony, the property as a whole, however, was in a state of neglect and overgrown with intruder plants. Although the Van Warmelo's cleared large areas to establish vegetable gardens, the western section adjacent to the Apies River was left unspoiled. Johanna approved of the 'wild' nature of the property and was especially fond of the tall weeping willow trees next to the Apies. Her mother soon befriended leading citizens of Pretoria, including the State Secretary, Dr. W.J. Leyds, Commandant-General Piet Joubert's family, the Reverend and Mrs Bosman of the Dutch Reformed Congregation of Pretoria, Domela Nieuwenhuis, the Consul-General of the Netherlands in Pretoria and other members of the diplomatic corps.[12]

Johanna's family and friends knew her as Hansie, a pet name that was a diminutive of Johanna. It is an old Afrikaner custom to call people by pet names that are diminutives of their actual names. She was 15 years old when she began corresponding with Andrew Brown, who remained a close friend for many years. He was probably the first love in her life, but her mother quickly ended the romance. Two years later she became involved in a serious affair with Karel de Kok. They became

[12]   J. Brandt, *Die Kappie Kommando of Boerevrouwen in Geheime Dienst*, p 6; F.G.M. du Toit, Brandt, Johanna, in *DSAB* IV, p 55; M.E. van der Merwe, *Johanna Brandt*, pp 13–14.

engaged and the marriage date was set for 7 April 1897.[13] However, the engagement was broken before that date due to an undisclosed reason. In the diary Johanna wrote extensively about De Kok and their engagement, which was obviously an emotional experience to her.

Johanna's first visit to Europe took place during the last six months of 1897. According to some sources, her objective was to further her studies in music, since she had a talent for singing and playing the piano and had attended lessons for both from an early age. However, according to the diary she kept for the duration of the visit, she and her mother merely toured through Europe, visiting inter alia Germany, Holland and England.[14] Johanna did express the wish that her mother would allow her to stay in Europe for a year to study music, but nothing became of that dream.[15]

It was while they were in Holland that Johanna first met her future husband, Louis Ernst Brandt. He was born in Zoeterwoude in South Holland in 1873 and came from a respectable Dutch family. Johanna's brother Dietlof became a close friend of Brandt while they were both studying theology at the University of Utrecht. Since Dietlof was not in Holland at the time of Johanna and her mother's visit, Brandt received the ladies and entertained them – taking them inter alia to Velp to meet his parents.[16] When Johanna and her mother left after a few days, she never expected to see Brandt again. He subsequently became a minister in the Dutch Reformed Church in the Netherlands.[17]

Johanna extensively described her activities and experiences of the Anglo-Boer War in the diary and it will not be discussed here. What should be mentioned is that her war experience and activities formed the basis of the first two of her many books, namely *Het Concentratiekamp van Iréne* (The Irene Concentration Camp), published in 1904, and *The Petticoat Commando* or *Boer Women in Secret Service* published in 1913. The latter was also published in Dutch and eventually also in Afrikaans as *Die Kappie Kommando, of, Boerevroue in geheime*

13	M.E. van der Merwe, *Johanna Brandt*, p 10; B. Roberts, *Those Bloody Women*, p 100.
14	NHKA, Diaries of Mrs Brandt-van Warmelo, script I.
15	M.E. van der Merwe, *Johanna Brandt*, pp 10–12.
16	NHKA, Diaries of Mrs Brandt-van Warmelo, script I.
17	M.E. van der Merwe, *Johanna Brandt*, pp 133–134; P.S. Dreyer, Brandt, Louis Ernst, in *DSAB* II, p 84.

diens (1958). Johanna herself made the translation. A noteworthy aspect of Johanna van Warmelo's war-time experience is that, even though dozens of Republican patriots were forced out of their houses after the British occupation of Pretoria, she and her mother were allowed to remain living in Harmony for the remainder of the war. Johanna herself speculated on the reason why they were left in peace in her book *Die Kappie Kommando*. She writes that neither she nor her mother was ever informed why, but it can possibly be ascribed to the influence of her brother-in-law, Hendrik Cloete, who formerly acted as British Agent in Pretoria.[18]

As is mentioned in the diary, Johanna left South Africa before the end of the war. She travelled by mail ship to England, and was probably one of only a few Republicans in the midst of a large number of pro-British passengers. They were near Tenerife in the North Atlantic Ocean when the news reached the ship that the war had ended. An extremely disappointed Johanna had no option but to witness the other passengers joyfully celebrating the news of the British victory.[19]

Soon after her arrival in Holland, Johanna became a celebrity, being publicly hailed as a heroine. Her admirers flocked to functions that were arranged in her honour, where she talked about the war and her experiences. At the same time her marriage to Louis Brandt was arranged and took place in August 1902, with only her brother Willem of her family present. It was a well-publicised event. She even received personal congratulations from Queen Wilhelmina of the Netherlands, as well as from President Kruger, who was at that time living at Menton on the French Riviera. The delegation of Boer generals who were visiting Europe at that time, namely Louis Botha, Koos de la Rey and Christiaan de Wet, also sent their congratulations. She and her husband enjoyed their honeymoon in Switzerland before returning to his congregation. Her own recollections of the period immediately after her marriage indicates that she suffered from severe post-traumatic depression. In *The Petticoat Commando* she wrote that after her marriage she at last found rest in her husband's parsonage in the Dutch province of Groningen, where she could finally sleep: "Hansie slept. Languid and

---

[18]   F.G.M. du Toit, Brandt, Johanna, in *DSAB* IV, p 55; J. Brandt, *Die Kappie Kommando*, pp 41–42.

[19]   J. Brandt, *Die Kappie Kommando*, pp 363–366.

Johanna and Louis Brandt, engagement photograph

more languid she became; drooping visibly, she sank into oblivion in that northern village home ... As the long winter months crept by, her sleep became more and more profound, less haunted by the hideous nightmares of the past, and though she at first rebelled, ashamed of her growing weakness, she was soon forced to yield to the resistless demands of outraged nature." Unbeknown to Johanna, her husband consulted a famous nerve-specialist about her condition. The advice was: let her sleep, she will eventually be restored. Supported by her husband she did rest, losing count of time, for a full 15 months before she gradually shook off the depression and took up the challenge to lead a meaningful life again. After the restoration of her mental health, Johanna soon became as active as she had been before the depression. She not only began preparing parts of her diary for publication, but convinced her husband that their calling lay in South Africa. He eventually agreed with her.[20]

In 1904 Louis Brandt accepted an invitation to the Congregations of the *Hervormde* Church in Soutpansberg and Waterberg in what was at

---

[20]   J. Brandt, *Die Kappie Kommando*, pp 370–374; B. Roberts, *Those Bloody Women*, p 261.

The Van Warmelo family in about 1904. From the left standing, Johanna and her husband Louis Brandt, Deliana and her husband Henry Cloete, and sitting, Willem, Dietlof, Mrs van Warmelo and Fritz

that time the Transvaal Colony. He and Johanna settled in Pietersburg (today Polokwane, the capital of the Limpopo Province). The Brandts soon became heavily involved in the uplifting of the Boer communities who were ruined by the Anglo-Boer War. In 1908 they moved to Johannesburg, when the Reverend Brandt accepted a call to that congregation. Here, too, they actively assisted in the social uplifting of especially the Afrikaans community.[21]

From 1923 to 1930 Johanna and her family (she and Louis Brandt had seven children) lived in Vereeniging, where her husband served as Minister for the local congregation of the *Hervormde* Church. By that time Brandt played a leading role in the church. In 1930 they returned to Johannesburg, where Brandt served as Minister for the Kensington and Turffontein congregations for the remainder of his life. He died on 23 June 1939 as a result of an accident in his home.[22]

[21]   P.S. Dreyer, Brandt, Louis Ernst, in *DSAB* II, p 84.
[22]   P.S. Dreyer, Brandt, Louis Ernst, in *DSAB* II, p 84.

Throughout this time, Johanna remained busy with a wide range of activities. Numerous manuscripts from her pen were published as books, including *The millenium* (1918), *Die Smeltkroes* (1920), *Die nieuwe wyn* (1921), *Patricia* (a novel in two parts, 1923 and 1928, under the pseudonym Marcus Romondt) and *Elinda*, also a novel (1938). She and her husband were at one time politically involved, he as (unsuccessful) candidate for the National Party in the general election for members of Parliament in 1915 and she as co-founder and honorary president of the Women's National Party in Johannesburg, also in 1915. Her sympathies were at that time solidly with the so-called Rebels, who opposed the South African government of General Louis Botha, who supported Britain in the First World War. She was one of the leading Afrikaner women who campaigned for the release of the Rebels, including General De Wet, who had been imprisoned for their participation in the rebellion. She also became a co-founder and honorary president of the World Harmony Movement in 1916, and in 1938 was presented with an award for literary work by the Eugene Field Society in the United States of America. She believed in natural treatment for diseases and wrote two books on natural treatments, namely *The fasting book* (1912) and *The grape cure* (1928). In 1938 she received an honorary degree from the American School of Natural Physics for her excellent writings on the topic.[23]

Johanna survived her husband by almost 25 years. She was relatively healthy and in a good physical condition up to a high age. She was 87 years old when she passed away on 21 January 1964. She lived in Cape Town for the last part of her life.[24]

Johanna in later life

---

[23] B. Roberts, *Those Bloody Women*, p 261; F.G.M. du Toit, Brandt, Johanna, in *DSAB* IV, p 55.

[24] F.G.M. du Toit, Brandt, Johanna, in *DSAB* IV, p 55.

Editorial notes

The diary was divided into 5 parts, as indicated in the table of contents. This is not a division used by the diarist, who merely wrote about her experiences of events in a more or less chronological sequence. All notes and editorial corrections are provided within square brackets [ ]. The diarist's insertions are provided within round brackets ( ) as used by her in the diary. The diarist often used only the first letter of a person's name or surname when writing about him/her. In most cases the full name is provided in this published version of the diary. Footnotes are used to provide more detailed annotations. The following changes were made without editorial comment:

- Since the diarist did not always clearly indicate new topics with new paragraphs, the editor inserted paragraphs at his own discretion where the diarist introduced new topics in the middle of lengthy paragraphs.
- The diarist often used the symbol & instead of the word *and.* In all cases & has been replaced by the word *and* in this published version of her diary.
- Incorrect spelling with regard to place names and names of persons were corrected, but contemporary spelling of place names was retained.

The original diary consists of 8 scripts, however, script V could not be traced. It is not in the Brandt Collection in the archives depot of the *Nederduitsch Hervormde* Church in Pretoria, where the other seven are preserved. Since the diarist regarded each script as a separate diary, the numbers of the scripts are indicated in square brackets. Script VI was used up to 8 September 1901, followed by script VII. Script VI was then used again from 16 March 1902 until the end of her diary on 30 April 1902.

Script VIII contains both her "Love-diary" and her "Secret diary". She wrote both using lemon juice. They run concurrently with her "open diary" – from 11 August to 19 October 1901, with inscriptions on only five days in this period in the case of the "Love-diary"; and from 17 August to 21 December 1901 in the case of the "Secret diary". In this published version the entries in those diaries are placed in chronological order with a note in each case to indicate that they were originally made in one of those diaries.

The use of the term 'kaffir' when referring to black South Africans is retained, as it was the custom in those days and not always used in a derogatory way.

I dedicate this book with sincere thanks to my wife Elize who spent countless hours in the archives to help bring this project to fruition.

Jackie Grobler

Part 1

"[T]he darkness of these days" – Pretoria, October 1899 to March 1900

[Script I]

September 30th 1899
Notes on the "Franchise" War[1]

On the 28th Sept[ember] 1899 the first detachment left Pretoria for the border. They were unfortunate enough to have a serious accident – in firing farewell shots a bullet rebounded from a rock, into a carriage and through a poor young fellow who is now lying at death's door.[2] The boys left today[3] looking very brave and manly in their warlike costumes. In bidding Fritz goodbye I found I could not reach him and was delighted when he leant far out of the window, took me in his arms like a doll and kissed me repeatedly. The dear boy! If he does not come back what a comfort this little bit of recollection will be to me.

---

[1]   The diarist's use of the term "Franchise" War for the Anglo-Boer War seems to indicate that she regarded the franchise issue as the major cause of the war. (See also her comment on 1901-01-18). Among her contemporaries no one else used the term "franchise" war. On the franchise issue in the South African Republic prior to the war, see I. Smith, *The Origins of the South African War, 1899–1902*, especially pp 240–242 & 305–315.

[2]   The Pretoria newspaper *De Volksstem* reported on 1899-09-30 that the victim was Artillerist Meijer, who was hit in the chest when his comrades fired a salvo at Irene on their way to the border. Fortunately he was, according to the report, making good progress in the Volks Hospital in Pretoria.

[3]   She means her brothers Dietlof and Fritz. Her other brother, Willem, was in Holland at that time. Dietlof also recorded that they left Pretoria by train on 30 September. See D.S. van Warmelo, *Mijn commando en guerilla commando-leven*, p 11.

Burghers leaving for the front from the Pretoria Station

On the 9th Oct[ober] our Ultimatum was despatched and less than 48 h[ou]rs afterwards England's reply came "We refuse to discuss the matter further." Before 5 o'clock on the 11th inst[ant] our Gov[ernmen]t formally declared war, proclaimed Martial Law and gave Mr Greene his passport. The Greenes left at 1.30 the following day under a strong police escort.[4] On the 12th the Pretoria commando crossed the Natal border, took Newcastle which was almost deserted and proceeded to fortify La[i]ng's Nek. We have heard nothing from them since but the Free Staters have commenced fighting on the other borders.

On the Western border Piet Cronjé[5] has done a great deal. The Railway line is broken up north of Mafeking and the Molani Bridge destroyed.[6] Yesterday (14th) a dynamite train was wrecked. The boers shot at the trucks of dynamite (2) with the result that an immense explosion and conflagration occurred. That same evening at 11 o'clock an

---

4   William Conyngham Greene was the British Agent in Pretoria before the war. See H.R. van der Walt, Greene, Sir William Conyngham, in *DSAB III*, pp 346–347.

5   In terms of the Republican strategy, Assistant Commandant General Pieter Arnoldus Cronjé was dispatched with a force of about 6 000 burghers to clear the Republican western borders of British forces. See A. Wessels, *Die Anglo-Boereoorlog 1899–1902. 'n oorsig van die militêre verloop van die stryd*, p 6.

6   She means the bridge across the Mogasane Spruit near Molani. See J.H. Breytenbach, *Die Geskiedenis van die Tweede Vryheidsoorlog in Suid-Afrika, 1899–1902, I*, p 390.

armoured train was captured, near Mafeking, with two wagons. The enemy hoisted the white flag and was captured. One captain and eight men seriously wounded – no casualties on our side – the prisoners are coming to Pretoria.

16th Oct[ober 1899]

On Sat[urday] 14th a fierce "skirmish" took place on the same place. An armoured train from Mafeking, full of troop, with heavy artillery, resisted the well-directed fire of the Boers, but was forced to return to Mafeking when help came from Cronjé. Two of our men were killed, one by accident, and one dangerously wounded, while 40 were disabled. The armoured train was coming to relay the dismantled lines but thanks to our efforts had to return without accomplishing anything. First victim on our side Ockert T. Oosthuizen.[7] Seven thousand Kaffirs plundered Charlestown. Our flag is waving over the telegraphic office there. A Natal guard of six police was captured. The Rev. Adriaan Hofmeyer[8] was taken prisoner at Lobatsi (9 miles north of Mafeking).[9]

October 19th [1899]

Mafeking has been surrounded and Colonel Baden-Powell[10] is in the

---

7 Oosthuizen, Ockert Jacobus of the farm Boschjeslaagte, in the Marico district. See A.P. Smit and L. Maré (eds), *Die beleg van Mafeking. Dagboek van Abraham Stafleu*, p 51n.

8 Adriaan Jacobus Louw Hofmeyr. She mentions him by name since he was a notorious character from the perspective of the Boers. He was a minister of the *Nederduitsch Hervormde Kerk* in Wynberg in the Cape Colony, but was suspended for alleged immoral conduct and subsequently resigned from the ministry. He became an agent of Cecil John Rhodes, who was regarded as an arch-enemy of the Boers, in Bechuanaland. After his capture he was held as a prisoner of war in Pretoria. In May 1900 he was put over the Portuguese border. He visited Britain before returning to South Africa to work for the British in the war. The Cape politician John X. Merriman's mother once referred to him as "that hypocritical sneak". See R. van Reenen (ed.), *Emily Hobhouse. Boer War letters*, p 448n; D.W. Krüger, Hofmeyr, Adriaan Jacobus Louw, in *DSAB III*, pp 401–402.

9 Closer to 45 miles (75 kilometres) north of Mafeking.

10 Robert Stephenson Smyth Baden-Powell was the commander of the British garrison in Mafeking that survived a siege of 216 days by the Boer forces before being relieved by a British force on 17 May 1900. He subsequently established the Boy Scout movement. See E. Pereira, Baden-Powell, Robert Stephenson Smyth, in *DSAB I*, pp 32–34.

besieged town. The bodies of ten Englishmen have been discovered on the battle-field [sic] near Mafeking. Rhodes[11] is in Kimberley. -* Last night our burghers were attacked by a large force, assisted by about 100 armed Kaffirs. No loss on our side but heavy blood spoors indicate casualties on the other side (*This was near Mafeking). The employment of natives is rousing the greatest indignation all over South Africa. Balloon observed over the Nigel. A railway accident is reported near Beaufort West. Ten men killed and ten wounded.

October 21st [1899]

Yesterday the Bethlehem and Heilbron burgers came upon 800 British outposts near Spitzkop. They fled without firing a shot leaving everything behind them – their ammunition, 80 tents and a wagon heavily laden with provisions. At v[an] Reenen's Pass fifty burgers had a heavy engagement with 150 Natal carbineers [sic] – it lasted from 10 in the morning until 4 in the afternoon and a man, Johnstone,[12] was killed on our side. The enemy fled to Ladysmith – seven Carbineers [sic] wounded and one taken prisoner, Gallwey,[13] son of the Chief Justice of Natal. The Zulus are friendly and supply our commandoes with cattle. Rhodes says he feels as safe in Kimberley as in Piccadilly.[14] We shall see. The water supply has been cut off and strong forces are gathering round the Diamond City.[15]

Last night Com Trichardt [sic], who composes the vanguard of the

---

11   Cecil John Rhodes was a famous South African mining magnate and politician. He was besieged with the British forces in Kimberley by Republican forces from October 1899 to February 1900. See N.G. Garson, Rhodes, Cecil John, in *DSAB III*, pp 713–714.

12   F. Johnstone. This engagement took place on 18 October in the low hills west of Bester Station, between Ladysmith and Van Reenen's Pass. See J.H. Breytenbach, *Die Geskiedenis van die Tweede Vryheidsoorlog in Suid-Afrika, 1899–1902*, I, p 196.

13   Lieutenant W.J. Gallwey, who was captured by the Free Staters when he fell from his horse. See J.H. Breytenbach, *Die Geskiedenis van die Tweede Vryheidsoorlog in Suid-Afrika, 1899–1902*, I, p 196. Sir Michael Gallwey was at that time chief justice of Natal. See J. Wassermann & B. Kearney (eds), *A warrior's gateway. Durban and the Anglo-Boer War 1899–1902*, p 353.

14   A famous square in central London.

15   Kimberley.

S[outh] E[ast] Forces, came into collision with about 250 English.[16] The engagement took place in a cattle-kraal and the enemy hoisted the white flag with the third cannon shot. One Fanie Minnaar[17] slightly wounded and four English killed – our prisoners number about 243 and about 20 horses shot.

Baden-Powell is in Mafeking – the besieged town will be subjugated by the Snyman-Botha[18] and de la Rey[19] commandoes as Cronjé has gone to the assistance of the Free Staters against Kimberley. Yesterday a patrol returned to camp with a booty of 49 cattle, 1 horse and 464 sheep and goats. – Dundee is now surrounded on three sides. An armoured train coming from D[undee] was captured as well as 800 head of cattle and a large quantity of provisions. Several prisoners taken.

A large balloon is said to have passed over Pretoria on the night of the 20th. Yesterday morning heavy fighting took place at Dundee. Gen Lucas Meyer[20] with a small force of 600 stood against more than 6 000 for seven long hours. He expected help from Gen Erasmus,[21] which, for some unknown reason, never came and he was forced to retire with

---

16   S.P.E. Trichard, Commander of the Transvaal State Artillery. This engagement occurred towards the end of the Battle of Talana on 20 October 1899. See O.J.O. Ferreira (ed.), *Geschiedenis Werken en Streven van S.P.E. Trichard Luitenant Kolonel der vroegere Staats-artillerie ZAR door hemzelve beschreven*, pp 120–121.

17   Possibly a son of J.C. Minnaar, the Registrar of Deeds of the South African Republic and an inhabitant of Pretoria. Trichard, quoted by J.H. Breytenbach, *Die Geskiedenis van die Tweede Vryheidsoorlog in Suid-Afrika, 1899–1902, I*, p 231, spells his name Phanie Minnaar.

18   Snyman, J.P., and Botha, J.D.L., respectively commander and second-in-command of the Transvaal forces for virtually the duration of the Siege of Mafeking. See Botha, J.P., *Die beleg van Mafeking tydens die Anglo-Boereoorlog.*

19   Jacobus Hercules (Koos) de la Rey, one of the most able and highly respected commanders of the Transvaal forces during the Anglo-Boer War. See J.S. du Plessis, De la Rey, Jacobus Hercules, in *DSAB I*, pp 214–218.

20   Lukas Johannes Meyer, former President of the Nieuwe Republiek (Vryheid), Chairman of the First Volksraad (Parliament) and commander of the Transvaal forces on the south-eastern front when the war began in 1899. See J.M. Schoeman, Meyer (Meijer), Lukas (Lucas) Johannes, in *DSAB III*, pp 607–608.

21   Daniël Jacobus Elardus (Maroela) Erasmus, respected Boer general when war began in 1899. See J.F. Preller, Erasmus, Daniël Jacobus Elardus, in *DSAB II*, pp 219–220.

the heavy loss of 31 dead on our side and 66 wounded and 30 missing. They had no chance against such overwhelming numbers, especially as the enemy was armed with 96 cannon and well protected by fortifications.[22] Dundee would have been taken if Erasmus had appeared, for large detachments had fled from D[undee] and we had captured one maxim. Those put to flight were eventually captured in the cattle-kraal by Com Trichardt [sic] – one a Colonel Miller.[23]

This morning's telegrams inform us that the roar of cannon is heard in the direction of Dundee so the attack has been renewed and a kommando [sic] has been sent to the assistance of our people. Tomorrow we shall hear news, I hope, for the dear boys are there; too, we think.

October 23rd [1899]

Yesterday (Sunday) the most terrible news reached us, of a whole commando of 600, utterly routed.[24] Today we received some details and things seem to be a little better than first reported – but quite bad enough. When General Meyer saw that the British were preparing to leave Dundee they decided that Gen Kock[25] with a commando of about 700 should go round D[undee] to cut off the retreat of the enemy to Ladysmith, but they were unexpectedly attacked from behind by a force of 6 000 British from Ladysmith and after a fierce and terrible battle they were utterly defeated and forced to flee – number of dead and wounded not officially known. Gen Kock and Col Schiel[26] are prisoners and Judge Kock[27] is supposed to be killed. Ninety men from the Hol-

---

22   The diarist refers to the Battle of Talana of 20 October 1899.

23   Lt-Col C.O. Möller of the 18th Hussars. See J.H. Breytenbach, *Die Geskiedenis van die Tweede Vryheidsoorlog, 1899–1902, I*, pp 218–231.

24   The diarist refers to the Boer defeat in the Battle of Elandslaagte of 21 October 1899.

25   Johannes Hermanus Michiel Kock, member of the Executive Council of the South African Republic; appointed general when the war broke out. See J.M. Schoeman, Kock (Kok), Johannes Hermanus Michiel, in *DSAB II*, pp 370–371.

26   Adolf Friedrich Schiel, commander of the German Corps of the Transvaal forces. See M.C. van Zyl, Schiel, Adolf Friedrich, in *DSAB II*, pp 628–629.

27   Antonie Francois Kock was the youngest son of General J.H.M. Kock and a judge of the Transvaal High Court. See P. van Warmelo, Kock, Antonie (Antonius, Antoine) Francois, in *DSAB IV*, p 283.

lander Corp went to their assistance – of the 90 only 12 returned – not known what became of the others.

Erasmus lost his way in a heavy mist and was unable to assist Meyer in his terrible fight against Dundee.

Oct[ober] 24. [1899]

Dundee has been taken but that does not mean much as it was almost entirely deserted.[28] The English only left their wounded and the ambulances behind, and some provisions – mealies, forage etc to the value of £2 000. Mafeking is being bombarded today. News of every description is so uncertain and the reports so conflicting that I don't know what to write down and what to leave.

Oct[ober] 25. [1899]

In the engagement under Kock 23 men were killed and over 50 wounded as far as we can make out, but a great many are missing still. Among the dead are Dr Coster,[29] D. Pronk,[30] E. Minnaar,[31] J.C. Bodenstein (Landdrost of Boksburg)[32] van Sittert[33] and Judge Kock (not quite sure). Gen Kock is seriously wounded and his wife has gone to Ladysmith to nurse him.

When Dundee was taken our men found 6 wounded comrades there, and the bodies of 250 English as well as 200 very seriously wounded. The dead have been buried by our burgers. Gen White[34] is

---

28   The Transvaal forces occupied Dundee on 23 October 1899. See P.G. Cloete, *The Anglo-Boer War a chronology*, p 45.

29   Hermanus (Herman) Coster, who was the State Attorney of the South African Republic from 1895 to 1897, was indeed killed in the Battle of Elandslaagte. See J. Ploeger, Coster, Hermanus (Herman) Jacob, in *DSAB II*, pp 148–149.

30   D. Pronk was probably a son of Isaac Jordaan Pronk, a Dutch medical doctor who had settled in Pretoria. See J. Ploeger, *Nederlanders in Transvaal 1850–1950*, p 105.

31   E. Minnaar was probably the eldest son of J.C. Minnaar, the Registrar of Deeds in Pretoria in 1899. See B. Theron (ed.), *Dear Sue, The letters of Bessie Collins from Pretoria during the Anglo-Boer War*, pp 27 and 82n.

32   No confirmation could be found in other sources.

33   Probably Hendrik van Cittert (1862–1899) of the Hollander Corps who was killed in the Battle of Elandslaagte. See J. Ploeger, *Nederlanders in Transvaal*, p 125.

34   General Sir George White did not die in the Anglo-Boer War period. He

dead, also his A.D.C. [aide-de-camp] on whose body very compromising documents were found containing instructions from the Imperial authorities. They were dated Aug[ust] last and referred to the use of D.D. [dum-dum] bullets. Gen Penn-Symons was wounded and is reported to have died.[35] Many prisoners (Hollanders) have escaped from their guards, who drank too freely of the whisky and brandy they found on their charges and were incapable of doing their duty – Mr. de Witt-Hamer was one of the lucky ones who escaped and found his way back to our camps.[36]

The prisoners here speak very gratefully of the treatment they receive – their requests for brushes, tooth-brushes [sic], clean clothes etc were

instantly granted. They say they hoisted a white flag thrice during the Dundee engagement, but owing to mist our side did not see it. Yesterday the bombardment of Mafeking has begun – only 30 shells were thrown into the Town but today they have gone on with the bombardment.

Oct[ober] 29[th.] [1899]

Uncle Paul Maré[37] has come back from Natal bringing all sorts of news from the boys. He could not endure the terrible hardships any longer and got lumbago[38] so

Paul Maré, the diarist's uncle

---

commanded the British garrison that was besieged by the Boers in Ladysmith, Natal, from the last day of October 1899. See T. Pakenham, *The Boer War*, pp 142–155.

[35] Major-General Sir William Penn-Symons was indeed killed in action in the Battle of Talana. See T. Pakenham, *The Boer War*, p 130.

[36] Probably wrong. The only De Witt Hamer mentioned in sources on the Anglo-Boer War is Boudewijn Gerrit Versélewel de Witt Hamer, who was captured by the British at Elandslaagte and remained a prisoner of war until the end of the war. See O.J.O. Ferreira (ed.), *Krijgsgevangenschap van L.C. Ruijssenaers 1899–1902*, p 193.

[37] Paul Maré, a brother of the diarist's mother. He was a former member of the First Volksraad for Soutpansberg, but owned a house in Pretoria. See *Longland's Pretoria Directory for 1899*, pp 151 & 227; D. van Warmelo, *Mijn commando en guerilla-commando leven*, p 17.

[38] Muscular pain in the lower part of the back.

he came home. The boys are quite well but had to suffer untold misery through cold, hunger, fatigue and drenching rains. I should like to write down all the wonderful tales he had to tell about his experiences but it would take too long.

There is no fresh news. Since the capture of Dundee our forces have been gathering round Ladysmith which will be attacked this week. The Free Staters had a small battle near Elandslaagte (Modderspruit) which lasted 8 hours – 1 000 against 6 000 English with 12 cannons and many Maxims. The enemy was forced to retire leaving 16 dead and a lot of ammunition (the Red Cross was busy over an hour removing the dead – 16 were left).[39] Mafeking has not yet surrendered.

Oct[ober] 31[st.] [1899]

Gen White is not dead as reported but Gen Penn-Symons has died of his wounds and was buried at Dundee by our men with all military honours. Judge Kock is living. Yesterday (30th) a great battle was fought at Modderspuit near Ladysmith – the enemy was totally defeated, heavy losses on their side, 60 wounded and dead on our side 1 300 were captured including 42 officers who are on their way to Pretoria.[40] The fight was almost entirely confined to artillery fire – Dr Hohls[41] and a son of Jacob Trichardt fell.[42] Com van Dam[43] slightly wounded. One of the imprisoned officers states that Gen White is seriously wounded. The fight began at 5 in the morning and by 12 the British were forced to retire into Ladysmith.

The fort to the east of Mafeking has been taken.

---

[39] This was the Battle of Rietfontein of 24 October 1899.
[40] The author is referring to the twin battles of Modderspruit and Nicholson-snek of 30 October 1899 in which the combined forces of the Transvaal and the Orange Free State defeated a British force outside Ladysmith and drove them into the town, where the Boers subsequently besieged the British for four months. The Boers lost a total of 16 men killed and 75 wounded, whereas the British losses amounted to 106 killed, 374 wounded and 1 284 captured. See P.G. Cloete, *The Anglo-Boer War*, pp 48–49.
[41] Höhls, Johan Otto, officer of health of the Transvaal State Artillery. See J. Ploeger, Höhls, Johann Otto, in *DSAB III*, p 408.
[42] Not identified.
[43] Gerard Marie Johan van Dam, commander of the Johannesburg Police Commando in the first phase of the Anglo-Boer War. See G.N. van den Bergh, Van Dam, Gerard Marie Johan, in *DSAB II*, pp 764–765.

Nov[ember] 2nd [1899]

Gen Kock died of his wounds at Ladysmith on the 31st Oct[ober] and was buried here with all military honours. His death was hurried on, or caused by the terrible suspense he went through when he heard the roar of cannon and knew that a fierce battle was raging just outside of Ladysmith.

Procession at General Kock's funeral in Pretoria

About 50 officers arrived here yesterday morning and are now lodged in the [Staats] Model School. On their arrival there were hundreds of people at the Station and one of the Boer authorities cried out "Hats off" and immediately every head was uncovered and the prisoners responded with the military salute.

At the Modderspruit battle nearly 1 300 were captured besides 6 cannon and 1 Maxim all in good order. Pres Steyn[44] wires that he lost

---

44   Marthinus Theunis Steyn, President of the Orange Free State, which fought
      in alliance with the South African Republic (Transvaal) against Britain in
      the Anglo-Boer War. See Anon, Steyn, Marthinus Theunis, in *DSAB II*, pp
      707–715.

about 30 men, killed and wounded, and Gen Joubert[45] has 40 wounded, two or three mortally. The English deserted their camps at Ladysmith and it is now occupied by our forces.

It is said that <u>Dr. Coster</u> was one of the 8 burgers who rushed out of cover at Elandslaagte, and by drawing the fire off their retiring comrades, sacrificed their own lives and saved 200 from capture or slaughter. Since the heavy British reverse Durban and P[ieter] M[aritz] Burg are in a state of absolute panic and 3 000 Blue jackets have been stationed there as a protection.[46]

The wagon bridge over the Orange River, which cost the C[ape] Colony £120 000, has been destroyed by the Imperial authorities.

The deserted camps at Dundee contained every imaginable luxury, fine table linen, silver and finger-glasses! – The prisoners here asked for so and so many bottles of champagne a day and some of the officers said they expected each to be put into a separate cottage ("it is done in civilized countries!") Durban has a population of 15 000 <u>more</u> than usual. Poor Durban!

November 8th. [1899]

Today I began my duties as nurse in the Volks Hospital.[47] I was busy from 9 until nearly 4 in the aft[ernoon] with 10 men – one Rompelmann[48] a Hollander is dying of dysentry [sic] and pneumonia. It was a hard days' work and I feel quite unstrung – tomorrow will be better.

December 2nd [1899]

Some of my Hospital experiences. I nursed the wounded every day until the 26th Nov[ember] and then I got very ill myself and had to give it up – am all right now but cannot go back until quite strong again.

---

45   Petrus Jacobus (Piet) Joubert, Commandant-General of the Transvaal forces when the Anglo-Boer War broke out in 1899. See J.S. du Plessis, Joubert, Petrus Jacobus, in *DSAB I*, pp 412–417.

46   The Colonial as well as Imperial authorities in Natal indeed took frantic measures to arrange for the proper defence of Durban, but at the same time decided that Pietermaritzburg would not be defended against a Boer attack. See J. Wassermann and B. Kearney (eds), *A warrior's gateway. Durban and the Anglo-Boer War 1899–1902*, p 32.

47   It was near the Artillery Camp, south-west of the city.

48   Not identified.

The Volks Hospital, Pretoria

Our wounded have nearly all recovered and gone away – there are only some serious cases left and a great deal of typhoid. One man Joubert[49] had a bullet under his knee-cap [sic] for 15 days and suffered untold agonies. Another (Zwanepoel)[50] was shot through the liver and thumb with the same bullet. Anderson[51] was shot through the arm and one of the main muscles was nearly severed and the doctors had to make deep gashes to get the two ends and sew them together again. He gets electricised [sic] every day and gradually life is coming back to his arm and hand. Kruiselberger[52] was at Elandslaagte and got a piece of shell in his foot – lost his way and roamed about 2 days with the sore foot. de Lange[53] was shot through the lungs but is also convalescent.

Van der Merwe[54] was shot through the right leg. I asked one man

---

49   Not identified.

50   Not identified.

51   Not identified.

52   Probably F. van Kruiselbergen, who seems to have been the only person with that surname who participated in the Battle of Elandslaagte. However, according to an official government notice, he emerged unscathed from the battle. See J. van Dalsen, *Die Hollander Korps tydens die Tweede Vryheidsoorlog*, p 63.

53   Not identified.

54   Not identified.

whether he had had chloroform when he had a bullet cut out of his leg and his answer was: "Chloroform! Not a bit of it! No one asked me to take C[hloroform] when I was shot, so the bullet had to come out as it went in – without chloroform." The men are very brave and one seldom hears one word of complaint and their only desire is to get back to the front as soon as possible – The worst cases are Lieut[enant] H. du Toit[55] whose leg is broken and left thigh almost shattered by a bomb and his whole body one mass of wounds; Coetzee[56] whose spine is injured and who can never recover; van Heerden[57] whose whole right leg is cut open; an Austrian[58] with 17 lance wounds; and Irishman[59] whose head is cut open and Cloete[60] who got a bullet above his left eye which entered right into the skull and had to be cut out. One sees the most awful suffering borne with the greatest fortitude and bravery. Coetzee tells how he was robbed of all he possessed while lying wounded and helpless on the battle-field [sic]. He remonstrated with the soldiers and afterwards began calling them names as he was quite paralysed and could not move, but they went on and he saw them going from one wounded and dying man to the other. Long after he was robbed of everything, soldiers kept coming along and rolling him over to examine his pockets and he was all the while enduring the most cruel pain. – There has been fighting almost every day but no big battles. The besieged towns are still holding out. Barnard, M.F.V.[61] has been killed. The boys are well and have had some thrilling experiences and narrow escapes. Willem[62] is coming home by the *König*.

Dec[ember] 15th [1899]

Willem arrived on the 8th inst[ant] looking very well and sunburned

---

[55] Du Toit, Heinrich Sebastian Davel, an artillerist, was seriously wounded in the Battle of Modderspruit on 30 October 1899, but recovered and remained in the field until the end of the war. See D.W. Krüger, Du Toit, Heinrich Sebastian Davel, in *DSAB III*, p 253.
[56] Not identified.
[57] Not identified.
[58] Not identified.
[59] Not identified
[60] Not identified.
[61] Not identified.
[62] Willem van Warmelo, a brother of the diarist.

after the long voyage, and left for Ladysmith this afternoon, after spending just one short happy week at home.

Dec[ember] 18. [1899]

More than a week ago the English attacked our "Long Tom"[63] near Ladysmith and blew it up with dynamite. Four Pretoria men were killed, Niemeyer, van Zyl, D. de Villiers and Spanier. Pott seriously wounded.[64] They made three attacks on different occasions during the night and spoilt two Howitzers as well. The guards were found sleeping – for the third time, once before at Mafeking and once at Kimberley. Treachery is suspected for it is impossible to find their way without a guide.

On the 10th inst[ant] (3.p.m.) Cronjé's forces of 8 000 were attacked by at least 20 000 English under Lord Methuen at Modderrivier or Scholtz Nek. They fought all afternoon until 10 p.m. and began again the next morning at daybreak, with the result that the enemy was beaten back three or four times with very heavy loss. 2 000 bodies were left on the field and the number of wounded was appalling. Our loss was 100 wounded and killed, the greater number being Scandivanians [sic],

---

63   Long Tom. The nick-name of the 155mm Creusot siege guns used by the Boers. They had four of these guns, which were initially used for long distance bombardment of enemy positions. From mid-1900, however, the Boer artillerists used them as field guns before demolishing them to ensure that the British would not capture them. See L. Changuion, *Silence of the guns. The history of the Long Toms of the Anglo-Boer War*.

64   The diarist confuses two separate incidents. The first occurred on the night of 7 / 8 December 1899 when a British patrol damaged the front of the muzzle of one of the Long Toms. It was subsequently repaired in Pretoria. See L. Changuion, *Silence of the guns*, pp 50–51. See also the diarist's entry on 1899-12-25. The second incident occurred three nights later, also at Ladysmith, when the British forces attacked a Republican gun emplacement. General D.J.E. Erasmus reported on this incident that two burghers (J.C. Niemeyr and Dèsiré Tieleman de Villiers) were killed, two (John A. Pott and E.J. (Sampie) van Zyl) died of wounds and eight others were either wounded or missing. See J.H. Breytenbach, *Die geskiedenis van die Tweede Vryheidsoorlog, II*, p 449. Van Zijl was a clerk in the office of the Master of the Supreme Court in Pretoria and Johan A. Pott a clerk in the office of the state secretary. See A.G. Oberholster (ed.), *Oorlogsdagboek* van Jan F.E. Celliers, p 43n. According to the diarist Pott recovered – see her entry on 1900-01-17. See also *De Volksstem*, Special Edition, 1899-12-12.

whose corp [sic] of 125 had bravely stormed a koppie and driven the enemy off. It was a reckless thing to do but very brave.[65] Before this great victory, the Colonial Boers had defeated Gen Gatacre at Stormberg, 1 800 against 8 000 – and captured 700 prisoners and some cannon.[66]

Our next great victory was at Colenso on the 15th when Buller's forces were utterly routed by the Boers under Joubert.[67] Then we took 150 prisoners, 10 splendid cannon and 13 loads of ammunition. The English fell in thousands and were driven back repeatedly. All the prisoners have been removed to Waterval[68] where a very strong "kraal" of barbed wire has been made for them. This week having been so wonderfully blessed the President[69] proclaimed Sunday (17th inst[ant]) a day of thanksgiving.

On Dingaan's Day[70] an armistice was granted for the English to collect and bury their dead and to attend to their wounded. On the 13th Van Zyl, Niemeyer and the other two were buried here with full military honours. It was a very impressive scene. Winston Churchill escaped

---

[65]   The author refers here to the Battle of Magersfontein which occurred on 11 December 1899. In this battle the Boer forces under command of Piet Cronjé repulsed a British attack on their position, inflicting serious losses on their opponents. Altogether at least 288 British soldiers of all ranks were killed, 700 wounded and 100 were reported missing. Boer losses amounted to 71 killed, of whom 43 were Scandinavians, and 184 wounded. See P.G. Cloete, *The Anglo-Boer War*, pp 67–69.

[66]   The Battle of Stormberg, the first serious British setback of the so-called Black Week, took place on 10 December 1899. See P.G. Cloete, *The Anglo-Boer War*, p 66.

[67]   The Battle of Colenso took place on 15 December 1899. In this confrontation the British forces under command of General Sir Redvers Buller suffered the loss of 143 killed in action, 756 wounded and 240 missing, as well as 10 guns captured by the Boers, when the Republican forces under General Louis Botha, not Joubert as the diarist alleges, repulsed their attack. Boer losses amounted to seven killed in action, 30 wounded and one drowned. See P.G. Cloete, *The Anglo-Boer War*, pp 71–73.

[68]   The prisoner-of-war camp at Waterval was about 20 kilometres north of the centre of Pretoria, next to the railway line between Pretoria and Pietersburg.

[69]   President S.J.P. (Paul) Kruger, the last elected president of the South African Republic (Transvaal). See D.W. Krüger, Kruger, Stephanus Johannes Paulus, in *DSAB I*, pp 444–455.

[70]   Annually on 16 December, the day on which in the year 1838 the Voortrekkers under command of Andries Pretorius defeated a Zulu force of King uDingane in the Battle of Blood River.

from the [Staats] Model School on the night of the 12th inst[ant][71] – it is suspected through the help of the Red Cross nurses next door, or through the sanitary boys. There is a great hue and cry but as yet he has not been found. The two Misses Boncker[72] were arrested the following day – one had thrown a note tied to a stone, over the fence to one of the officers. It fell into the hands of a policeman and contained highly treasonable matter to the effect that she hoped to have him out before Christmas. There is a great deal of treachery in our camp and the Red Cross is doing more harm than good.

Mafeking is still holding bravely out. The Colonel, Baden-Powell seems to be a bit of a wag for he is constantly sending us funny messages. When first we bombarded Mafeking he sent us word that if we did it again he would regard it as a declaration of war; on another occasion he said he was not aware that the bombardment had commenced. Once, some of our men sent to ask him for a bottle of whiskey for a wounded comrade who was far away the lager and he sent them two cases of whiskey – perhaps to show that his supply was so plentiful that he had enough for his enemies too. His last joke was a long letter in awful Dutch asking the Boers to lay down their arms and go quietly home, for the Transvaal would be in the hands of the English before the 14th inst[ant] and promising them his protection if they ceased hostilities. Our answer was as brief as his was long and very much more to the point. He is a very brave man, as wily as an Indian – it is said that he is his own scout and glides about like a snake in the very midst of the enemy.

December 24th [1899]

Nothing.

---

[71]   Winston Leonard Spencer Churchill, the famous British statesman and politician. He arrived in South Africa soon after the outbreak of the Anglo-Boer War as correspondent of the *Morning Post* and was captured by the Boers when he actively participated in military operations when a British armoured train was captured by the Boers at Chievely in Natal on 15 November 1899. Churchill was sent to Pretoria where he was held as prisoner of war with British officers in the yard of the Staats Model School from where he escaped on 12 December. See S.B. Spies, Churchill, Sir Winston Leonard Spencer, in *DSAB V*, pp 126–129.

[72]   Not identified.

Dec[ember] 25. [1899] Christmas.

We had dinner with the Potgieter family[73] today and enjoyed ourselves very much notwithstanding the darkness of these days.

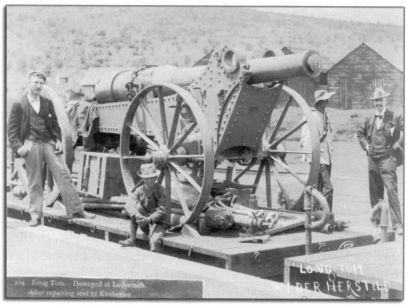

The Long Tom that was repaired in Pretoria

On the 23rd we went to the Engineering Works to see "Long Tom". It is a magnificent cannon and is in repair after the damage done to it by dynamite;[74] also the two Howitzers. L[ong] T[om] is going back to Ladysmith this week. They are working at it night and day. We also saw some locomotives captured from the English and we were told that they have no less than 400 trucks. Six of the cannon captured at Colenso are at the Artillery Camp – the other four at Ladysmith and Colenso.

Dec[ember] 28. [1899]

A desperate attempt was made to escape from Mafeking on the 26th. 109 English were killed and wounded and they were beaten back. 2 killed on our side and several wounded.

---

[73] Possibly P.J. Potgieter, the first full-time mayor of Pretoria and his family.
[74] See entry on 1899-12-18.

January 11th 1900.

On the first day of this new year the English tried (under Gen French)[75] to force their way through Colesberg. Schoeman[76] and his brave band of men beat them back but each day the battle was renewed and lasted five or six days with the result that the enemy was forced to retire.

At Ladysmith on the 6th our burgers tried to take the forts on the Platkop (Platrand*)[77] and succeeded for a time but had to give them up again. It was a terrible fight and our losses were 52 killed and about 135 wounded.[78] The boys were in the thick of it but escaped unhurt.

January 13. [1900]

Today I began my duties at the Staats Meisjes School hospital where we have nearly fifty wounded patients.

Jan[uary] 17. [1900]

One of our patients v[an] d[en] Heever from the Heidelberg district[79] had both eyes destroyed by splinters of rock struck off by a bullet. He is blind for life. Another, Truter,[80] was shot by a bullet that exploded ten of the cartridges in his bandolier mauling his right arm and hand about in an awful manner. While a comrade was binding up his wounds he was shot again clean through the right shoulder. He told me yesterday that at Elandslaagte he saw a friend of his shot down deliberately by an English man, after he had thrown up his hands and cried "Pardon". His gun had been shattered by a bullet and he was quite defenceless. Truter told me that he revenged his friend by taking steady aim and sending a

---

75   Major-General John Denton Pinkstone French, one of the most able British officers in the war. See S.B. Spies, French, John Denton Pinkstone, in *DSAB II*, pp 242–243.

76   Hendrik Jacobus Schoeman, former member of the Volksraad, commander of the Republican forces on the Southern Front. See S.B. Spies, Schoeman, Hendrik Jacobus, in *DSAB II*, pp 633–634.

77   * This was later added as footnote by the diarist herself.

78   The Battle of Platrand took place on 6 January 1900. The Boer forces lost 56 men killed and 116 wounded in their failed assault on the British position. British losses amounted to 148 men killed and 301 wounded. See P.G. Cloete, *The Anglo-Boer War*, pp 80–81.

79   Not identified.

80   Not identified.

bullet through the murderer. Pott,[81] who was all but killed at Ladysmith during the canon episode, is getting slowly better. He told me yesterday how he was transfixed by a bayonet through the lower part of his body, <u>after</u> he was lying helpless on the ground with a bullet through his breast. Such things force one to believe that the English finish off their wounded enemies. I saw a youth in the Bourke Hospital[82] with a Dum-dum bullet wound through his hand – an enormous hole that will perhaps necessitate amputation.

February 15<u>th.</u> [1900]

Fritz came home today on 18 days' leave – a fearful and wonderful sight.

Feb[ruary] 21<u>st</u> [1900]

Dietlof is home too – arrived on the 18th inst[ant] with a sore knee. For a time I am not going to the Hospital. On Sat[urday] 17th , the last day I was there, I assisted at the operation on Coetzee's foot (Baby).[83] They took out some dead bones and the poor boy suffered agonies when he came to. He nearly died under the influence of chloroform, turned black and ceased breathing entirely, but with artificial means the doctors and nurses restored respiration. Left Hospital on the 17th. Fritz went back to Ladysmith on the 24th Feb[ruary].

March 2<u>nd.</u> [1900]

Received news that Willem is a prisoner of war – captured at Tugela 27 Feb[ruary].[84] A curious case we had was a man called Erasmus[85] who

---

81 See her diary entry on 1899-12-18.

82 The school hostel on the south-eastern corner of Van der Walt and Schoeman Streets was converted into a hospital after the closure of the Staats Model School, which was immediately south of the hostel. It was done on the initiative of the brothers George and Eddie Bourke, who were prominent businessmen. See B. Theron, *Pretoria at war 1899–1900*, pp 102–103.

83 Not identified.

84 This happened when the British broke through the Boer line on the Tugela River at Pietershoogte Station. The Information Bureau of the Red Cross in Pretoria confirmed in a letter to Mrs van Warmelo dated 20 March that Willem had been captured, was in good health and held in Pietermaritzburg. (See Archives of the *Nederduitsch Hervormde Kerk van Afrika* in Pretoria, Brandt Collection, IX/168, file 5, Diverse dokumente, unsorted).

85 Not identified.

was shot through the wrist. The bullet went between the muscles, arteries and bones inflicting only a slight flesh wound.

The news of the relief of Kimberley and Ladysmith and the surrender of Cronjé with his whole force of nearly 4 000 has plunged us all into the deepest gloom.[86] Things look bad enough now but we do not despair.

March 3rd. [1900]

Went to American consul[87] about letters.

March 7th [1900]

Dietlof went to Glencoe.

M[ar]ch 13th [1900]

D[ietlof] and F[ritz] came home unexpectedly.

M[ar]ch 15th [1900]

Went to J[o]h[anne]sburg for the day with the Morices[88] – enjoyed myself immensely.

M[ar]ch 16th [1900]

D[ietlof] went to Warm Baths for knee. Received two letters from Line.[89]

March 20 [1900]

Miss Mitchell[90] went to Durban. Fritz got ill on the 18th inst[ant].

---

86   General Piet Cronjé was forced to surrender with his force of almost 4 000 burghers at Paardeberg in the Orange Free State on 27 February 1900. See A. Wessels, *Die Anglo-Boereoorlog 1899–1902. 'n Oorsig van die militêre verloop van die stryd*, pp 25–26.

87   The American Consul in Pretoria in 1899 was C.E. Macrum. See *Longland's Pretoria Directory for 1899*, p 228.

88   Probably Judge G.T. Morice and his family – the only Morice listed in *Longland's Pretoria Directory for 1899*, p 154.

89   The diarist's only sister, Mrs Deliana Cloete.

90   Not identified.

March 29th [1900]

Gen Joubert's funeral.[91] Heard the death-watch [sic] that night in bathroom.

March 31st [1900]

Dietlof came back from Waterberg. Consulted Dr Eugen.[92]

[This is the last entry before the British occupation of Pretoria on 5 June 1900].

---

91   Commandant-General Piet Joubert died on 27 March 1900 in Pretoria. A memorial service for him was held in the city two days later, but he was buried on his farm near Volksrust. See J.A. Mouton, *Genl Piet Joubert in die Transvaalse geskiedenis*, pp 263–265.

92   Not identified.

Part 2

"[I]n this lying, slanderous, evil town"
– Pretoria, June 1900 to May 1901

June 5th [1900]

(Fritz's birthday). Dear diary, you have been much neglected but the war ceased to interest me and it is only now that we are becoming aware of the reality of the war. It is only too true, the enemy marched into our beloved town in thousands this morning. On the 30th of May Mama[1] and I heard the roar of cannon for the first time and yesterday the bombs began to burst in Sunnyside[2] and we had to flee to Town for safety. The boys instantly rode to the scene of action.[3] Our forts[4] were being bombarded and Harmony[5] was directly in the line of fire. The bursting of the great lyddite bombs on our hills caused terrific shocks and we fled leaving our dinner standing on the table. The shells went shrieking and whistling through the air over our heads and we were not one moment out of danger. Everywhere were great clouds of dust and smoke and the fragments of rock and shell fell like hail on the iron roofs. We have picked up fragments in our garden and behind the stable. We stayed with friends in town and came home when darkness fell. That

---

1 Mrs Maria van Warmelo.
2 A Pretoria suburb, southeast of the city centre.
3 This sentence was inserted later on. The original here is written in pencil, but this sentence is in black ink in the space between two written lines.
4 Fort Schanskop and Fort Klapperkop, the two fortresses south of the city that were erected in 1897–98 to protect Pretoria against possible attack from the south. Ironically the fortresses were never used, since the Transvaal authorities decided not to defend the city since the unstoppable British commander, Lord Roberts, threatened to destroy it by a bombardment. See J.H. Breytenbach, *Die Geskiedenis van die Tweede Vryheidsoorlog in Suid-Afrika, 1899–1902, V*, p 546.
5 The house in which the author lived with her mother at this time was called Harmonie, or Harmony in English. See J. Brandt, *Die Kappie Kommando of Boerevrouwen in Geheime Dienst*, p 1.

night our dear boys rushed home from the fight, slept here a few hours and cleared at break of day. They have gone to join the commandoes out Lydenburg[6] way where we hope our President is in safety with the Government. As long as the war lasts we shall probably not hear from them, for we are all prisoners and cut off from the whole world.

I went to Town this morning to watch the troops marching in – the mother declined to go but I think such things will become historical and everyone ought to see them, so I carefully put on my Transvaal colours[7] and went to Town on my bicycle – met some friends with whom I stayed all the time while the marching and parading and shouting and band-playing went on. Sick at heart I watched all this – with boiling blood I noticed the jubilations of the half-breeds and blacks, the sporting of the red, white and blue[8] by people who have been strictly "neutral" during the war and even by some who were red-hot Republicans not long ago (after Colenso, Magersfontein, Spion Kop).[9] At first I shed some bitter tears but afterwards my pride came to my aid and I had the satisfaction of "cutting" the wearer of the red, white and blue right and left. I watched our own people a great deal more than the Tommies[10] and I know all the loyal ones. The poor soldiers were really not worth looking at, covered with filth, footsore, weary. I can't say I admired them and yet one must admit that the discipline is perfect. At about 3 o'clock the Union Jack was hoisted on the Government Buildings,[11] the bands played "God save the Queen",[12] the soldiers cheered, and all the world seemed to go mad, only this poor child stood like a marble statue and soon afterwards she nearly fainted, what with heat, emotion and fatigue.

---

6   A town some 280 kilometres east of Pretoria.
7   The flag of the South African Republic (Transvaal), the *Vierkleur* (Four Colour) consisted of three horizontal lanes, red, white and blue, with a vertical green lane on the left.
8   The colours of the British flag, the so-called Union Jack.
9   Famous Boer victories in December 1899 and January 1900.
10   British soldiers.
11   The *Raadzaal* (Council Hall, called Government Buildings in English) on the southwest corner of Church Square, Pretoria.
12   The national anthem of the United Kingdom.

British troops marching into Pretoria, 5 June 1900

My friends let me out of the crowd and I came home – it was more than flesh and blood could bear, but I shall never regret having seen what I saw today. There were some funny things, some pathetic things and many very touching things that helped to make this bitter day bearable. The greatest comfort to me was my Transvaal ribbon – everyone saw it, everyone knew my sentiments and in all that crowd of thousands I was one of the only women with enough courage to sport the "Vierkleur". One of our people – a young man – stopped beside me and looking earnestly at me cried "Hoera, ver onze Vierkleur – daar het ik nou respekt voor"[13] and he took off this hat almost reverently. I was quite touched and gave him a friendly "Good morning". Oh, dear diary, if ever we shall require courage and patriotism and loyalty it is now and <u>now</u> I shall stick to my colours. I think there is a bitter time before us.

Tonight we are surrounded by thousands of armed Tommies – they are camped out at our very gates and their fires are to be seen all along the roads and railway lines. We asked the men at the gate to see that no one came into Harmony and the officer was very respectful and promised that no one would molest us. The mother promptly sent them a

---

[13]   Hurray for our Four Colour – I have respect for it now.

The parade on Church Square, 5 June 1900

basket of oranges by way of gratitude. I saw Lord Roberts[14] today – also Kitchener[15] I think.

June 9 [1900].

An English officer came to ask us whether we could take in three officers for a week or two! Of course we refused and I told him that we were red-hot Republicans and that we didn't want to have anything to do with them.

We are surrounded by Tommies and yet we have had no trouble with any of them. At our front gate are camped the military police and at the back are the Montmorency Scouts, with Capt McNeil[16] in com-

---

14   Field Marshal Lord Roberts, commander-in-chief of the British forces in South Africa from the end of December 1899 to November 1900. See S.B. Spies, Roberts, Frederick Sleigh, in *DSAB II*, pp 598–602.

15   Major-General Kitchener, Roberts' chief of staff and from November 1900 commander-in-chief of the British forces in South Africa. See S.B. Spies, Kitchener, Horatio Herbert, in *DSAB II*, pp 365–368.

16   A.J. McNeill. He was a veteran of the Nile Expedition of 1898, staff officer of the Seaforth Highlanders and later commander of Montmorency's

mand – the officer who wanted us to take him in. As if we would let them sleep in our two poor dear boys' beds, while they are wanderers on the face of this earth – fugitives, homeless! No, indeed.

The British Agency in Sunnyside, Pretoria

Khakis, Khakis everywhere – in the streets, in the stores, in every open spot in Sunnyside. Lord Roberts is living in the British Agency so there are hundreds of "Tommies" in our immediate neighbourhood and we are quite safe, for perfect order is kept. The Duke of Westminster[17] is living in Wierda's house[18] and Lord Kitchener in Blumlein's[19] and

Scouts. See Savannah Publications, *Boer War Services of Military Officers of the British and Colonial Armies Imperial Yeomanry Mounted Infantry Local Units &cc 1899–1902 including Earlier Services*, pages unnumbered.

[17] Hugh Richard Arthur Grosvenor, the Duke of Westminster, was an Aide de Camp to Field Marshal Roberts. See Savannah Publications, *Boer War Services of Military Officers of the British and Colonial Armies Imperial Yeomanry Mounted Infantry Local Units &cc 1899–1902 including Earlier Services*, pages unnumbered.

[18] S.W. Wierda was a well-known architect. He designed inter alia the Government Buildings and the Palace of Justice on Church Square and the Staats Meisjes School in Visagie Street. His house was situated in Mears Street in Sunnyside. See *Longland's Pretoria Directory for 1899*, p 176; F.J. du Toit Spies, Wierda, Sytze Wopke, in *DSAB III*, pp 842–843.

[19] S.J. Blumlein's house was in Rissik Street in Sunnyside. See *Longland's Pretoria Directory for 1899*, p 118.

there are three lords in Plate's[20] house so we have very grand people for our nearest neighbours. Lord Roberts' nephew, Colonel Maxwell,[21] asked Mrs Morice to bring him to Harmony. She had told him all about us and he wanted to meet us, but he has gone to Bloemfontein now. The mother says I must ask Mrs M[orice] whether she thinks this is a menagerie – she does not want to be <u>looked at</u>, but I think she will try to be civil if any of these folk come and see her.

June 14th [1900]

This morning I got a permit to ride a bicycle – no one is allowed without.[22] A patrol of soldiers passed through Harmony this afternoon and helped themselves to oranges. They wanted to commandeer horses and mules. Miss Cinatti[23] tells me that one of the English officers asked her whether she knew who the young lady is who rides about in a grey dress, with the Transvaal colours round her hat, accompanied by a big black dog. Miss C[inatti] told him my name and then he said: "I wish she knew how we fellows respect her". Miss C[inatti] said she would tell me and she did and I was quite pleased, because I have been feeling painfully conscious of my "Vierkleur" lately.

---

[20]   C.L. Plate was the Traffic Manager of the Nederlandsch Zuid-Afrikaansche Spoorweg Maatschappij (NZASM). His house was in Joubert Street in Sunnyside. See *Longland's Pretoria Directory for 1899*, p 159.

[21]   Major-General John Grenfell Maxwell came to South Africa as brigade commander in Roberts' army. After the occupation of Pretoria he was appointed military governor of the Transvaal. He served in that capacity until the end of the war. See D.S. Augustus, Maxwell, Sir John Grenfell, in *DSAB IV*, pp 496–497.

[22]   In terms of a police notice issued by the Military Governor all civilians in Pretoria were required to remain in their houses between 19:00 and 06:30 unless provided with a pass signed by the Military Commissioner of Police and was not allowed to ride a bicycle within the town unless provided with a similar pass. See *Government Gazette Extraordinary*, 1/1, 9 June 1900, p 2.

[23]   Probably the daughter of D. Cinatti, the Portuguese Consul-General in the South African Republic. See *Longland's Pretoria Directory for 1899*, p 123.

Harmony, the Pretoria home of the Van Warmelo family

June 17th [1900].

Was introduced to two officers at Mrs Morice's yesterday. Got into a heated argument with one, Capt Walker,[24] who persisted in talking war-talk. This morning I went to fetch a book for the mother and there they were again – it was very annoying because I am determined to have as little to do with these Khakis as possible.

June 25th [1900]

A great indignity has befallen me. This morning an officer rode up to me in the street and ordered me to take off my Transvaal colours. I said "you must first conquer the Transvaal before you dictate to us." "Well, I have told you now and if you don't take them off I shall be obliged to

---

24   Not identified. There were at least three Captain Walkers active in the British forces in the Pretoria area in June 1900. See Savannah Publications, *Boer War Services of Military Officers of the British and Colonial Armies Imperial Yeomanry Mounted Infantry Local Units &cc 1899–1902 including Earlier Services*, pages unnumbered.

send someone to do so." Soon afterwards two soldiers came to take my "Vierkleur" by force and I went in to Miss Cinatti who gave me a white ribbon to put on. When I came out again they were waiting for me and smiled smiles of devilish glee when they saw me minus the Vierkleur. England is making herself ridiculous by this small-mindedness. The mighty British Empire afraid of a bit of ribbon round a girl's hat!

June 28th [1900].

We have had an eventful day. Yesterday a mounted policeman stopped Mama for her pass. She was very angry and said she did not know that women had also to carry passes, so he let her go with a warning. She went to town to get a pass and an officer said it was a mistake and that he would write about it.[25] This morning the same man stopped her and was very impudent and before she had a chance to explain to him he said "I have a good mind to march you off to the Charge Office this minute!" "I should like to see you try", the mother valiantly declared.

Afterwards when he had heard about the mistake he was quite polite but the mother took his number and this afternoon we went to report him. We had a lot of experiences. First we went to see the Military Governor, General Maxwell, about our rifle.[26] The officers in charge of this rifle department had declined to give us permission to keep it so we decided to go straight to the Governor. He was most affable and took us into a room where he keeps the guns that are placed under his especial care. I told him that my brother had given it to me as a parting present and I must get it back. He promised to look well after it and to give me a written promise signed by him. To-morrow I will get it. We spoke to him about the colours and he said they had found such a step necessary

---

25   In terms of a government notice issued by the Military Governor on 1900-06-25, no male person above the age of 16 years would be allowed to reside within the town or suburbs of Pretoria, unless in possession of a pass signed by an officer authorised by him. See *Government Gazette Extraordinary*, 1/7, 25 June 1900, p 93. There was no mention of passes for women.

26   In terms of a government notice issued by the Military Governor on 1900-06-19, all rifles and other firearms and all ammunition had to be surrendered at the office of the Provost Marshal in Pretoria on or before 1900-06-23. It was added that sporting rifles and guns should be surrendered properly labelled and the receipts would in all cases be given. See *Government Gazette Extraordinary*, 1/4, 20 June 1900, p 38.

because women complained that the men insulted them. Ridiculous! We were never insulted until this nonsense was started.

General Maxwell

Mevr[ou] van Alphen[27] told me this morning that she went to Lord Roberts, with the Vierkleur on, to ask if <u>he</u> had given these orders. She was stopped three times by the police on her way but she showed them her revolver and dared one of them to lay a finger on her. They allowed her to pass when she said she was on her way to Lord Roberts. One of them said "Don't interfere with the madam." (Revolvers have a way of inspiring respect, especially in the bosom of a Tommy). Lord R[oberts] received her courteously and she sat alone with him in a room with a small table between them. She told him everything and objected to the way young girls had been taken to the Charge Office and forcibly deprived of their colours, and he said he thought himself that it was an unnecessary proceeding but the Governor wished it and he thought she had better obey. In her house and on her property she could do as she pleased but in public she must not expose herself to insult. "You are under British protection and for the time being I think you had better not wear your colours". "Well", she said, "if you wish it I shall take them off" (here she unpinned her Vierkleur and laid in on the table, from where Lord R[oberts] took it up and sat playing with it)

27 Mrs Alida van Alphen, born Rousseau, was married to Isaac Nicolaas van Alphen, the postmaster general of the South African Republic. They had six children. See J. Ploeger, Van Alphen, Isaac Nicolaas, *in DSAB V*, pp 788–789.

"but I have threatened to shoot the first soldier who lays a finger on me, and that reminds me ..." (here she got up in her slow and stately manner and drew her revolver from her pocket. Lord Roberts started up and stood erect before her, with staring eyes and crimson face). "Madam, you know ladies are not permitted to walk about with firearms". "Yes, I know, and that is what I have come to see you about. Will you give met a permit for it?" She put it on the table and he sat down and examined it. When he saw that it was unloaded the colour slowly left his face until it was as white as death. Poor old gentleman! He thought his end had come and he had escaped all these months only to fall by the hand of this formidable woman. When he had regained his composure he told her where she could go for a permit. She went at once by cab and found someone waiting to receive her and was shown every attention. Lord R[oberts] had telephoned at once. I don't think he will ever forget her but what an <u>awful</u> fright she must have given him.

Lord Roberts

From the Governor's we went to get a permit for my pocket-pistol. Met Lieut Majendie,[28] who asked whe-ther he would be allowed to call. The mother had to say "yes" – she who has so often vowed that no English officer would ever cross her threshold! – I bought two copies of the "The Pretoria Friend" (a new English paper) and a Kruger sove-reign with two *disselbooms*[29] – the coin cost me £4, but is very rare.

---

[28]   Lieutenant B.J. Majendie of the Kings' Royal Rifles was a member of the staff of the Commissioner of Police in Pretoria. See *Government Gazette Extraordinary*, 1/2, 16 June 1900, p 9.

[29]   Disselboom (Afrikaans): the draught-pole of a cart or wagon. This coin is still regarded as extremely rare by collectors and one in mint condi-tion is worth around $2 000. See *The 1892 Double Shafted pound that nearly brought down the Kruger Government*, http://www.tokencoins. com/zar03.htm, accessed 2 June 2006.

We were driving in Oom Pieter's[30] carriage when a sentry stopped us for our permit. We were at once taken to the police station because the permit was only for the horses not for a carriage – it was no good my asking what good the horses were to us without a carriage – we had to go and report ourselves and escaped with a warning. So it goes – you can't put your nose out of doors without being asked if you have a permit for it.

Monday 16th July [1900].

"Rampie"[31] arrived here. A dog bit Kleinbooi[32] on his way to Aunt C[33] with our washing.

Tuesday 24th [July 1900].

We have had a dreadful experience. Poor old Kleinbooi died quite suddenly on Sunday. He was with us for nearly six months and was a fairly good boy at first but got steadily worse during the last few months. We often said to one another that he was getting duller, lazier and dirtier by the hour and we worried and harried him from morning to night. If his life was a burden to himself ours [sic] certainly was to us, but who could dream that it was <u>death</u> at his heels. He never complained and it never entered our heads that he was slowly dying of Bright's Disease.[34] On Sunday Mama heard him cleaning the stove rather late (about 7) so she went to see and came back to say he was drunk on something for he was behaving so strangely – could hardly speak and was lying on the ground laughing because he could not get up again. I dressed quickly and when I got there he was almost unconscious, rigid and cold and gasping for breath. We forced some brandy between his teeth, asked Mr Leliveld[35] to go for a doctor, and threw some blankets over him. Dr Mulder[36] came, examined him and said he was nearly gone – carried

---

30   Probably Pieter Potgieter, the former mayor of Pretoria, who was a friend of the Van Warmelo family. See diary entry on 1899-12-25.
31   Rampie. A domestic servant employed by the Van Warmelo's.
32   Kleinbooi. A domestic servant employed by the Van Warmelo's.
33   Probably Clara, the wife of Paul Maré, who was the brother of the diarist's mother.
34   Nephritis – inflammation of the kidneys.
35   Not identified.
36   Not identified.

him to the stable, where he lay on some nice fresh hay until about 3:30 when he drew his last breath, without having regained consciousness. I went to the hospital to get two Kaffirs and a stretcher to carry him away to the Volks Hospital where a post mortem was held. We were so nervous and wretched that night that I, for one, hardly closed my eyes. The thought of how we scolded and hurried him will haunt me for the rest of my life – and he was always so good-tempered. Just the day before he died he touched my black silk skirt gently and said he thought it very beautiful – he always admired me so much when I was dressed for going out. We never could make out what had come over him – his appetite was always so good and he seemed to grow fat. Afterwards we saw that his face, hands and feet were swollen but his arms wretchedly thin. We thought he was lazy when he rested so often in carrying water and chopping wood and often called him a "mesarri" (old woman). He stuttered and stammered lately and forgot everything – oh, it has been perfectly dreadful. To think that he should have died in harness!

July 26th [1900].

The Hollanders are going over the border wholesale – very often in open trucks. Khaki is dreadfully afraid of *Kaaskop*.[37] Lord and Lady Roberts are living in Hey's house[38] with their two daughters. Our nearest neighbours have nearly all gone away – a great relief to us. Had a telegram from Line on the 19th inst[ant] to say that Willem had left for South Africa.[39] Heard the next day that our boys were with Gen[eral]

---

[37] A derogatory term commonly used by Afrikaans-speaking South Africans to refer to people of Dutch descent.

[38] Widely known as Melrose House. It served as Roberts' and later as Kitchener's headquarters. The Peace of Vereeniging, by which the war was ended, was signed there on 31 May 1902.

[39] In the original it was Holland. The word Holland, written in pencil as the whole first script of the diary is, was subsequently crossed out and South Africa was written over it in black ink by the diarist herself. It should be Holland. Willem van Warmelo was a prisoner of war in British hands after his capture at the end of February 1900. His brother in law Hendrik Cloete secured his release on parole and he returned to Holland to resume his studies. See J. Brandt, *The Petticoat Commando*, p 3 and B. Roberts, *Those Bloody Women. Three Heroines of the Boer War*, p 98.

Botha.[40] His wife[41] had a letter from him in which he mentions their names – they are safe and well.

August 6th [1900]

Dear diary, I would write in you every day if we did not hear as many lying reports that we never know what to repeat and what not. The English seem to be getting beans every day. They become stricter and more severe by the hour – a sure sign that things are going badly with them outside. We are always made to suffer for their reverses. I hear that Baden-Powell is dead. Poor Willie McLaren[42] died of exposure at Balmoral some weeks ago. It was a terribly sad case. He and his men were caught in a fearful storm after a long day's march, and crept into some shelter, where he was found dead that day with three of his men. The cold must have been intense. His poor mother! My heart aches for her.

Great excitement prevailed at Harmony last week. Mama discovered that our fowls were diminishing by the day and we suspected Khakis or coolies[43] so we asked the Military Police to keep watch every night. They did so, but only for a few hours, not at dawn. The mother was quite sure the thief came at dawn, so one morning when the finest cock was missing, she traced him by the white feathers he had dropped in his struggles, right through Harmony and C. Joubert's[44] property to the

---

40   General Louis Botha, who succeeded Piet Joubert as commandant-general of the Transvaal forces in March 1900. After the war he became a leading politician and from 1910 until his death in 1919, he served as the first prime minister of the Union of South Africa. See D.W. Krüger, Botha, Louis, in *DSAB IV*, pp 41–51.

41   Mrs A.F.B. Botha, born Emmett, the wife of General Louis Botha. See T.C. Pienaar, Botha, Annie Frances Bland, in *DSAB III*, p 89.

42   In her book *The Petticoat Commando*, p 111, the diarist wrote that W. St. Clare McLaren was a former school friend of hers in Heidelberg. He became a lieutenant in the Argyle and Sutherland Highlanders and died with five of his comrades when a snow storm swept over the Highveld in the winter of 1900. However, there is no mention of any W. McLaren in Savannah Publications, *Boer War Services of Military Officers of the British and Colonial Armies Imperial Yeomanry Mounted Infantry Local Units &cc 1899–1902 including Earlier Services*, pages unnumbered.

43   A derogatory term commonly used by whites in Transvaal to refer to people of Indian descent.

44   C.J. Joubert's property was in Preller Street, south of Harmony. See *Long-*

river, where she came upon the den – an ideal place, in a little hollow, surrounded by trees and bushes and with the river flowing by: There were a few old sacks, a little fire-place with some tins etc – evidently the haunt of kaffirs. Heaps of feathers and fowl bones were lying scattered all over the place. Mama told the police about it but they thought it would be better to catch the thief red-handed, so they watched in the fowl-run again. Next morning two fine hens were missing so the mother sent Rampie at once (6.30 a.m.) to the den. If he found anyone there he was to say he was looking for his nonnie's little dog. Not long afterwards he came in great excitement to say that a Kaffir was sitting beside a fire, eating the fowls! The police went at once armed to the teeth and brought the culprit. Such a sight! Glimmering all over with fat, covered with feathers, and as the corporal said in high glee "With a corporation like the Lord Mayor". He was handcuffed and dragged to the police camp just next-door to us. It was too amusing to see the way every soldier went up to examine him and how each one in turn gave the "corporation" a dig, or felt it all over. Evidently the corporation is going to prove conclusively against him. While the police were having breakfast before taking him to the Charge Office, my fine gentleman slipped one hand cuff [sic], crept through the wire and flew like the wind over Harmony to the river. We were having breakfast too when we heard a fearful commotion, yells, and the barking of dogs. Carlo[45] flew madly after them and away they all went – the Kaffir with the hancuffs [sic] dangling from one wrist, jumping over furrows and bushes, tearing past trees and fences and long grass, and after him five soldiers, three Kaffirs and I don't know how many dogs. Mama and I stood watching it all in the greatest excitement and suspense. No, thank goodness, he has not escaped – here he comes with his hands securely fastened on his back and blood running from his mouth – the corporal had caught him just as he was climbing up the bank of the river and had given him a knock when he offered resistance. He was taken to the Charge Office at once, where Mama has just gone to give evidence against him.

All this happened on Dietlof's birthday. Poor boy, I wonder where he was then. We hear no word from them now-a-days but I don't think they can be very far from here for we hear the roar of cannon almost daily.

---

land's Pretoria Directory for 1899, p 139.
45   Carlo, the Van Warmelo's dog.

Today I am sending letters to Holland by the De Jongs[46] – neatly packed behind a photo frame. Something must be done to cheat Khaki. The Hollanders are being treated shamefully. Adelaar,[47] who was a typhoid patient while I was at the Volks Hospital, was sentenced to six years hard labour for saying that he did not consider his oath of neutrality binding because it was forced from him. Another man scratched out a nought on an official bulletin, making 500 of 5 000 Boers captured, and was arrested – I don't know what his punishment was.[48]

August 30th [1900].

The fowl thief got only one month, to everyone's amazement – the corporal told us it would be two years or 18 months. Someone else is stealing our fowls now so we are keeping them in the stable. About 19 are left of over 60!

Dear diary, this book is nearly full now and I suppose I shall have to begin another one because I don't see the end of the war yet. So much has happened lately that I don't know what to write down first. Of course this plot against Lord Roberts is the most important thing. An American detective, in the service of the Khakis, got into some disgrace and was discharged. In order to get back into favour again he led some people into a conspiracy which he very cleverly "discovered" afterwards. The young leader, Cordua,[49] was shot and all the others transported to

---

46 Not identified.

47 Probably the hairdresser H. Adelaar of Market Street, or H.A. Adelaar, the hairdresser of Church Street, since these are the only two Adelaars in Pretoria listed in *Longland's Pretoria Directory* for 1899, p 109.

48 On 1900-08-01 it was reported in the Government Gazette Extraordinary (1/11, p 472), that General Prinsloo, with 5 000 burghers had surrendered to Lieutenant-General Sir A. Hunter near Fouriesburg in the Orange Free State. According to more reliable sources about 4 300 burghers surrendered at that time. See T. Pakenham, *The Boer War*, p 444.

49 Hans Cordua was a 23 year old German who came to Transvaal in 1896. In the early part of the war he served in the State Artillery, but after the fall of Pretoria he took the oath of neutrality. He did indeed attempt but failed to persuade a number of surrendered Boers in Pretoria to assist him in a scheme to kidnap Roberts and hand him to a Boer commando. The chief witness in Cordua's trial was one Gano, a British secret agent of Spanish origin who had lived in South America for some time. As the diarist recorded, Gano seems to have been notified that he would be dismissed from the secret service. Since he wished to avoid that penalty, he assisted

Ceylon. Cordua was a German by birth, but a full burger of this State, young (22, I think) well-born, clever, rich; – in all respects a splendid man, and the trial, which was publicly held, showed him to be quite innocent. His fate was left in Lord Robert's [sic] hands and the next thing the world heard was that he had been shot. Everyone is furious about it and calls it a "murder", for not even his most intimate friends knew that he had been sentenced to death. This is the <u>English</u> way of doing things. Ah well, some day they will be punished for all their cruelty and injustice.

Hans Cordua

They are destroying farms wholesale, blowing up houses with dynamite, cutting trees down to the ground, burning cornfields and everything else that they can lay hands on – on the pretence that the Boers take shelter in the houses and fire on them. Strange! I thought we were in a desperate war and that each one had a right to take shelter where he could. Some time ago an English officer, Colonel Hilyard,[50] went hunting with his orderly

---

Cordua in his scheme, thus acting the part of an *agent provocateur*. Cordua was sentenced to death and shot by a firing squad on 24 August 1900. See S.B. Spies, *Methods of Barbarism? Roberts and Kitchener and Civilians in the Boer Republics January 1900 – May 1902*, pp 161–162. B. Theron (ed.), *Dear Sue*, pp 61–62 contains a moving account of Cordua's last hours. In the *Government Gazette* (1/14, 29 August 1900), it was reported in a government notice that Lieutenant Cordua was charged with violating his parole in taking "part in a movement against the British Government"; with being found and arrested "disguised in a British uniform"; and for conspiring "with certain persons with a view of seizing certain officers of Her Majesty's forces". He was found guilty of all the charges.

[50] There was no officer with the surname Hilyard (or Hillyard) in the British Forces in South Africa in the Anglo-Boer War. See Savannah Publications, *Boer War Services of Military Officers of the British and Colonial Armies Imperial Yeomanry Mounted Infantry Local Units &cc 1899–1902 including Earlier Services*, pages unnumbered.

right in the Boer lines outside Pretoria. Of course they were both shot and when the English found their bodies they destroyed the farms on which it happened, in the way described above. Our own cousins, the Jordaans,[51] were living there and the father and son were sent to Ceylon, the mother with seven children and an old grandfather of 82 were brought to Pretoria, where they are living between four bare walls, and all they possessed in the world destroyed. They have nothing to sleep on and nothing to eat except the rations they get – mealie meal so bitter that no one can touch it. We have done what we could for them but of course they are utterly ruined. There are many similar cases – we don't know the half of what takes place around us.

Since the conspiracy the English are in a state of the most abject terror – invalids, women and children are going over the border wholesale – one really gets quite sorry for Khaki in his fearfulness and misery.

We have begun our vocal society again under ten Brink.[52] Mrs Carl Hoepner[53] is President and yours truly Secretary and Treasurer. Our first meeting was held on the 22nd inst[ant] and the first rehearsal on the 29th. We have about 15 members. I had to go to the Governor to get a permit for our rehearsals, for two and three may not gather together except in the name of the Governor, so last Sat[urday] aft[ernoon] I went and had quite a long talk with him. He was alone and disengaged for a wonder and in a very gracious mood. I got our permit without much difficulty but had to answer a dozen questions and to promise that no politics would be discussed and that the members would be home before 7 p.m.[54] The Governor is very charming but I don't trust him

---

51   Not identified.

52   Ten Brink, Jan Hendrik (1856–1920). He was born in Amsterdam in the Netherlands and received his musical training there and in Paris, France. After emigrating to South Africa in 1896 he settled in Pretoria where he was one of the founders of a Music School. He gave singing lessons and did much to advance chamber music. See J. Ploeger, *Nederlanders in Transvaal*, p 119; C.G. Henning, Ten Brink, Jan Hendrik, in *DSAB IV*, pp 643–644.

53   Probably the wife of C. Hoepner, who lived in Skinner Street. See *Longland's Pretoria Directory for 1899*, p 136.

54   In terms of a proclamation issued by the Military Governor on 1900-06-25, the convening or holding of all meetings and assemblies of more than six male persons above the age of 16 years in the open air of any place, without his consent having first been obtained, was forbidden. See *Gov-*

– he tried to fish all sorts of things out of me, but oh, I was so hopelessly
ignorant whenever he tried to jump me. He even asked in a fatherly "I-
take-such-an-interest-in-you" way whether I ever heard from my brothers and murmered [sic] something about "a very trying time" when I
answered in the most innocent surprised "No, of course not, how are
we to hear?" We discussed music and politics and parted quite friendly
to all appearances but I wonder whether he guesses how I measured
him. He is false.

Last Sunday we got a photo from Line and a lovely long letter
through a Mr Secretan.[55] Poor thing, she looks so ill and sad and is so
discouraged. Two of her friends called on us, Captain Buckle[56] and
Colonel St Clare[57] – the first Khakis to cross our threshold as visitors
and equals – So have the mighty fallen! The mother declared that she
would <u>never</u> entertain a Khaki and this is the end of it. – There is something quite new now – every bicycle has to be registered and to carry a
ticket – I am no 636.[58]

They say Lord Methuen[59] is dead – wonder if it is true.

[For the next four months until the beginning of 1900 there is no entry
in the diary. Very little evidence on her thoughts and actions in this
period survived. It seems that she contemplated going to England, since
her friend J.S. Blumlein wrote in a letter from South Hampstead (near
London) on 12 October 1900: "You can't imagine how pleased I am

ernment *Gazette Extraordinary*, 1/8, 5 July 1900, p 101.

55 Can perhaps be Mr Searetan – not identified.

56 Not identified. A number of Captain Buckles are mentioned in Savan-
    nah Publications, *Boer War Services of Military Officers of the British and
    Colonial Armies Imperial Yeomanry Mounted Infantry Local Units &cc
    1899–1902 including Earlier Services*, pages unnumbered.

57 Probably Colonel J.L. St Clair, who was at one time the deputy judge ad-
    vocate to General Buller. See L.S. Amery (ed.), *The Times History of the
    War in South Africa 1899–1902 VI*, p 547.

58 Johanna van Warmelo was given a handwritten note signed by Captain
    R.W. Morley, Assistant Commissioner of Police, on 28 August 1900 that
    legalised her possession of her brother's bicycle. See Archives of the *Ned-
    erduitsch Hervormde Kerk van Afrika*, Pretoria, L.E. Brandt Collection,
    IX/160, unsorted, note signed by R.W. Morley, 28 August [1900].

59 Lord Methuen (Paul Sanford) served virtually throughout the war in the
    British forces. He only died in 1932. See B.J.T. Leverton, Sanford, Paul,
    third Baron of Methuen of Corsham, in *DSAB II*, pp 616–617.

to think that you are really coming to stay with me." [60] It is possible that she suffered from some ailment at this time, since on 28 November one of her relatives wrote from Holland: "I sincerely hope that Johanna is better. It would be the best if she could come to Europe as soon as possible, since that will brighten her up."[61]]

January 1901

In another book will be found the continuation of this most erratic diary.

[Script II]

[On front cover, on the inside:]
Firing heard by us:

Nov 17th 1900	direction of Johannesburg
Nov 18th	Middelburg
Nov 22nd	Scheerpoort
Nov 23rd	Krugersdorp from 5 to 11 am
Dec 13th	Nooitgedacht camp taken
Dec 16	Bronkhorstspruit, Paardekraal Nooitgedacht
Jan 1901	Nearly every day round Pretoria
Jan 12th	heaving [sic] firing Irene and Middelburg
Jan 16th	all afternoon Mundt's farm direction
Feb 25th	Heard three heavy shots at about 8.30 in the evening – sounded like cannon

January 1901.

Dear diary, With the new year I am going to make another attempt at writing down all my daily experiences, but this time you must under-

---

[60] Archives of the *Nederduitsch Hervormde Kerk van Afrika*, Pretoria, L.E. Brandt Collection, IX/160, file titled 1894–1902, Aan JB – vriende, ens, unsorted, J.S. Blumlein – J. van Warmelo, 12 October 1900.

[61] Archives of the *Nederduitsch Hervormde Kerk van Afrika*, Pretoria, L.E. Brandt Collection, IX/160, file titled 1894–1902, Aan JB – vriende, ens, unsorted, Emilia – Dear Mrs and Johanna, Lith, 28 November 1900, translated from original Dutch by editor.

stand when I say "we hear" or "it is said" that I am only quoting the rumours that reach us, and that I cannot vouch for the truth of any of the said rumours. I also intend making this more a <u>personal</u> than <u>political</u> diary because I feel the need of some means of relieving my heart. I have no intimate friend, dear diary, to whom I can speak freely and I fear you will have to put up with fearful and wonderful confessions, but you must just be patient and remember that I am passing through a never-to-be-forgotten stage of my existence. Month after month this terrible war is dragging on and not even the most sanguine of us can see the end of it, and the longer it lasts the less strength we have to endure it. I feel some days that all my will-power is going and that I shall break down utterly before long, but human beings are endowed with an extraordinary power of endurance and it takes a great deal to break a heart and blight a young life. Some day I daresay I shall look back on this time trial with an interesting feeling of self-satisfaction – as if I had done something wonderful; perhaps (and this is more likely) the marks of this war will remain with me to the end of my days, tinging [sic] my life with melancholy.

"Stop moralising, J[ohanna], and tell me the latest news".

Well, if you will keep in mind what I said about "rumours" I can go on writing for hours, but first let me tell you some "true news". On Old Year's Day we had a visit from Dr Mulder, who had been allowed to come in from the Boer lines, on his way to Holland. He brought us glad tidings from our boys, for he had seen Dietlof in the English camp at Nooitgedacht immediately after its capture (on Dec[ember] 13th)[62] and both boys were in perfect health and the highest spirits. From him we heard every detail of that great reverse the English had. Gen Beyers[63] with 2 000 men (amongst whom were D[ietlof] and F[ritz]) attacked the camp in the early morning and took everything in it, killing and wounding hundreds of English and capturing a great many. De la Rey failed to put in an appearance at the appointed time and when he arrived

---

[62]   The Battle of Nooitgedacht took place on 1900-12-13 and ended in a victory for the Republican forces led by General de la Rey. For Dietlof van Warmelo's own account of the battle, see his memoirs titled *Mijn commando en guerilla commando-leven*, pp 125–137.

[63]   Christiaan Frederik Beyers, one of the Boer commanders in the Battle of Nooitgedacht. See Anon, Beyers, Christiaan Frederik, in *DSAB III*, pp 64–67.

there all was over. Through this a great many of the enemy escaped and our own losses were heavier than usual – 15 killed and 63 wounded, of whom only about 14 were too badly injured to go away with the commandos again. Seven loads of ammunition were taken and partly destroyed.[64] Amongst the prisoners taken were two or three of our own Government officials and they were released along with the rest! The Boers are as lax and indifferent as ever. No question of shooting spies and rebels – nothing of the stern discipline which characterizes the English army. "I hear" that Kitchener had 30 outposts shot the other day for being drunk on duty! Fancy a Boer shooting <u>one</u> man in cold blood! It is very foolish of them to be so lax and yet I am thankful that they err on the side of mercy. Dr M[ulder] said he was present at Pres Steyn's address to the burgers and there was not any question of false hopes being held out to them. Pres S[teyn] said plainly that the men who were holding out in the hopes of intervention could go home – they must expect to triumph by their own unaided efforts – <u>he</u> personally did not for a moment build on foreign help.

This is exactly the opposite of what the English say. They declare to all the world that the Boers are kept in the field by means of false hopes and promises held out to them. Ah, dear diary, <u>I</u> can tell you what is keeping them in the field – faith in a God of Justice, love of independence and a determination to have it, and a bitter hatred of British rule, to which they will <u>never</u> bow after all that has happened. Those noble, lion hearted men, the flower of our nation, would rather die than give in. What inducement have they for surrendering? Their homes are burnt to the ground, their farms destroyed, their women and children carried away. Heaven only knows where! They have nothing left to live for and nothing more to lose and as long as they have strength they will

---

64   She is rather harsh in her criticism of De la Rey. Even though the Boers failed to capture the whole British force, the fact remains that De la Rey planned the Boer attack at Nooitgedacht and achieved considerable, although incomplete, success. A total of 109 British soldiers were killed, 186 wounded and 368 captured, as well as a booty of 70 fully loaded supply wagons, 200 tents, a large supply of ammunition, 400 horses, 300 mules and 500 cattle. The Boer loss amounted to 32 dead and 46 wounded. See A. Wessels, *Die Anglo-Boereoorlog 1899–1902*, p 40 and G. van der Bergh, *24 Veldslae en slagvelde van die Noordwes Provinsie*, pp 103–112.

struggle against their mortal foe. Our hearts may bleed for the innocent victims of England's "drastic measures" but we and our children will thank God for them in the years to come, for nothing can wipe out the bitter feeling now.

"But J[ohanna], your writing is getting worse by the day. Please don't hurry so".

"Is this better? Thank you for the reminder, dear diary, but my feelings run away with me and my pencil, when I get on the subject of politics. However, I shall try to do better in future. You are going to be a good and true friend, I see, and I feel glad of the happy thought that inspired me to cultivate your acquaintance.

Today I began my painting lessons again (January 18th) and now I want to tell you how my days are spent. Who knows how interesting it will be fifty years hence for my grand-children to read of my occupations during the dreadful war of – I wonder what it will be called. I always say "Franchise War", for was not that the lame excuse England offered for endeavouring to take our country?

Well to begin with Monday (I like to end with the first day of the week – the sweet day of rest) I get up at 5 o'clock every morning, have a shower-bath and begin at once with my house work so that most of it is done before the worst heat comes. On Monday morning I have no special house-work so I mend and darn, attend to the flowers and do all sorts of little odd jobs. Have a nap after dinner – always – because one can't keep one's eyes open from 5 a.m. to 10 p.m. without a rest – give one music lesson at 4 o'clock and spend the rest of the afternoon in calling or shopping. My evenings are all the same – reading, writing or studying French – and we go to bed early.

On Tuesday morning turn out drawing-room – afternoon 1 music lesson and vocal rehearsal, of which more anon. Wed[nesday] morning, dining room, afternoon, tennis or cycling. Thursday morning, French lesson and one music lesson – afternoon "At home". Friday, turn out bedroom, afternoon – painting lesson and give one music-lesson [sic]. Saturday morning vocal practice with two girl friends – afternoon – holiday. Sunday morning Church – afternoon, "At Home". There is not one moment during the day that I don't know what to do with and I think that has a great deal to do with my contented frame of mind.

My house-hold duties are innumerable – sewing, dusting, sweeping, cooking. Just now we are canning fruit for the winter season – great jars of apples, pears, peaches, grapes, etc[etera]. Of course our thoughts stray lovingly and longingly to the two hungry fellows in the field while we are working with those immense baskets of fruit. The figs and grapes are very fine this year and Harmony is a picture just now, after the rains. Yesterday the mail brought me a photo from L[ouis] B[randt][65] – such a nice one. I wonder whether he wrote at the same time – it appears that Khaki is keeping back our letters again. My friend has a fine face, so good and strong – a face that every woman must trust instinctively. I wonder whether – never mind J[ohanna] leave off wondering and write down what you have to tell. Oh yes, I also received a magnificent badge from James Incl[66] a stag's head in a wreath of ivy leaves – in solid silver – the badge of the Seaforth Highlanders – or Gordons, I forget which. A Khaki doctor brought it from James and I am afraid he had a cool reception, for the mother and I had just made up our minds that not another Khaki would cross our threshold – at least not visits of pleasure. That same afternoon (Thursday) Captain B[67] came again and I had to perform the painful task of asking him not to come to us as long as the war lasts. He has been a regular visitor here for nearly six months and we have shown him in every way how we disliked his coming, but to no avail – he could not or would not see how unwelcome he was. We had many quarrels and many a hot dispute on the subject of the war and I was often furious with him for his tactless and unfeeling remarks. He is a great Jingo[68] and has the thickest skin I have ever came across and yet there were many things I admired in him – his great love of animals and of all nature – flowers, birds and insects. He is well informed on almost every subject, has travelled and read and seen a great deal and is most observant, but for all that we could not get on with him. Dangerous topics were always cropping up and more than once I saw his handsome

---

65   Louis Ernst Brandt, the diarist's future husband. He was born in 1873 in Holland and became a minister in the Dutch Reformed Church. In January 1901 he was still waiting for a call to a congregation. The diarist met him when she visited Holland before the war. See P.S. Dreyer, Brandt, Louis Ernst, *DSAB II*, p 85.

66   Not identified.

67   Presumably Captain Buckle, who first visited Harmony in August 1900.

68   Jingo – supporter of British war policy.

face go white with rage when we mentioned cases of English brutality, which we knew to be <u>facts</u>, but which he absolutely refused to believe. He has a passionate temper, which he has well under control, I must say, and we always knew, by the way his bold black eyes blazed, how angry he was. Yesterday when I asked him not to come again, his face was a study, but he said nothing except "I am very sorry. What have I done?" I put our reasons before him nicely and courteously but he only shook his head and said he failed to see what they had to do with him. However, he bade us goodbye very tragically and I saw him clench his right hand as he walked down the garden path. He looks very nice when he is angry. It was a wretched business but it had to come some day and I am thankful it is over. Mama would not do it – she hated the idea and is afraid we may want him some day when we are in trouble. Well, I would rather die than appeal to <u>him</u>, especially now.

Our friends are leaving Pretoria wholesale. On the 16th inst[ant] Mrs Carl Hoepner went to Europe. I do miss her so – she was so very good to me. Yesterday Mr Hay[69] and Mrs de Zwaan[70] left – they will join Mrs H[oepner] in Durban and travel together from there. What are we going to do without Mr Hay? For nearly a year we have been receiving letters from Line regularly through him – and from many other people as well. He was perfectly charming about doing favours for people and never made us feel under any obligation to him – but he is coming back – perhaps within a few months and in the meantime Mr Gordon,[71] American Consul at Johannesburg, will see about our letters.

Now that Mrs Hoepner is gone Mrs Esses[72] has been chosen Presi-

69   Probably Adelbert H. Hay, the Consul of the United States of America in Pretoria from the end of 1899 to the end of 1900. See L. Changuion, *Uncle Sam, Oom Paul en John Bull: Amerika en die Anglo-Boereoorlog, 1899–1902*, pp 77, 162.

70   Probably the wife of Willem Johannes de Zwaan, an architect from Holland who settled in Pretoria before the war. See J. Ploeger, *Nederlanders in Transvaal 1850–1950*, p 63.

71   Hay never returned. William D. Gordon, the American consular agent in Johannesburg, became the acting US Consul in Pretoria in Hay's place. Gordon was an outspoken supporter of the Boer Republics. See L. Changuion, *Uncle Sam, Oom Paul en John Bull : Amerika en die Anglo-Boereoorlog, 1899–1902*, pp 45, 162.

72   Should be Esser, probably the wife of J. Esser, a judge in the supreme court of the South African Republic. See J. Ploeger, *Nederlanders in Transvaal*

dent of our Vocal Society, and the rehearsals are held in Mrs Ueckermann's[73] house in Schoeman St[reet]. Ten Brink is still conductor and I am Secretary and Treasurer. We have only about 12 members now, but I think some new ones will soon join us. – It is late, dear diary and I want to go and sing just one little song before going to bed, so goodnight.

January 19 [1901]

As today has been very uneventful I want to go back a little to some things that were neglected during the months that I did not keep a diary. Today we only went to see Oom P[74] and had a fine old talk about the war. He drove us home because it rained heavily while we were there and the streets were in a frightful condition.

During the last few weeks Khaki has been very anxious because Pretoria was almost entirely surrounded by Boers. An attack on the Town was expected and every night the search-lights were used from the forts. We are even told that a week ago two trains were standing ready all night to remove Kitchener and his staff in case of danger. Trenches have been dug all round the Town, electric wires put up and every hill is bristling with cannon – in fact every imaginable precaution has been taken against the re-capture of Pretoria. It is delightful to us to see Khaki in such a state of terror and we all long for the time when the Boers will sweep into the Town. Of course they would do it in the night but most of us think there is not the slightest possibility of such an event taking place. I do. Some fine night we shall hear a great commotion and Botha will be here – if only to release our prisoners; – they will not try to keep Pretoria, that would be impossible against those heavy siege-guns.

It is three days now since last we heard any firing and everything seems quieter, although a great many troops went out this morning on the Eastern line. We can see every train that passes and we generally make a rush for doors and windows when the whistle is heard. Some-

---

1850–1950, p 63.

73 Probably the wife of Carl Ueckermann, Jr., an attorney, notary and conveyancer in Pretoria. According to *Longland's Pretoria Directory for 1899*, p 172, he was the only Ueckermann with a residence in Schoeman Street.

74 Can be either Oom Paul (Maré), the uncle of the diarist, or Oom Pieter (not identified).

times the trains consists of hundreds of Khakis, coming back or going out to some great fight, sometimes of open trucks heavily laden with women and children who are being brought in from their ruined homes, and sometimes the train creeps slowly and softly in with its sad burden of sick and wounded. The long white carriages with their bright Red Cross glide into Town noiselessly, bearing so many innocent victims – the victims of England's greed of gold – and one would be heartless indeed if such a sight failed to sent a thrill of pain through one. I know that our salvation depends on the number of English killed and wounded and yet I can never see those Red Cross carriages without a feeling of intense sadness.

The hospitals here are full to overflowing and just now there are so many cases of typhoid fever and dysentery. Typhoid is so bad this year that most cases terminate fatally – perhaps the patients are in a very low state after all they have endured – perhaps because so few luxuries are obtainable now – good wine, milk, eggs, etc. But, dear diary, I have not told you yet of the saddest thing (to me) that has happened during this whole war. In November my friend and playmate, Minnie Goodwin[75], died at Barberton ten days after having given birth to a baby-girl. It does not sound so very bad, does it, but you must know what it means. Not only is her babe left motherless and her young husband desolate and lonely after not quite eleven months of married life, but a mother mourns her favourite daughter, her pet, her darling, a sister has lost her best friend and companion and two old people, her grandparents, who adored her, are left to bear their heavy grief in their old age. And I have lost a friend, the friend on a life time, for Minnie was only five years old when first I met her. Minnie cut off in all the pride and beauty of her one and twenty summers! Minnie dead! Ah no, I <u>cannot</u> believe it even after these three months, and what is hardest of all to me is to think that my darling friend, Edith, is bearing the great loss of her only sister and I can do nothing to help her. Edith will never, never get over it and yet she is bearing her grief nobly and bravely, and doing all she can to comfort her broken-hearted parents. Minnie's baby is with them poor little motherless girl! It seems too cruel that she should have come into

---

[75] The diarist knew Minnie Goodwin and her sister Edith well since they were childhood friends in Heidelberg in the 1880s. See B. du Toit, *Die verhaal van Johanna Brandt*, pp 18–24.

the world with an affliction that embittered and saddened her mother's last days – an affliction that must grieve and humiliate her for the rest of her own life – a terrible hare-lip! Oh, when I heard about it my whole being rose up against it in bitter rebellion – the thought seemed more than I could bear. How then does poor Edith bear it? All around us nothing but misery – is there to be no more joy and beauty in our lives? I remember so well how Minnie looked when I saw her at the railway station not one year ago. She confided her sweet secret to me with many blushes and drew herself up with great dignity when I teasingly said "But Minta, you are such a baby yourself still!" That was the last time I saw my friend – strange that I had not even the shadow of a presentiment of what was going to happen. And now I have vowed that my home will be a second home to her baby and that I shall do all that lies within my power to sweeten her young life – Minnie Goodwin Skirving – she has been christened. Poor little darling!

We are all very much troubled to hear that the prisoners at Ceylon and St Helena are dying in hundreds of all sorts of diseases. They say the Information Bureau here gets long lists of the dead. Can it be true?[76] I must make enquiries, for this is too terrible. I suppose the islands are over-populated now and the sanitation bad – some reason there must be, for they used to be healthy enough. In the camps here we have more than 500 prisoners. Mama's youngest brother was there for many weeks, but has been released on parole. We can never be thankful enough that Willem is free and back in Holland again. Lucky fellow! How dreadful it would have been if he had been at Ceylon all this time, it may have ruined his whole career.

January 20th [1901]

On this most perfect Sabbath morn, dear diary, you find me sitting under the verandah, surrounded by my books and flowers, Carlo, the Faithful, by my side, an exquisite view before me and the sweet summer air filled with the fragrance of innumerable buds and blossoms. After last night's storm the atmosphere is crisp and cold and very clear – overhead the sky is the deepest, richest sapphire blue, paling away towards

---

[76]   It was not true. The Information Bureau was a section of the Transvaal Red Cross.

the horizon to the most delicate tints, against which the distant hills show in bold relief. And before me is a perfect view of our fruit-laden garden, the great pear-trees with their burden of yellow fruit, the vines with their bunches of purple and white grapes, the orange trees with their thousands of dark green, unripe oranges, and in the distance the apple-trees with their fruit in every imaginable shade of crimson and yellow – the whole a perfect picture to rest one's weary eyes upon. Of course, I do not dwell upon the weeds and unseen reptiles that do abound so plentifully in our little Paradise, nor do I describe the military camp upon which I have carefully turned my back. Why should our thoughts be poisoned on a day like this? Why indeed? Why then is my heart so full of anguish and unrest? Ah. Lord, the beauties of nature have, in my case, failed in their endeavour to atone for the evil passions of mankind and they only serve as a bitter contrast to the awful strife that is being waged in our fair land.

The Reverend H.S. Bosman

We are not going to Church today because someone told us that Mr Bosman[77] is preaching in the women's camp at Irene this morning.[78] That camp is one of the most disgraceful things

---

[77] The Reverend H.S. Bosman was the minister of the Dutch Reformed Church in Pretoria from 1876 to 1926. See F.G.M. du Toit, Bosman, Hermanus Stephanus, in *DSAB I*, pp 104–105.

[78] The British established one of their notorious refugee camps (later on called concentration camps) at Irene, about 20 kilometres south of central Pretoria on the eastern side of the railway line to Johannesburg in December 1900. It was used to accommodate Boer women and children whose farms had been destroyed, or who had no means of subsistence. See T. van Rensburg (ed.), *Camp diary of Henrietta E.C. Armstrong. Experiences of a Boer nurse in the Irene Concentration Camp, 6 April – 11 October 1901*, pp 45–47.

in this war. Can you imagine any civilized nation, dear diary, forming camps for women and children in the principal entrances of a town and sheltering behind them with their armoured trains and cannon. That is what the English have done, knowing very well that the Boers dare not make an attack when their own wives and children are in such exposed positions. Things go badly with them in the camp, I hear. They do not get full rations and there is much sickness. They live in tents – whole families of them with little children. The worst is that sometimes they have to stand in open trucks at the railway station until they can be removed to Irene. Someone told me that one trainload stood there from Friday until Sunday, in the blazing sun by day and pouring rain by night, and that the skin was peeling from the children's arms – for they are turned out of their homes in such haste that very often they are not even properly dressed.

A horrible rumour is afloat of a woman and seven or eight children who were burnt alive in their home near Krugersdorp – but I can't find out how much truth there is in it. It seems that a woman here says that she and some of her friends had notice to be ready to leave within ten days and one night she woke to find the roof in flames over her head. She managed to save her children and rushed out to warn her neighbours and about six families escaped, but when they came to the last house everything was in ruins and the whole family burnt to death. This is supposed to have happened somewhere near Doornkop – the scene of Jamieson's fall.[79] The rumour is so persistent that I cannot help thinking that <u>something</u> of the sort must have happened. – I wonder whether there is any fighting out Middelburg way – another train load of troops has just gone out – looked like reinforcements. – Some young people are coming to eat fruit here this afternoon; we often give what we call "fruit parties" during the summer.

---

[79]   L.S. Jameson and his Freebooters were captured at Doornkop west of Johannesburg by Boer forces on 2 January 1896 at the end of the ill-conceived so-called Jameson Raid. It is generally acknowledged that this unsuccessful attempt to overthrow Kruger's government in Pretoria irreparably damaged the trust between the South African Republic and British authorities both in South Africa and in London and thus contributed significantly to the eventual outbreak of the Anglo-Boer War in October 1899. See T.R.H. Davenport, *South Africa. A Modern History*, p 188.

Sunday evening: Harmony was overrun with young people this afternoon – Consuéla Minnaar[80], Sarah Rood[81] and her brother, a Miss Buyskes[82], Gustav Fichardt[83], Archie Truter[84] and Fred Niemeyer[85] – Mama also had companions, Mrs van Eeghen[86] and the French Consul[87]. The young folks disappeared into the garden and lost themselves for the rest of the afternoon. They roamed under the trees and ate as many figs and grapes as they possibly could and seemed to enjoy themselves immensely. They told us that three trains were taken near Balmoral – one of provisions and two of coals. The Boers are having a fine time.

January 21st [1901]

Today news arrived from England that Queen Victoria[88] is on her death bed and all her children have been summoned to her side. I don't think she will die – if she gets better, dear diary, I'll tell you my reasons for thinking so. The poor old soul may be dead by this time and then it would not be kind of me to say what I think. All day reinforcements have been going to Belfast – whole trains of them. I sometimes counted over 30 trucks, laden with horses and carts and troops and cannon, and I heard a few very distant cannon shots. They say a great battle is raging

80   Consuéla (Connie) Minnaar was probably the daughter of J.C. Minnaar, the Registrar of Deeds, whose house stood in Schoeman Street, Pretoria. See *Longland's Pretoria Directory for 1899*, p 153.

81   Sarah Rood and her elder sister Annie were friends of the author, as was their brother Karel. Their father, Karel Rood, was the owner of Parkzicht, a fashionable mansion in Maré Street next door to Melrose House.

82   Not identified.

83   Not identified.

84   Probably A. Truter, the post office clerk who lived in Market Street and who is the only Truter mentioned in *Longland's Pretoria Directory for 1899*, p 172.

85   Not identified. There were, according to *Longland's Pretoria Directory for 1899*, p 156, at least four Niemeyer families living in Pretoria at that time. He could have belonged to any of those families.

86   Probably the wife of H.M. van Eeghen, secretary of the Pietersburg Railway Company, who is the only Van Eeghen mentioned in *Longland's Pretoria Directory for 1899*, p 128.

87   The French Consul in Pretoria was V.S. Aubert. See *Longland's Pretoria Directory for 1899*, p 228.

88   Monarch of the United Kingdom of Great Britain and Ireland from 1837 to her death on 22 January 1901. See A.L. Harrington, Victoria (Alexandra Victoria), in *DSAB V*, pp 841–842.

at Belfast – I wonder if our two dear boys are there. Paulus[89], our Kaffir, told us this evening that Mr Jasper Aitchison[90] told him that somebody else told him that the boys were safe and well on the 7th inst[ant]. My kitten's got cats.[91]

January 22nd. [1901]

Thousands of troops with carts, horses and cannon have been going to Belfast today again. It breaks my heart to see those great reinforcements going out and to know what their object is. Someone told me today that the English were getting paddy-whacks where they are fighting and I must say it looks like it when so much help is needed.

The Queen is not dead yet – she is even a little better today. I told you she would not die and now I'll tell you why – because she is pre-served in spirits and will only shake off this mortal coil by a process called "spontaneous combustion". Some fine day the English will wake up to find their beloved old Queen has disappeared leaving no trace be-hind her, but this won't happen soon because *"Onkruid vergaat niet"*[92]. Dear diary, I know you are shocked at me but tonight I feel positively wicked so you must excuse me if I close this chronicle – at least until I am in a more charitable frame of mind.

January 23rd. [1901]

The Queen is dead. Last night while I was writing those words she died, at about 9.30. I am in more charitable frame of mind, dear D[iary], so

---

89   A domestic servant employed by the Van Warmelo's.
90   Probably a member of the family of E. Aitchison, grocer and general deal-er, who is the only Aitchison mentioned in *Longland's Pretoria Directory for 1899*, p 111.
91   Probably the cat which the diarist, according to her own admission, "kid-napped". In her book *The Petticoat Commando*, pp 283–284, she reveals this history. Shortly after the British occupation of Pretoria, she and her mother were returning home one afternoon. As they passed the house occupied by a senior British officer, they saw a black kitten with a ribbon of blue satin round her neck. The diarist exclaimed 'I wish you belonged to me!' In jest her mother answered: 'She does,' picked the kitten up and placed it in her daughter's arms. The diarist refused to put the kitten down again, but claimed it as a "trophy of the war". She called it Mauser, after the rifles used by the Boers.
92   Onkruid vergaat niet (Dutch) – Ill weeds grow apace.

I shall tell you the latest news. Belfast is in the hands of the Boers and things are going very well over there, but they say that the Heidelberg commando made a fearful blunder and suffered heavily – I know no details. Reinforcements are still going hourly – train after train and it seems as if the trouble is by no means over yet. Until definite news reaches us, I can tell nothing.

I spent the afternoon with Connie Minnaar whose birthday it is. There were a great many young people.

January 24th. [1901]

This afternoon Archie Truter took me for a long drive – it was delightful. We were out <u>spying</u> and went to nearly all the boundaries of the Town and of course were stopped by half a dozen Tommies. No one may go beyond a certain limit without a special permit, which we had <u>not</u> so we amused ourselves by going as far as we could and making many important observations on the way – where the English

Queen Victoria

camps are, the situation of the different cannon, the extent of the field hospitals etc, etc. This morning, when I was at my French lesson, Henriette Aubert[93] told me that our dear old President had dined with the Dutch Queen[94], he and Dr Leyds[95]. Her mother[96] was also present and this remarkable quartette [sic] spent the evening amicably together.

---

[93]　Probably a family member of the French Consul in Pretoria.

[94]　Queen Wilhelmina. See J. Ploeger, Wilhelmina (Helena Paulin Maria), in *DSAB IV*, pp 780–781.

[95]　W.J. Leyds was the South African Republic's Special Envoy and Minister Extraordinary in Europe at the time of the Anglo-Boer War. See D.W. Krüger, Leyds, Willem Johannes, in *DSAB III*, pp 516–520.

[96]　Queen Adelheid Emma Wilhelmina Theresia. See J. Ploeger, Wilhelmina (Helena Paulin Maria), in *DSAB IV*, p 780.

The Hollanders have collected money in order to send teachers to Ceylon, for the benefit of the youths, who have given up their studies for *"land en volk"*[97] – a very good idea. What has Holland not done for us, dear diary, in this bitter war? Can we ever repay her? And then it grieves me to the heart to hear them being run down by our own people. Has our nation no sense of gratitude? And what has Holland done to deserve the hatred and distrust of the Africanders? It is one of the greatest and saddest problems to me. If I don't marry an Africander I shall look for some nice young Hollander, just to show the other girls what a mistake they are making in looking down on *"Kaaskop"*. Good heavens, who are <u>they</u>, I wonder, to look down on anybody. I am afraid they have never had the chance of meeting the kind of Hollanders I know – men like my father was, and .... and .... ever so many others.

Queen Victoria's death has cast a great gloom over her soldiers. They go about with black bands round their arms, the flags are all half mast and every shop and office is closed. Today the big cannon boomed triumphantly at mid-day when the king was crowned – so goes it ever – *"La reine est morte, vive le roi"*[98] – change and decay all around us and the greatest change of all, within our own breasts, daily, hourly, as each new experience or emotion builds up our characters, as each new grief purifies and sweetens – or embitters – us, as each new joy brightens our sad existence. Our joys are few and far between now and I sometimes wonder whether we shall ever again be free from care on this side of the grave. – I had one joy today, dear D[iary], – a sweet, long letter from mine Sister. An angel must have brought it to Pretoria for we know not how it came here. I only know that a ragged little boy brought it to Harmony and handed it to me with the grave enquiry *"Woon die menschen hier?"*[99] pointing with one dirty little finger at the address. When I said "yes", he disappeared. Our darling is well and begs us to be of good cheer, for all is going in our favour. The rising in the Colony must be getting serious, but of course she says very little about it. Mrs Gen[eral] Botha has had a letter from her husband through Kitchener. He says he has never been so well and she must just keep cheerful – *"alles zal*

---

97   Land en volk (Dutch) – country and people.
98   "The king is dead, long live the king!" The diarist is wrong. Victoria's successor, King Edward VII, was only crowned after the war.
99   "Do these people live here?"

reg kom"[100] – but when? We <u>can't</u> endure it much longer – but then, I said the same thing a year ago. Will this time next year find us in the same condition? Ah no, it <u>cannot</u>, it cannot. I think I would rather die this minute than go through another year of this misery.

The Boers have damaged the dynamos of the Johannesburg electric light and all the mines and some of the suburbs are in total darkness. They must have come pretty near in order to do a thing of that sort.

Mama saw Jasper Aitchison this morning and he said <u>his</u> boys were well on the 7th inst[ant] not ours. I wonder where they are tonight, my poor, dear, homeless, hunted-down brothers.

January 25th [1901], <u>midday.</u>

As I write, the great guns on the forts are booming every minute. Is the Queen being buried, I wonder, or what <u>can</u> it be? The mother has gone to Town and will be able to tell me perhaps when she comes home. Strange! Last night when I was writing those last words I had such a terrible fit of the blues – my whole being was plunged into the deepest sadness and I felt too utterly "down" to speak even to my mother, and then I read our evening portion Ps[alm] 88, every word of which came straight from my heart, for it seemed as if it had been specially written for <u>me</u> – and I felt better. How often it has happened during this dreadful war that the evening portion has been exactly suited to my needs! I never understood and appreciated the Old Testament as I do now – every word is a revelation to me as seen in the light of recent events.
<u>Evening.</u>
Vocal rehearsal this afternoon. The day has been changed to Friday now as some of the new members could not come on Tuesdays. I paint on Tuesdays now. "Oom Willie"[101] told me that Maria M[aré][102] is in Town and that she says she saw our boys in Pietersburg a month ago. Fritz was suffering from fever. I must get hold of her and hear further particulars. I suppose the boys went back to Zoutpansburg after the battle at Nooitgedacht – how I long to know for certain. This everlasting suspense is enough to kill one. – Horse-sickness is very bad this year

---

[100]   "Everything will be alright"
[101]   Not identified.
[102]   Should be Maria Knevitt – see the diarist's entry on 1901-01-31, where she herself gives that surname.

and the worst time is till to come. Mama went to the Governor this morning to ask him not to allow anyone to commandeer our fruit – or at least only a part of what we send to the market. He was most affable and gave her permission to sell as much fruit out of hand as she pleased – although the last proclamation strictly forbids it.

January 26 [1901].

This afternoon we had the loan of Margaret's[103] carriage to take fruit to the Volks Hospitaal (Pretoria Hospital, Khaki calls it now). We were stopped under the great railway bridge (Pre[toria]-Pietersburg Railway) by a sentry, who said we could not pass without a special permit. When asked where the permit was to be got he informed us "at the Gov[ernmen]t Buildings" right in the Town, to which we drove full speed. I enquired first of a small boy, who referred me to No. 7, who referred me to Major Hoskins[104], who referred me to Pass Office, Pretorius Street. There I eventually got a permit, with orders to go back to Gov[ernment] B[ui]ld[in]gs, as it had to be signed by the Governor. By the time we got away all our pleasure was spoilt for us and we had only a few minutes to spend with the patients. That is what is called "Red Tape", dear Diary, and may you never have the misfortune to become acquainted with it. The patients had a lot to tell us but of course one does not know how much to believe – De Wet[105] had joined Botha at Belfast – of 15 000 Khakis, 4 000 were killed and wounded and 2 000 captured – de la Rey's little son[106] has been sent in to Pretoria by his father, who (he says) was slightly wounded in the head etc etc. Afterwards when I went to see the Cinattis. I found the French Consul there also and they all say the English have had a terrible reverse – but 6 000 men killed and wounded must be an exaggeration.[107] M. Aubert says there

---

103   Not identified.
104   Major A.R. Hoskins was the aide-de-camp of Governor Maxwell. See National Archives, Pretoria, TAB, T115, Inventory to the Archives of the Military Governor, Pretoria, p vii.
105   Christiaan Rudolph de Wet, the Chief Commandant of the Orange Free State, was not in Transvaal at this time, but was preparing for his second invasion of the Cape Colony. See De Wet, C.R., *Die Stryd Tussen Boer en Brit*, pp 203–204.
106   Jan de la Rey. See J. Meintjies, *De la Rey – Lion of the West*, p 69.
107   It was a gross exaggeration.

was an accident to a goods train at Zuurfontein this morning – went full speed round a curve and capsized over an embankment. <u>Nothing saved.</u>

I think I have heard firing in the direction of Arcadia this morning. Maria M. [Knevitt] came here this afternoon with her baby boy, just before we went out. She is married to an Englishman and was put over the border by the Boers in Pietersburg. Strange that Pretoria should be other side of our own borders now! Verily the world is turning upside-down. She says the Boers have no food or clothing in that part of the world and that Fritz was in tatters when he came there. Dietlof was not so bad. The Boers live on mealie porridge and meat and make clothes of table-linen and sheets. Fritz was very ill with fever but had quite re-covered when she saw him – <u>before</u> they were at Nooitgedacht. Maria was very angry because Mama said she had better not bring her English-man to us – she flared up and went away in a great temper, vowing not to come here again. Well, well, no one can expect us to be very tolerant after all that has happened.

In a letter I had from John Rabie[108] this morning through the Ameri-can Consul, he says that Martial Law has been proclaimed throughout the Colony, except in a few sea port Towns.

January 27th. [1901]

Another Sunday at home. I did not go to church because I do not feel very well today – spent the morning on the couch, dozing and reading. I think an occasional day of perfect rest does me good. In the afternoon we had many visitors – it was quite an effort to me to entertain them and yet these Sunday visitors are becoming a regular institution and there is no getting away from them. Gustav Fichardt brought me a 1900 Kruger sovereign – a lovely present.

I have just written to L[ouis] B[randt] to thank him for the photo he sent me and then I went out into the cool night air to <u>think</u> – wonderful thoughts, so sad and sweet, with the sadness predominating for what is there sweet about my life now? The night is perfect. I shall go out again and fill myself with its beauty, before we retire. The sky is covered with heavy clouds, through which only the Southern Cross is blazing in all

---

108   Not identified.

its splendour and the young moon shows its modest half-crescent occasionally.

I have often noticed that the finest sun-sets and moonlight nights are when great clouds are drifting about. Is it so with us too? Is no life perfect until it has been darkened by the clouds of sin and suffering? Yes, even <u>sin</u>, for what influences character more than the memory of some deeply regretted act of folly?

Look here, dear diary.[109] This is the way the English are trying to make peace. They are actually punishing Boer women and children for the "sins" of their husbands and fathers. I would not have believed it unless I had read it with my own eyes in an English paper. What I wonder most about is that this scandalous paragraph is headed "Kitchener's Appeal". Appeal to what and for what? One can hardly call "reducing the rations" <u>an appeal</u>. I call it a threat, pressure, force, anything you like – but then I am only an uncivilized little Boer girl.

January 28th. [1901]

I have done a foolish thing this evening – I have actually been playing

---

[109] In the original diary a newspaper cutting from the *Natal Witness* of 21 January 1901 is pasted here. The contents of the cutting reads thus:
LORD KITCHENER'S APPEAL
INDUCEMENTS TO SURRENDER
HOW BOER REFUGEES ARE TREATED
Pretoria, January 17th (Reuter) – The system of gathering in all the Boer families and stock from outlying districts is proceeding regularly and vigorously.
Rest camps are being established all over the country, at all convenient centres where Boer refugees, voluntarily or otherwise, are kept and fed.
Those voluntarily surrendering are supplied with full rations, while, when husbands are still on commando, families are provided for on a reduced scale, which is raised when the husband surrenders, to the full allowance.
Every opportunity is offered refugees to obtain work for pay, and other privileges are accorded.
Prominent surrendered burghers are allowed to visit the camp to ascertain the treatment of refugees.
Reports that unnecessary hardships are inflicted are still assiduously spread.
The male refugees continue willingly to assist in guarding stock. As the number grows, steps will be taken to extend their usefulness in this direction.

the piano – yes, and Grieg's music into the bargain – soul-stirring, weird and strange – the kind of music that has most effect on me. I cannot touch the piano without being filled with a passionate longing and regret – longing for the music that is to be heard all over the world – regret for my wasted and wasting youth. All day I have been spending my time (in thought) in some great conservatoire in Europe, learning and listening, and now I feel as if the hard realities of life are more than I can bear. It is not good to dream, but just let me tell you this once what I dream about, dear diary, what <u>my</u> castles in the air are, and then I shall try to drop the subject and forget it. First of all you must know that when the war is over I am going to Europe to study music for a year. This is a promise from the mother but there are many things that <u>may</u> happen to prevent me from going. We may be ruined financially when this war is over – our boys may be killed or wounded and then I could not dream of leaving Mama – and last of all, I may get engaged and married.

I am not very much afraid of that last "eventuality" because I have made up my mind that if Mr Right <u>does</u> come along soon I shall only engage myself to him on condition that he lets me go away for a year – not only for my music, but also because I am in a very low state and not fit to marry until I have had a thorough change. I daresay I shall meet with many objections, for I am no longer very young (25 next birthday) but my mind is made up on that point. To study music has been the one ambition of my life and I shall never rest until it has been satisfied to a certain extent. Once I wanted to go to Dresden, then to Zurich, and now at last I have built my castle in Brussels – partly because it is near Holland and I can always escape to my relatives in any trouble, and chiefly because Dr Leyds is there and he will be a great help to me with the choosing of teachers etc. Brussels is healthy and – cheap! A great consideration, for I shall not have too much money. I am going to take a tiny room, hire a piano and take lessons in music and singing and, if my finances will allow me, I shall take French lessons as well. How I <u>shall</u> work! My mouth waters at the very idea and I am just going to dream of it even if nothing comes of it – so there!

Last night when I went out again the Southern Cross was hidden by heavy clouds and the moon had disappeared altogether and I felt chilled and disappointed, for alas! I am a slightly superstitious soul and it seemed to me an omen of my own future – a life ever darkened by the clouds of adversity. Am I not foolish? Let us hope so.

This afternoon I went to the Grand Hotel[110] to see Maria [Knevitt] and when I got there I found to my dismay that I did not know her married name, so I described them to the porter as a young couple from Zoutpansberg, with a baby, but as there were not less than <u>four</u> couples from Z[outansberg] with a baby each, and I declined the porter's suggestion that I should inspect them all in turn, I came away "empty" – looking and feeling very foolish. To comfort myself I went to Dobbies[111] for some tea and cake – found the ladies' room full of officers – one can't go anywhere now without falling over them.

Grand Hotel, Pretoria

When I had refreshed the inner woman I took a cab up to the Cottage Hospital[112] to see poor [Albert] Schilthuis[113], who is recovering from a serious attack of typhoid, called at Rood's on my way home, gave little M.[114] a music lesson and by that time it was nearly dark.

---

110   The Grand Hotel was situated on the south-eastern corner of Church Square, the central point of Pretoria.
111   Dobbies was the popular name of W.H. Dobbie's tea rooms in Church Street. See *Longland's Pretoria Directory for 1899*, p 183.
112   Cottage Hospital
113   Not identified.
114   Not identified.

Mrs Gen Botha was at Rood's and she told me that after she had received that letter from her husband through Kitchener, she wrote one in reply and sent it to his secretary by Mr Fisher[115] – Mama says I <u>must</u> go to bed now, so I'll tell you the rest of this story tomorrow.

January 29th. [1901]

Well, Mr Fisher took the letter to Colonel Somebody – perhaps Col nobody will be a more suitable name – Lord K[itchener]'s sec[retary] and he said with a drawl, "I do not think Lord Kitchener will like being made a post master of". Mr F[isher] took up the letter and turning on his heel walked away without a word. "But", the courteous Colonel called out after him, "you may leave the letter here and I'll see about it". "No, thank you" "Well, call in again tomorrow with it." "No, thank you" and away he marched with his head in the air. I wonder now whether they will apologise or call for the letter – I think not and yet I am sure Kitchener will be angry if he knows about it because they have all along done their best to make friends with our generals' wives.

This morning Mama and I gave the dining-room a thorough cleaning and ten Brink tuned the piano and this afternoon I went to my painting-lesson and had to stay there until quite dark because a great storm of rain and hail swept over the Town. There was no cab to be had so I had to come home on my bicycle in all that mud – it was hard work but I got here safe and sound and only had to dismount twice on the way. There was a meeting of the Consuls at Mr N.'s[116]. I wonder what weighty subjects were discussed. I am sure Khaki was reviled for all his sins because the whole Diplomatic Corps is terribly against him. Young Mrs Jorissen[117] came to say goodbye while I was there – they have <u>all</u> been put over the border for being too Anti-English – full burgers of our State! It is disgraceful. Mr Nieuwenhuis[118] wrote to Kitchener twice on the subject – once to ask the reason of it and once to ask for an interview and he <u>received</u> no <u>answer</u>. Then he went to the Governor to complain

---

115   Not identified, but on 1901-02-25 the diarist described Fisher as "A great friend of Mrs Gen Botha".

116   Probably at F.G.D. Nieuwenhuis, the Consul-General for the Netherlands in Pretoria.

117   Not identified.

118   Certainly F.G.D. Nieuwenhuis.

and eventually a reply came, curtly refusing an interview – not even a word about the first letter. The Governor told him that – "We must make room for all the Boer women and children and the Jorissens have nice, large houses!"

What do you think of that? Ugh! I am so sick of them all – they just torment us from morning till night and the poor Hollanders have a harder time than anyone else. To me it is the greatest marvel that Mama and I are still here, for we are "notorious" for our fierce Republicanism and yet we are never interfered with in any way.

January 31 [1901].

The end of the first month of the first year of the new century. Yesterday I made no entry in this remarkable document because for a wonder I spent the evening away from home (How foolish of me to call this a "remarkable document" – the words are about as appropriate as "Kitchener's Appeal".)

I must first finish off yesterday. Spent the whole morning in housecleaning and rested all afternoon, for I was very tired, had a nice book to read and – it was raining – three excellent reasons for taking a nice holiday. A stately old medical officer called here while I was "lazing", to see our fruit and get as much as we could spare – Mama took him to the garden and seemed as much charmed with him as he was with Harmony.

In the evening A[rchie] T[ruter] and G[ustav] F[ichardt] called for me on their way to Rood's, where we spent a very delightful evening. I am quite in love with Sarah R[ood], the dearest girl you ever saw – tall, slender, graceful, with a pure creamy-white complexion and lovely soft, brown eyes – a face to lose one's heart to – so winning and sweet and merry. She was dressed in a fresh white muslin – simplicity and girlishness personified. Her elder sister, Annie, is also a beauty in her own way but has not the half S[arah]'s charm of manner. There were about 10 of us in all and we made music and walked in the moonlight and chatted and partook of the good things so plentifully provided for us. I was quite happy for a few hours.

So much for yesterday. This morning I went to French (not the general – my lesson, dear Diary) and this afternoon I had to go to Town

<u>again</u> to do a thousand and one commissions. I dressed myself very prettily in a cream dress trimmed with lace and pink ribbon, a large shady white Leghorn hat and a dear little pink silk sunshade. You will wonder why I mention these details – perhaps you think I am becoming very vain and frivolous – but have patience, my dear. This stylish young lady hailed the first cab she saw and found to her surprise and delight that the driver was one of the old hospital patients – Dietloffs.[119] You should have seen the shaking of hands and heard the tender enquiries, and then we drove away together, my driver sitting half turned to me with an arm over the back of his seat, watching the horses with the tail of his eye and talking sixteen to the dozen. How the people stared and how I enjoyed myself, to be sure! He drove me to the Pass Office where we had a lively argument, he absolutely refusing to take the fare from me because – *"Ik het zoo banja liefde en vriendschap van Zuster van Warmelo ondervind in die ou dagen – nee, dankie, ik neem dit nie".*[120]

I had to give in and parted from him with a friendly shake of the hand that made the Khakis stare. At the Pass Office I got a permit for Mama to go to the Hospital tomorrow, with fruit for the patients, and the officer there said he had a message for me from Lord Athumlie[121] (or something) who had ordered him to keep duplicates of all sorts of passes and permits for my collection. Then I remembered that about six months ago I had asked an officer to give me a few duplicates and he had said he could only do so when the war is over, but had taken my name and promised not to forget me. So this was Lord Athumlie! I was so pleased and told the young man I hoped he would carry out his instructions! Lord A[thumlie] left Pretoria four or five months ago.

I then went with my permit to the Governor to have it signed and while I was there Major Hoskins (his A[ide-]D[e-]C[amp]) asked me to thank Mama for the lovely fruit she had sent him. You must not think we are in the habit of sending things to Khakis – oh, dear no, but he and the Governor are always so good to us and do anything we ask them, so Mama said she would send them some of our lovely fruit as specimens

---

119 Not identified.
120 "I experienced so much love and friendship from Sister van Warmelo in the old days – no thank you, I do not accept it."
121 Not identified.

of the Transvaal produce. Major H[oskins] asked me whether the card that went with it was written or printed and when I told him it was written by my brother (Dietlof) he joyfully informed me that he had won a sovereign over it, for the officers had betted and examined the card with a magnifying glass and no one could tell whether it was handwriting or not. Dietlof does all my calling cards, so beautifully that no one ever can find out that they are not printed.

I then went to the Grand Hotel to see Maria (her name is Mrs Knevitt – I found out at last) and heard that she was living at "The Laurels" now.[122] Her husband, who seems a nice, gentlemanly fellow, gave me her address. Visited Mrs Usher[123] and was told that her baby (a girl) was born last Sunday. I did not see the happy young mother.

February 1st. [1901]

At our vocal rehearsal this afternoon there were five new members – a very good thing, for we have been going steadily down-hill since Mrs H[oepner]'s departure. There are now 17 members – a fair number if only their voices were a little stronger.

I hear that the English have had a great reverse in the Free State – at Wepener, lost two batteries, according to Dame Rumour.[124] Tomorrow Queen Victoria is to be buried and all civilians are ordered by proclamation to wear deep mourning. Am I a civilian, I wonder? Or can't a woman be civilian. Well, no matter what I am I shan't wear black. The heat today has been terrific and I feel utterly knocked up tonight. We did so hope that it would bring rain but alas! The night is perfectly clear and the brilliant moonlight is flooding our garden making a little paradise of it. Harmony always looks lovely in the moonlight.

Mrs Nieuwenhuis told me a few days ago that Dr Leyds no longer lives in Brussels. Am I to break down my castle again and remove it to some other musical city? That would be a great disappointment to me and yet I cannot go tot Brussels unless I have friends there. No, I begin to think that my fate will be Zurich or Dresden.

---

122   Not identified.
123   Probably the wife of O. Usher, a transport rider, the only Usher listed in *Longland's Pretoria Directory for 1899*, p 172.
124   "Dame Rumour" was mistaken – no truth in that news.

February 2ⁿᵈ [1901]

Another day has passed – another day of such pitiless, unbearable heat that the evening finds us quite prostrate. I don't know whether this is an unusually hot season or whether I only feel it more than at other times, but to me it seems as if we have never had heat like this before. I suppose my ill-health has a lot to do with it – but at mid-day today I did not feel able to lift a finger. My back has been aching cruelly all day – got up with it and wondered how I was going to get through the long, long day. And still no blessed rain falls to relieve us – everything is parched, shrivelling up like dead leaves under the sun's scorching rays. And the mother and I had hard work to do this morning – re-arranging the fern stands under the verandah, cutting out the old stems and leaves, giving each pot fresh ground and manure – tiring work on a blazing summer's day. There is still much to do – two other stands with begonias etc, and all the large tins with ivy geraniums. I suppose the Queen was buried this afternoon, for a great deal of firing was heard from the forts at about 5 o'clock.

February 4ᵗʰ [1901]

No entry yesterday. That is a pity for, like a lost hour, it can never be retrieved – I cannot write today as I would have written yesterday.

It was not a bit like Sunday. Early in the morning, immediately after breakfast, I found Schilthuis under the verandah. He had crept over from the Cottage Hospital – a ghost of his former self, poor boy. He stayed until about 10 o'clock and then it was too late for me to go to Church. Soon after he left ten B[rink] came to see what was wrong with one of the notes of the piano and in the afternoon we had our usual visitors – G[ustav] F[ichardt] and A[rchie] T[ruter] and Mr Hoepner,[125] who came to say goodbye. He is leaving on Wednesday and we are busy writing some letters to send by him. The two boys had all sorts of wild rumours – Cape Town in the hands of the Boers – Gov[ernmen]t B[ui]ld[in]gs razed to the ground, Milner[126] fled in a man-of-war, 45 000 Boers in arms (Colonials) there was no end to their stories. In

---

125   Probably C. Hoepner, whose wife was the former president of the Vocal Society to which the diarist belonged.

126   Sir Alfred Milner, British High Commissioner in South Africa. See A.L. Harrington, Milner, Alfred, First Viscount, in *DSAB III*, pp 613–617.

the evening M[ama] and I went to see Oom Piet and aunt Bessie.[127] It was such a lovely moonlight night and the stroll did us good. Aunt B[essie] told us all about her experience in a coal-truck from Florida to Barberton. She can talk of war. I don't feel up to writing tonight or I would tell you some of the things she went through.

Today has been quiet and uneventful. Went to the Roods late in the afternoon. Kitchener passed me quite close on horseback and I had a good look at him. What a face! Cold, cruel, bloated; with bloodshot eyes. It made me shudder to think that we are at the mercy of such a man. They say he drinks hard now and is as cross as a bear and I must say his appearance gives one that idea.

Lord Kitchener

February 5th [1901]

Today the English are exactly eight months in Pretoria. Eight months! Can it be possible that eight months after that terrible, never-to-be-forgotten day, we find ourselves still under Martial Law and apparently as far as ever from the end of this bitter war? If anyone had told me that day how it would be today I would have answered "Impossible!" And now nothing seems impossible to me.

There is some news. Some Duke or other is dead – the royal family is unlucky lately. I <u>think</u> it is one of the late Queen's sons.[128]

Yesterday Mrs Gen Botha went to ask Kitchener to let her go to her husband. Someone there said "I don't think you can see Lord K[itchener]" and she just went off in high dudgeon and drove to Town to do some shopping. When she came

---

127   Not identified.
128   The news was false.

home she found that they had been hunting all over the place for her with a message that Lord K[itchener] would be pleased to see her at any time, so she went again in the afternoon and got permission to go to her husband. K[itchener] was most friendly to her. – She went this morning and now I wonder what news she will bring home.

Four or five collies attacked me this afternoon and nearly pulled me from my bicycle and a brave Tommie, armed to the teeth, saved my life.

February 7th [1901]

Today the Queen of Holland[129] was married and all her subjects here celebrated the happy event – and many others as well, who are not her subjects, like Mama and myself for instance. There was a reception at the Dutch Consul's and I went to help with serving refreshments. It was very full at about 5.30 and I was at my wits' end for we had not nearly enough "hands" and sometimes there was not a single clean glass or plate or fork to be had and I fear many of the guests went home hungry and thirsty. But it was great fun all the same. Many young men came with flaring orange ties on and orange handkerchiefs and rosettes. I had on the Vierkleur with just a touch of orange.

I heard scraps of war news there – Krugersdorp again in our hands (ours, dear Diary.)[130] J[o]h[anne]sburg in a great state of anxiety and all civilians warned to flee when a certain steam whistle blows, as there will be fighting in the streets of J[o]h[anne]sburg in case of attack. How I should like to have it all my own way with that steam whistle just for five minutes. Wouldn't I make the people run! Our President's wife[131] has sent the young Queen a cable in the name of all Transvaal women. The Consul sent it, so Khaki had to let it pass.

I made no entry yesterday because I felt so ill and there was nothing to say. We were going to drink tea in the garden (eight young folks) and a thunderstorm came up and spoilt everything – no one turned up. We must have it some other day.

No one is dead and the report was false, – only the Duke of York

---

129 Queen Wilhelmina married Count Hendrik van Mecklenburg-Schwerin on 7 February 1901. See J. Ploeger, Wilhelmina (Helena Paulin Maria), in DSAB IV, p 781.
130 The news was false.
131 Mrs Gezina Kruger, the second wife of President Paul Kruger.

has measles. The President's little grandson, Tjaard's son, is dead – his namesake – and of course the news flew over the Town that the old man was dead. You have no idea, dear diary, how very busy Dame Rumour can be in time of war. One learns to be very sceptical and unbelieving and I don't suppose I shall ever hear news again without enquiring "But it is true?"

February 8th [1901]

Have been in bed all day feeling most wretched. I have never had such a backache in my life as all last night and today. Mama went to Town and got me some port wine – got it with the greatest difficulty, had to get a permit from the Commissioner, and I don't know what not. Oom Piet came to see us this afternoon and he had some strange "reports" to report. Kitchener had fallen from his horse and had concussion of the brain – some said DT's[132] – (oh no, this was the news the mother brought from Town). Oom Piet said K[itchener] had sent in his resignation and was going home, refusing to finish Lord Roberts's "dirty work". Dynamite Factory in the hands of the Boers. Boxburg[133] re-taken as well as Krugersdorp. Oh, how I wish one knew what to believe.

It has been raining all day, a soft, gentle penetrating rain that will do everything a lot of good. I wonder how the vocal rehearsal went off without me. (conceit)

February 10th. [1901]

The English sent reinforcements to Krugersdorp (2 000 men) and took it again, Boers quietly retreated to the *"randjies"*,[134] where they are staying until they see another chance of taking the place. They took two trains heavily laden with goods, during the last few days – one on the Cape and one on the Natal line. Yesterday the Cinattis came with Mr Philipp[135] to see how I was. They caught me under the verandah with

---

132   DT probably stands for delirium tremens, a disease of the brain caused by the excessive and prolonged use of intoxicating liquors. See *Webster's Comprehensive Reference Dictionary and Encyclopedia*, p 142.

133   Should be Boksburg, an East Rand mining town. The news was, as most rumours were, false.

134   randjies (Afrikaans) – low hills.

135   A. Philipp of the South African Dynamite Company. See *Longland's Pretoria Directory for 1899*, p 159.

hair hanging down and in a general state of undress. Mr P[hilipp] said the Dynamite Factory was <u>not</u> in the hands of the Boers as far as he knew, and he ought to know, for he is one of the directors. On Friday night Mama dreamt that Mr von Wichmann[136] was killed – I make a note of this, for dreams are strange things and one never knows what fate can befall one's friends in a war like this. The last news we heard from him was that he was at Wakkerstroom with his gun. Poor fellow! he has had a rough time of it. This afternoon four young people came and we decided to have our picnic next Wednesday.

February 11th. [1901]

We are very busy canning yellow peaches and have at least 50 jars to fill. Someone asked me this afternoon who was going to eat it all and the tears came into my eyes as I answered "The boys". We think of them – at least I do – with every peach we peel and I often wonder where they are and when they will come home again. I cannot get rid of the thought that Fritz will never come home again, hence these easy-flowing tears. I want to cry at every trifle now-a-days. It seems as if we lose all control over ourselves in a war like this – I, for one, have no more will-power left and every day I seem to be less my old, strong self. I know that trouble is supposed to build up one's character and <u>strengthen</u> one but surely not <u>war</u>! War is an evil that brings so much bitterness to the surface, that nourishes so many passions and above all, that <u>wears one away</u>, body and soul, until one is a perfect wreck. At least so it is with women, because they can't fight and so get rid of some of their bitterness. Those men in the field will come out of this struggle, ennobled and purified, <u>men</u> in every sense of the word, or they ought to – while we – what is to become of us if we go on bottling everything up? You must really not mind, dear diary, if I "let fly" to you occasionally – it

---

136   Probably Captain Friedrich Wilhelm von Wichmann, who was an officer in the German Army before coming to the Transvaal. He joined the Transvaal State Artillery in 1897 and participated in many battles in the Anglo-Boer War. In the latter half of the war he was active on the Transvaal Highveld where he served with distinction to the end of the war. See F.V. Engelenburg and G.S. Preller, *Onze Krijgs-Officieren. Album van Portretten met Levens-schetsen der Transvaalse Generaals en Kommandanten e.a.*, pp 213–214. See also the entry in the "Love diary" on 1901-08-20.

does me a world of good. This afternoon I went to see Mrs Morise[137]
– Khakis were playing tennis there so I only stayed quarter of an hour.
Now I want to go and play just one little tune.

February 12th [1901]

Such a day as we have had! All the fruit is getting ripe <u>together</u> and we
don't know how to get rid of if fast enough. Mama works with it from
morn till eve and today I had to help her, for someone came to buy
to the value of £8 for our prisoners. Mama gathered great baskets of
grapes and I picked out all the *"vrot korrels"*[138] (in our own expressive
taal)[139] and packed them in a big bath, 100 lbs weight – it took us the
whole morning. They are also getting about 3 000 peaches and I don't
know how many figs. The grapes when cleaned and arranged presented
a magnificent appearance – some bunches weighing 3 lbs and 4 lbs.
This drought is very good for them, but the peaches are small on account of it. All day long kaffirs come to buy fruit for their "bass" or "mis-
sis" – in baskets and bags and boxes. The poor mother is simply worn
out at night, for she does everything herself and allows no one to cut
the vines. Young Rood also came to get fruit this afternoon and as I was
just ready to go to Town he drove me there. He is a nice boy with a soft
voice and gentle manners and such a Boer! This morning Paulus, our
kaffir, ran away (of course they always run away when one is particularly
busy) but the funny part of this episode was that he ran back again when
he came to himself. Paulus has a history. Some months ago he left his
home and wife and four children to visit a friend a little way off (he lives
other side of the Magaliesbergen) and was caught by the English as a
spy and brought to Pretoria. There was no proof that he was not a spy
and he refused to tell the English anything about the Boers so he was
kept a prisoner and given to us to work here until the war is over. Some
days he is very miserable and longs for his wife and children and thinks
they will think he is dead, and on these days Paulus is rather trying. He
"cheeks" the mother and shirks his work and generally ends in being
very penitent. Then he is angelic for a few days, until "next time". He
is a good-looking kaffir and has the heart of a white man – honest as

---

[137] Should probably be Mrs Morice. See entry of 1900-03-15 on p 42.
[138] vrot korrels (Afrikaans) – rotten grapes.
[139] taal – language.

gold, faithful and devoted. I suppose he got up in a temper this morning for when M[ama] called to him he gave no answer and afterwards we missed him, found all his things gone and Paulus cleared! I was amazed, for although natives have a pleasant little way of disappearing when things are not to their liking, he was the very last one we expected it from. But I was more amazed still when he came back after breakfast and meekly took up his work. On being questioned he confessed to having gone to Town, without permission, to take a blanket to a friend – such nonsense – he had carefully hidden all his belongings with the idea of striking terror to our hearts. I told him he had better not play with us like that and the next time he walked off he need not come back again. All day he's been a jewel. About a month ago he asked me to teach him to read and write so I got him a copy-book and Dutch spelling-book and every evening I teach him for half an hour. Of course he is delighted and I think that has a great deal to do with the queer way he came home again.

Feb[ruary] 13th. [1901]

The wild rumours that are afloat now are enough to turn one's head. I shall not repeat them – it would only be waste of time. The picnic was very nice, only three of the party could not come. Annie R[ood] has gone to J[o]h[anne]sburg, Connie M[innaar] was not well and Gustav F[ichardt] had to work until six o'clock. Sarah Rood and her brother came, Fred Niemeyer and Archie Truter. We five spent a delightful afternoon under the trees, boiled a little kettle, had tea and cake and fruit and sweets – (Gustav sent me an enormous box of Canadian sweets to make up for his non-appearance) while the men smoked cigarettes and we "lazed".

Feb[ruary] 14th. [1901]

Mama is not feeling very well and has gone to <u>bed</u> early, leaving me all by my lone – and lonesome it is in our quiet house with a heart full of sad thoughts. Some days I feel so crushed, so despairing. When one hears of the misery and suffering around one, the devastation of one's own land and when one realizes <u>why</u> it all is happening – no wonder our courage fails us. Why are we being ruined? Because we love our

country, because we want to be free and independent, because we refused to bow to the tyrant's yoke. The more I think of it the more
forcibly the injustice and cruelty of it all comes home to me. I feel sad
tonight because there is a bulletin announcing the capture of a large
convoy from the Boers somewhere near Ermelo – over 100 wagons.[140]
Of course it must be an exaggeration but I am afraid there is <u>some</u> truth
in it. We hear such dreadful tales of suffering and sorrow and we can do
<u>nothing</u> to relieve our poor country-women. There are hundreds and
hundreds of them with their children, who have been brought in from
the farms and it is pitiful to hear what they have had to endure from the
hands of our "civilized" enemy. One old woman, an old friend of ours
from the days when Papa was still with us, told Mama yesterday that the
soldiers had orders to destroy her farm and the house with everything
in it and she was an eye-witness to the way they smashed her stove with
hammers, tore albums to pieces, cut open bags of grain and scattered
them about the yard and finally put fire into the wreck. Is it not <u>terrible</u>?
Can anyone believe that the mighty British army has fallen so low as to
destroy albums and photographs and all the little cherished belongings
of a life-time. Is it not trivial, small-minded? What have these poor old
women done that they should have to stand by and see all their possessions ruined like that? It makes my heart very, very bitter and I realize
how helpless we are – how utterly powerless to put a stop to this awful
state of affairs. And then these poor women and children are packed
into open cattle-trucks and brought to the Towns, where they are thrust
between four bare walls and get a miserable portion of food every day.
They are herded together like wild beasts on a show – many of them
the families of wealthy farmers, accustomed to fine homes and every
imaginable luxury. Oh God, Thy ways are dark and mysterious to us
– give us wisdom and strength to leave all in Thy hands and trust to
Thee to do all for our own good. The human heart cries out against all
this seeming injustice – no wonder there are people who are becoming
hard and reckless – and that is the saddest part of it all. We <u>ought</u> to
become good under our afflictions, but alas! The effect is more often
the exact opposite.

[140] On 10 February 1901 a British unit overpowered a Boer convoy near
       Chrissiesmeer, northeast of Ermelo, capturing 50 wagons and about 30
       burghers. See P.G. Cloete, *The Anglo-Boer War*, p 222.

Today brought me another letter from L[ouis] B[randt] sent, as I thought, along with his photo. I wonder where it has been all this time, for it was <u>not</u> censored. He was ordained or "consecrated" (I don't know the exact term) on the 6th Jan[uary] and is now in his own *"pastorie"*[141] and has his own congregation in a small place near Groningen.[142] They are lucky in getting such a good man – for he really is to my mind a <u>good man</u> – and I hope he will get on very well there and do a lot of good.

This evening we had a most magnificent sunset, I gazed and gazed and lost myself in its beauty and glory, until it all faded away and became grey and lifeless, leaving us only the memory of it to dream over.

<u>Feb[ruary] 16th</u> [1901]

Yesterday, I made no entry because there was nothing particular to tell. We canned peaches in the morning and I washed my hair and in the afternoon went to vocal rehearsal. Was escorted home by G[ustav] F[ichardt] and F[red] N[iemeyer] two very nice young men. Fred N[iemeyer]'s conversation interests me very much and I think he and I are going to be good friends. – Yesterday morning no less than five dead horses and mules were carried away from the little camp at the back of Harmony. This morning the Hollenbachs[143] came to sing as is our custom on Sat[urday]. I was in very good voice – took the high g and a without the slightest effort and clear as a bell. When my voice is good I get so sad, so restless, and long to go away where I can have it trained – it breaks my heart to think that my youth is fast slipping away and my one talent has not been cultivated and developed. When will that most blessed time come? If not very soon, it will be too late. – Schilthuis came in a cab and took us to van Wouws's Exhibition of Art this afternoon.[144] It was very interesting. He has the most costly bronze and

---

[141] Parsonage.

[142] His congregation was centred in Niëzyl.

[143] Either the family of J.H. Hollenbach, professor of drawing at the Staats Model School, or that of G.H. Hollenbach of the public works department – the only two Hollenbachs listed in *Longland's Pretoria Directory for 1899*, p 136.

[144] Probably Anton van Wouw, the well-known sculptor who came from Holland and settled in Pretoria in 1889. Created inter alia the statue of President Kruger on Church Square in Pretoria. See J. Ploeger, *Nederlanders in*

marble figures, exquisite Venetian glass, old paintings and drawings and curios of every description and everything is draped artistically with rich brocades in gold and silver. It is high time someone opened an exhibition like that in Pretoria and I shall certainly advise all my friends to go and see it.

Feb[ruary] 17th. [1901]

So little seems to be happening that I am often tempted to make no entry in this diary. "Seems to be" I say, because of course we know nothing of what is going on around us. I can't believe that the Boers are sitting quiet now. Now is their time to act, for the English are suffering terrible losses through horse-sickness and are so handicapped that I am sure we could do them great mischief. Mrs Botha has not come home yet. The weather is strange – sky overcast and a strong wind blowing since yesterday morning. I hope the worst heat is over now – one can begin to live again as soon as the cool weather comes on. It sounds like winter this evening with the wind howling through the trees and round the house, but it does not feel cold enough.

One of my ex-patients, van der Westhuysen, came to see me this afternoon. He had a broken arm, which is still stiff and will never be quite cured.[145] Mrs Bodde[146] was here with her dear little baby-boy, and some young folks.

Feb[ruary] 19th. [1901]

Since yesterday we have had rain – today it was a steady, refreshing downpour which seems as if it is going to last all night. I gave Sarah Rood her first music-lesson yesterday.

Transvaal 1850–1950, p 140; G. Dekker, Van Wouw, Anton, in *DSAB I*, pp 841–844.

[145] He was a cab driver who was employed by Mrs Hendrina Joubert, the widow of the late Commandant-General P.J. Joubert. See G.D. Scholtz, *In Doodsgevaar. Die Oorlogservarings van Kapt. J.J. Naudé*, p 190. Van der Westhuysen features again later on in the diary. See entries on 1901-08-22, p 325, 1901-09-14 (p 354) and 1901-12-20, p 408.

[146] The wife of either G.R.Y. Bodde, who originally came from Holland but settled in Pretoria in 1888 (see See J. Ploeger, *Nederlanders in Transvaal 1850–1950*, p 45), or F.A. Bodde, an architect, since they are the only Boddes listed in *Longland's Pretoria Directory for 1899*, p 118.

The mother would not let me go out today although I should have gone to my painting – and I do so love walking about in the rain. When I am my own mistress I shall make a point of going for long walks on rainy days, to make up for being kept like a lump of sugar now.

Colonel St Clair called here yesterday afternoon. He is such a perfect old gentleman that we simply <u>cannot</u> ask him not to come again so we have just decided to put up with an occasional visit from him. He comes seldom enough, only I hope none of our friends will ever catch him here. When I told him that we never hear from Line since Mr Hay left, he said we could write through him and tell her to address our letters to his care. He gave me an envelope with his name in the corner, so I have written to her. Poor dear sister! How she must long for news from us. I have also asked her to send me half a doz[en] bottles of pink pills through him. It is the only tonic that agrees with me and is not to be had in the Transvaal just now.

Feb[ruary] 20th [1901]

Went to get a permit for Mama to go to the Volks Hospital and found that they had done away with those permits – I am thankful, for I hate going to the Gov[ernment] Buildings. Got a special permit from the Governor to visit van Aardt[147] – one of my ex-patients – in the Rest Camp.[148] He said it was a great favour and quite against regulations, as only people who have relatives in the Rest Camp are allowed to go there. I did'nt [sic] even say thank you – I feel so wild when they come to me with their "special favours". All sorts of rumours are afloat – I cannot even remember everything I picked up in Town this afternoon – My back is aching again tonight so I want to go to bed. Got two letters today – Tante Nelly[149] and Mrs McLaren,[150] who is at Wijnberg. She

---

147   Not identified.

148   A concentration camp in Pretoria which existed from January 1901 to January 1902 and was used as a transit camp. Boers were transported from here to prisoner-of-war camps. This camp was situated to the west of a drift called Vanderhovensdrift in the Apies River north-west of the centre of the city. See P.J. Greyling, *Pretoria and the Anglo-Boer War. A guide of buildings, terrains, graves and monuments*, p 82.

149   Mev Nellie van Eeden, the sister of the diarist's father. She lived with her husband Frederik in Haarlem, Holland. See B. du Toit, *Die verhaal van Johanna Brandt*, p 12.

150   Not identified.

came to S[outh] A[frica] for her health. I am surprised at anyone coming <u>here</u> to get well at a time like this.

The British Rest Camp in Pretoria

Feb[ruary] <u>22</u> [1901]

We have a visitor – an old Boer woman one of the refugees – Juffrouw Breedt.[151] She was one of Papa's congregation and we used to know her very well and have great respect for her. She arrived here this morning without a single thing – no brush, no comb, not even so much as a nightdress. We have to give her all sorts of necessaries. Some evening when I have more time I shall make a note of the things she told us – <u>her</u> experiences of the war. – Let me see, I made no entry yesterday. Went to French lesson in the morning and paid Mrs van Alphen a visit to find out about a woman who came in from the Boer lines to get medicine for the ambulance. She is a wonderful creature, with a deep, <u>man's</u> voice and all the ways of a man. She walked 40 miles and was caught by the out-posts here who thought she was a man in disguise. She was marched

---

151   Not identified.

into Pretoria between two armed Tommies and is kept as a prisoner now – at least until it pleases the Gov[ernor] to release her. She told Mrs v[an] A[lphen] that she was at Paardekraal on 16 Dec[ember] and heard Dietlof making a short speech to the burgers. Our boys joined Gen Botha at Ermelo afterwards and are no longer with Beyers.

Aling Tulleken[152] was here, from J[o]h[anne]sburg. It must be terrible the way people are rationed there and the worst of it is that no one is allowed to take food. Aunt Clara [Maré] gave him a tin of butter and a loaf of bread but she had to open the tin to show that it was *"pad-kos"*[153] and cut the loaf into sandwiches. He took some fruit and vegetables also – things that can spoil are allowed. Went to Cinatti's yest[erday] afternoon and in the evening Mr Philipp came to see us about stamps. There was a most remarkable sun-set. First of all the sky was covered with grey clouds, heavy and lifeless, and some time after the sun had disappeared the sky began to get crimson – deeper and deeper – until the heavens were ablaze with a flaring, burning, vivid, <u>blood</u>-red. It was almost too strange to be beautiful – there was something awesome about it, and it was a rest to turn one's dazzled eyes to the grey, crimson-tinted clouds on the opposite side of the sky. Long, long after dark these warm, rich tints hung in the heavens fading away very gradually.

Today I went to vocal rehearsal – good attendance – and delightful Schumann music. The night is dark and stormy. Great gusts of wind are tearing round the house filling my sad heart with many strange, undefined forebodings. We may well be anxious, for there seems to be a great deal of fighting lately, and news came yesterday of the death of Mrs Koos Smit's son[154] – a boy of 16 or 17. K[oos] S[mit] was Railway Commissioner here formerly and is now with the Pres[ident] or still in the field – I am not sure.[155] I believe Mrs Gen Botha came home yesterday.

152　Aling Albert van Hoogenhouck Tulleken was appointed postmaster of Johannesburg, the largest post office in the South African Republic, in 1896. It is not known what he did after the British occupation of Johannesburg (Personal communication by Joh Groenewald, postal historian, Pretoria, 4 July 2005). Tulleken was the brother of Clara Maré, the wife of the diarists uncle Paul Maré.

153　"pad-kos" (Afrikaans) – "food for the journey".

154　She was wrong. See the last sentence of her diary entry of the next day, 23 February 1901.

155　Smit was not at that time fighting for the Boer cause. On the contrary,

Feb[ruary] 23rd [1901]

This afternoon a party of young people went to the Art Exhibition. We met at Harmony at about 4 o'clock – two Roods, Connie Minnaar, Fred Niemeyer and yours truly. I don't know whether they appreciated it very much because none of them have ever seen anything of the sort before, but I enjoyed it even more than last time and want to go again. F[red] N[iemeyer] is very clever – he appreciated all he saw – But we are sad tonight – bad news from the front. The English have taken a whole convoy from De Wet in the Colony – ammunition, provisions, horses, etc and about 20 prisoners – an official bulletin.[156] It is not Koos Smit's son who is killed, but some other Smit – I am very glad for the mother's sake, but I suppose the other one has a mother too.

Feb[ruary] 25th. [1901]

Yesterday was Sunday and nothing out of the way happened. G[ustav] Fichardt] and A[rchie Truter] were here in the afternoon. Today our old Boer *tannie*[157] departed. I don't think she was quite happy here – things are too grand and too – too – clean for her and though we were as homely as possible I think she felt like a fish out water and nothing could tempt her to stay longer with us. She is a dear, good, gentle old soul and it cut me to the heart to see her weeping stealthily sometimes when her sorrows were too much for her. What sufferings our old folks go through at a time like this!

---

he was involved in the activities of the Burgher Peace Committees that worked hand in glove with the British military authorities in an attempt to overpower the Boer republics. In other words he was what the diarist would have called a joiner. See A.M. Grundlingh, D*ie "Hendsoppers" en "Joiners". Die rasionaal en verskynsel van verraad*, pp 82–83, 90, 107–113 and 184.

156 During the night of 15/16 February 2001 a British force indeed compelled De Wet to abandon a large part of his convoy, including ammunition wagons that got stuck in a muddy marsh north of Strydenburg in the Cape Colony. See C.R. de Wet, *Die stryd tussen Boer en Brit*, pp 211–213.

157 *tannie* (Afrikaans) – auntie (Mrs Breedt).

But I must tell you what I heard today, dear diary. When I had given Bertha M.[158] her music-lesson I went to speak to Mrs M.[159] and found Mr Fisher (Mr) with her – a great friend of Mrs Gen Botha. He told me all her experiences. She was a week with her husband and his staff on Bothasberg – somewhere near Ermelo I think[160] – and when she was coming back she was informed that she would have to travel by rail as the farms had been destroyed and consequently there was no "touching-place" for her. In going she had travelled by carriage, as her husband did not think the line safe, and she

Mrs Annie Botha, the wife of Commandant General Louis Botha

had done it by easy stages – resting at several farms on the way. Before her return – that is within ten days – those farms had been devastated and she was obliged to take the train home. It took her a long time to get here, for the train just before the one she was in was blown up by the Boers and she had to spend two days and three nights in the railway carriage while the line was being repaired. She went to "report" herself to Lord K[itchener] who received her kindly and apologised that the officials had not sent her back to Middelburg instead of keeping [her] in the train while the line was under repair. He asked her no questions and only said as she was going away that he supposed there was no sign of surrender yet and when she said "no" he said it was only what he expected. She says

---

158 Probably a daughter of S. Michaelson, of Bellevue House in Pritchard Street. See *Longland's Pretoria Directory for 1899*, p 153.
159 Probably Mrs Michaelson. See diary entry on 1901-03-02 on p 103.
160 Bothasberg is north-east of Middelburg in what was then the Eastern Transvaal – not near Ermelo.

the Boers know <u>everything</u> that is happening in Pretoria. Her husband knew that she was dining with Lord Roberts, the same evening, and he quite approved because he knew it was only a matter of etiquette.

While I was there someone brought news from Town – an official bulletin pasted on Gov[ernmen]t Buildings – great victory over the Boers, Gens Christiaan Botha and Tobias Smuts "smashed up" – horses, wagons, provisions, ammunition and prisoners taken, 280 dead Boers left on the field[161] – something grand and wonderful. Of course I don't believe anything until the news is definitely confirmed and their official bulletins are so much waste paper to me. – Went to Dr Kolff[162] this afternoon and got him to prescribe for me. I am only very much run down and require nourishing food, plenty of milk, eggs, wine and a preparation of bullocks' blood and iron.

Feb[ruary] <u>26</u>th [1901]

Letter from Mr Boord, who is on his way to S[outh] Africa and writes to ask whether we are still in Pretoria as he wishes to see us. He is an English aristocrat, very wealthy, who travelled out with us in the "Gaika" more than three years ago. We were very good friends then but I doubt whether we shall be able to "get on" <u>now</u>. [163]

Feb[ruary] <u>27</u>th [1901]

A bitter day of sad memories for us – Cronje's surrender, Pieters Heights and Willem's capture – just a year ago. This year we are again anxious and depressed on this memorable day. The air is full of rumours of Boer disasters – some people even go so far as to say that

---

[161] This was false.

[162] Dr J.W.C. Kolff came from the Netherlands where he had been trained as a physician. He arrived in the South African Republic in 1895 and settled in Pretoria in 1898, working both as a private practitioner and at the Volks Hospital. His home was in Skinner Street. See J. Ploeger, *Nederlanders in Transvaal*, p 81; *Longland's Pretoria directory for 1899*, p 143.

[163] Mr Percy Boord. He never made it to Pretoria, but wrote to the diarist from Cape Town on 18 March 1901 that "the authorities will not let casual people go north just now." He probably returned to England. See Archives of the *Nederduitsch Hervormde Kerk van Afrika*, Pretoria, L.E. Brandt Collection, IX/162, file titled *1894–1902, Aan J.B. – vriende, ens*, unsorted, P. Boord – J. van Warmelo, 18 March 1901.

Botha has surrendered with all his men and is expected in Town today, and that the war is over. It is certain enough that things have been going rather badly, but <u>what</u> it is and where and with whom, we cannot find out. This suspense is wearing our very lives away and the worst of it is that one never gets used to it. <u>We think</u> our boys are where the fighting has been – Ermelo district. If so, have they come out unhurt? If we only knew that!

M[ama] and I went to see Uncle Paul this afternoon. I killed a little black snake on our way home – it crawled right under the mother's skirts. Began with my new medicine today – now we shall see if I don't get well soon.

March 2nd. [1901]

Two days since last I made an entry. Come, come, Johanna, this will never do – you are beginning to get slack, and it is my painful duty to refer you to the first few pages of this book with their good resolutions and earnest endeavours to "do well" this year. – On the 28th Feb[ruary] nothing of importance happened. I went as usual to my French lesson and was told by Mrs Michaelson[164] that Mrs Gen Botha had said our boys were safe and well – at least as far as her husband knew. She did not seem to know <u>where</u> they were.

Yesterday, vocal rehearsal in the afternoon and in the evening a delightful musical gathering at Mrs Minnaar's, which I enjoyed very much. The moonlight night was perfect, and the walk home through the deserted streets, with only an occasional "Pass, please sir" from the sentries, was most charming, especially with such a good companion as F[red] N[iemeyer]. For a boy of his age his mind is wonderfully mature and our long conversations are generally on rather deep subjects. He is very earnest and takes life seriously and yet he is full of fun. This afternoon we had a picnic in the "forest" in honour of Archie Truter's 23rd birthday and F[red] N[iemeyer] kept the party going all the time. Sarah Rood was not well enough to come and sent a letter of apology addressed to "Little Hanner, Garden of Eden, Paradise" and signed by "Long Tom". It took me some time to find out who the sender was and even now I am puzzled to know how the letter ever reached its destination. I am called Little

---

164   See diary entry on 1901-02-25 on p 101.

Hanner because of an epitaph that runs – "We have lost our little Hanner, in a very painful manner, etc". The rest I don't know, but they have promised to put that on my grave if ever I break my neck on the bicycle or come to some other untimely end. You see, dear diary, young folks will be young folks and they <u>will</u> have their bit of fun even with this deadly strife raging around them and I assure you it is by no means due to heartlessness or indifference but is just nature having its own way. Small blame to us if we indulge in a little harmless amusement now and then, during these bitter days. The feeling of death in the air seems to become more defined to me lately – more as if it is approaching us or our dear ones. I cannot shake it off and spend many sleepless, anxious nights, but I must try not to yield to these forebodings for we shall need all our strength and courage when the blow falls. Yesterday when I was at the Dutch Consul's I found some Boer women and children waiting under the verandah to speak to Mrs N[ieuwenhuis]. I spoke to one of them and she told me that they had received notice that morning to go to the Irene Camp the following day, because they could not pay house-rent! You must understand the deep tragedy of those words, dear diary. Unable to pay a few miserable pounds of house-rent! The wives and families of wealthy Rustenburg farmers! The woman told me that she was turned out of a fine house and not allowed to save a thing and had to stand by and see all her worldly belongings reduced to ashes – furniture, waggons [sic], carts, 200 bags of grain besides all her other provisions. And here she is today – totally ruined! When I asked her what reason the English gave her for the act, she said, "None. They are laying the country waste – *voor die voet*".[165] She had a letter for Mrs Nieuwenhuis from someone asking her to give the woman a chair to sit on, as she had nothing in the world and could not sit on the bare floor. When I went away Mrs N[ieuwenhuis] was just coming out with armfuls of childrens' clothing for her little ones. Oh, my heart was filled with bitterness too intense for words! What <u>right</u> has our "civilized" enemy to wreak their spite and rage on defenceless women and children! Mrs S. Eloff[166] told me that a few days ago a woman died at Irene after having given birth to a child, and to her last breath she was

---

[165]   *voor die voet* (Afrikaans) – without exception.
[166]   Possibly Stefina Petronella Eloff, the wife of S.J. Eloff, a grandson of President Kruger. See J.H. van Dyk, Eloff, Sarel Johannes, in *DSAB III*, pp 270–271.

pleading for a morsel of meat. They are being starved to death there, especially the relations of men who are still in the fields.

This evening we received a letter from Line through Mr Dyer[167] – the first we have had for a long, long time. All well at Alphen.

March 3rd [1901]

Sunday morning in the "Forest".
I was always rather inclined to agree with the poet, [168] who says: -
"The myriad-faced multitude, that pass
An ever changing, never ceasing show,
Drive deep the blade of loneliness. Alas!
Amid the thousands, not one face I know",
but this morning I realize how true those words can be amid surroundings of the most intense solitude. I am sitting near the spot that was the scene of so much laughter and fun yesterday – but what a contrast! Instead of the clatter of tea-cups and the incessant chatter of six busy tongues, I hear the gentle wind swaying the branches overhead with a soothing sound that is beginning to make me feel a little - - - sleepy! I hear the buzz of industrious bees that know of no day of rest, I hear an occasional chirp and warble from the birds that are my sole companions. But no, I am forgetting the faithful Carlo, who is ever by my side – fast asleep now, it is true but turning a watchful eye on me at every slight movement. – What a perfect day! What soul-stirring, never to be forgotten beauty of nature! Can it be true that this fair land is being soaked with the blood of thousands of noble young lives, that not far from us the air is rent with heavy roar of musketry and cannon, that men are standing up against their brothers and fathers and sons – slaying one another! O God, o God, canst Thou in Heaven look down and see it all without laying a calming hand on the bitter, surging, murderous hearts of men? In Thine own good time, I doubt not, but we pray Thee, do not let us wait too long.

I have been reading over some parts of this diary and I find that it gives one the impression that the writer is rather good and pure-minded. I don't know how this has come about because I am not good, and have

---

167   Not identified.
168   Not identified.

not the slightest intention of allowing anyone to run away with such an idea. I honestly meant to write as I feel and the only thing I can think of to account for this deceptive chronicle is that my bad thoughts and actions are <u>too</u> bad to be put down on black and white. You must ask my mother what she thinks of me and then you will condemn this whole diary as a most finished piece of hypocrisy and deceit. If there is a thing in the world that will keep me humble and modest it will be the remembrance of my mother's opinion of me – lazy, extravagant, careless, insolent, cringing and sweet to outsiders, selfish and short-tempered at home. Nature has given me a soft voice and winning manners, and they have been a curse to me. Outsiders fall in love with me at first sight and go into raptures over me – "sweetest girl in Pretoria", "The most charming and womanly young girl I have ever met", "What culture, what refinement!" – these are the <u>outside</u> opinions that reach me every day of my life, for there are always people unwise and indiscreet enough to repeat what has been said of you. But I go by the opinions of the people I live with and according to the one with whom I spend the greater part of my life, I am the faultiest creature in existence, and she ought to know. So I refer you to her, dear diary, whenever you detect a vein of insincerity running through my writings. – Two Tommies with butterfly-nets have just disturbed my meditations. They were just going to pass without a word so I gave them a friendly "good-morning" and they stopped to speak to me and show me their "finds" – a rather poor show, because there are not many butterflies at this time of the year. One asked me whether I was "sketchin" and when I said "No, writing", he seemed very curious and wanted to know whether it was poetry. I did not enlighten him. They told me they were of Lord Kitchener's bodyguard and encamped near Berea Park,[169] and with a few more friendly words they went away. I have just asked "Gentleman Jim"[170] to go up to the house and get some grapes for me. G[entleman] J[im] is another character of note, living in the tin cottage not far from where I am sitting. He is nothing but a pitch-black Kaffir but such a gentleman! Speaks nothing but English and that in a deliberate, aristocratic drawl that "fetches" everyone. It is as good as a play to see Jim taking off his cap to me with a princely flourish and to hear him say "good morning, little mis-

---

169   A sports ground on the western side of the Apies River immediately op-
        posite Harmony.
170   A domestic servant employed by the Van Warmelo's.

sie". He is very lazy and does nothing but go to the market with the fruit every morning, and keep an eye on the lower part of Harmony, but he is honest and faithful and good to send on messages, so we keep him on.

Later. One of the Tommies came back and as he passed I offered him a bunch of grapes. He squatted down in the grass and saying something about "Hope I'm not intrudin'", began to talk. He told me many interesting things. Last week he went to Middelburg with Lord Kitchener. They asked Botha to come into the town and have an interview with Lord K[itchener]. He came with his brother Christiaan and five or six other men – arrived at nine in the morning and stayed until about 4.30 pm.[171] Had lunch with Lord K[itchener] and this soldier was their orderly. He said the first thing Botha asked him was water for a good wash. He thinks Botha a "fine, well-set-up man", tall and broad-shouldered. They had long interviews, he and Lord K[itchener] and when they went away he shook hands with Lord K[itchener] and said "I hope you will have good luck". The soldier says he thinks Botha meant good luck in Natal, for Lord K[itchener] went away yesterday and he thinks it is on an errand of peace. This poor fellow told me something of what they went through coming up from the Colony. Fighting nearly every day and marching at least thirty miles a day on one biscuit. For three days not one drop of water passed his lips and he heard the wish from his fellow-sufferers – not once but a thousands times – "Would to God that a bullet finds me before night". And their officers are so cruel and selfish. More than once when the water carts came the Tommies had to look on with parched tongues hanging out of their mouths while water was being carried into the tents for the officers' baths. He is very discontented and says he doesn't care who gets the country. He won't benefit by it and he'll be hanged if ever he lets himself in for another war – on his return home he will leave the army and take up his old work – carpentering. He wants to know why the "bloomin' capitalists" don't come and fight when they want the country with its gold mines. What a sensible Tommy Atkins![172]

---

171 Botha and Kitchener did in fact meet for negotiations in Middelburg in the South African Republic on 28 February 1901. See S. du Preez, *Vrede-spogings gedurende die Anglo-Boereoorlog tot Maart 1901*, pp 166–209.

172 The name Tommy Atkins refers to ordinary soldiers in the British army, also called Tommies.

Sunday evening

We had quite a lot of visitors this afternoon but from no one could I hear any war news. Everyone is talking about Lord K[itchener]'s interview with Gen Botha, and Uncle Paul says every word the Tommie told me is true. What <u>can</u> it mean? Is it possible that we are going to have peace at last? God grant it, but – peace with honour – nothing less will satisfy us. But I have written enough for today and want to go to bed now, so goodnight, dear diary.

General Botha and Lord Kitchener, accompanied by members of their staff, meeting at Middelburg, 28 February 1901

March 4th [1901]

I am not feeling quite well, so the mother is keeping one in bed for a day or two. Oom Pieter was here this morning on behalf of some people who want to buy "Harmony". Mama named a big price (£25 000) in the hope that they will not be foolish enough to pay it, for we have no wish to sell this beautiful property. I wonder what their answer will be. Oom P[ieter] told me something interesting. He says he went to see his brother-in-law in one of the hospitals and there was a young Africander with a bullet wound in the calf of his leg, a boy of 17 or 18 – and this youth told him that last week he was on a train out Delagoa way, that was captured by the Boers. It appears that he and a friend of his, also a young Boer, were working for the Cold Storage Co[mpany] and left Pretoria in connection with some business for the Company. On their return to Pretoria, his friend was in one train, and he was following, not far behind, in another. The first train was blown up and plundered by the Boers, who came galloping towards the second train just as the engine of it also flew into the air. Then the fight began. The Boers bore down on the wrecked train, firing as they came, while the English returned the firing with interest, until they saw that all was lost and the officer in command held up a white handkerchief in token of surrender. The Boers rode up, someone asking him playfully whether that was all white flag he carried about with him, and then they set to work on the provisions and fruit. The train was laden with bananas and pineapples, of which the Boers soon made short work, tearing up the banana skins, cutting open whole pineapples and burying their teeth in them. How they must have enjoyed themselves! I hope my own two boys were there! But now comes the strangest part of the story. In spite of the heavy firing that had come from both sides, not a single Boer was wounded, not even a horse had a scratch, while a good many of the English were wounded and a few killed. The young Africander had this bullet-wound in his leg, for which the Boers apologised profusely. His friend, who had been in the train before him, was with the Boers, mounted and armed! Quick work, was'nt [sic] it? Soon afterwards some trolleys arrived, and everyone set to work, loading them with what remained of the spoil and they rode away singing and shouting at the top of their voices, leaving this poor boy behind with a sore leg. And so he comes to be in the hospital![173]

---

[173]   She is probably writing about an incident that occurred on 1901-02-13, when Commandant Trichard and Captain Slegtkamp derailed a British supply train near Brug Spruit on the Eastern Railway Line. Since the Boers captured a huge booty of inter alia sugar, they called it the Sugar Train. Trichard mentions in his memoirs that a jongetjie (Youngster) who was on the train, was wounded in the incident. See O.J.O. Ferreira (ed.), *Geschiedenis Werken en Streven van S.P.E. Trichard*, p 183.

Evening.

The Roods came over this afternoon to ask me to spend tomorrow evening with them – an invitation I had regretfully to decline. K. Rood[174] told Mama that Sir A[lfred] Milner has arrived in Pretoria – they think in connection with Kitchener's interview with Botha. Something is brewing, but what can it be. If we only knew!

March 5th. [1901]

Oom Pieter was here again today. Those people offer £20 000 for Harmony and no more, so that question is settled, for the mother will not "come down, come down". He told us that Gen[eral] Botha is expected in Town – tonight. I believe – to interview Sir Alfred M[ilner]. All this shows that something is happening – some great event is hanging in the air. Tonight I am going to begin my correspondence to send with Mrs Bodde, who is leaving for Europe at the end of this month.

I feel unfit for anything but sitting under the verandah in the brilliant moonlight. It is an exquisite night – even Paulus was impressed by the beauty of it for he drew my attention to it with the words *"Allah! Kyk daardie mooie wolke, nonnie".*[175] Last week we had great "ructions" with Paulus again and now he is as meek as a lamb: He caught three Tommies in the vineyard this afternoon and struggled with them, but while he was holding one, the others tackled him from behind and so he lost them all. They stole a lot of grapes but dropped nearly all in their flight to the "Forest". – Am reading "Hyperion", a beautiful book by Longfellow,[176] lent me by F[red] N[iemeyer].

March 7th. [1901]

Yesterday nothing but rain, rain, keeping me a close prisoner all day. My poor old Carlo has been fighting again – his face is swollen to twice its normal size and he howls dismally and mournfully. Today the sky was heavy and overcast, but as it did not rain, I went to Town – more for exercise than anything else, as I have been shut up for nearly a week.

---

174   Probably Karel Rood of Parkzicht.
175   "Oh! Look at those beautiful clouds, little missy."
176   Henry Wadsworth Longfellow (1807–1882) was a famous American poet. His novel Hyperion was first published in 1839. See *The Consolidated Webster Encyclopedic Dictionary*, p 501.

Had a delightful walk and talk with F[red] N[iemeyer] through Berea Park. – There is no news from the front. – It is raining steadily tonight. Had letters today from Miss Prinsmann,[177] Mrs Dawson[178] and dear Marie,[179] and a postcard from Cornelis Beelaerts.[180]

March 9th. [1901]

Went to vocal rehearsal yesterday in spite of very threatening weather. Strange that we have this rain at the end of the season. For days now we have not seen the sun and it rains almost incessantly. Today has been the same and the streets are in such a frightful condition that I have had to say at home – which I dislike very much. I must have exercise every day. As far as we know, there is no war news – only rumours, one more wild and extravagant than the other.

March 10th [1901]

Our dear Willem's 27th birthday. What a dreary one – nothing but rain and wind and storm – not a glimpse of a fresh face to cheer one up. It has been a very lonely day. I wonder how much longer this rain is going to last. Our poor men in the field! How my heart aches for them on a wild night like this. – Seven saloon carriages passed today, I suppose Sir A[lfred] Milner returned from Middelburg. What was the result of his conference with Botha? If we only knew! Ah, if we could have peace before the winter comes!

March 12th [1901]

When it rains night and day and one sees very few people, it is not easy to keep a diary. Yesterday afternoon it cleared up a little and Anna

---

177   Not identified.
178   Not identified.
179   Probably Marie van Eeden, a cousin of the diarist who lived in Holland, the daughter of Frederik and Nellie van Eeden. See B. du Toit, *Die Verhaal van Johanna Brandt*, p 44.
180   Probably C. Beelaerts van Blokland, a prominent inhabitant of Utrecht in the Netherlands, who corresponded with the diarist earlier on in the war. See Archives of the *Nederduitsch Hervormde Kerk van Afrika*, Pretoria, L.E. Brandt Collection, IX/165, unsorted, C. Beelaerts van Blokland – J. van Warmelo, 22 November 1899.

Fockens[181] called with Céleste C[inatti][182] and F[red] N[iemeyer] came to tell me that I was expected at a "Party" given in honour of his birthday at Consuéla [Minnaar]'s that evening, so I went and we had great fun – half a doz[en] young folks. The walk home was terribly muddy. To-day was wetter than ever but I put on thick boots and tramped to Town – one must have exercise. Went to Mrs Michaelson and *Mevr[ou]*[183] Nieuwenhuis – heard that the Boers refused to accept the terms of peace offered them. I believe the English offer them "fair treatment" and nothing more. They say there is much discord in the English House of Parliament. The Bubonic plague in the Colony is spreading rapidly. We received a long letter from Line today through Col St. Clair. Also had a "military" telegram from Mr Boord from P[or]t Elizabeth say-ing that he is unable to come to the Transvaal.[184] I thought as much! Of course the poor thing thought war was over and the road clear for every-one.

March 13[th.] [1901]

Persistent rumours are afloat as to the capture of Gen French (as to? – it sounds wrong, but I am sleepy, dear Diary, and my brain is not very clear, so you must please overlook grammatical errors – or is it ungram-matical errors? I really don't know. The one sounds as ungrammatical as the other and it strikes me that with each word I am going deeper into the labyrinth. Never mind, let's try something else) ((what a long aside!))

I spent the afternoon with the Boddes. It was such a perfect day. Fetched Sarah [Rood] on my way home to call on Connie [Minnaar] – where I made my "indigestion visit" for two evenings spent with her. After the rains, (oh, I forgot to tell you that the sun shone brilliantly today and that we think the rain is over) the roads were hard and lovely

---

181 Anna Fockens was the wife of Willem Jacobus Fockens, who was the Secretary of the First Volksraad (People's Assembly) of the South African Republic before the Anglo-Boer War and served in the Republican forces during the war. See J. Ploeger, Fockens, Willem Jacobus, in *DSAB III*, pp 300–301.

182 Probably the daughter of the Portuguese Consul-General, D. Cinatti. See J. Brandt, *Die Kappie Kommando*, p 46.

183 Mrs

184 See footnote 163.

and walking was a great delight. Mama had visitors, Anna F[ockens] and Mr Phillipp – and Mr Dely[185] came to take out the honey. The whole house is full of honey – great boxes as full as they can bee – I mean <u>be</u>. No, this will never do. When one is so sleepy that one makes <u>puns</u> then it is time to go to bed. I suppose you know, dear D[iary] that some wise man once said that "puns are the flickering embers of a decayed mind." I quite agree with him, don't you? – There is more war news but I can't remember the details so it is best to say nothing – only things seem to be going rather well! Let us hope so. I am dying for some good news.

March 15th [1901]

Yesterday I went to my French lesson in the morning. H[enriette Aubert] and I had so much war news to discuss that we had precious little French. She told me many interesting items of news from Europe – that our President gave the young Queen a gold thimble for a wedding present, which everyone considered very simple and appropriate – her Majesty not excepted; that the crazy German Emperor [Wilhelm II] presented her with a cut-glass scent bottle, with gold stopper, filled with the waters of [the River] Jordaan(!) to christen her children with, which greatly shocked the old Queen mother, who is something of a prude; that the Queen of Portugal, who is of French descent and consequently bitterly against "perfidious Albion" and all that pertain to it, bestowed all the *"Ridder-ordes"*[186] of Portugal on the young Queen Wilhelmina, and the highest honour of all (I forgot what it is) on her consort, during the King of Portugal's visit to England. He went to attend Queen Victoria's funeral and during his absence his wife was Regent and committed all sorts of *"katte-kwaad"*[187]; that the consuls at Pretoria have protested to the Military Government against the ill-treatment of our women and children, especially those who have husbands etc still fighting – I can't remember all she told me. The Boers have had victories all over the country and took three trains recently – Bubonic Plague in

---

185   Probably H.W. Dely who lived in Meintjes Street, Trevenna, Pretoria. See *Longland's Pretoria Directory for 1899*, p 125.

186   Orders of knighthood. These rumours were probably not true, since it was unlikely that the Queen had the power to independently bestow orders on foreign dignitaries.

187   Mischief.

Durban – 30 000 new troops coming out – French's capture, or at least, great defeat, almost a certainty – De Wet in the Free State now (the French call him the Napoleon of South Africa). Great dissatisfaction in the English Parliament. How much of it all to believe is more than I can say – I give it for what it is worth. In the afternoon Mr and Mrs Bodde came to Harmony. They are very charming people. I am now reading Thackeray's "Vanity Fair".[188]

Friday evening. Vocal rehearsal was a failure today, only about six members turning up. The weather looked very threatening but cleared up later on and the afternoon ended beautifully. I have nothing special to write this evening so I am going to do my French exercise and then practice a little before going to bed.

March 16th. [1901]

Went to Céleste [Cinatti] this afternoon. There was tennis – two Khakis were present and Mr Philipp and Mrs van Eeghen. I don't know what was the matter with me – I had not a word to say for myself and followed each remark addressed to me with the greatest difficulty. I believe the most brilliant remark I made was about the weather. I suppose those who knew me will put it down to the presence of the Khakis but it was nothing of the sort. I am not at all shy before any of the enemy, as a rule. The whole thing is that I am feeling rather depressed. I have been "looking mournfully into the Past" – a fatal error when the Present is so dreary. One can afford to look back on the troubles and struggles of the Past, if they are past, but not when the Present is just as bad – if not worse. Longfellow's book, "Hyperion", opens with these words – "Look not mournfully into the Past. It comes not back again. Wisely improve the present. It is thine. Go forth to meet the shadowy Future without fear, and with a manly heart." Can anyone have a better life motto than that? The book has had a great effect on me. It is so pure and good.

---

[188] William Makepeace Thackeray (1811–1863) was a celebrated British novelist. Vanity Fair, issued in monthly parts between 1846 and 1848, was his greatest success. See *Consolidated Webster Encyclopedic Dictionary*, pp 527–528.

March 17th. [1901]

Another Sunday morning of peaceful meditation in the Forest – Carlo at my side, "Vanity Fair" at hand when I am tired of writing and thinking. It is not an exceptionally fine day – there is a fresh breeze blowing, the sky is dull and covered with great white clouds and all around me are signs of approaching winter. And yet it is all so infinitely calm and restful. How one's thoughts do travel on a day like this and in these hours of solitude! I find that these Sabbath morns do me more good than all the church services in the world, or am I deceiving myself? Can it be that they are only <u>pleasanter</u>? "The heart is deceitful above all things and desperately wicked" and perhaps I am only edified by the beauty of the scene around me because it is so much nicer sitting here than tramping to Town through dust and heat and sitting for two mortal hours in a close church. The question now is, which is the better for my soul? I am afraid I cannot tell.

I hope no one will disturb my solitude this morning. There is a chance that my Tommy of two weeks ago will come and look for me because he promised to bring me some buttons and badges for my collection, but I shall not allow him to sit and converse with me again – that is, not unless he has some news to tell me. I suppose there is church parade or something, for I hear the military bands playing – how their music jars on me! how I hate the sight of the enemy flouncing about our Town, officers out riding with our girls, promenading in our Parks! O, the bitter pain it is to me. Shall I ever get used to it? I think not; there will be no living here for us if the English remain in possession. For my part, I don't care if I never see the Transvaal again, much as I love my own dear native land. Several Tommies have been prowling about the river but they all depart in a hurry when they come upon me. I am not exactly in a mood to write this morning so I shall read a little now.

<u>Sunday night.</u> No adventures this morning. The usual lot of young visitors this afternoon. Archie Truter had a wild story to relate – a Boer commando swept down on the refugee camp at Irene last night and carried away all the women and children – took them to Pietersburg, I believe. He seemed to think the story true but we all laughed at him. What would the Boers do with so many helpless creatures? How are they to feed them? how get them under cover? It would be a most fool-

ish and reckless thing. Paulus tells me that a train came in this evening at 6 o'clock with a white flag. I wonder what that means.

March 20th. [1901]

On the 18th we got a letter from Line through the post – censored. It seems as if one can write as usual now, but of course there is always a chance that de Wet might get our letters. I don't mind his censoring anything I write. Yesterday (19th) I went to see Mrs Gen Botha. She gave me the loan of the De Wet and Steyn manifesto[189], which Mama has copied. Khaki does not like it that it is becoming public. Mrs B[otha] has many interesting things to tell of her visit to her husband. She is very angry because people still talk about her, even now that she has quite given up receiving Khakis. I think she is acting very well under most try-ing circumstances and it is a shame that our own people run her down. She did wrong in the beginning by allowing herself to be seen in public with Khakis, by entertaining them at home and by dining with Lord Roberts, but she soon found out her mistake and is quite different now. The story is abroad now that she has taken in Khaki boarders! That she went to her husband with a bribe from the English!! – one worse than the other. No wonder the poor little woman is bitter against her slanderers.

From there I went for a delightful drive with the Roods yesterday. We drove out to the cemetery and saw all the new graves – rows upon rows of childrens' [sic] graves, our own poor little ones – innocent vic-tims of England's gross neglect and starvation. One's heart is very, very bitter at the thought of all the needless misery. War is such a calamity at the best of times – why should our "civilized" foe make it so much hard-er for defenceless women and children? No one can form an idea of the terrible sufferings around us. These people would have been safe and comfortable in their own homes if the English had only left them there,

---

189   A statement issued by President Steyn and Chief Commandant De Wet in Fouriesburg in the Orange Free State on 1901-01-14. It was printed in the form of a handbill for distribution to the Republican commando's. A translated version was later published by the Natal Witness. See diary entry on 1901-03-25 and also M.C.E. van Schoor (ed.), 'n Bittereinder aan die woord. Geskrifte en toesprake van Marthinus Theunis Steyn, pp 177–180.

and now they are going through privations too terrible to describe. The stories that reach us every day! But no, I cannot dwell on them.

I spent this afternoon with the Roods. Annie has come back from J[o]h[annes]burg – in a very low state of health, pale and thin and frightfully melancholy. She suffers from great depression and is low-spirited to the verge of morbidness. Poor girl, I have promised to come and cheer her up sometimes.

March 21st [1901]

This morning Mama and I went to Town together and on our way to Hen[riette] Aubert we passed some of those tin shanties crowded with women and children. At the door of one of them was an old woman looking very sorrowfully out into the street. We stopped to speak to her and it was heart-breaking to hear her sad story. Her husband has been at Ceylon for nine months and another young woman who was with her had lost her husband in the war, and her only two children had died of measles last week, three days within one another. The poor old mother told us they were Rustenburg people and from her farm alone ten children had died of measles here in Pretoria.

Every day we hear of the most dreadful cases no human being can imagine how bad things are and it seems they are getting worse daily. I hear that the people are on half rations now. I cannot believe it.

Mama and I went to have dinner at Aunt Clara's, where the rain kept us until quite late this afternoon. Wanda Schuart[190] told me of a brother of hers who is one of Kitchener's Scouts[191] – another brother is fighting on our side. That is what makes this such a terribly cruel war – the differences in families.

Brother No. 1 was at Krugersdorp when a sergeant, an ex-carpenter, shot a bullying young lieutenant with a carbine. He (Schuart) was one of the four men who led the man to jail where he was kept for ten days and then hanged for the desperate act. Poor fellow, he was goaded on to it and knew very well that it would cost him his life but he told his com-

---

[190]   Not identified.
[191]   Former burghers who joined the British forces and fought against their own people. More commonly known as National Scouts or "Joiners". See A.M. Grundlingh, *Die "Hendsoppers" en "Joiners". Die rasionaal en verskynsel van verraad.*

rades that he had rid the army of a great scoundrel and he had done it calmly and deliberately. The officers are sometimes such selfish tyrants that one is quite glad to hear of a case like this, but it is very sad to think that the brave sergeant had to pay for it. His comrades admired him and said he was one of the bravest and most fearless of men in action.

Bubonic Plague is spreading rapidly in the Colony. Several dead rats have been found lying in the streets of Pretoria – a very bad sign. I read an announcement today in which the Mil[itary] Government offers 3d for every dead rat – won't our little ragamuffins and street boys do a roaring trade now? – Letter from Oom Pieter informing us of the birth of another son and heir – one from Edith [Goodwin] in which she mentions some of the Heidelberg men who have been killed recently – Dolf Spruyt, Okkert Spruyt, Johnnie Biccard[192] and some others.

March 23rd. [1901]

Yesterday was rather uneventful. I went to vocal rehearsal in the afternoon and was disappointed to find so few members present – a few clouds in the sky, one or two drops of rain are sufficient to keep away half of the "sweet songstresses". I was told that the Boers have re-taken Middelburg and Rustenburg and today someone told Mama that it is De Wet who is out Middelburg way. That something is going on in that direction is evident from the number of trains going out on the Eastern line – laden with troops, cannon, horses and provisions.

Today has been a red-letter day to me, not because of anything extraordinary that has taken place but simply because I have been so _inwardly_ contented and happy. There are days like that, when not all the misery in the world can affect our deep sense of _"levenslustigheid"_[193]. The first thing I noticed was the exquisite beauty of the sky, a beauty ever changing and increasing as the day passed on, ending finally in a glorious sunset of blue and white and gold. No one _can_ be sad on a day

---

192   Wilhelm Mangold of the Heidelberg Commando recorded the events surrounding the death of the two Spruyts and Biccard, who were close friends of his, in his diary. These three, as well as three other Heidelbergers were killed in action at Chrissiesmeer on 6 February 1901 and were, according to Mangold, buried on the battlefield. See T. van Rensburg (ed.), _Vir Vader-land, Vryheid en Eer. Oorlogsherinneringe van Wilhelm Mangold 1899 – 1902_, pp 329–330.

193   Cheerfulness.

like this, at least I found it impossible today so I just let myself go and gave myself up to the mere joy of living – The two girls came to sing as usual this morning and I sang like a bird, as happy and free from care – and this afternoon I went to the Roods and we (MF[194] and I) we went for a lovely, never-to-be-forgotten walk in the park. Do you know why I am so happy now-a-days, dear diary? Just look at the first page of this book – "I feel the need of relieving my heart, for I have no intimate friend to whom I can speak freely." That was my state not three months ago, and now? Well, now I <u>have</u> a friend and a very dear, good sympathetic friend it is. I shall not mention names because it does not concern anyone but myself – it is enough that I am more content and that my mind is much healthier and that even <u>physically</u> I am much improved since I met my friend.

Sunday. March 24th. [1901]

The following is a "poem" on De Wet and Kitchener.

Kitchener to Secretary of State for War.

Sunday.

I am taking measures once for all to clear my reputation,
I swear to give de Wet a fall that means annihilation.

Monday.

A brilliant action by Brabant, the enemy has fled.
Their loss was something dreadful; ours – a single Kaffir dead.

Tuesday.

De Wet is short of foodstuffs; his ammunition's done,
His horses are all dying, and he's only got one gun.

Wednesday.

The cordon draws in round de Wet; he now has little room
He only can escape one way, by road to Potchefstroom.

---

194   Not identified.

Thursday.

De Wet is now caged like a rat; he's fairly in a box,
Around him grouped are Clements, Clery, Methuen, French and
Knox.

Friday.

An unfortunate event occurred – I report it with regret.
A convoy with 500 men was captured by De Wet.

Chief Commandant
Christiaan de Wet

Saturday.

A kaffir runner says he saw de Wet's
men trekking West
With ammunition for 2 years and
food supply the best.

Sat[urday]: (later)

A loyal farmer told our scouts, de
Wet was riding East
Each man, beside the horse he
rode, was leading a spare beast.

Rock Ferry 20.1.01.
J. McKeown.[195]

There you have the latest war news
– official reports – I wonder who
made the above lines? Would'nt
[sic] Khaki be wild if he got hold of
them! It is a glorious morning and
I have been enjoying it to the full.
Young Dely[196] came to attend to
our bee-hives this morning. I have
just been writing and amusing myself with doing nothing in particular.

---

195 Not identified.
196 Obviously a member of the Dely family whom the diarist mentions on 13
March 1901.

We hear that Gen Botha's brother Philip[197] has been killed and two of his (Philip's) sons wounded. How dreadful that would be!

Sunday night –

Of all my young friends only Annie Rood turned up this afternoon and we two had nice little confidential chat under the trees. She told me many of her Johannesburg experiences. An old Major told her that Gen Hart[198] was sent home because he refused to destroy farms. He said he had come out to do his duty, not to fight against women and children and destroy private property. What a pity that there are not more men in the English army courageous enough [to] come out boldly with their own opinions!

March 25th. [1901]

This afternoon I had a little adventure. Some time ago Mrs Gen Botha gave me the de Wet and Steyn manifesto to read with strict injunctions to say nothing about it to anyone. This manifesto's appeared in the "Natal Witness" some weeks ago and was carefully cut out of each copy by the English. Imagine the excitement and curiosity of Pretorians when they found their morning's paper so cruelly entreated – how they wondered and wondered what the forbidden article was, and what excitement prevailed when it became known that a few of the cuttings stuck fast in the papers and were discovered lying loose within the sheets. Everyone burned with desire to see and read these remarkable cuttings the mother and I not excepted and we were very much pleased when Mrs B[otha] gave us the loan of hers (I don't know where <u>she</u> got it and did not like to ask). We read it and made a copy of it for our own use, keeping it very secret and only showing it to our most trusted friends, as we had been told that a terrible fate was in store for everyone found in possession of it.

---

197   General Philip Rudolph Botha, the eldest brother of Commandant-General Louis Botha, was killed in action on 1901-03-06. He was regarded as one of the foremost commanders in the forces of the Orange Free State. See J.P. Brits, Botha, Philip Rudolph, in *DSAB IV*, pp 51–52.

198   Probably Major-General A.F. Hart. He served in the British forces in South Africa to the end of the war and was not sent home. Rumours probably false. See O.J.O. Ferreira, Hart (later Hart-Synnot), Arthur Fitzroy, in *DSAB III*, pp 374–375.

Today I put Mrs B[otha]'s cutting into an envelope and went to return it to her, putting it into my sunshade while I was fastening my gloves and – promptly forgetting all about it! Near the bridge I suddenly remembered with horror – the manifesto! I do believe the people in the street thought I had gone mad for I turned round suddenly, caught up my skirt in one hand and ran like the wind to the spot where I had first opened my sunshade. There was nothing to be seen so I ran on and presently came upon the envelope crushed and open. I snatched it up eagerly and found it "full of emptiness"! Then I saw a Tommy walking slowly up the street reading something so I ran after him shouting "Stop" Tommy, Soldier, Hullo. Some officious little street boys stopped him and he came towards me. "Did you pick up an envelope?" I demanded. "Yes, with de Wet's manifesto in it". "It belongs to me", I said, "give it back", and then he slowly took it out of his waistcoat-pocket. I was very thankful that it had fallen into hands of an ignorant person – an officer would have refused to return it. M.F.[199] The mother is not well. She has a touch of malaria.

March 26th [1901]

A lovely long letter from mine own sister through Col St Clair. There is an official report that de la Rey has had a great reverse at Vredesburg – (I am quoting English figures) 200 prisoners, between 3 and 400 dead, eight maxims and pom-poms taken and one 15 pounder, 300 round of (cannon) ammunition, 15 000 of small ammunition and I believe a whole convoy.[200] We are feeling just a little anxious because there may be some truth in the reports but not for a moment do I believe that it is as bad as they say. – I went to Mrs Nieuwenhuis and from there to see the three typhoid patients in Pretorius St[reet]. Am too tired to write much this evening – I have not been able to sleep for three nights in succession.

---

[199]   It is not clear why the diarist wrote the letters M.F. here.

[200]   On 1901-03-24 a British force indeed captured De la Rey's convoy after a running battle near Ventersdorp in the Western Transvaal. The British took 140 prisoners, 77 wagons and carts, two Armstrong guns that the Boers had captured at Colenso, a Maxim Nordenfeldt gun and six machine guns. See P.G. Cloete, *The Anglo-Boer War*, p 231.

March 27th. [1901]

I spent the afternoon with Annie Rood and we went for a walk together. Someone told me today that Prof Mansveld's son, prisoner since the battle of Elandslaagte, has died of typhoid at St Helena.[201] Also that a son of Ds Goddefroy,[202] was shot when trying to escape with Sarel Eloff from Ceylon. I do hope it is not true, for there is one Goddefroy dead already and another wounded I believe.[203] Some families have been very unfortunate, and <u>we</u> have been wonderfully blest and can never be thankful enough for Willem's escape, first out of that awful fight and then the long exile at Ceylon or St Helena. I often think of it and thank God for His great goodness to us. When we remember the dangers our dear boys have gone through and compare our lot with that of thousands of others, we can only marvel at the great mercy that has been shown us. Our time may still come; no doubt we too shall be called upon to give up our best-beloved for *"land en volk",*[204] but at least we have been spared all these weary months, although I must say there is something <u>awful</u> in having such a sword hanging over one's head day after day. The suspense is sometimes more than one can bear and I wonder whether it will not be easier for us when once we know the worst. Well, we must just be brave and patient to leave all in His hands.

---

[201] Cornelis Willem Eduard Mansvelt, the son of Prof N. Mansvelt, the Superintendent of Education in the South African Republic, was taken prisoner of war at Elandslaagte on 21 October 1899 and sent to St Helena, but he did not die there. See O.J.O. Ferreira (ed.), *Krijgsgevangenschap van L.C. Ruyssenaers*, p 186.

[202] The Reverend M.J. Goddefroy of the Hervormde Church congregation in Pretoria. He joined the Republican forces at the outbreak of the war. See A.D. Pont, Goddefroy, Marius Joseph, in *DSAB III*, p 329.

[203] Goddefroy, Marius Theodoor, the son of the Reverend M.J. Goddefroy, was shot by a guard on St Helena on 9 February 1901. Goddefroy, who was only 19 years old, did not attempt to escape but was shot for allegedly throwing stones at the guard. His one brother was also a prisoner of war on St Helena. See A.D. Pont, Goddefroy, Marius Joseph, in DSAB III, p 329. Sarel Eloff, who was the grandson of President Paul Kruger and husband of Stefina Eloff who is mentioned by the diarist on 1901-03-02, did indeed attempt to escape from St Helena, but failed. See O.J.O. Ferreira (ed.), *Krijgsgevangenschap van L.C. Ruijssenaers*, pp 158–160, 162, 198.

[204] "country and people".

March 29th. [1901]

I went to Town yesterday and met M.F. coming up Andries St[reet] and
he asked me to go and have some refreshment with him in Dobbie's
old tea-rooms. I went. I meet him very often now-a-days; sometimes by
accident, sometimes by appointment and I say nothing of these meetings to anyone, because they are <u>my</u> business and no one else's. Even
my mother does not know and that simply because she has forfeited all
right to my confidence by some unpardonable accusations with which
she has charged me. It is enough for me that my meetings with him
are perfectly innocent. There is never a suspicion of love-making about
them and there never will be, of that I am certain and he always does me
a lot of good so why should I not see him? He is a boy of 20 and I am a
woman of nearly 25 – there could never be any question of anything but
friendship between us – and I would <u>never</u> meet him again if I thought
there was the slightest danger of his falling in love with me. That he likes
me is evident and I have come to have a very sincere affection for him,
but <u>that is all</u>. I am going to take you into my confidence, dear diary,
because you understand me so well. I would not give up my friendship
with M.F. for <u>anything</u>, because it has done so much for me. He may
be a boy in years, but he is a man of thirty in experience and I never
feel the difference in our ages, on the contrary, I am a perfect child in
many things compared to him. Intellectually he is miles above me and
yet I am never oppressed with a sense of inferiority, because I am sure
there is much he can learn from me, in the same way as I am a wiser and
happier woman after every interview with him. I want my influence over
him to be all for his <u>good</u>, for I think he is easily influenced, in spite of
his strength of character, by those he likes. I admire him very much.
He is not wonderfully good-looking and yet there is much strength in
his face combined with a certain soft beauty that is indescribable. His
eyes are a dark brown, veiled by long lashes like a girl's and his voice is
expressive and on occasions, full of feeling. Altogether he is to my mind
the most sympathetic of men and we get on very well together. I hope I
don't like him <u>because</u> he is so sympathetic and spoils me so and draws
me on to speak about myself, but I think we are all influenced by selfish motives to a far greater extent than we are aware and perhaps I am
only flattered by the evident interest he feels in me and my concerns. It

certainly is very comforting after all the loneliness I have gone through. He is studious and thoughtful, his very appearance is scholarly, and his conversation always charms and interests me. His quick appreciation of things is most refreshing after the languid indifference of the ordinary young man of today. And that he leads a pure life is <u>certain</u> - of that I am as sure as a woman with good instincts usually is about these things – (it sounds a little conceited to talk about "good instincts" in connection with oneself, does'nt [sic] it? but I think I am beginning to have quite a wonderful opinion of myself - Someone else is to blame for <u>that</u> however).

Mama has gone to Town and I am supposed to be looking after the dinner and here I am scribbling away.

Friday night.

I was in the park with M.F. this afternoon and Mama went to see Oom Paul and when she came home she asked whether I had been alone and when I said "no" she asked who had been with me. Of course I told her and then we had a little bit of a scene. She said I was making a fool of that boy and that I was just like all other girls – bent on making as many conquests as I could, regardless of the pain I gave others. Such things cut me to the heart, for I have never flirted with anyone in my life and no one knows that better than the mother. She laughed me to scorn when I spoke of him as a good friend and asked what I knew about him. I told her plainly that I would not give up his friendship and would meet him when and where I liked and I am rather glad that this happened, for I am perfectly free now. There is no question about secrecy now and his name will be mentioned less than ever now. There are people who <u>cannot</u> understand such a thing as Platonic friendship and M[ama] is one of them. She says people will talk about me – and she herself is the first to talk. I am seen in public with Schilthuis and Gustav [Fichardt] and Karel Rood and a host of other young men – why should I be talked about for going out with M.F.? I am <u>not</u> going to worry my head about Mrs Grundy[205] at <u>my</u> time of life. I shall look after my own reputation and even that is not necessary, for M.F. will look after it for me.

---

[205]   Mrs Grundy = a grumpy old woman.

March 30th. [1901]

Today is Gustav's [Fichardt] birthday and I have written to congratulate him, for he has come of age and I am afraid the important event will not be taken much notice of. It will be his own fault, however, for he declined a "fuss" – like M.F. What a modest, retiring pair of youths! It is just as well that I did not give a pic-nic this afternoon, because it rained hard and I would only have been disappointed. Went to Town this morning and bought a new diary because this one is nearly full. Dear, soft, shiny, black friend, how fond I have become of you! and how sad I shall be when I write the last words in you. I tried to get another book like you but alas, I was unsuccessful and your rival is an unsympathetic looking thing with a hard back and reddish coat. Perhaps I shall learn to love him too but that will depend greatly on the confidences I have to make to him. What will their nature be? Shall I be sad? Or glad? Shall I grow in grace and in beauty of thought and feeling – in short, will my confidences be <u>worthier</u>? There is one thing I have made up my mind to and that is – no more "looking mournfully into the Past" for me. After next month I am going to put the Past away from me completely – with all its bitterness and grief, all its struggles and failures and disappointments – and live only in the present. I shall also give up trying to penetrate the mysterious Future. To what purpose these restless longings, these vague yearnings after I know not what? I want my life to be serene and calm but that can only be when the "World Beautiful" is to be found in my own breast.

But April is upon me with its "memory-laden hours" and until it is past I cannot, and would not if I could, enter into the fair, new life that seems to be opening before me. These April anniversaries! How they wring my heart and take me back to the years of my unhappy girlhood. The first chapter of any life closed on the 21st of April 1892 when I knelt beside my dead father and gazed on those beloved features, so still and white, that silvery hair, that figure, calm, majestic, noble. Was there ever a father like ours? I think when I am an old, old woman, the memory of that sainted being will be with me still, and his loss as fresh as today. Nearly nine years have passed since I gave up my dearest and with every year I worship him more and long more for his presence. And then there are people who would have us believe that we have no immortality – that when we lose our dear ones they are lost <u>for</u> <u>ever</u>. How the thought hurts! How cold and cruel it is! And yet I know people who have lost their dear ones, too, and have reconciled themselves to the thought that they will not meet again in all eternity. What a hopeless grief theirs must be.

But April contains more than anniversaries of death and desolation – memories more bitter than death – hopes of a starry future unfulfilled, shattered ideals, broken promises of love – all this and a great deal more. Yes, I realize more keenly every day that I have "wasted all the purpose of my youth".

But why so sad tonight? Is it because the wind is moaning drearily round the house, or because the friendly moon is obscured by heavy clouds? My soul is sorrowful unto death tonight and I am filled with many dark forebodings. My brothers, my brothers! Sometimes I remember with a thrill of horror that my own flesh and blood is in deadly peril and then I see – Fritz lying face downwards on the cold earth. Oh how wicked and ungrateful I am when God has been so merciful to us. But it is no wonder when one dwells on the fate of so many noble young lives. Why should Stuart[206] fall and be buried in an unnamed, unknown grave and my own brothers be spared?

I saw a youth today with eyes just like Stuart's and all day I have been haunted by his tragic fate. And then Minnie's image is before me, young and beautiful, glowing with the fervour of life and love, only to be cut down ruthlessly in all her pride – oh no, I cannot, <u>cannot</u> dwell upon it. – Edith writes that her (M[innie]'s) little daughter is thriving and that her lip has been most successfully operated on. Two tiny scars will remain, but nothing very disfiguring. If only dear Minnie had known that before she died, how it would have comforted her! But how foolish of me! She knows <u>now</u>, of course, and is serenely happy where there are no mysteries. And now I think I ought to stop writing – at least for tonight. The morrow may find me in a less melancholy frame of mind and then I shall try to take away the memory of these few last pages. And yet – no, that can never be while they remain in this book. The hand that wrote them must tear them out and fling them in the fire – <u>then</u> perhaps the memory of them will disappear.

---

206   Not identified.

March 31ˢᵗ· [1901]

I have been spending this Sunday morning in bed because I don't feel very well and the mother always insists on my keeping quiet – but now I must get up, for presently my usual visitor will arrive. I am sorry I was such poor company last night, dear diary, but I feel much more cheerful this morning. How could it be otherwise on a glorious day like this? Yesterday I forgot to tell you that I met Captain Buckle and spoke to him for the first time since that memorable afternoon when I sent him away from Harmony. I have often seen him since and greeted him quite friendly but yesterday I met him on the bridge and he stopped the driver and asked me whether I would speak to him. I looked up and down the street and said grudgingly "Yes, I don't mind, because there is no one in sight".

B[uckle]. (shaking hands) You are looking very fit and what a pretty ribbon that is round your hat (pointing mischievously to my crossed flags).

J[ohanna]. Yes, do you want it?

B[uckle]. (eagerly) I should like very much to have it.

J[ohanna]. (with a sneer) I thought as much. You always want everything you see.

B[uckle]. (after a pause) I have written another story. May I send it to you to read?

J[ohanna]. Um - yes, as long as it is'nt about S[outh] Africa.

B[uckle]. Oh no, it is'nt. I am sick of South Africa.

J[ohanna]. But not quite as sick as S[outh] A[frica] is of you – still it does my heart good to hear it. –

And so on, and so on. We fly at one another immediately after the first words of greeting and I am often thankful to think that our disagreeable tussels are over. Sometimes I rather enjoyed them but there were days that I could have scratched his eyes out joyfully.

How lovely Harmony is this afternoon! how blue the sky and how dazzling white the clouds! The cosmos is in full bloom and the whole of Harmony is covered with the delicate flowers – pure white, mauve and deep magenta. –

Sunday evening. Only two visitors this afternoon, Gustav [Fichardt] and Archie [Truter]. No news. Sunset something too grand for words. –

April Fools' Day. [1 April 1901]

I have not made a fool of anyone today – not in a mood for nonsense. I heard this afternoon that de la Rey had been captured – <u>that</u> I don't believe, but I do believe that the Warm Baths are in the hands of the English again, because Frikkie Grobler[207] has been sent into Town with his family. Oom Paul sent us word that F[rikkie] G[robler] says he saw our boys a few months ago at Waterberg, where they joined Kemp's[208] commando and left for Ermelo – from there to Krugersdorp and now probably with the other commandos in Waterberg. I have not yet told you, dear diary, that the English are trekking in thousands to Zoutpansberg. That is their latest move – to take Pietersburg and all the other places in the north and then I suppose they think the war will be over. People say the Boers are running rather short of ammunition, in spite of the large quantities they take from the enemy. If that is so I am afraid they won't be able to hold out very much longer, and if the English take Pietersburg I don't know what is to become of our cause, for there the Boers make ammunition and there all their stores and provisions are kept.

I cannot write tonight – heart and hands are heavy as lead, for I have looked deep into a man's soul today and seen the awful skeleton kept there. And I have thought <u>my</u> lot hard! I have said it was more than I can bear! God forgive me. I do not know yet what the word "calamity" means and I have had a lesson today, which I shall not soon forget.

April 2nd [1901]

A very uneventful day – rain and nothing but rain – no chance of going out, no chance of seeing a new face. I have been reading hard at Pope's

---

[207] Not identified.

[208] General J.C.G. (Jan) Kemp was a prominent Boer commander in the second half of the Anglo-Boer War. He was especially active in the Western Transvaal, often in conjunction with General Koos de la Rey. The Van Warmelo brothers were indeed with Kemp's commando in the Ermelo area by the end of January 1901 and participated in the abortive attack on a British camp at Chrissiesmeer on 6 February, to which the diarist referred on 1901-03-21. See J.C.G. Kemp, *Vir vryheid en vir reg*, pp 365–366; D.S. van Warmelo, *Mijn Commando en Guerilla Commando-Leven*, pp 177–189; S.B. Spies, Kemp, Jan Christoffel Greyling, in *DSAB I*, pp 420–421.

Essay on Man,[209] lent me by M.F. I don't know what to make of it yet for I do not grasp half of it, but I have promised to read it carefully and thoughtfully and what is incomprehensible to me, <u>he</u> will have to explain.

This morning Paulus went to the Pass Office to get permission to go home. It was refused for not a soul is allowed to leave Pretoria and so my gentleman had to come back to us again.

April 3rd [1901]

The dreary, sunless day has ended in a night of unparalelled splendour. I think the moon must be full tonight, and all nature is serenely beautiful – like my thoughts. Why I am so light-hearted this evening? Can it be because of the load that was taken from my mind today? There was such a shadow over me and this morning it was removed and I who seldom weep, shed tears of joy and thanksgiving. I have secrets from you, dear diary, you see, but they are not mine, so I have no right to tell you. There are many things I cannot tell you – my inmost thoughts, for instance, because I never know into whose hands this book may fall: – and many things that pass between me and my friends. And this evening I have to part from you. The two blank pages must remain for the rest of Marie's verses and so I am afraid you and I must bid one another "good-bye". My next "diary" will, I hope, be a healthier and happier production, for am I not richer than when I opened this volume three months ago? Something has helped to "adjust the focus of my vision, and has changed our "sad world" into "The World Beautiful" and never can I be so desolate, so lonely as I was not many weeks ago.

I received a letter from Edith this morning saying that she is down with enteric and will not be able to write soon again. I hope she is not going to be seriously ill – those poor creatures have had more than their fair share of trouble. I would be very anxious about Edith if I did not know how sound her constitution is, but on the other hand, she is to terribly run down since Minnie's death that one does not know whether she has enough strength left for such a long illness. Typhoid is no joke.

---

[209] Alexander Pope (1688–1744) was an English poet. His *Essay on Man* was published in 1733. See *The Consolidated Webster Encyclopaedic Dictionary*, p 512.

I have just written her a very cheerful letter asking whether I may have the extreme pleasure of nursing her. Our old Boer *Tannie* can come and stay with the mother, the change would do me good and I have had a little experience. If anything were to happen to my dearest girlfriend and if I never saw her again I think I would go out of my mind. What Edith is to me no one can imagine – least of all herself. I don't know why I love her so much – I suppose it is because she gives, and always has given, so very little in return.

<u>Later</u>. My evening has been very satisfying and satisfactory. A little reading – *Essay on Man* – a little French and a good hour's music – one of Beethoven's[210] sonatas and then I wound up with a little promenade in the moonlight. Here endeth the second lesson.

[Script III]

"Harmony." Sunnyside. Pretoria. April 4th 1901.

Dear new Diary. Last night I took leave of my old friend – tonight I greet the new. There is really no difference, except perhaps that one always enters more thoughtfully into a clean, new book. In the first place I intend writing in pen and ink in future – it is so much more satisfactory than pencil – secondly I intend making this a still more personal diary than the last – for many reasons. Of course I shall follow the events of the war as closely as possible, but when there is no war news I shall write about myself, my friends and studies and recreations and enjoyments, and – my troubles! The last always forms an interesting topic to one as self-absorbed as I am, and if I have no troubles I shall just to invent a few in order to keep myself entertained.

---

210   Ludwig van Beethoven, the famous German composer.

The events of this day are as follows:–

French lesson this morning – nothing this afternoon – writing this evening. Now I defy anyone to keep a diary on material of that meagre description. Oh yes, we killed a snake on the verandah this afternoon – that is, Mama killed it with a stick, while I looked on and gave directions. When the deed was done I condescended to approach a little nearer and even offered to take the reptile by the tail and cast him into the roaring torrent: viz: the furrow.

Harmony is undergoing great changes. The lower part has been let to two Italians, who are going to lay out vegetable and fruit gardens; Gentleman Jim has been turned out of the tin cottage, to make room for Italiana, and is now in a room next-door to Paulus. He is going to cultivate the upper part of Harmony, and fetch and carry for us when we have no one else.

But I am sure I heard some news today. When I came home from Town a Mr v[an] Schalkwyk[211] was here and he told us that the English have burnt thousands and thousands of bales of wool in the Free State. Now that is nothing but wilful destruction. The Boers can't eat wool, no matter how hungry they are and they can't shoot with it, so there is no excuse for Khaki, who says all this destruction is necessary in order to starve the Boers into an unconditional surrender. Their real object is to ruin the Boers, to lay the country waste and impoverish it to such an extent that our poor people will be entirely dependent upon them.

The march to the north is continuing steadily and today a great many families passed through Pretoria on their way to Irene – some from the Warm Baths, others from Nylstroom. It is horrible to think that the districts, that have escaped so far, must now also be devastated. Some time ago we heard that an end had been made to this wholesale destruction but it seems as if it is not so.

This afternoon there is such a glorious sun-set again – they seem to be the order of the day, and tonight the moonlight is, if possible, even grander than last night. I wish my pen were powerful enough to describe at least something of the beauties I have the privilege of revelling in every day, but I find myself saying over and over again: Grand, Exquisite, Magnificent, etc words used by every little miss fresh from school.

---

211   Not identified.

And it is not because I do not appreciate what I see – that is certainly not the reason of my poor little attempts at describing – no, I am afraid I am not born to write, whatever I may be born to do. I am still trying to find out – in the meantime the mother wants me to go to bed, for it is nearly 11 o'clock p.m. My usual hour for retiring is ten.

April 5th. [1901]

Good Friday. Spent a delightful afternoon on the "Bomb Hill"[212] with some of the young people. Mr de Zwaan[213] was our chaperone. It was such a lovely day and the air was so pure and fresh where we were – I enjoyed myself very much, but feel a little tired and sleepy and not in a mood to write. Perhaps tomorrow I shall have some news to tell.

April 6th. [1901]

Yes, indeed I have news to tell tonight. Dietlof has been taken prisoner![214] This now the second van Warmelo. Where is the third and last? The feeling of impending sorrow which has been growing on us, is becoming a tangible something. Try as I will I cannot shake it off and I must frankly confess that my heart is full of dread – but the mother must not know, for she is quite miserable enough as it is, and I do all I can to cheer her up and see the bright side of things. This morning I went to Town to do some shopping and to send a wire asking how Edith is and when I came home the mother told me she had received a note from the Governor enclosing a telegram from the Assistant Provost Marshal at Ventersdorp, in the name of Gen Babington, to say that D[ietlof] was captured – quite well – and Fritz was also well when last seen. "When last seen", what does it mean? When and where was he last seen, and how do the two brothers come to be separated? Why are they not both caught? My brain is in a whirl with all these guesses and surmises and oh, I am so anxious. If Fritz had been caught I would have been quite content, because I have always had such forebodings about him, and as prisoner he would have been all right, but now? Why is he the last? Oh, I am so anxious! This afternoon Mama and I went to the Governor to

---

212   Not identified.
213   Probably Willem Johannes de Zwaan. See diary entry of 6 August 1900.
214   He was captured on 3 April 1901. See D.S. van Warmelo, *Mijn commando en guerilla commando-leven*, p 210.

see whether there is any chance of getting Dietlof home on parole. He promised to ask Lord Kitchener and to say a good word for us, but he seemed to think there was not the least chance of success. It depends on the way D[ietlof] surrendered. If he was caught fighting, there was no hope for him and Ceylon was his fate, if he surrendered of his own free will there was just a chance of his being let out. We had quite a long conversation with the Governor and he was perfectly charming and promised to help us in every way. He will allow us to go to Johannesburg to see Dietlof when he passes through on his way to Ceylon and I am afraid that will be our only crumb of consolation.

Oom Paul and several other people told us that over a hundred prisoners have already arrived at J[o]h[anne]sburg from Ventersdorp. Dietlof is with them, I suppose, for the wire is two days old and he has had time to arrive. Now we are so afraid that he will be whisked away before we can see him. That would be dreadful, because Mama wants to take a portmanteau of food and clothing to him and the poor boy must have money. Oh, I hope we shall see him before he goes. Perhaps Mama will ask permission to send him to Holland, as he cannot be let loose in South Africa. We must see him – if only to hear what has become of Fritz.

The Governor seemed to think that the war is all but over – but then the English thought so ten months ago. Yesterday it was exactly ten months since Pretoria was taken.

Dietlof van Warmelo

Can it be possible! How the time has flown and yet – and yet – how it has <u>dragged</u>! When we came home late this evening, so tired and so sad, I was cheered by a wire from the Goodwins – Edith better. She has a nurse so I am not going to Heidelberg and it is just as well now that we may have to go to J[o]h[anne]sburg any minute. – Annie Rood told us that two of Gen Botha's staff had been captured, on their way to de Wet with dispatches; someone else told us that the English have been driven back from Nylstroom and I heard many other rumours, but nothing definite. What I can repeat for "certain sure" is what my own eyes have seen – one train after the other on the Eastern line, laden with cannon, troops and horses.[215]

April 7th. [1901]

Mama gave me no peace today until I had been to the Governor to see whether he had any news. I went to his house feeling very bad about troubling him on Sunday, and found him all alone. I thought Mrs Maxwell would be there and perhaps a crowd of officers, but she has left Pretoria and I was pleasantly surprised at having the General all to myself. He says he asked Lord Kitchener yesterday to let Dietlof out on parole, but he refused, because he is afraid to begin making exceptions. Gen Maxwell advised us to go to Johannesburg by first train tomorrow, because the prisoners arrived there some days ago, and he gave me a special permit there and back and a letter of introduction to the Military Governor at J[o]h[anne]sburg, asking him to help us.[216] So we are going tomorrow afternoon at 4 o'clock, that is if we do not receive a wire before the time that Dietlof has already left for Ceylon. The Gov[ernor] does not seem to think he is still in Johannesburg. He was so kind and good and has done all he can to make things easy for us. He did not

---

215   The British undertook a major offensive against the Republican forces in Eastern Transvaal in the first half of April 1901. See P.G. Cloete, *The Anglo-Boer War*, pp 232–234.

216   Archives of the *Nederduitsch Hervormde Kerk van Afrika*, Pretoria, L.E. Brandt Collection, IX/168, file titled *Briewe aan Mev van Warmelo 1878– 1915*, unsorted, Special permit for Mrs van Warmelo and her daughter, 7 April 1901. In terms of a notice issued by the Director of Railways in June 1900, all civil passengers on trains between Pretoria and Johannesburg needed written permits. See *Government Gazette Extraordinary*, 1/8, Pretoria, 5 July 1900, p 116.

seem to mind being troubled on Sunday – took me about the garden and showed me the flowers and when I went away presented me with one of his buttons and a Colonel's crown – for my collection. Everyone says he is so courteous and considerate and I apologise for having called him names in my "black diary". From him I went to see Mrs Morice, who is back from J[o]h[anne]sburg, and told her the news of D[ietlof]'s capture. Mr Cinatti was there, dear old soul, and much concerned when he heard it. When I told them of the Governor's kindness he kept on saying – "General Maxwell is very well – very well" – meaning very good, and when I went away he said he hoped I would see my "husband" in J[o]h[anne]sburg. I did not understand at once that he meant my brother – he is always full of nonsense.

It was a stormy afternoon and we did not have our usual Sunday visitors – for which I was devoutly thankful. I am not in a mood to entertain anyone just now – in fact I should like nothing better than to get away from everybody until this month is over. Today it is my wedding-day that should have been and I cannot help thinking of what I went through four years ago. I wonder whether everyone makes such a fuss of anniversaries as I do. It is very foolish to dwell on what is past for ever, especially when the present requires all one's patience and energy. When I am an old woman I can afford the luxury of "looking back" but not now, when the future holds so many fair hopes and promises. Just now I am very sad about M.F. He is in great trouble and I may not help him – I may not even see him for a week or two and in the meantime I am tormenting myself with many unanswerable questions. As soon as confidence is restored I shall be quite happy, and until then you must put up with confessions of melancholy and depression. It is good to have a dairy, when human friends fail one – not that M.F. has failed me yet, but "circumstances over which we have no control" have raised a barrier between us. Let us hope that it will only be a temporary one. At present I have enough to bear, what with anxiety about Fritz, poor Dietlof's capture and the mother's low spirits. She feels this thing dreadfully and can't shake off her fears regarding her youngest born. Poor mother! how my heart aches when I see her lying on the sofa in that attitude expressive of so much hopeless misery. I often think I must be a most unsympathetic companion with my endeavours at brightness and cheerfulness – perhaps it would be better to see things in their proper light and admit that they are "very bad". We young folks simply cannot realize what mothers have to go through at a time like this, and that is what makes us appear unfeeling. She is asleep now and it is nearly 11 o'clock. Shall I disturb her or go on writing until she wakes? We ought to go to bed and I think I ought to wake her, for I am also tired. For a wonder my back is aching again tonight – I thought I had got rid of it, but as soon as I am worried it comes on again. Mental distress has a great influence over my health.

April 8th. [1901]

After all, we have not gone to Johannesburg yet. All day wires have been flying over the country and no one can find out what has become of Dietlof. His name does not appear in the list of prisoners who arrived at J[o]h[anne]sburg a few days ago and no one seems to know where he is. This morning Mama went to Major Hoskins and he at once sent telegrams in every direction, but nothing has been found out and it is late – tomorrow perhaps. I spent the whole morning in darning and mending the dear boy's old clothes, to wear on board. We are taking a big portmanteau full of all sorts of little luxuries, and I am going to put in a book like this, for him to keep a diary. He is fond of writing, it will give him something to do and will be most interesting for us afterwards. While his experiences of the war are fresh in his memory he must write them down, as well as everything about Ceylon. All day the mother has been trotting about, packing little things for our hero – nothing is too small to think of – no detail too trivial for his comfort. I am wild with impatience to see him and if he is carried away, before we can get to Johannesburg, the disappointment will be too great to bear.

I went to some friends this afternoon to tell them the news – it does one good to see how interested and sympathetic people are. At the Roods I met M.F. and he walked home with me. We had a little chat that ended in the clearing up of some disturbing doubts – little things that have been worrying me so much lately – and this evening I am feeling quite relieved and happy. It is not dreadful when one has a nature like mine – full of ups and downs? I always envy those people with even temperaments – people who remain calm and placid under the most distressing circumstances and who do not torment themselves with a thousand needless doubts. For mine generally turn out to be "baseless", as F. said they were in this case.

I have not touched the piano nor sung a note since – since I felt so worried – a sure sign with me that something is wrong – and this evening I had a lovely time. Scales and exercises were an exhilirating recreation for half an hour or so and then I spent an hour with the great master. I played his beautiful Sonata (the fourth) in E flat, and it moved me to the very depths, but not sorrowfully – I cannot touch Beethoven when I am sad; he is my fair weather friend, unlike Chopin and Schubert.[217] – The mother wants me to go to bed, but first let me think what war news I have to tell. They say the English have taken Pietersburg and that Ermelo is again in the hands of the Boers; also that the English got "paddywhacks" somewhere near Marabastad.[218] The line to Johannesburg has been destroyed in several places and we don't know now when we shall be able to go.

April 9th. [1901]

We have been looking out all day for news from our prisoner – in vain. It seems as if he has disappeared from off the face of the earth – at least no satisfactory answer to our telegrams can be had. I begin to think he has escaped from the clutches of Tommy Atkins. Would'nt that be a lark, dear diary? I went to Mrs Nieuwenhuis this afternoon and from there to the Cinattis, where I heard that Pietersburg has been taken "with but slight resistance". That is a very good sign, for it shows that the Boers did not intend to defend it and I am sure they are coming back here as fast as they can, to do all the mischief that lies within their power. There are no troops worth speaking of, to protect the lines and towns, and if the Boers are sharp they can do a lot of harm. I wish they would take Pretoria. I think I would kiss every Boer I saw in the street – at least I would shake hands all round. – There is positively nothing I can think of to write down this evening. Had a letter from Tante Nelly [van Eeden] through the Dutch Consul. Dear old aunt! how very kind and sympathetic she has been all the time! I did not expect it from her,

---

217 F.F. Chopin and F.P. Schubert were famous composers of piano music.
218 A small settlement in the northern part of the South African Republic (Transvaal) some 20 kilometres south of Pietersburg.

but it is wonderful how some people have come out during the war. But as it seems that that is the most brilliant thing I can think of to say, I shall just read a little and go to bed. I have been practising a little but there was no "inspiration" this evening My throat is burning and I feel I am in for a bad cold – nice prospect with Friday's rehearsal so near at hand.

S.[219] walked with me from Town to Cinattis' – I wonder how I am to get rid of his attentions. It is quite three years now that he has been hovering round me and I know that one word of encouragement would be enough for him – but I cannot give it and I wish I could show him once and for all how useless it is to "hover" round this candle. He is such a good fellow, one can't help feeling sorry for him and that is just where the danger lies – if you don't <u>dislike</u> a man it is almost an impossibility to snub him – at least I find it very difficult. I always was too soft in this respect, in fact I have been accused of "drawing" men on purposely, on account of this very softness. The mother, for instance, fully believes I encourage men for the sake of "conquests" and we have had many a tussle on this point.

April 10th. [1901]

We had news from Dietlof this morning. He is on his way from Ventersdorp to Potchefstroom from where he will be sent by train to Johannesburg, so now we may expect a telegram any moment. Mama went to Town this morning to see Major Hoskins and ask why we heard nothing and found that he had sent a letter yesterday already,[220] but the little boy had taken it to the wrong house – Major Poore's[221] – and he had put it in

---

219   Not identified.

220   In this letter, on the letterhead of the Military Governor's Office, Pretoria, Hoskins wrote on 9 April: "Dear Mrs van Warmelo, I have just received an answer to my wire to Ventersdorp which says 'Van Warmelo left here this morning stop will be forwarded from Potchefstroom to O.C. Troops Johannesburg' – so you have plenty of time to get to Johannesburg to see him. I return you the first telegram. Please let me know if I can do anything further to help you. Yours sincerely, A.R. Hoskins." Archives of the *Nederduitsch Hervormde Kerk van Afrika*, Pretoria, L.E. Brandt Collection, IX/165, file 1, titled *Briewe aan Ds en Mev L.E. Brandt 1892–1911*, unsorted.

221   Major R.M. Poore was the Provost Marshal or chief of the British military police. See *Government Gazette Extraordinary*, 1/4, Pretoria, 20 June 1900, p 40. He lived in a house across the street from Harmony's main entrance. See J. Brandt, *Die Kappie Kommando*, p 40.

the post. Just like him – he is always so disobliging and indifferent. Fancy sending a letter to the post when we live immediately next door to him! And he knows Harmony quite well, so there is no excuse for him. I shall not forget in a hurry that he came to see Mama on business one morning and marched into our drawing room with a pipe! and he did'nt [sic] even salute when he addressed my mother! Some of these beauties have the most perfect manners in the world, really. – My afternoon has been such failure. Just think, dear diary, I was invited to a pic-nic in Berea Park – Connie M[innaar] asked me on Monday and I promised to go if we had not left for Johannesburg. Well, I had nothing to do this afternoon so I left home with Carlo at about 3.30 and will you believe it, I roamed about the forest until 5 o'clock and fell in the river, and tore my skirt, and scratched my face under a thorn-tree, and got myself covered with black-jacks and came upon two Kaffirs bathing – in fact I did everything except find the pic-nic party. In despair I walked over to Connie's to see whether there really was a pic-nic or not and was told that there <u>was</u> and that they were all in Berea Park. Comforting, was'nt it? And then to "cap the climax" I must needs pass the S.G. Hospital[222] just as they were carrying in a poor, dead Tommy Atkins. That finished me completely and I came home sad and weary and in a very bad temper. But it is all over now. My tempers never last very long and after I had poured my woes into the mother's sympathetic ear and we had had a good laugh over them, I felt better. – Had letters from May and Joan Metelerkamp[223] today. They say Line and the children are quite well – I wonder why she does not write. We have not had a letter lately. Good night.

April 11th. [1901]

This evening I am writing with a fountain pen, a gift from M.F. this afternoon. It is expressly meant for this diary. He has one too – a diary <u>and</u> a fountain-pen – and we are going to see which of us will keep it up longest. I have not much time for writing this evening and I have a good deal to tell, so I shall at once proceed to business. This morrow's morn I went to the Government Buildings to see whether there was no news

---

222   Not identified.
223   Probably members of the Metelerkamp family with whom the diarist lodged when she attended school in the Cape Colony before the war. See B. du Toit, *Die verhaal van Johanna Brandt*, p 25.

from Dietlof. There was nothing, but Major Hoskins promised to let is know as soon as a wire came and he gave me our pass-ports and made everything in order so that we can leave without a moment's delay when news of Dietlof's departure from Potchefstroom arrives. Everything is packed now and if the dear boy receives the portmanteau and box in good order he will be surprised at all the little comforts and luxuries the thoughtful mother has put in for him. We are so awfully afraid he will arrive in J[o]h[anne]sburg and be sent away before we can get there – it would be a most bitter disappointment for us, as well as for him.

This afternoon Mr Philipp came to show us his beautiful collection of old Transvaal stamps. M.F. was here too and Schilthuis who came to see if he could help us with anything as he is going to Johannesburg tomorrow. He will wire to us if he can find out about Dietlof. He made me furious by running down a friend of mine and I gave him a bit of my mind. A thing like that ruffles me for several days, for I am very staunch in my defence of absent friends and do not easily forget disparaging remarks made about them. In this case it was most unfair because he does not know the man at all (A.B.)[224] and I told him to wait until he had reason to say such things. Never mind! it is a little thing and I don't even know why I should have mentioned it – it is not worth while. M.F. says the English have announced the death, in action, of our State Attorney, Mr Smuts.[225] That would be terrible – such a young man and they say he was such a splendid general. I do hope it is not true. There seems to have been a lot of fighting again. Someone told us the Boers were near Middelburg and that the Gordon Highlanders[226] had lost heavily again.

Hundreds of families are pouring into Pretoria from Waterberg and Zoutpansberg. Mama's youngest sister is coming tomorrow, with her five children. I wonder what is to become of her – a poor widow – I suppose she will go to Irene. Mama won't take her in because our house is not large enough and we would have to keep her as long as the war lasts – years perhaps. Just now our finances are in a very bad

---

[224] Probably Andrew Brown. See diary entry on 1902-04-22.
[225] Jan Christiaan Smuts, State Attorney of the South African Republic, achieved fame as a Boer general and later as politician, serving inter alia as Prime Minister of the Union of South Africa for two terms. The rumour was false. See J. van der Poel & S.I.M. du Plessis, Smuts, Jan Christiaan (Christian), in *DSAB I*, pp 737–758.
[226] A famous Scottish regiment.

state. We have no cash, not a penny income and heavy expenses. Of course Mama could have sold Harmony and then we would have been very rich but I think she felt she ought not to do it without consulting the boys. I don't care how we have to economise as long as we can live peacefully at Harmony. – Oom Paul Maré told me this morning that the Information Bureau here demand a list of the names of our killed and wounded whenever the English announce "heavy losses – so many Boers found lying dead on the field, so many wounded" and they can never get a single name.

It seems as if only the live Boers carry cards of identification, at least there is never one found on them by the English. I was so glad when I heard about this – it is splendid that the Intelligence people have such a hold over lying Khaki. Now whenever an official report speaks of "ten dead Boers found" or "fifteen" or "twenty" (an everyday occurrence) the Bureau confronts them with, "produce the cards of identification". Oom Paul says that in all the fighting there has been in Waterberg lately only the name of one wounded man has been reported by the English, at least that was all the In[telligence] Dep[artmen]t got out of them. The stream of troops, cannon, horses, etc continues on the Delagoa Line. Every hour almost there is a train and the mother and I make a rush to see what it contains and look at one another miserably. How is our poor little hand-full of burgers to stand against such overwhelming odds? Oh, it is so cruel – and one cannot help wondering how such things can be permitted. It is not always easy to keep one's faith in these dark and dreadful days but please God, I shall not yield to these sinful doubts that assail me now and then. It would be sad indeed if my great love of fatherland had to be the cause of my disbelief – and that is what it would be, for only those who really love their country feel its desolation and ruination enough to lose faith in a God of Justice. I hope you understand what I mean, dear diary, it <u>does</u> sound rather vague but I am not good at expressing my inmost thoughts – and it is very late and of course my brain is not clear, so I shall just go to bed. I wonder whether we are going to Johannesburg tomorrow or not.

April 12th. [1901]

The long-expected telegram has come at last and Mama and I are leaving tomorrow by the 8.40 am train. Mama had a note from Major

Hoskins[227] enclosing a telegram from Potchefstroom – "Van Warmelo leaving tomorrow for Fort Johannesburg". Now I wonder whether he will arrive there before us or if we shall have to wait for him. If there is a hitch anywhere we shall have to stay over one night in J[o]h[anne]sburg and if we are delayed on the road we shall miss him altogether. For once in my life I pray that the Boers will not take it into their heads to blow up the J[o]h[anne]sburg train. I wonder what adventures are in store for us. I shall take a note-book and write down everything interesting. Today's news from the front – let me see, I heard so many rumours this afternoon at the Vocal rehearsal (we did not sing but had a sort of consultation because our society is dwindling down to nothing and something must be done to stir up our sleepy members). I have a terrible cold "i by dose" and look an awful fright. Is'nt [sic] it unfortunate that I have to go to J[o]h[anne]sburg with boiled gooseberry eyes and a tomato nose? Poor Dietlof will say I have "aged perceptibly" since last he saw me. Oh yes, the news – Bubonic plague very bad in Cape Town – people just falling down dead in the street – Kitchener says the war will last another nine months, at least. Comforting thought, but as long as we keep our country I don't care. Good-bye – I hope to have a lot to tell you when we come home.

April 15th. [1901]

Monday morning. Our visit to the Golden City is over and done with and we are back at Harmony, safe and sound. My mammie has gone to see old *Juf[frou]*[228] Breedt, leaving me to see about dinner, which I have done and have now a quiet hour before me to devote to you, dear diary. I am sure you want to know everything about our trip, so I shall begin at the very beginning. We woke up at 3.30 am on Sat[urday] and did not sleep again because we were too excited and so afraid of missing the train, so we got up before dawn and had all our preparations made in plenty of time, arrived at the station about half an hour too soon – a very good thing, we found out when we got there, for when we presented our passport, tickets were refused us because it had not

---

227 Archives of the *Nederduitsch Hervormde Kerk van Afrika*, Pretoria, L.E. Brandt Collection, LIX/168, file titled *Briewe aan Mev van Warmelo, 1878–1915*, unsorted, G.R. Hoskins – Mrs van Warmelo, 12 April 1901.

228 Miss.

been signed by us at the Gov[ernmen]t B[ui]ld[ing]s before the issuing officer! Imagine our despair and consternation. How we blessed Major Hoskins for not having told us it had to be signed! We asked them to telephone to him at once, which they did, but could get no answer and the train was ready to depart. At last I thought of producing our letter to Col MacKenzie (Mil[itary] Gov[ernor] of Johannesburg) and telling them that a great deal of trouble had been taken to find out the whereabouts of my brother, who would be sent away without our seeing him if we missed that train. Our letters were duly inspected and as a "great favour" we were allowed to get our tickets. Thank Heaven! We got into the train and had a carriage all to ourselves to the end of the journey which was most delightful and interesting. All along the line one sees signs of the war; here a blown-up bridge, there, the ruins of a whole train of trucks and carriages. We had great fun over the fortifications at the various stations – underground passages, covered with bags of sand, with *"schiet-gaten"*[229] protected by plates of iron, and all round them a perfect net-work of barbed wire, ornamented with thousands of empty tins, meat-tins, butter-tins, milk and jam tins! The idea is that when the Boers get entangled in the wires at night, Khaki can know exactly where he is by the jangling of the empty tins. *Ons het ver hulle banja gespot.*[230]

At Irene, just beyond the station, we saw the women's camp, a very large one where thousands of women and children are kept in tents, the families of men who are still fighting. At a distance it looks very nice, rows and rows of white tents surrounded by the beautiful green forests of Irene, and they could not have chosen a prettier spot, but I believe the sufferings those poor people have to go through, are indescribable. They sleep on the hard ground and the food they are provided with is of the poorest – no meat, no vegetables – in fact nothing that a child or delicate person can live on. The small farms lying along the line are all deserted but I saw no signs of devastation. At Elandsfontein[231] we came upon the largest field hospital I have ever seen. I should like to know how many patients it can hold. It is very picturesque and looked quite

---

[229]   Loopholes.
[230]   We laughed endlessly at them.
[231]   Important railway station and railway junction east of Johannesburg, later named Germiston.

Irene Concentration Camp

inviting with its snowy tents and hundreds of Tommies in regulation hospital uniform, loose suits of red and blue flannel. The nurses with their white aprons and red crosses reminded me of my own hospital days – I should like to nurse again if I can get hold of a lot of wounded Boers – no Tommies for me, thank you. A deathly silence reigns in and round the mines, no busy natives, no roar of batteries, hardly a sign of life anywhere. In Johannesburg itself things are livelier than when I was there nearly eleven months ago, but the suburbs are almost deserted and one can see whole streets without a living thing in them. It gets on one's nerves, I can tell you, and made me feel horribly depressed. We drove in a cab to Heath's Hotel,[232] where we took two rooms and then set out for the Mil[itary] Governor's office – Exploration Buildings, Commissioner St[reet]. I don't think we had gone twenty yards when we came upon Aling T[ulleken] on a bicycle and while we were talking to him, S.[233] drove up in a cab! Curious, is'nt [sic] it, to meet practically the only people one knows in a big place like J[ohannesburg]. It shows how very few people there are to meet. Aling promised to look us up at the hotel and then we drove with S[chilthuis] to the Governor. We sent in our cards and General Maxwells' letter of introduction and got

---

232 At 78 Pritchard Street in Central Johannesburg. See *Donaldson & Hill's Transvaal and Rhodesia Directory 1899*, p 689.

233 Probably Schilthuis – see diary entry on 1901-04-11.

in return a letter from Col MacKenzie to the Officer in command of troops, asking him to help us. The Governor was very busy so we did not see him. As the O[fficer in] C[ommand of] T[roops]'s office is in Doornfontein[234] we had to take a cab again – cabs are twice as dear as in Pretoria and we spent a small fortune on them – and were told that the O[fficer in] C[ommand of] T[roops] had gone away for the day, but a sergeant advised us to go to the Provost Marshal with our letter, so we drove to the Fort[235] where Captain Short, the P[rovost] M[arshal] (he is short of three fingers, which a Boer bullet carried away) told us he had not been informed of the arrival of prisoners from Potchefstroom, but a train would be coming in at 5 o'clock and if D[ietlof] arrived by it we could see him for half an hour on Sunday morning. Mama and I looked at one another in dismay, because we had hoped to see D[ietlof] at once and come home the same day by the last train, but there was no help for it so we went back to the Hotel trying to look as if we did not mind the delay. The faithful S[chilthuis] trotted about with us all the time and when I asked him where he was staying he confessed that A[ndrew] B[rown] (the very man he had run down a few days ago and to whom I had given him a letter of introduction) had been very good to him and asked him to take up his quarters with him at Doornfontein, for as long as he cared to stay. "He is a jolly good fellow", said S[chilthuis] with a shame-faced air. I only sniffed in reply and tossed my head to show that I had not forgotten nor forgiven. (The sniff was perfectly natural, though, for my cold was getting worse every moment.)

We had lunch at the hotel – a very good meal, considering the scarcity of provisions in Johannesburg but after the exhorbitant [sic] prices that were charged we had a right to expect the best of everything. Fancy, 20 shillings per day for each person! It is an unheard of price in this country but Heath's Hotel is unusually good – everything so beautifully clean and fresh, lovely rooms and good attendance. We discovered an acquaintance in the ladies' drawing room, Mrs. Pieter Botha,[236] after

---

234   A suburb of Johannesburg.
235   The Johannesburg Fort, erected by the government of the South African Republic after the Jameson Raid of 1895–96. Today part of Constitution Hill.
236   According to the diarist Mrs Pieter Maritz-Botha, who was a close friend of Mrs van Warmelo, was a sister of (Sir) David Graaff, the well-known Cape politician and businessman. See J. Brandt, *Die Kappie Kommando*,

lunch, and she and the mother began to talk while I was left to myself. Then my misery began. I had been feeling ill for days and now the excitement and fatigue began to have their effect on me. (Monday evening) My cold had been greatly aggravated by the keen air of Johannesburg and now a nervous headache came on that did for me completely and the worst of it was that I was expecting a visit from A[ndrew] B[rown] and I could not go and lie down. He came at about 3.30 and the wretched porter told him we were out and he went away again without my seeing him.

While I was waiting a brilliant thought struck me. Why should we not go to the Braamfontein Station to see the prisoners arrive? The mother was charmed with the idea, so we took a cab at about 4 o'clock and drove to B[raamfontein] Station. When we arrived there we were informed that the Potchefstroom train had been delayed and would be more than an hour late. It was cold and windy and there was no ladies' waiting-room and I shall never forget that time – it seemed like an eternity to me. My nerves were in such a state, my head was raging and all the miseries of our country came crowding upon me. Mama discovered an old friend, who was waiting for the same train, the Rev[erend] Martens[237] of J[o]h[anne]sburg and they sat there talking, leaving me to my own sad reflections and I don't think I have suffered so much during the whole war as in that endless hour. Thank God, there the train is! In one moment everything was forgotten and we were breathlessly scanning the crowded carriages. Armed troops and a great many passengers, but no sign of prisoners. We were just running along the platform to the front part of the train when I heard a well-known, highly-excited voice shouting, "Ma, ma", and there was Dietlof, tumbling out of a carriage with an armed Tommy at his heels. I shall draw a veil over that meeting. I don't remember much more than a passionate embrace and have a faint recollection of astonished stares all round us, and all I know for certain is that I was "quite well, thank you" for the time and that Dietlof's Tommy discreetly turned his back on us and walked away until the

---

p 132 and B.J.T. Leverton, Graaff, Sir David Peter de Villiers, in *DSAB II*, pp 267–269.

[237] Rev J.N. Martins of the Dutch Reformed Church on Von Brandis Square lived at 65 Jorissen Street. See *Donaldson & Hill's Transvaal and Rhodesia Directory 1899*, p 746.

worst was over. Blessed, thrice blessed Tommy – I am so sorry now we did not shake hands with him. Dietlof told us afterwards how very good he had been to him. We asked permission to walk with them as far as the Fort, which was instantly granted, Tommy leading the way. How everyone stared at us and turned round in the street to stare again! Now that I come to think of it, it must have looked very remarkable; a ruffianly-looking man, with a disreputable little bundle, with a well-dressed lady hanging on each arm and an armed soldier guarding the whole!

Dietlof was a sight. He had on an old felt hat, full of holes, through which his hair was sticking, a greasy black suit and dirty top-boots and his beard and moustache wild and unkempt-looking. Of course the first thing we asked him was how he had been caught and why he was alone, and he told us that for many months he had been going about the country, commandeering things for the commandoes. About two weeks ago he left his people again, on the same errand, and when he was far from them, his horse got horse sickness and died, leaving him to tramp back to the commando, carrying as much of his baggage as possible. He came to a farm where a woman was very good to him and warned him that the English were quite close by. He fled from there and, I believe, got into their lines. I don't remember exactly how it came about – all I know is that he was hunted like a wild beast for three days, that he crept into mealie-lands and hid behind rocks and on the third day a Kaffir saw him lying behind a big stone and told the English there was a Boer. A soldier came towards him and he levelled his gun at him and could easily have killed him when he fortunately remembered in time that more would follow and they would shoot him if he harmed the soldier – so he surrendered. There was nothing else for him to do and they told him afterwards that they would have shot him like a dog if he had fired. I believe they took him to Ventersdorp and that he found Mr Barry[238] there, who saw to the telegram that was sent to us. (Mr B[arry] is a Pretoria advocate, a young man of whom I saw a great deal the winter before the war.)

Dietlof has promised to write down all his experiences in the exercise-book we put into his portmanteau, so I shall be as concise as possible. Besides, I don't remember one half of the details. He left

---

[238]   Advocate A.J. Barry. See *Longland's Pretoria Directory for 1899*, p 115.

Fritz under General Kemp not two weeks ago, with a few good friends – Izak[239] and Jan Celliers,[240] the Boshoffs[241] and some others – and he says we need not be anxious about him. He is very well and very dirty (that he won't mind – I do believe he is only happy when he looks like a savage) but just now he will be awfully anxious about D[ietlof] because of course he does not know what has become of him. He will think he has been killed – I wish we could get a message away for him.

Well, we walked with our dear hero until quite close to the fort, and there we took our leave, thanking the good, kind Tommy for his leniency and consideration. Very few guards would have allowed us the privilege of walking with a prisoner and I shall never forget this man's kindness. We talked Dutch all the time and could have asked him everything about the war, but we did not, and have regretted it ever since. It is always so when one has so much to talk about that one does'nt [sic] know where to begin. We told him all sorts of insignificant home news and try as I did I could not remember a single important question I had intended asking him.

Mama and I walked back to the hotel and then I found that I was very ill – could not touch a morsel of food at dinner and went to bed at about 10.30 after having spent the evening with Mr Heath, the proprieter [sic] – a very nice, fatherly old man – who took us into his private sitting-room and doctored me with – shall I confess it? – hot toddy,[242] and showed me his curios and photos. I was thoroughly exhausted and soon sank into a deep, refreshing sleep, from which I woke next morning feeling much better. My cold was still very bad but the sick-headache had disappeared altogether. After breakfast S[chilthuis] called for us and we all drove up to the Fort. Mama had been thinking over the

---

239   Isaac Bisseux Celliers (1874–1948), a geologist, son of Jean (Johannes) Francois Celliers and his wife Magdalena Bisseux, a daughter of the French missionary Isaac Bisseux. Isaac was a member of the Pretoria Commando at the beginning of the war and is often mentioned in the diary kept by his brother, Jan Celliers. See A.G. Oberholster (ed.), *Oorlogsdagboek van Jan F.E. Celliers 1899–1902.*

240   Johannes Francois Elias (Jan) Celliers (1865–1940), the famous Afrikaans poet. Jan kept a diary that was subsequently published as *Oorlogsdagboek van Jan F.E. Celliers 1899–1902.* It contains biographical detail on Jan and Isaac as well as references to both Dietlof and Fritz van Warmelo.

241   Not identified.

242   Popular name for an alcoholic drink with sugar or spices.

meeting at the Station and came to the conclusion that we had done something very wrong, that the Tommy would be court-martialled and Dietlof transported for life and that we would perhaps be put over the border. I felt anxious too, especially as we had letters from the Governor. There seemed to be something underhand about the way we sneaked off to the Station without telling anyone or asking permission, so we made up our minds to explain the whole thing to Captain Short and tell him that we had only gone with the intention of waving our greetings from a respectful distance – it never entered our heads that we would have a chance of speaking to him. When we arrived at the Fort D[ietlof] was standing in front of the P[rovost] Marshall's office, between two Tommies. I jumped out of the cab and was just going up to him when one of them said "You may not speak to the prisoner". "But I may kiss him" I answered sharply, and before Tommy could prevent me I had thrown my arms round Dietlof's neck and given him a kiss that could be heard all over the fort. There was a general laugh and the mother followed suit and then we stood aside and waited impatiently for the P[rovost] M[arshal]. Soon D[ietlof] was called into his office where he went trough an examination that lasted quite an hour while we walked up and down outside getting more nervous every minute. We thought he was being questioned about the previous evening's escapade and we fully expected our turn to come before D[ietlof] was allowed to speak to us. How needlessly we do torment ourselves sometimes! The P[rovost] M[arshal] was interested in D[ietlof]'s experiences of the war and was only questioning him about some fights he had been in. I suppose he was trying to fish things out of D[ietlof] but D[ietlof] is prudence personified and would not give our people away in any one particular. At last he came out with a soldier who said we could talk for half and hour in English. Imagine being ordered to talk, to know that the time is limited, to know that a stranger is waiting to catch up every word and to grope desperately after the hundred and one things that must be said! I do believe we lost about five minutes on trying to find our tongues, but when once we found them there was such a babel [sic] that I doubt whether Tommy understood one word. Dietlof had asked permission to tell us about Mozelikatz Nek [sic] in which fight he had taken a prominent part.[243] I shall not repeat all he told us because he will do it himself and far more accurately than I can. It must have been wonderful. D[ietlof] and F[ritz] and five others – seven Boers in all, fought against 250 English who surrendered after one third of them had been killed and wounded. It does not seem possible but I know that D[ietlof] has never told a lie in his life and to me his every word is gospel truth. During that fight he came upon a dying officer, Captain Pilkington,[244] who called him and asked for help. D[ietlof] stayed with him as long as he could, put grass under his head and held his hand until Fritz and the others joined him and the poor fellow died soon afterwards. D[ietlof] says he knows of four Khakis that he has shot – one at a distance of not more than 100 y[ar]ds.[245] One's hair rises at the narrow escapes he has had – he does not know how he and Fritz have come out of all those dangers unhurt. One thing comforted us very much – they have always had plenty to eat – sometimes only mealie-porridge, it is true, but never has starvation stared them in the face. When our time was up we all went into the office where Capt Short asked Mama if she could assure him on her word of honour that the box of food contained no arms. She did, and he allowed the things to be carried into the fort without being examined. They only opened the portmanteau and glanced over the contents and then we bade the dear boy good-bye and everyone considerately left us alone a few minutes. Mama asked D[ietlof] hurriedly whether the Boers had plenty of ammunition but he refused to say a word. He is the most honourable and conscientious man I have ever

---

243 In the Battle of Silkaats Nek, that took place on 11 July 1900 in the Magaliesberg Mountains about 30 kilometres west of Pretoria, Republican forces under the command of General Koos de la Rey overpowered a British unit and captured two field guns. See P.G. Cloete, *The Anglo-Boer War*, p 169.

244 Not identified. In her book, *Die Kappie Kommando*, pp 98–100, the diarist writes that the officer was Lieutenant Pilkington and adds that Dietlof van Warmelo received a letter a few weeks later in which an English officer informed him that Pilkington was a famous cricket player. See Officers died: South Africa 1899–1902, on http://redcoat.future.easyspace.com/BoerP.html, accessed on 2003-04-25, where it is recorded that Lieutenant Thomas Pilkington, of Lancashire, England died of wounds on 11 July 1900. He is not mentioned in county cricket records in Britain. (Search of British county cricket records undertaken on behalf of the editor by Dr G.P.J. Grobler in April 2003).

245 About 90 metres.

come across – in fact I often think he over does it a little. For instance
he thinks it very wrong of the Boers to take clothes from their prisoners before releasing them. I don't see why they should not take all they
require in return for the freedom they give Khaki. We can't keep our
prisoners and they ought to be thankful to escape so easily.

It is getting late so I shall go to bed and think of the rest – there is not
very much to tell and I can finish it tomorrow.

April 16th. [1901]

Mama had gone out again – she is getting quite demoralized, but I am
glad, because she stays at home too much as a rule. My work for the
morning is done so I shall try to finish about our J[o]h[anne]sburg trip
this morning. The mother seems to think I am writing far too much
about it and yet I have not told one half but perhaps I had better cut it
short now. It will become wearisome if I don't take care, and that would
be a pity because this diary is already quite uninteresting enough.

– The first thing I noticed when we met D[ietlof] was his little black
Bible. I was much touched by this proof of the dear boy's piety for
there are not many young men who would carry a Bible about with
them through so many hardships and dangers. D[ietlof] is <u>good</u> if ever
a man was, and the best of it is that with him religion goes so deep that
he cannot speak about it. I have more faith in that silent, intense religion
that only shows itself in purity and nobility of thought and deed, than
in all the words and protestations of piety in the world. But it is often
very hard to live with these very good people. They are so terribly scru-
pulous and exact and generally have a good many worrying little faults
and foibles that greatly detract from the worth of their characters. So it
is with mine brother. He has faults that are utterly unworthy of one who
stands as high as he does and I often find it very difficult to get on with
him – especially as I am no saint myself. But I think we have all learnt
so much during the last two years that we shall be far more forbearing
and generous to one another if ever we have the chance of living happily
together again. After all, there is no school like the School of Suffering
– a truth I have learnt to value and appreciate at its proper worth. But
instead of moralizing I think I ought to finish my story.

Dear diary, can you believe it that my fastidious brother D[ietlof] should have fallen so low as to have "gogga-bibbies"?[246] It is a fact. He confessed as much to us and was exceedingly thankful when he heard that the wonderful Indian juggler of a portmanteau contained a tin of insect-powder as well as a bran[d] new fine-comb. (Please excuse the indelicacy of this subject, but war is war and this is no time for mincing matters). He asked Mama whether she knew those woollen Kaffir blankets with yellow stars and red and green half-crescents and when she said "yes" he told her that he once had a pair of breeks[247] made of that material! He gave us six banknotes, of £1 each, printed in Pietersburg by our Government and given to him in payment of a part of his salary, on Feb[ruary] 1st 1901. Of course we were awfully glad to get them and Mama gave him cash in exchange. They will become very valuable. He left a lot of money in Oom Jan's[248] care at Middelburg, some more bank-notes, printed, I believe at Lydenburg and seven blank sovereigns. It is very curious about these sovereigns. They were weighed and in perfect order to be stamped when the Gov[ernment] had to flee. There was no time to finish them so the men were paid out in these remarkable coins – I believe with nothing on them but a date.

When we had said goodbye to D[ietlof] we walked slowly and sadly back to the hotel, where Aling was waiting for us, and soon A.B. arrived on the scenes too and I had a nice little talk with him. We had lunch at the hotel and left by the 3.30 train, which was very late. Mrs Botha and her little son travelled with us. She is a very nice women – tall and very stately and exceedingly well-read. S[chilthuis] said she reminded him of a sailing vessel in full sail, and that exactly describes her. But she can talk! I wish I had time to repeat one half of the stories she told us – perhaps on the days that I have nothing to write about I can go back to her and her war-experiences. When we arrived in Pretoria it was pitch dark and not a cab to be had so I had to carry our portmanteau which was fortunately very light – to Oom Paul's. They were awfully glad to see us and had many questions to ask – we had tea with them and were escorted home by a large party afterwards.

---

246   Probably head lice.
247   Breeches or trousers.
248   Not identified.

Tuesday evening 16 April 1901

Mama came home this morning from the wife of J[an F.E.] C[elliers][249] (it is best not to mention names in this case) to whom she had gone with a message from Dietlof, and told me that Mrs C[elliers] had been so very thankful to hear of her husband's safety – oh, I forgot to say the message was that J[an] C[elliers] and his brother [Isaac] were with Fritz and in perfect health – because he had escaped from Pretoria ten weeks after the occupation and that the English did not know yet that he had gone. She refused to tell how he got out.[250] But even if they found out what can they do to him? It is their own look-out if they allow men to escape from Pretoria and they can't put her over the border by way of revenge.

Jan F.E. Celliers

Today there are many rumours afloat – 2 000 Boers have taken Dundee and Newcastle, a whole train-load of Henwood's[251] goods has been taken, Pietersburg being destroyed as well as all the farms in the north, and last of all Kitchener about to propose other terms of peace. That may be true because Mrs Gen Botha has gone to her husband again and I am sure she means business this time. She told me herself that she would not go for pleasure in a hurry again. I do wish the English would do their work them-

---

[249] Mrs Susanna Jacoba Celliers (born Dürr).

[250] Celliers himself wrote about his escape in his war diary. See Oberholster, A.G. (ed.), *Oorlogsdagboek van Jan F.E. Celliers 1899–1902*, pp 119–125.

[251] Henwood & Company, general merchants and importers in Church Street, Pretoria. See *Longland's Pretoria directory for 1899*, p 135.

selves and not apply to women for assistance – how degrading for the mighty British nation to have to stoop so low.

This afternoon Capt B.[252] overtook me on the bridge as I was walking to Town – he was riding and did not even dismount when he addressed me, ill-mannered wretch! – and told me that he was leaving for Pietersburg tomorrow. I hated him so much at the moment that for the life of me I could not help hoping that he would never come back again. Oh, how I loathe them all more and more very day! It breaks one's heart to hear of the misery all over our poor country. Khaki seems to be very anxious about the entry into Natal and I believe the Boers are quite near Pretoria because the search-lights are being used from the forts every night. Dietlof told us that our only chance now would be to go deep into the Colony and Natal and cut off the lines of communication if possible.

April 17th [1901]

This morning we had long visit from Mrs Morice, who came to hear news about D[ietlof]. It was a surprise, for we see very little of her now. She told me it was true that the Boers were in Natal and I suppose she hears reliable news from her "ossifer"[253] friends. Mama and I went out calling together this afternoon – for a wonder – and heard all sorts of rumours. We first paid a visit to the wife of our old President. Poor old lady, she was not at all well but brightened up a good deal before we went away. She told us that some time ago a man in Khaki arrived at her house at night and asked the guard many questions, whether she had plenty of food and if the English treated her well and all sorts of things about affairs in town. He spoke English and the man (sentry) answered very guardedly because he suspected foul play and just as the man was leaving he said in Dutch "With us everything is going well too" and disappeared, and then he only found out that he had been talking to one of our own spies. It is marvellous the way those people slip in and out of the towns! Mrs Kruger was so sorry she did not see and speak to him. She says our prisoners escape daily from the rest-camps – no one knows how – sometimes as many as 25 in one week. It does one good

---

252   Probably the Captain Buckle whom the diarist mentioned in her entry of January 1901.
253   Officer.

to hear her talk – one would really think that things have never gone so well with us as now – she has never lost her faith. They had just received a letter from Holland saying that the President is in perfect health.

From there we went to a Dutch family – Postemus Meyers[254] – that Mama used to know in Heidelberg. They told us that young van Alphen[255] had told them that Pietersburg was in the Boers' hands again and [Pieter]Maritzburg taken – very improbable yarns – also that the Boers had taken enough ammunition for a whole year – Mrs Kruger said for seven years. I am getting tired of repeating all these wild reports but it may be rather interesting afterwards to go over these days of excitement and unrest, and up and downs.

Then we went to see Mrs Pieter Botha – our Heath's Hotel friend. She showed us a newspaper which one of the Zoutpansberg refugees had lent her – the last one printed before the English arrived in Pietersburg.[256] I only glanced over it and was rather amused to see a notice that the holidays of the Gov[ernmen]t schools had been "prolonged indefinitely" – good news for the children – on account of Khaki's expected arrival. The paper contained proclamations by Gen Botha and many other interesting items. How I should like to possess a copy! But it is most difficult to get hold of such things – the English snap up every mortal thing – I was even told some days ago that many of the curios of our museum have been conveyed to England. Already? You may well ask, dear diary. Khaki is in such a mighty hurry to get things in safety that I begin to think he is afraid there will be no chance later on. Maddening thought! All our relics (and goodness knows they were few enough) on view in English exhibitions!

– We had a nice letter from Line through the post – uncensored, for a wonder. It was written just about the time of D[ietlof]'s capture and she was in a great state of nervous dread and apprehension – looking out for bad news every day. It is very strange that Line always knows

---

254 Foscus Leonard Posthumus Meyjes was born in 1841 in the town Sneek in the province Friesland in Holland. He was a farmer. In 1890 he settled in Heidelberg, Transvaal where the Rev Van Warmelo was the Minister of the Dutch Reformed Church. Later on he farmed in the district Rustenburg where he died in 1911. See J. Ploeger, *Nederlanders in Transvaal*, p 103.
255 Probably a son of I.N. van Alphen, who was the postmaster general of the South African Republic before the war.
256 Probably the *Zoutpansberg Wachter*.

when something is going to happen – she seems to have the gift of second sight.

Bubonic Plague is getting very bad. Mrs P[ieter] Botha says she had news from Cape Town this morning of the death of a young cousin of hers and his whole family has been quarantined. Cape Town has been declared an infected port and yellow flags are to be seen waving all over the town.

This is the 17th of April again, and again have I lived over certain events of the past, but this particular event happened seven years ago and I find that the remembrance of it only calls up feelings of sad regret and none of pain. I have wondered all day where he is and whether he has thought as much of me as I have of him – that is, if he remembered this day at all – he always was careless about dates, but I never had reason to complain of carelessness and forgetfulness where our anniversaries were concerned. – I have too many duties to attend to this evening, to waste any precious time in "looking mournfully into the Past" (how those words crop up every time! – I cannot get them out of my mind) so I shall just go and practice a little, do my French exercise for tomorrow, write for the European mail and then, if it is not too late, read a little.

I have just begun Charles Kingsley's beautiful book "Alton Locke"[257] (lent me by M.F. – it seems as if everything I read now-a-days comes from him and you can judge his character pretty well by the samples I have mentioned) and I am so deeply interested in it that I should like to read and read until the end, but, as you see, I have many little duties, and find my evenings all too short for the "work and play" I should like to get through. But winter is fast approaching and that means long cosy evenings – spent, in any case, I am thankful to say, most pleasantly and profitably. They are much longer already – this evening I lit the lamp at about 6.15.

April 18th [1901]

I was told today that some time ago there was a panic amongst the guards at the rest-camp (one dark night) and they all fled into the Town.

---

[257] Charles Kingsley (1819–1875) was a famous English author. His best known books were Alton Locke (published in 1850), *The Water Babies* and *Hypatia*. See Harvey, P (ed.), *The Oxford Companion to English Literature*, Fourth, Revised Edition, Oxford, 1973.

Our prisoners first thought of making use of the opportunity by escaping but some prudent old *"tak-haar"*[258] suggested that it might only be a ruse on the part of the English, to try them, so they decided to stay quietly "at home". I suppose the guards <u>would</u> run away if the Boers took Pretoria – but I don't believe a word of this story. I have been wondering whether it is not a great waste of time to write down all these reports, but if I only had to repeat what I know to be <u>facts</u>, I would have nothing at all to write about. It is a fact that Mrs Gen[eral] Botha has gone to her husband again, but <u>not</u> on business for the English, as folks say. She wants to leave Pretoria and has gone to consult her husband – I think she is going to Europe or, if he does not approve of that, to her people in Greytown.[259] I shall keep my opinions to myself until I know more about the matter. It seems utterly incredible that our Generals wife can go away and leave her country and people at a time like this. The name of the Africander woman has already been dragged in the dust to such an extent that I cannot bear to think that an important person like Mrs Botha will do anything to create more scandal.

I have written to thank A[ndrew] B[rown] for his kindness during our recent visit to J[o]h[anne]sburg. I wonder how he and S[chilthuis] are getting on together. They are both clever men and good, and I am sure they will be friends, but I cannot help being amused at the thought of my two admirers living under one roof – brought together by me – but that was quite unintentional, for it did not enter my head that A[ndrew] B[rown] would treat him with so much hospitality.

– This morning in Town I met M.F. and we had tea at Minnie's[260] and a very nice little chat. I see him seldom since – and it seems as if the barrier is not going to be removed for some time. I am ever unlucky with my friendships and wish I could learn to be independent and do without friends altogether. Afterwards I saw Eddie Cooper[261] in the street, but he did not see me so I had not the chance of cutting him. If ever we come near enough together I have my speech ready for him – a very long one – viz *"Land-verrader"*.[262] You know the shameful

---

[258] Backvelder.
[259] A rural town in Natal.
[260] Not identified.
[261] Not identified.
[262] Traitor.

story of E[ddie] C[ooper] don't you, dear diary? How he went with the English, soon after Pretoria was taken, to show them where the Boers had taken their cattle for safety. The first time he came home safely, but the second time he went out, there was a fight and he was seriously wounded and taken prisoner by the Boers. Of course they could not finish off a wounded man – traitor or no traitor – so they nursed him back to health and lugged him about with the commandos. It seems as if he has escaped, because he is here now and I am sure he was not re-leased. The Boers <u>are</u> lenient and forgiving, but that would be carrying it too far altogether – I have known him nearly all my life and sat on his knee a hundred times as a little girl, but now I only know him as a traitor and look forward to the time when I can draw my skirts away from his polluting touch. When our cannon were destroyed that terrible night at Ladysmith, everyone knew that there had been treachery and everyone knew that the Coopers were the traitors, but there were unfortunately no proofs against them. I believe it was Dietlof who told me that he saw Eddie Cooper coming from the enemy's lines <u>unarmed</u> that night. M.F. lost a beloved brother through him, for it was then that our Pretoria men defended the guns so bravely and so bravely gave their lives.[263]

April 19th. [1901]

This afternoon we had a meeting instead of vocal rehearsal. The society is going "to pot" altogether – in fact we have not had a single rehearsal this month, on account of the irregular attendance of the ladies – and this afternoon Mrs Esser sent in her resignation and we had to choose a new Pres[ident]. Mrs Eloff[264] was chosen but as she was absent I don't know whether she will accept. I suggested that, as it is too much for one person to be both Secretary and Treasurer, I resign my position as Sec[retary] and asked leave to keep the post of Treasurer only. There is not very much for the Treas[urer] to do but I often help with copy-

---

[263] See her diary entry of 1899-12-18, p 36. Dietlof van Warmelo writes about this incident in his memoirs (*Mijn Commando en Guerilla Commando-Leven*, p 33), but merely mentions that Cooper and another Boer were suspected, arrested and taken to Pretoria, where the enquiry did not result in anything conclusive.

[264] Probably either Mrs Elsje Francina Eloff, a daughter of President Kruger, or Mrs Stefina Petronella Eloff, the wife of Sarel Eloff, a grandson of President Kruger.

ing music and that runs away with a lot of my precious time. We also proposed getting some honorary members. They must pay £2 or £3 a year and have free admittance to any concerts, public or private, that we may give, and in this way our funds will be increased and the monthly subscriptions of the members reduced. We shall have twice as many members if the fees are lower – people have no money now and they are always grumbling about the 5/- a month. It seems little enough but folks need all their spare cash for charity now.

I shall write no more this evening. Paulus's lesson took up so much time – I often grudge the half hour spent in educating our "nigger's" mind but he is so eager to learn that I can't disappoint him. If only it does him any good! I don't quite approve of teaching Kaffirs to read and write, but he is an exceptional Kaffir with quite a remarkable character of his own. I have seldom come across anyone with such a passionate temper and yet there is no one who repents more quickly. Yesterday he flew out at the mother so I refused to give him a lesson in the evening and this morning he besought Mama to let me teach him again. He said he did not know what possessed him and was very "heartsore" about it.

Well, I am gong to practice an hour now. I am learning Rubenstein's [265] beautiful Valse-Caprice – a brilliant and very difficult piece, just what I want after those heave sonatas of Beethoven. I heard it played most magnificently in London, in Albert Hall, at one of Patti's[266] concerts, and have often thought of it since. The player was a slender little German girl and I wondered where all the strength came from, and the passion and power she put into it. There is not a bar in it that I shall not be able to master, with hard practice, but some of the chords have such long stretches that my hands can hardly make them. I often wish they were a little larger – or at least that my fingers were longer – Filled my pen for the first time.

---

[265] The Russian composer Anton Rubinstein.

[266] Adelina Patti (1843–1919), a celebrated soprano, who was called the Queen of Song at one stage of her long concert career. See P.A. Scholes (ed.), *The Oxford Companion to Music*, pp 484 & 771.

April 20th. [1901]

O gift of God! O, perfect day!
Whereon shall no man work, but play;
Whereon it is enough for me,
Not to be doing, but to be!

Through every fibre of my brain,
Through every nerve, through every vein,
I feel the electric thrill, the touch
Of life, that seems almost too much.

Longfellow's "Day of Sunshine".

A day like this is indeed the gift of God and I feel, with Longfellow, disinclined for work of any sort. I am as lazy as lazy can be – something quite unusual with me, so early in the day. I have opened every door and window in the house of Harmony and am now revelling in deep draughts of pure, fresh air, that send the life-blood flowing through my veins and fills me with an intoxicating consciousness of the delight of mere existence. It is the first time during the war that I have been so keenly alive to the joys of life. I was beginning to think that <u>that</u> feeling had gone from me for ever, but why should it? I have often been told by people long past middle-age that they enjoyed life more than in their youth, and who knows what happiness the future has in store for me. But my heart is too full for words this morning. What is it that Kingsley says? "Our mightiest feelings are always those which remain most unspoken". Great thought! The utterance of a great man's mind! And if a powerful writer like Kingsley felt the inadequacy of mere language in expressing his inmost thoughts, how much more do I not the powerlessness of my poor little pen. I must do something to give vent to my "levenslust".[267] What shall it be? There is only one thing I can think of – oh, happy thought – Beethoven's Sonata Pathetique –

---

[267]   Exuberance.

Sat[urday] evening

I have had my fill of music today and shall not soon forget this Day of Sunshine. This evening I practised hard for more than an hour and find my new study more difficult than I thought at first. When played a tempo it is impossible for one to "make" those long stretches without looking at my hands, so I shall have to learn the thing off by heart. I never do know a thing thoroughly until I can play it without music, which I fortunately can do with ease, especially with a piece like this Valse-Caprice. It is one of my greatest gifts – this learning of music by heart – my only gift, alas, for I do not compose and read music at sight slowly and with difficulty.

This afternoon I called on Mrs Bodde and went from there to the Roods, who saw me home through Berea Park. M.F. was there. They told Mama that the newspapers tell a story of a plot against our old President – someone stabbed him with a knife, I believe, because the war does not come to an end. If there is any truth in it,[268] I wonder whether anyone is foolish enough to think that the poor old man can bring the war to an end if he wants to. Poor old soul! his power has long ago passed into other hands and I think it is time he was left in peace.

April 21<u>st.</u> [1901]

This is the ninth anniversary of my dear father's death. It is not possible to feel sad on a day like this and I am just lying about under the trees enjoying the soothing solitude and great beauty of our dear Harmony. Each day seems more perfect than the last. If I thought yesterday beautiful what must I think of this day? I can write and think of nothing else, it seems, but "the weather". I remember how annoyed Dietlof always was when anyone said "fine day" or made any remark at all about the weather – he said it was so "banal", especially in our country where the weather is nearly always fine, but I don't quite agree with him, for we are already too apt to ignore the beautiful in the common. What is there sweeter, more wonderful in our world than the words, "I love you"? And yet, they are so common, so "every day".

I have just been reading over that part of "Alton Locke" where old Sandy Mackaye takes the budding young poet into the filthiest slums of

268　There was no truth in the rumour.

London and points out to him the hidden poetry in all that seems most revolting. That book has been a revelation to me. It has opened my mind to a whole train of new thoughts, new ideas; it has shown me the life of the "people" of London in an entirely new light and filled me with new gratitude for my many advantages and privileges.

– This afternoon my "young folks" are coming to see the new summer-house, which has at last been finished. I am sitting in it now – Carlo at my feet, books at hand, writing in a rather uncomfortable position, I am sorry to say, as you can see by this scrawl. It is under such circumstances that I appreciate my fountain-pen most of all.

Sunday evening.

We had quite a number of visitors this afternoon. The Hon[ourable] Stopford,[269] for a wonder, Mr Phillipp with a friend of his and the usual young people. Ernest Niemeyer[270] called here for the first time, a very charming young man, with an unusually refined, thoughtful face – his Christian name suits him to perfection. "Dickie"[271] told us that Baden-Powell had been sent home – he was "no good" he said. Really the English are funny people! If you only knew what a fuss has been made to "the gallant defender of Mafeking", how every news-paper was full of him, how he was praised and made much of! It was quite disgusting the way they went on about him and now quite suddenly he is "no good" and someone else has been put at the head of the S[outh] A[frican] Constabulary and he is sent home in disgrace.[272] I wonder what he has done or not done to deserve this treatment. I feel inclined to defend him now that his own people are so hard on him. Mr S[topford] also told us the Bubonic Plague is decreasing in the Colony, but I don't believe it. They always try to hide from us how bad things really are. I

---

269   Probably the Honourable James Richard Neville Stopford, who was the private secretary of the political secretary of the Military Governor in Pretoria. See *Government Gazette Extraordinary*, 1/8, 5 July 1900, p 116.

270   Not identified.

271   Not identified. The remark by the diarist in this paragraph, namely "Mr S also told us the ..." indicates that "Dickie" could have been Stopford.

272   Baden-Powell was not "sent home in disgrace", but returned to England on sick-leave. While he was there the Companion of the Bath (CB) was bestowed on him. See E. Pereira, Baden-Powell, Robert Stephenson Smyth, in *DSAB I*, p 33.

think the Boers must be quite near Pretoria – the search-lights are being used all night and a lot of cattle were brought into Town today – I suppose because they were not safe outside.

April 22nd. [1901]

I heard something this afternoon that filled my soul with dread and horror unspeakable. Mrs General Botha has come home from her husband and she says he told her that the English put the Zwasies against the Boers and they murdered thirty families – men, women and children.[273] Thirty Boer families! That is no small matter in a young nation like ours – and the horror of it! O God, O God, where is it all to end? We call upon God, but in our heart of hearts we know it is in vain. The hand of the Lord is against us – there is no hope for us, no help in Heaven or on Earth – struggle as I will I am beginning to realize the bitter truth. The enemy will triumph over us but – by the Lord we shall rise again – ten, twenty, fifty years hence perhaps, but I shall live to see it. I shall live to send my husband and sons as I have sent my brothers, to fight for land and people and independence.

Mrs Botha told this fact about the Zwasies to a great friend and she confided it to me. I promised strict secrecy, for it could bring Mrs B[otha] into great trouble if the English knew it. Her husband has the proofs on black and white and will move heaven and earth to get them published, but to what avail? There is not one power that will move a finger to help us. Even Derdepoort has already been forgotten.[274] We are powerless – our commandos are diminishing daily and there is no way of wreaking vengeance on the treacherous, dastardly cowards who murdered our women and children in cold blood. I have all my life heard so much from Mama about the awful Kaffir wars of the past that I am filled with the horror of this thing. I dare not dwell upon the agony

---

[273] This was not true. However early in April 1901 the British did employ Zulu regiments to loot cattle from the Republican forces. See P.G. Cloete, *The Anglo-Boer War*, pp 232–233.

[274] On 25 November 1899 Kgatla-Tswana warriors armed by the British attacked a Republican outpost at Derdepoort on the Transvaal western border. They also invaded the village, leaving 20 people, including two women and a German trader, dead. They also kidnapped 17 women and children. The latter were returned to Republican lines unhurt after 5 days. See P.G. Cloete, *The Anglo-Boer War*, pp 58–59, 62.

and terror of those poor, helpless beings when they found themselves face to face with savages armed with assegaais and other barberous [sic] weapons – it is enough to drive one mad. &&

The brutes captured thousands of sheep and what they could not take away with them, they slaughtered wholesale and left lying all over the country. Mrs Botha is going to make everything public in Europe. Her husband wishes her to go – in fact he always wanted her to leave Pretoria since the English came and she refused – but now he has persuaded her. After all, her husband is never in any great danger and why should she not go and try to do our cause some good, if she can. I am glad she is not going on a "pleasure trip" and I am very glad that I did not give my opinion of her hastily. I shall defend her now, more than ever. She has had a terrible time in this lying, slanderous, evil town and I do not wonder that she can endure it no longer. Of course it must be hard for her to go away – I could not do it, I am sure. Nothing will take me from the Transvaal – no, not even if the war were to last another ten years.

Sara[h] Rood walked home with me from Minnaar's. She is a dear, sweet girl, with many beautiful thoughts and ideas. We talked a lot, but my heart was so full of this new misery that I fear I made but a poor companion – and of course I could not tell her about it. No one knows yet but I suppose it will be made public when Mrs Botha is safely out of the country. My soul is exceeding sorrowful, even unto Death, and I feel the contrast between tonight and the last few gloriously peaceful days.

April 23rd. [1901]

An eventful day. First thing this morning I received a lovely letter from Marie [van Eeden] through Mr Gordon, American consul at J[o]h[anne]sburg. If I have time later on I shall say more about this letter. Then the mother went to Oom P[aul] and brought home a letter from Line, which someone had kindly brought from Cape Town. There was also a beautiful pair of gloves for me. The letter was "highly treasonable" and therefore most interesting to us – it was smuggled in – shall I tell you how? I have a certain dear little morroco [sic] watch-case, with a maroon velvet lining – a gift from Papa when I was about twelve years old – and this wonderful case has been travelling backwards and forwards with correspondence snugly tucked under the lining! Whenever anyone leaves Pretoria we ask him or her to take a small parcel to Mrs Cloete – a watch that she has to forward to my brother – and by the next opportunity she returns it with a message to the effect that it is the <u>wrong</u> watch. I am afraid it never will be the right one – and it is going back to her with the same man who brought it – an Englishman, into the bargain! We are writing as hard as we can – on tissue-paper and with the finest of nibs. She tells us much news and seems to be full of hope and courage, but as we are keeping her letter it is not necessary for me to repeat its contents here. And this evening when I came home Mama put a letter into my hands and asked me to read it over to her again – pretending that it was Line's of this morning. Imagine my bewilderment when I found that is was bran[d] new letter, which Col St Clair had brought – two in one day! This seems an unnecessary fuss about letters, but you don't know what they are to us, in these days, especially Line's – she is such a heart and soul patriot – every word she says does one good and she has such wonderfully sound views! I rather admire a woman-politician when she is sensible and knows what she is talking about. I wonder where Line gets all her information from.

Today Pauline Bernsmann[275] was married – at least I hope the event came off without any hitch – and I sent her a wire. Today is also the 31st birthday of K.[276] He is getting old and I wonder if he is not thinking of getting married. Nothing in the world would give me more pleasure than news of his engagement – it would oppress me all my life if he remained single on account of our past unhappy engagement – and I know he longs to hear that I too have forgotten and forgiven. I shall not forget how earnestly he begged me not to let our past mar my future. Poor boy! I can never think of him without a throb of pain. And now Marie writes about L[ouis] B[randt] in a way that plainly reveals her suspicions – and yet, if she only knew how <u>little</u> there is to suspect! He has never made love to me, and if a young man corresponds with a girl and

---

275   A friend of the diarist who lived in Johannesburg. Her husband's surname was probably Ramme – see diary entry on 1902-01-10.

276   Karel de Kok. The diarist was briefly engaged to him about five years before the outbreak of the war. See B. du Toit, *Die verhaal van Johanna Brandt*, pp 39–40.

asks for an exchange of photos and talks about his "lonely *pastorie*",[277] there is no reason to suspect a "romance", is there, dear diary? At least I am never in such a hurry to think a man is in love with one, and why should an innocent question from me call forth a small lecture on the subject of the future wife of L[ouis] B[randt] – the qualities she ought to possess, her chances of happiness with him etc[etera] etc[etera]?...

Tante Annie[278] has come back from Irene with her five children and Mama says it is too dreadful to hear from her what our "refugees" have to go through in that hell on earth. I shall see her myself and get facts and details from her and write them down. Line begs us to make a note of everything – I am sure she will want to read this poor diary of mine some day. Can I ever let anyone read it? I think not. In the first place it is too utterly insignificant and trivial; secondly, it is made up of rumours and lies; thirdly, my own personal little thoughts and experiences don't concern anyone. (This sounds rather as if "my own personal thoughts and experiences" are the "rumours and lies" – but I hope you know what I mean.)

I forgot to tell you yesterday that we received a letter from our dear prisoner, written just before he left Johannesburg. This afternoon when I passed Lord Kitchener's house I saw Mrs Botha's carriage waiting outside. I suppose she had gone to ask him to let her go to Europe. Last night when I had finished writing those bitter words I read our evening portion, Is[aiah] 41:1-14. What greater reproof could I have had than this! "Fear thou not; for I am with thee; be not dismayed; for I am thy God; I will strengthen thee; yea, I will help thee; yea, I will uphold thee with the right hand of my righteousness" vs 10 and further on, "they that war against thee shall be as nothing, and as a thing of nought. For I the Lord thy God will hold thy right hand, saying unto thee: Fear not; I will help thee" – and this "Fear not, thou worm Jacob, and ye few men of Israel; (revised ver.) I will help thee". I was much struck by these words, which I had read scores of times in happier days without being impressed in the least. Again and again, during the war, has our evening portion been exactly what we needed. A little while ago Mama and I were talking about the way our nation is being exterminated, how the

---

277   Parsonage.
278   Probably the youngest sister of the diarist's mother.

young and strong are mowed down on the field of battle, how our prisoners are dying of disease and neglect, how our women and children succumb to the exposure and privations in those infernal (please excuse the word) camps, and that evening our text was "And the remnant that is escaped of the house of Judah shall again take root downward, and bear fruit upward". Is[aiah] 37 v[er]s[e] 31. We always read a Dutch Bible and to me the words seem more impressive, more dignified, in that language than in English.

April 24th. [1901]

Today I am playing the invalid. That usually means getting through a lot of darning and I have just finished a lot of stockings, with a French grammar by my side. It is a good idea, I find, sewing and learning dry French rules at the same time. I wish the mother would leave off keeping me in bed on the very least provocation – I grudge the time and today it is so beautiful outside that I am longing to go for a walk. Through my window I can see the sky so blue and bright and the great clouds, so dazzlingly white – it is most tantalising. I have nearly finished "Alton Locke" – it is so beautiful and yet so intimately sad. I wonder what news there is today. Mama says there is a great bustle and confusion at the war office this morning – horses, cabs, Tommies, telegraph messengers in unceasing flow. The head-quarters are in Tom Bourke's house[279] just in front of Harmony, so we can always see when there is some excitement going on.

Mrs Botha had to leave her husband in a great hurry because there was a battle coming off, and before she had gone very far she heard the roar of cannon. That was somewhere near Ermelo. Yesterday I was asked whether I would go to Irene for a month to nurse our invalids. How I should like that! I would give anything I possess if I could go and help those poor creatures, but Mama does not seem to like the idea. She could easily get someone to stay with her for a month but she thinks the life will be too hard for me. It would certainly not be very delightful but I am well and strong now and able to endure any amount of hardship. I shall coax and wheedle her into letting me go and <u>then</u> won't I have a lot to tell? That is just what I have wanted all along – an oppor-

---

[279] Exact location not identified.

tunity of coming into close contact with the <u>real</u> victims of the war, of hearing their personal experiences, of seeing things as they are at Irene and of relieving as much of the misery as I can.

April 25th [1901]

Tonight I have nothing at all to say and as I am very behindhind [sic] with my correspondence I shall just neglect my dairy for once and devote this evening to writing letters. Connie and the two Rood girls spent the afternoon with me and Mrs Bodde was here too. She is leaving at the end of May – much later than she intended – and is willing to take any number of "treasonable" letters for me. I have a pile ready for her and am now going to write to Mr Stead of the "Review of Reviews" [280] – Mama has so begged of me to send him <u>facts</u> for publications and now I have made up my mind to do so and I am busy collecting all sorts of information.

April 26th. [1901]

Tonight I can write a little more than usual. The mother went to see Mrs Botha this morning and came home with quite a lot of news which she repeated to me for the express edification of this book. In after years, dear diary, you will have to testify to Mrs Botha's innocence and loyalty. One's blood boils at all the lies that are spread about her and the English are to blame most of all, for they speak of her as "Mrs Botha, the Peacemaker". She has <u>never</u> tried to make peace, she has <u>never</u> tried to influence her husband in any way. The only message she ever took from Lord K[itchener] was when he wanted that interview with Botha at Middelburg. She merely gave the message as any one would do in return for Lord K[itchener]'s kindness in allowing her to visit her husband. Yesterday someone told me that she was with Lord K[itchener] an hour and a half – someone must have watched her carriage and timed it! – and that no end of treachery and treason had been concoct-

---

[280] Stead, William Thomas (1849–1912) was a prominent British journalist and editor of the Review of Reviews. He severely criticised the British Army in South Africa and often revealed what he regarded as brutal methods employed by the British. He furthermore published the weekly journal *War against war in South Africa* and a treatise *The truth about the war*. His attempt to organise a national Stop the War Committee, however, failed. See D.W. Krüger, Stead, William Thomas, in *DSAB II*, pp 704–705.

ed. Now let me tell you what the interview was about. Lord K[itchener] told her that her husband had written him an awful letter about this murder in Zwaziland [sic] – this never-to-be-forgotten wholesale slaughter of women and children – and roundly accused the English of having put the Zwasies up to it. He told her that <u>he</u> knew nothing about it, that <u>he</u> had never given such orders and he did not think any English officers would have taken such a responsibility upon themselves, but he did not know what the soldiers might have done. His orders had been that the Swazies were to defend themselves within their own boundaries and not set foot beyond them. The Boers go into Swazieland [sic] every year to get good winter pasturage for their cattle and they have never yet been molested – on the contrary, the Swazies have always been most friendly – but this time they attacked thirty families and wiped them out completely. Whether they "misunderstood" Lord K[itchener]'s orders or whether they were secretly told to kill every Boer that entered their country – who can tell? how is it ever to be proved? Botha says he is investigating the matter and will make it public.

Then Mrs Botha spoke to K[itchener] about the Irene camp. She said our women are <u>starving</u>. "Starving?" repeated his lordship with uplifted eye-brows – "how is that possible? They get enough to eat". "Yes, <u>enough</u>." she answered "if it were <u>eatable</u>. The meat they get is rotten – quite unfit for use" – and then she told him some disgraceful facts – how the sugar is full of clotted blood – yes <u>blood</u>, as the wounded Tommies lie on the bags! how the coffee is nothing but roasted acorns etc, etc. I think his eyes were opened a little, but the question is whether he will do anything to improve matters. She says he seems the most humane and kindest of men. He told her how people talk about <u>him</u>, how, when first he came, everyone said he was so cruel, so inhuman, and would murder right and left, how the tone changed gradually and the latest thing he heard was that he was pro-Boer!

While Mama was with her Mr Fisher came from Lord K[itchener] with the news that he gave her gracious permission to leave the country – to go to Europe, or wherever she pleased. She is leaving on Monday, with only her youngest child. The girls are at school and her eldest son, "the little General", as he was called by the Tommies, she left with her husband, who was very glad to have him.[281] He can ride and is nine years old, so his father wished to have him "to bear him company". When she left her husband the English were on his heels and he was attacked from four sides at once – she heard the cannon roaring before she got very far. She says her husband knew nothing about the [British] occupation of Pietersburg – she told him the news.

This afternoon at the vocal rehearsal someone told me that Holland has sent out five nurses for the Irene Camp: Zuster Bakkes,[282] our dear, energetic matron, who was turned out of the Volks Hospital by Khaki, is at their head. She went to Holland a few months ago and I suppose she worked hard until she got this chance of coming out again. I never saw such a wonderful woman. Very small and slight – even fragile – but with a marvellous will-power, strength and determination written on every line of that delicate face, and with powers of endurance beyond belief. She slaved from

Commandant-General Louis Botha and his son Louis on commando

morn till even and was always bright and sweet. She dispensed stores and attended to the linen; she attended the operations and superintended the kitchen and wards; she was at the head of the native hospital; received the visitors and relations of the patients, wrote letters, etc – her duties were innumerable and yet one never saw her out of temper. But I always knew by her flushed cheeks when she was tired. The patients adored her and so did the Africander nurses, but the Dutch ones did not seem to get on very well with her. I could never understand why. And this woman was turned out for an English bit of frivolity, who must have her tennis-parties and "afternoons" and private sitting-room

---

281 General Louis Botha's eldest son, Louis.
282 Not identified.

(a luxury Zuster B[akkes] never indulged in) who acts in "Charley's Aunt"[283]; who drives out daily with the Hon[ourable] S.[284]; who dresses most elaborately instead of wearing her uniform, and who is out morning, noon and night to luncheons, parties, theatres etc[etera]. Such is the new matron of the Pretoria Hospital, as it is now called, and I know my description of her to be true – every word of it – for I have seen her myself, not once but many times. I believe she acted very well indeed in "Charley's Aunt" – ahem!

Our vocal society is now in a very flourishing condition – twenty-one members! We have never yet had so many and long may it continue so! Mrs Botha refuses to take letters for us, so I suppose we shall have to wait until Mrs Bodde goes.

We had very nice letters from Holland yesterday, from Tante Kee, Emilia and Cornelis.[285] How sympathetic and loving our friends across the sea have been during the war! Their invitations to me are so warm, so cordial – they are all longing to have me as their guest for as long as ever I care to stay. I could live a whole year and more in Holland just by going from place to place, but when I do go I shall have very little time there, because I am going to study as soon as possible. Dreams, dreams growing fainter every day – sometimes I quite give up hope.

Ms Kee ten Bosch, an aunt of the diarist who lived in Holland and regularly corresponded with her

– Oh, by the way, Mrs Botha says it is quite true that

---

283 *Charley's Aunt*, a play by Walter Brandon Thomas.
284 Probably Stopford.
285 Dutch relatives and friends of the Van Warmelo's. Emilia Frijlinck later married the diarist's brother Willem. Cornelis was the well-known Cornelis Beelaarts van Blokland.

our State Attorney[286] has been killed – her husband told her. It is a dreadful thing and I pity his young wife from the bottom of my heart. Dietlof often told me how they loved one another – he never came from there without speaking of the way they looked at one another, with a world of mutual understanding in their eyes. I cannot help thinking of Eleanor in "Alton Locke" when I think of this poor stricken wife. May God comfort her! It may be our turn next. Who knows when the blow will fall, for fall it must – I cannot believe that we shall be permitted to come through this war without losing one or more of our dear ones; and there is only one left that I love – though I have many friends in the field still. Why is Fritz the last of our boys? Why was he not captured? I have had forebodings about him all my life. When he went to Europe and we bade him goodbye at the Station I was sure we would never see him again, and when we parted again at Southampton a year later I had the same feeling and every time he went to the front I said "this is the last time", but that morning, nearly a year ago – that 5th of June, his birth-day, when he had to flee from Pretoria and leave us in the hands of the enemy, when he looked so broken-spirited – oh God, it was more than I could bear. That day, that parting will haunt me for the rest of my life and I know as surely as if an angel from Heaven had prepared me for it, that I shall never look upon his face again. Perhaps even now he is lying in an unknown grave – but no, I dare not dwell on such things. I feel as if my heart would burst with its burden of unrest and dread – these quiet evening hours, in our lonely home I can be so desolate, so desolate – as I am tonight – as if I am alone on the face of this earth – friendless, yea even God-less, for He seems very far away and there is not help for us wherever I look. The wicked triumph and crush the weak and helpless under foot – do you think I would mind giving my best-beloved brother if in the end our cause triumphed? Ah no, I would glory in my sacrifice, but if it were in vain – no, a thousand times no – it shall not be in vain.

But am I mad? Fritz is not dead – for all I know he is watching tonight under God's silvery moon that is shining so peacefully and radiantly – thinking of home perhaps – of me – no, more likely of his little Sweetheart. Does he love her still? I wonder, I wonder. Or does he only care for her in a placid, careless way – or is he indifferent? No one will

---

[286]   General Jan Smuts. The rumour was false.

ever know, for he will marry her for the sake of his word of honour, if for nothing else. Oh, if boys only <u>knew</u> what they are doing by binding themselves when their characters are still unformed! How many young lives have been ruined by one false step! If I thought that Fritz no longer cared for M.[287] I would pray God to let him die a soldier's death sooner than go through the mockery of a loveless marriage, for Fritz will never break his word to that little girl, who is eating out her heart in Cape Town and clinging to the memory of his boyish love. –

Today is the anniversary of my dear father's funeral.

April 27th [1901].

It is a stormy night, cold and dreary. Winter is coming very early this year and I am afraid it is going to be a hard one. On a night like this one is full of all sorts of sad forebodings but I do not mean to dwell on <u>my</u> feelings again – I had a dreadful night last night because I had been brooding, brooding, Heaven knows what on! Let me think of something cheerful to write this evening. This afternoon as I was going to see Mrs Botha I met a Tommy on horseback who stared very hard at the two tiny flags on my hat. He kept his eyes fixed on them until he reached me and then he reined his horse in and stopped almost in front of me. I thought I was in for it and just glared at him and would you believe it? – he rode away after one glance at my face. Now I know how to frighten away Tommies in future. It is very strange. Every evening when I come home I meet Lord K[itchener] and his A[ide]-D[e]-C[amp] on or near the bridge, on their way home from their daily ride. The[y] know me by sight quite well already – I can see it by the way they look at me. Once there was very little room for them to pass – there was a cab on one side of them and an open drain on one side of me and I had to pass so close to Lord K[itchener] that I could have touched his horse. He looked very keenly at my flags and passed on with some remark to his companion – I was so sorry I did not catch it but I felt myself getting quite hot, because after all, it <u>is</u> cheeky of me to wear our colours after we had been expressly ordered not to do so. But I am quite sure no one will interfere with me. I walk about alone in the streets every day of my life and never do I hear an insulting remark – seldom do I even

---

287   Not identified.

meet an rude stare. I have often noticed that the common Tommy is not nearly as ill-mannered as those conceited young officers. Preserve me from the little lieutenant! He never takes his pipe out of his mouth, he never makes way on the pavement – oh no, my lord thinks far too much of himself for that. But Tommy generally removes his pipe and very often Tommy gets quite off the pavement when ladies approach. Of course the politest of all are the dear old grey-headed colonels and generals – the real soldiers who have seen a lot of the world and know what true courtesy is.

– Mrs Botha was out, so I left word that we would see her at the Station tomorrow evening and went to the Cinattis. There I heard that Lady Maxwell (by the way, the Governor is Sir John now) had written to the American papers appealing for help for the Irene women and children, and one man alone sent £400. I had often heard that she was such a pro-Boer but I did not quite believe it. I beg her pardon humbly. I liked the look of her – she always drove about in a carriage filled with the dearest little dogs and she looked so sweet; and more than once I met her driving to the cemetery with wreaths of white flowers – always alone, she seemed to have no friends here.

Mr Cinatti says the English say the Boers are surrendering in hundreds. I am sure it is another of their lies. They catch all the old men and boys they can find and get patients out of the hospitals and bring them into town as "surrendered Boers". Mrs Botha told Mama yesterday that some time ago the Boers took a train at some station or other. The first case they opened contained whiskey so they gave the Tommies each a bottle and told them to drink. Tommy refused because he has strict orders on the subject but when Tommy is threatened by a remorseless foe, what is he to do? He drank (most unwillingly of course) and got quite drunk. Only the sergeant refused to touch a drop. The next case they opened contained a magnificent assortment of dressed dolls (originally intended for the firm of Messrs Henwood and Co.) and what do the naughty Boers do but put a large doll in the arms of each drunken Tommy and decorate the whole station with dolls of every description. And then they rode away. I think the sober sergeant must have enjoyed the joke immensely.

Yesterday morning Mama cut Eddie Cooper. It happened thus wise.

He was coming up the road and she was walking down and she fixed him with her eye (and an awful eye it is when it is blazing with righteous indignation) and he stared at her like one fascinated, and at last, in a sort of desperation, took off his hat. When he got no response he looked away in a mighty hurry and she went on her way pleased and satisfied. In the afternoon when I went out I met him on the same spot, but he had had such a lesson that he thought it safer not to look at all, and so I had no chance of following my mother's example. But I daresay my turn will come some day. And now, for my French exercise - I waste a lot of time over this silly book.

April 28th. [1901]

We had a great crowd of visitors this afternoon, several of them being people who are soon going away. It is simply dreadful the way folks are clearing out of the country - we shall soon be the last at this rate. S[chilthuis] has returned from J[o]h[anne]sburg and told us of his intention of also leaving for Holland soon - that is, he informed me when we had a few moments alone, if some plan or other he is meditating does not come off. He was so nervous and so incapable of saying more that I quickly changed the subject, for I know only too well what he means. I am afraid there is no help for it and before he goes away there is a painful ordeal for us to go through. He says my friend A[ndrew] B[rown], who is now his friend also, is in very bad health. Poor fellow, and there is no chance of his going away for a change just yet. Gustav [Fichardt] and Archie [Truter] told us that the Boers wrecked an ambulance train somewhere near Kroonstad last Thursday. I remember now that Mrs Botha told Mama about it but then no particulars were known. It appears that they laid a mine on the railway-line and the first train that came along was an ambulance full of doctors, nurses and patients. The Boers warned them and did what they could to stop them, but in vain, with the result that everything flew into the air and - so they say - everyone was killed.[288] We shall never hear the end of <u>this</u>.

Our kaffir Jan, a new boy, was telling us this morning that when he was working at the Hatherly Distillery,[289] or at least in that direction,

---

[288] The rumour was false.
[289] The Heatherly Distillery was at Eerste Fabrieken on the Eastern Railway Line about 30 kilometres east of Pretoria.

about a month ago, the Boers took a whole train of horses, carts and waggons. He says they sent back the engine and driver with two soldiers to tell the English what had happened. Paulus has disappeared again. He always goes out visiting on Sundays and this morning he said to me that he was going *"anderkant* Daspoort"[290] and if he did not come home I must know that the English had caught him. I laughed and said "all right" and forgot all about it. Later on as he was leaving I heard him at the bedroom window and then he came to the bathroom door, where I was busy, and said softly *"Dumella nonnie, thlala kathla."*[291] I called out goodbye and thought it rather strange but forgot that too, until this evening, when all our visitors had gone, I went to the kitchen and found the dishes unwashed, no fire, no sign of Paulus. It is late and he has not come yet and we think he meant to be caught or that he has found some means of getting out of Pretoria – his "things" are all here still – I don't understand it.

Mama and I are now going to the Station to say goodbye to Mrs Botha and Mrs Michaelson.

April 29ᵗʰ· [1901]

I am very tired this evening and yet there is so much to do that I can't go to bed early. I have had a hard day and have lots to tell. Last night we went to the Station and found a regular gathering of all our friends there. Everyone was full of the good news that had just come in – how, I don't know, because Khaki does not announce his reverses to this most unsympathetic public. Judging by the excitement prevailing at the war-office today something wonderful must have happened, I shall give you the news as it reached me. Gen Badenhorst[292] has taken seven can-

---

290 "to the other side of Daspoort". Daspoort was some three kilometres north-west of the city centre.
291 Good day little miss, stay well.
292 There was no General Badenhorst in the forces of the South African Republic and it is not clear to what incident she refers – probably a false rumour. Commandant C.P.S. Badenhorst was at that time commander of the Pretoria Commando and indeed active in the western Magaliesberg Mountains. However, J.F.E. Celliers, who was a member of that commando and kept an extensive diary, mentions no such incident in March or April 1901. See A.G. Oberholster (ed.), *Die Oorlogsdagboek van Jan F.E. Celliers*, pp 215–237. No evidence suggests that Commandant C.J.J. Badenhorst of the Orange Free State was at that time active in the Mag-

non, 400 prisoners and I don't know how many horses on the Magaliesbergen - Skurveberg, I think; Ben Viljoen[293] has taken two cannon at Bronkhorstspruyt [sic] and in the Free State de Wet has taken two large trains laden with food and ammunition. This is the talk of the Town. Wherever I went this morning I was told the same story, with variations, and where I was not told, I told, so doing my share towards the spreading of anti-English reports. R. Hollenbach[294] and I spent the morning in getting honorary members for the vocal Society - we were most successful and have about twenty already; all the consuls and many leading men of the Town. Our dear old President's wife is "*Bescherm vrouwe*"[295] - if you know what that means - I don't quite, but never mind, it sounds fine and will make a good impression. Mrs P.M. Botha (our J[o]h[anne]sburg friend) joined too. She told us that she hears that a train-load of prisoners was taken by the Boers. That would be lovely. Talking of prisoners reminds me that we got a letter from Dietlof this afternoon, through Col St Clair, from - where do you think? Ladysmith.[296] Yes, of all places. Oh, the irony of fate when one thinks how many months Dietlof tried in vain to get into Ladysmith! And now he is there willy-nilly, and there he will stay until the war is over, or the Boers release him. But Ladysmith was so well fortified in the days of the siege that I am afraid it is un-takeable. Still I heard a wild story this morning to the effect that it was in our hands. How glad D[ietlof] would be to get out of the land of bondage into the free veld!

By the way, our Paulus has come back - he only stayed out a night "for fun". I was very glad to see his honest old face this morning again.

Dear diary, can you keep secrets? Because I have a great one on my

---

aliesberg Mountains or for that matter present anywhere in the Transvaal.

293 Ben Viljoen was a well-known general and at this time commanded the Republican forces in the Eastern Transvaal. See D.W. Krüger, Viljoen, Benjamin Johannes, in *DSAB IV*, pp 740–742.

294 Probably a family member of either G.H. Hollenbach who lived in Joubert Street, very close to Harmony, or of J.H. Hollenbach, who was the professor of drawing at the Staats Model School. These are the only two Hollenbachs listed in *Longland's Pretoria Directory for 1899*, p 136.

295 Patron lady.

296 Dietlof van Warmelo spent only a few days in the prisoner-of-war camp at Ladysmith before being taken to Durban and from there by ship to India, where he spent the remainder of the war as a prisoner of war. See D.S. van Warmelo, *Mijn commando en guerilla commando-leven*, p 213.

mind and am longing to confide in someone – but oh, it is too dangerous. You are trustworthy enough but what can you do to guard our
secrets if you fall into the hands of the enemy? I am very much excited
and perhaps I may tell you soon. It is so interesting that I am dying to
write it down in detail – before I forget all the ins and outs.

But I am too sleepy and tired now and there is my French exercise
to do still. I gave Annie Rood her first music lesson this afternoon.
Sarah [Rood] only had one from me and then I gave her up because
Mama is against my teaching but now little [Bertha] Michaelson has
gone and I have some time to spare so I have taken Annie. I must have
someone to teach music – it is good discipline for me and keeps me in
pocket-money. For nearly seven years now I have been entirely independent of the mother through my own exertions, not because it was
necessary but because I believe every girl ought to be able to support
herself in case of need.

– Today is Mama's wedding-day and now we have come to the end
of our April anniversaries and I am not sorry. Goodnight now, my dear
little friend. Oh, I had such a dear letter from Edith [Goodwin], so confidential and sweet, so unlike her everyday business-like epistles.

April 30ᵗʰ [1901]

11.30 am. My work is done and I have a quiet hour before dinner. It is
a most glorious day and I feel so content this morning – goodness only
knows why. How shall I devote – no that's wrong – how shall I spend
this unexpected spare hour?

Later. Oom Pieter has solved the problem for me – he has only just
gone and now I have no time to settle down to anything before dinner.
But I think I can tell you about my secret, dear diary. You remember
perhaps that I told you some time ago that J[an F.E.] C[elliers] escaped
from Pretoria 10 weeks after the occupation. His wife told Mama a
week or two ago that men get out of town every fortnight – she would
not say how – and if we knew of anyone who was very anxious to get
to the Boer lines we had to send him to her and she would refer him
to someone else and so on until the fourth person was reached. He
would work the rest. Everything had to be kept as still as death and only
the most trustworthy men had to be offered their liberty. Of course

we were deeply interested and wondered how it was done but we did not speak to any of our young men about it because it seemed such a terribly dangerous thing. The young men have all taken the oath of neutrality and will be shot like spies or traitors if caught in an attempt to escape. They had to choose between Ceylon and the oath and most of them preferred the oath because there is always some chance of their being set free by the Boers, whereas at Ceylon there is no possibility of getting away. If the Boers took Pretoria the oath of neutrality would be "null and void", as soon as British protection is withdrawn it falls to the ground and so our young men took it in the hope of speedy deliverance. But it is nearly a year now and many of them feel as if they can endure this state of affairs no longer, in which feeling I sympathise with them heart and soul. A great many of this "hands-up commando" as we call them, are being sent away lately; we don't exactly know why but we are afraid it is because the English have found out that men are continually escaping – but they cannot find out how it is done. Pretoria is so well guarded that one would think it an utter impossibility for even a mouse to get in or out unseen.

But now the mother thinks it is our duty to try and get some of our young friends out. I told her that G[ustav Fichardt] and A[rchie Truter] would go like a shot, oath or no oath, and so on Sunday when they were here she told them that there was just a chance, if they were willing. She mentioned no names and made them swear the utmost secrecy and both of them expressed their eagerness to go, taking all risk and responsibility on their own shoulders. Mama asked me if M.F. would go and at first I said I thought not, but the whole truth is that I am a coward where he is concerned and I am selfish too, but it worried me so much that yesterday morning I took the law into my own hands and told him about it. The effect rather alarmed me. He became so excited that I realized at once how hopeless it would be to stop him now – he is coming this afternoon to discuss the whole thing with Mama and I am sure he will be the next man to go away to the Boers. What have I done? How shall I live through the time of suspense that must follow his escape – until we know whether he has reached the Boer lines safely or not? We may never hear from him again and for the rest of my life I shall be haunted by my own evil conscience – evil, because the memory of that oath will rise up against me, for I am not sure that what we are doing is right. Most of the young men say that they do not put any store by their oath and will break it as soon as they can – it was forced from them, they say, but there was always the alternative offered – Ceylon, and Khaki can't help it that they preferred the oath of neutrality.

Yesterday afternoon Mama went to see Mrs C[elliers] again and she told her of the three young men who are eager to go. Mrs C[elliers] told her how the thing is worked but, dear diary, this is such a secret that I am quite afraid of putting it on black and white. Spies help the men out of Town – our own spies, who come in when there is no moon and always take one or two men with them. They have to pass through untold dangers and suffer untold privations, but they do it, and as far as we know, they have always reached the commandos in safety. Her husband went out dressed as a woman and for six long weeks she did not know whether he was dead or alive. They make holes in the ground and creep out under the electric wires that are round Pretoria. I am going to see Mrs C[elliers] myself soon and get all particulars from her.

Evening. Karel Rood says a man told him that the Boers are surrendering daily in hundreds. That is very nice, because now the war must be over soon, for how can a "hand-ful of farmers" go on surrendering every day without coming to an end? It is really very comforting to think that we shall not be living in this state of misery much longer. Karel's informant was an Africander who works in the Military Governor's Office, so the news comes from an extremely reliable quarter, for how can an Africander who works for the English possibly tell a lie? There is no "true news" to tell tonight and I want to finish some of my correspondence so well shall bid one another a very good evening.

Two letters from Holland – uncensored.

May 1st [1901]

A new month. What has it in store for us? I have begun it badly and sadly and feel as if it can bring us any amount of trouble. I am overwhelmed, oppressed by the misery around us, which is becoming worse every day. Let me tell you where I have been this morning and what I have done and seen and heard. I promised Mrs Nieuwenhuis to watch beside her little Johan for a few hours while she rested, but when I got there I found a trained nurse who had been called in because he was so seriously ill – with measles – so my services were not required and I persuaded Mrs M[297] to come out with me for a little fresh air. She then told me that she had received £150 from Holland for the women and children, with permission to cable for as many hundreds more as she required and she wanted to go to Town to get some things that were absolutely necessary. We bought 40 mattresses for £20 and she deposited £10 in the Koedoe Apotheek[298] to be used for Dr Kolff's poor patients. He is so wonderfully good to our people – gives not only his time and energy, but provides the needy with medicine and luxuries at his own expense. He is ruining himself, for he is by no means well off and has a wife and child in Holland to support. For a long time there was a "free dispensary" where everything was procurable on "tickets" given by some Dutch doctors, who prescribed free of charge at certain hours every day, and when the "Hollandsche Ambulance"[299] was dissolved they gave all their cases of surgical instruments, bandages, wines, medicines, etc to this free dispensary, which our humane foe has now closed. No free consultations are allowed either, that has also been put a stop to; in fact, everything that helps to make the lot of our poor people a little easier, is sure to meet with every imaginable discouragement and opposition.

Evening. Let me see, where was I? There is so much to tell but I am almost too sad, too miserable and tired and broken-spirited to write. May God have mercy on our land and people! Things are getting worse daily and the terrible stories I heard today are enough to break one's heart. When I was at the Consul's this morning there were a crowd of women who had come to him for protection. We have no consul of our own – for us there is no help from the persecution, the ill-treatment of our enemy and Mr Nieuwenhuis is besieged all day with these poor, defenceless creatures who implore him to defend them. The lat-

---

[297]   Probably Mrs Nieuwenhuis.

[298]   The Koedoe Pharmacy was situated in Pretorius Street near the centre of the city. See *Longland's Pretoria Directory for 1899*, p 143.

[299]   Dutch Ambulance. There were altogether three Dutch ambulances that were sent out from the Netherlands soon after the outbreak of the war to assist the Republican forces. See J.H. Breytenbach, *Die Geskiedenis van die Tweede Vryheidsoorlog I*, p 73, and G.L. Kepper, *De Zuid-Afrikaansche Oorlog. Historisch Gedenkboek*, p 97.

est thing is that all women who are unable to support themselves and their families must go to Irene. Hundreds have gone for how can they support themselves when everything they possessed on earth has been taken from them, but these women have sick children who will die if they are moved now – they are in a very weak state and could not possibly live in those tents now. Mr N[ieuwenhuis] told the poor, half-crazy mothers that all he could do for them would be to write a private letter to the Governor – as consul he could do nothing for they are not Dutch subjects. He read the letter to me. It was very good. In it he reminds Gen Maxwell of his own words to him yesterday – that so many children are dying – and says that these delicate little ones must surely die too if they are exposed to the open air in their present state, and begs him to leave them where they are – at least until they are out of danger. I do not know what the result was, but he would be an inhuman brute if he ignored such an appeal. Last week a woman lost three children – all she had – and yesterday she was buried – sank under her grief I suppose and her husband is still fighting and does not know what an awful calamity has befallen him. O God, have pity – there are so many similar cases – it is more than we can bear. I know of another woman who has lost six children. What the mothers have to go through now no pen can describe. I have heard stories that I cannot even repeat – of the neglect and brutal ill-treatment of women when they require most care. But these things I store away in my heart of hearts and it is just because they are so bad that I take courage and remember that it is darkest before dawn and that crimes like these will not be allowed to go on for ever. There is a God of Justice still – I know it, I feel it though everything is so dark and incomprehensible to me just now.

Mama and I went out this afternoon to make a few duty calls, and wherever we came we found the people in the same state of nervous dread. There is something, some calamity brooding and no one seems to know exactly what it is. The English are becoming daily more rigorous, more severe in their laws and regulations. Crowds of young men are being sent away – for no apparent reason, new proclamations are being made, the latest being that no one may take a single private letter out of the country. I have not read it myself but it must be very severe and has struck terror into the hearts of all the people who intend leaving, at least they all refuse to take my correspondence to Holland. I don't know about Mrs B[odde] yet but hope to see tomorrow afternoon. If she is also afraid I shall just keep my letters until I find some chance of smuggling them away[300] - M.F. said I would smuggle myself into trouble if I did not look out, but I am getting reckless and don't care what I do as long as I can feel that I am doing something for our cause. I hear today that Zuster Bakkes has been stopped at P[or]t Elizabeth with the nurses and can't get through. And that in spite of a letter she has from Lord Roberts personally that she must be allowed to go where she pleases. Khaki does just whatever he likes and seems to be supremely sure of at least one thing in this world, viz: That Might is Right. M[ama] and I wound up our afternoon by going to wish Mr Cinatti many happy returns of his birthday. He read something to us from "Le Temps" which did our hearts good. It seems that in Europe one Congress after another is being help to stop the war and give us our independence and in a great international congress in Paris,[301] which was attended by delegates - if that is the word - from every part of the globe. The reasons that were given for the necessity of bringing the war to an end were worded magnificently - concisely - strikingly. They made a deep impression on me and I wish I could remember them - all I do remember is that the

---

[300] Mrs Bodde was indeed prepared to and did smuggle the correspondence out. The diarist recorded the details of this smuggling operation in her book, *The Petticoat Commando*, pp 173–176. The correspondence consisted inter alia of a report by a Mr Spoelstra, a Dutch citizen, on the hardships and ill-treatment of Boer women by British soldiers while they were being transported from their farms to concentrations camps. Spoelstra himself was arrested by the authorities when his own attempt to smuggle the report out failed. He was sentenced to one year in prison. Mrs Bodde was prepared to attempt to smuggle the report, as well as a report on Spoelstra's trial, to W.T. Stead in London. It was a bulky document, 60 pages, closely typed. The Van Warmelo ladies bought a one-pound (about 450 grams) tin of cocoa, unfastened the paper wrapper carefully, removed the lid without damaging the paper around it, shook out the cocoa and placed the tightly rolled packet containing the documents in the tin. They then filled the tin up with cocoa again until it weighed exactly one pound as before, replaced the lid and pasted the paper wrapper over the lid to make it look like new. The tin arrived safely in London and Stead published the contents of the report in three successive pamphlets.

[301] An international congress of delegates of committees for the independence of the Republics was indeed held in Paris, France early in 1901. See G.D. Scholtz, *Europa en die Tweede Vryheidsoorlog*, p 145.

little State that was thought unworthy of joining the Hague Conference, that was bound by no laws, no Geneva Convention, has nevertheless preserved those laws from purely humane motives, and that the might British nation, at the head of the civilized world, has violated one and all the most sacred laws of the Convention, from which the small State had been excluded in view of this very war – there was something else that struck me as being so <u>true</u> – I must get the paper from Mr Cinatti and copy that wonderful paragraph word for word. My brain is so muddled this evening – I can hardly think and yet there is so much I wanted to write this evening. As we were coming home I suddenly exclaimed to Mama "Look at that funny star with a little tail", pointing to the West. "Why" quoth the mother, "that is a little comet", and so it was. We are going to watch it very night and see it grow – its tail was <u>barely</u> noticeable this evening and I wonder whether anyone else has observed it.[302]

Oh, I forget to tell you yesterday that we have bought a goat with two dear little ewe-lambs.[303] She gives us just about enough milk for our tea but is a great acquisition to the family, especially on account of her beautiful Khaki colour. Her children are white and black. Mama bought her from the Tommies next-door, who have plenty of goats and sheep and even cows which they take unto themselves whenever a flock or herd is driven into Town from the farms. We have often watched them standing by the roadside when the poor wretches come by and choosing the best for their own use; they just catch them by the hind leg and drag them to the camp, and there is no one to say them nay – and then they sell them to us.

I cannot tell you how it hurts us to see the poor animals brought in in thousands, to hear their bleating and lowing, to see their weariness and sufferings. Sometimes they are hurried along so fast that the little ones are left behind, and all over the country one can pick up the dead and dying little lambs and calves. Oh, the sufferings of dumb animals in a

---

[302] The comet was observed all over South Africa and even by the Boer prisoners of war on St Helena Island. It was simply known as the "Great Comet of 1901" and was visible for about a month. It was commented on by several burghers, including Jan Celliers (Oorlogsdagboek van Jan F.E. Celliers 1899–1902, p 239) and J.F. Naudé (Vechten en vluchten van Beyers en Kemp "bokant" De Wet, pp 238–239).

[303] The diarist made a drawing of the goat in Script III of her diary.

101

quoth the mother," that is a little comet," and so it was. We are going to watch for it every night & see it grow – its tail was barely noticeable this evening & I wonder whether anyone else has observed it. Oh, I forgot to tell you yesterday that we have bought a goat with two dear little ewe-lambs. She gives us just about enough milk for our tea but is a great acquisition to the family, especially on account of her beautiful khaki colour. Her children are white and black. Mama bought her from Ye Goat. the Tommies next-door, who have plenty of goats & sheep and even cows which they take unto themselves whenever a flock or herd is driven into Town from the farms. We have often watched them standing by the roadside when the poor wretches come by and choosing the best for their own use; they just catch them by the hind leg & drag them to the camps, and there is no one to say them nay – and then they sell them to us. I cannot tell you how it hurts us to see the poor animals brought in in thousands, to hear their bleating and lowing, to see their

A page from the diary where the diarist
made a sketch of "Ye Goat" on 1 May 1901

war! Is it not enough that we human beings kill and wound one another and break one another's hearts? Why must we punish God's helpless creatures for our own evil passions? I dare not think of the horses. Dietlof once told me that when a bomb burst over his head in a battle his horse screamed like a human being! But I shall never close my eyes tonight if I go to bed with such thoughts – I must think of something good and sweet and beautiful – there are plenty such, only sometimes we have to go out of our way to seek them – they do not always come to us.

May 2nd. [1901]

We had a nice letter from Line today. She says she has been told that Fritz has surrendered and she advises us to make inquiries. I am quite ready to believe that he has been captured but that he has surrendered – never! And we shall not even trouble to make inquiries. I am sure her informant is thinking of Dietlof. In Town this morning I saw something about 500 Boer casualties – great victories for the English all over the country, but I am so sick of their lies that I shall waste no time in repeating them. I prefer dwelling on a very good piece of news that M.F. told me this morning – he is out of his trouble, thank Heaven, and has come out of better than I could ever have expected. Now he is very happy and our friendship can continue undisturbed by the "clouds that have rolled by, Johnnie". It is a great comfort to me for I have been terribly worried – a way I have when I am interested particularly in anyone. It was none of my business and yet I could not get it out of my mind night and day – but it is all over now – I am thankful to say.

May 3rd. [1901]

There is absolutely no news to tell and as I am rather behindhand with my correspondence I shall waste no time over this book tonight. We had another letter from Dietlof this morning. He is quite comfortable in Ladysmith and hard at work with his "book" on the war. He says he has already written 33 pages in the exercise book I gave him and has only got as far as the relief of Ladysmith. Our vocal rehearsal was a great success this afternoon, about 20 members being present. M.F. escorted me home. It is necessary for me to have an escort now because it is quite dark by the time the rehearsal is over. But now I really must go and practice for an hour – my Rubinstein is getting on very slowly but surely – and then I have a French exercise to do – I wish the evenings were twice as long again. "My" comet appears every evening after sunset and is growing very much.

May 5th. [1901]

Our dear Minnie's 22nd birthday. Poor Edith [Goodwin] will be very sad this morning. I have just written her a long letter, also to Dietlof from whom we hear often. Today the English have been exactly eleven months in Pretoria; and that memorable day (June 5th) they said the war was "practically over". I wonder how they feel this morrow's morn, the darlings. I feel particularly cheerful, I suppose because it is such a magnificent day. I have been sitting in the summer-house since breakfast and now it is nearly dinner-time and I feel very little inclined to budge from my comfortable seat.

Dear diary, I am going to Irene – not now, as soon as the next batch of nurses goes – perhaps within a fortnight or three weeks. The mother has consented at last and at last the desire of my heart is to be fulfilled. It is rather a queer "desire" but I certainly do not wish to go because I think I am going to enjoy myself. Oh dear no – it will be very hard work and very sad; but I may be able to do a great deal of good and the discipline will be good for me. I am longing to set to work and feel grateful now for my past hospital experiences. I am sure we do not appreciate our home comforts sufficiently – we are too often discontented and irritable and it will do me a world of good to see what real suffering is. But when I look round at our beautiful Harmony and draw in deep breaths of pure, sweet air and see myself sitting so comfortably on cushions and surrounded by so many luxuries then I cannot help being afraid that the discomforts of a life in camp will be harder for me to bear than I anticipate. But what matter? I shall require all my time and energy and patience for the poor sufferers and shall not think about myself at all.

I did not make any entry yesterday. That was because we had some young folks at Harmony last night and I had no time to write. We sat here, just where I am sitting now, in the bright moon-light, with the scent of the orange-blossoms in the air and a band playing in the Park.[304] It is certainly not the time of the year for orange-blossoms, but strange to say, there are a few branches simply covered. I hope, when I get married, our trees will be considerate enough to burst into bloom, even if

---

[304]   Probably either Berea Park, immediately next to Harmony, on the western side of the Apies River, or Burgers Park, about one kilometre northwest of Harmony.

the event takes place at such an unseasonable time of the year as May – then I can wear _real_ orange-blossoms – very unlucky, according to some superstitious people, but very romantic and appropriate, to _my_ mind. I shall hate to have even an artificial flower about me that day – I must go to _him_ as real and natural as God made me, with nothing false about me. I wonder who he is and where he is this lovely Sabbath morn, and when shall I meet him? Sometimes I think it is going to be that somebody far across the seas who writes me such charming letters.[305] There is only one objection – he is far, far too good for me. I don't love him _yet_ but I think I could if he tried very hard to win me – perhaps he will when the war is over and I go "across the seas" too.

Sunday night. Aunt C[lara] was here this afternoon with her brother Aling [Tulleken] from Johannesburg, who told me that K[arel de Kok] is in J[o]h[anne]sburg again; that he is a British subject now and has taken the oath of allegiance; that he works for the English; and (and this is to me the most wonderful) that he _runs the Boers down_!!! What a miraculous escape I have had. Is _this_ the man I was engaged to for three long years with whom I was prepared to spend my life? Was I so blind and inexperienced and trustful that I could not see in those days what manner of man it was to whom I gave my love and faith and confidence? Verily, the hand of the Lord has been guiding my through mysterious ways; His eye has been watching me; His loving Father's heart has protected me and brought me out of all my dangers unharmed. And now my life is before me – its pages are fair and white and it lies in my power to inscribe upon them a history as spotless. What must I do with my wonderful, God-given freedom? How shall I devote my life? For years I have been brooding over the events of the past, I have deplored its faults and follies and that one great mis-step; I have thought and spoken of my "ruined life" – but now I see how wrong it was of me. I am only twenty-four and my life is _before_ me – to make or to mar, and I realize now more than ever how important it is that I should marry a _good_ man, how much depends upon the choice I make. I am influenced so greatly by the people I love that everything – my whole future – will be in the hands of the man I marry. I am talking a lot about "marrying" today – silly little girl! I suppose it is the moon and the scent of orange-

---

[305]   She means Louis Brandt.

blossoms and perhaps the comet – who knows <u>what</u> it is.

The following interesting conversation reached me in the street a few evenings ago:

First urchin (pointing sentimentally to the comet) That 'ere star means peace.

Second urchin (more contemptuously than politely) Bosh!

F[irst] U[rchin]. Well, then it means war.

I passed on and heard no answer, perhaps because that last statement was unanswerable.

Mr Cinatti was here this afternoon also and he told me that the English regard the comet as an omen of ill; he made a good pun on the subject. He said that if the English had to watch the indications "*des astres*"[306] it was because they had reason to fear "disasters". He is a very dear, good man and I am very fond of him, a feeling he seems to reciprocate (ahem! is that word spelt "good"? I am not sure). His English is so funny; he calls penalty, "penality", and cough, "cuf", and alter "alternate", etc[etera]. We often lose a good deal of his always interesting conversation on account of this funny "*taal*"[307] of his and Mr Cinatti reading English is too comical. He says there is a lot of fighting going on and he seems to think that if the Boers held out another six months England would have to give in. He thinks a great deal of these European congresses and meetings and is sure they must have effect soon. God grant it, oh, God grant it – it is my one cry, my one hope and prayer and longing night and day, before which all else sinks into insignificance.

May 6th [1901]

The night is wild and stormy – at least what we call stormy in our land of fair weather, and I am wondering how I shall feel at Irene in a thin tent on a dismal night like this. Sometimes my heart fails me, especially when the mother talks as she did this afternoon – that I am going against her wishes, that I shall ruin my constitution and regret this step to the end of my days. They all said the same when I proposed becoming a Red Cross nurse and yet there is no experience in my whole past that I value more than that – I would not be without it for <u>anything</u>. After all,

---

[306]   of the stars.
[307]   Language.

I find that "my way" is the best and in this one particular case I am determined to have "my way". The mother has a pleasant way of throwing cold water over every plan and I am so used to it that I no longer worry my head over it. When I make up my mind to do a thing, I do it and I seldom regret it.

The comet was rather peculiar this evening. It was very large and bright and had two tails, one very distinct and the other a sort of reflection of the first – like so – a regular V which might stand for *Vrede*[308] or Victory or anything else that begins with a V. We take a great interest in it and watch for it eagerly every night. As far as I know there is no news and if Khaki has "no news" then it generally means good news for us.

The diarist's sketch of the comet in script III of her diary

This evening as I was busy teaching Paulus there was a fumbling at the door and Gentleman Jim stumbled in with a chair, slate and pencil and two Royal Readers – "Coming to learn too, little Missie". It is becoming a regular night school and I am not sure whether I quite like it because it takes up a good deal of my time. Paulus certainly was not pleased, for now he is no longer "cock of the roost" but I don't see how I can refuse to help Jim. His reading is something fearful and wonderful.

Had a letter from Katie M[309] today – she is to be married on the 5th June. I wonder whether she chose that day of memories purposely. I am afraid there will be no more friendship between us in future – she is too "Engelsch gezind"[310] – "her and me" won't be able to agree.

May 7th. [1901]

We have found out now what the meaning is of that mysterious V in

---

308   Peace. The diarist made a drawing of the comet in Script III.
309   Not identified.
310   pro English.

the heavens – why, "Vrijheid"[311] of course. I feel quite happy since the problem has been solved. This evening we had a visitor to tea, viz the redoubtable S[chilthuis] who has only just taken his departure – 9.30 pm and so I have done nothing that I ought to have done tonight. Never mind, evening visitors are such a rarity with us that I need not grumble. But now I am off to bed – it is cold and windy and miserable and I have sung and played myself tired. The Town was unusually full of ossifers (sic) and men this afternoon – I wonder what it means. I cycled for the first time for about two months and expect to be stiff all over tomorrow.

May 9th. [1901]

Yesterday no entry and tonight I have so much to tell that I don't know where to begin – I am tired unto death and have a raging headache.

Mrs A.H. Bosman

Dear diary, I am leaving for Irene on Saturday. And this is, let me see, Thursday night, and I have only one day clear for a thousand preparations. It is not fair to give me such short notice but it seems that the need is most urgent. I went to Town this morning to do some shopping and when I came home Mama told me that Mrs [A.H.] Bosman (wife of Rev[erend] B[osman]) and Mrs Malan[312] had been here to say I must get ready to go immediately, but I cannot be ready before Sat[urday] afternoon – impossible!

---

311   Freedom.
312   Mrs H.S.J. Malan, a daughter of Commandant General Piet Joubert and his wife Hendrina and a member of the Irene Hulpkomitee (Relief Committee). See T. van Rensburg (ed.), *Camp Diary of Henrietta E.C. Armstrong*, p 61n.

Mrs C[elliers] was here this afternoon with news from Fritz. There are two spies in Town and they brought her a letter from her husband in which he says F[ritz] is well and safe and informs us of Dietlof's capture. So they know that too. The spies are going out tomorrow night with four Pretoria men! Oh heavens, dear diary, if you fall into the enemy's hands I am done for. This is an important and most dangerous secret. We had just a line from Dietlof today – "am leaving for Bombay presently" 3rd May. So the poor dear boy is on the briny ocean now. And now I really must go and snatch a few hours' sleep.

May 10th. [1901]

Tomorrow afternoon at 4 o'clock I am leaving – that is to say if the line is not broken – one can be sure of nothing in these tempestuous days. I am nearly ready now but have still a good many little things to attend to tomorrow. It is now my sad duty to bid you goodbye, for I cannot take you with me, my beloved; it would not be safe – you contain too many secrets to be lugged about in these days of danger. You must just stay quietly at home and when I come back I shall take you up again.

I am taking a bran[d]-new exercise book and note book "to the front", and this dear fountain-pen and a small bottle of ink, all gifts from M.F. who has been so awfully kind and thoughtful. He has brought me some books to read when I am "off duty" and he has helped me in every way imaginable. He is one of the few people from whom I have had no opposition – no discouragement to put up with – on the contrary, he thinks my Irene plan an excellent one and says he wishes there were more girls ready to make such a sacrifice. Not that I regard this as such a great sacrifice, but of course one does give up something by going into camp-life for a month, and very likely I shall stay much longer, if it agrees with me and the mother does not require me at home.

Let me think, what war news have I heard during the last few days? That de la Rey has had a great victory; that Col Kitchener has been killed; that two regiments have come in and laid down their arms, refusing to fight any longer; (volunteers I believe;) that Potchefstroom has been taken by the Boers; that Smuts is not dead; that [the Reverend] Goddefroy's eldest son is not dead, but a prisoner, brought in last week; that the Boers are "hands-upping" in hundreds (strange that they don't "get done" and that the *Natal Witness* can still announce, as it did a few days ago, that "a great battle is expected. Boers concentrating under de la Rey". The English tell so many lies that they sometimes quite forget "where they are" and the result is confusion worse confounded. There is plenty of other war news but I can't remember all.

Uncle Paul told Mama that last night there was a sudden call to arms – about eight bugles at once. How I wonder whether it was only a false alarm or if there really was something wrong (or right?) At about noon today there was a great explosion somewhere – the whole house shook and we are still trying to find out what it could have been. The spies who brought news from Fritz say that all is well on the commandos – they have plenty of food and are full of hope and courage. Thank God for that. Tonight they are going back taking four of our men with them – may Heaven protect them and bring them safely out of all their dangers. Mama wrote a short letter to Fritz, which they are taking to him – she disguised her hand and mentioned no names in full, it was a very funny little letter and I hope the dear boy will be able to understand it. And now, little friend, goodnight and goodbye. I shall have seen and heard and done, and maybe, <u>suffered</u> much before we meet again, but I am going "vol moed"[313] and hope to do my duty under <u>all</u> circumstances.

Harmony <u>again</u>. May 11th 1901.

Dear diary, I see some heroic remark about "doing my duty", above but I don't see anything about "keeping cheerful" and it would be as well to make many good resolves on the subject, because doing one's duty is often very much easier than keeping cheerful. If you knew how savage I am tonight! Instead of sitting in a draughty tent I am in my cosy home perhaps you think I ought to be grateful and want to know what I am grumbling about, but just listen to this chapter of woes. I went to Mrs Bosman this morning and was told to be ready to leave by the 4 train this afternoon – Mr D[314] would call at her house for my permit and give it to me at the Station, where I would meet the two other nurses – Well and good. I made my preparations and left home soon after three o'clock – in plenty of time, as I thought – but alas, as I got out of

---

313   in high spirits.
314   Probably Mr Dürr.

the cab the train steamed out of the station. I was informed that the time had been changed and there would be no train until tomorrow and I was on the point of getting into the cab again when I saw a man whom I imagined must be Mr D from his likeness to his sister Mrs C[elliers].[315] Of course there was no time for ceremony, so I pounced on him, introduced myself and poured my woes into his astonished ear. He told me the two nurses were gone, that he did not know he was expected to call at Mrs Bosman's and that he did not even know I was going by that train. He offered to go to Mrs B[osman] at once and find out what the "mischief" it all meant and come and tell me – so I came home bag and baggage, feeling very foolish and greatly astonishing the mother. He came later on with more complications. Mrs B[osman] had given Miss C[316] a message for him yesterday to the effect that he must call at her house. Dear miss [sic] C forgot and when he did not turn up for my permit she (Mrs B[osman]) sent it to the Station with a kaffir, who lost it on the way, if you please – so I could not have gone by that train in any case. He then offered to take a note to the Governor from me asking a special permit to go tomorrow, as all the offices were closed this afternoon. I gave him a letter and he promised to bring the answer this evening. I must now possess my soul in patience and see what my fate is to be. Gen[eral] Maxwell is always so kind to me that I am sure he will do what he can to help me.

Later. Of course he will. I might have known that the dear man would do anything for me (you see, I am beginning to think quite a lot of myself, and no wonder) Mr D[ürr] has been here with a special permit, written and signed by the Governor and – what do you think? – four packets of some nourishing stuff to make soup for my patients, and two tiny bottles of tablets for sweetening tea and coffee. I have just written to thank him and tomorrow and 2.30 Mr D[ürr] will call for me in a cab. If I don't get off then I am sure I won't know what to do. It is

---

315 Probably Mrs Susanna Celliers, the wife of J.F.E. Celliers, since her maiden surname was Dürr.

316 Probably Miss Hessie Celliers (1879–1956), who was a sister of J.F.E. Celliers and therefore a sister-in-law of Mrs Susanna Celliers. She was one of the Pretoria women who helped with voluntary nursing services in Irene in 1901. See T. van Rensburg (ed.), *Camp diary of Henrietta E.C. Armstrong*, pp 59n and 82n.

very miserable having all one's things packed and having to dive to the bottom of my great trunk for every trifle, but I daresay there are worse things in store for me. Old Tante Breedt is here and has promised to look well after the mother for an indefinite period. [Gentleman] Jim says my going away is a "bad business, little missie". Paulus says nothing but looks a lot. I am afraid they are thinking regretfully of their "night school".

I was to have gone to a pic-nic today – "my last frivol", I called it – and had to give it up because I was going away. The Roods, Connie [Minnaar] and I gave this picnic and we invited about 16 people and at the very end I was obliged to back out of it. I must take care that no one sees me tomorrow or I shall never hear the end of it. I sent my contribution of cakes, jellies, tongue etc to Annie with a huge jar of canned fruit but they were all very wild with me for not coming myself. If I had known how the train would go off without me I would not have gone to the Station at all, but have surprised the pic-nic party just about lunch time. I was looking forward so eagerly to a whole day on "Bomb Hill" in the lovely plantations, but alas, it was not be. The mother did not approve of this pic-nic at all – she thinks we ought to keep perfectly quiet while there is so much misery around us, but I think a day in the open air, with some friends, can do no harm. I would certainly not go to balls and parties and theatres, but this is something quite different. Well, never mind, I am going to another sort of pic-nic tomorrow.

Mrs Bosman tells me that things are very bad in the camp. They have no luxuries, not even comforts for the patients and many invalids die because they get no nourishing food. How shall I endure it when a dying child implores for milk and I have not the power to give it? The stories I heard today made my hair rise and I am beginning to feel horribly nervous. And now, dear diary, I hope this is really goodbye. When I come home, maybe a sadder and a wiser woman, I hope to tell you all my experiences. Good-bye, dear dumb friend.

Notes

1. Contemplated destruction of mines
2. Highest praise "not bad for an Englishman."

[End of Script III]

Part 3

"[T]hat hell on earth" – Irene, 12 May 1901 to 7 June 1901

[Script IV][1]

"Het eind zal zeker zalig zijn."[2]
"Casualty Ward". Irene Camp.
May 12th 1901.

Dear Diary, I am beginning my new life with a thousand good resolutions – one of them being to make an entry in this book <u>every</u> night – no matter how little I write. But as I am writing in the warmest place I can find (viz: <u>bed</u>) you may be sure my writing will be something dreadful, especially with the pale candle-light flickering and casting shadows on the white tent walls. Last night I was at home surrounded by every luxury and <u>now</u> – ? Well, I am comfortable enough but it is not <u>home</u> and everything is so new and strange. But I shall soon get used to this life and I am sure it will agree with me. The girls are all looking so well and are sun-burnt and jolly.[3] This morning I was at home, washing my hair and making all sorts of little preparations for this journey and at 2.30 Mr D[ürr] called for me in a cab, took me to the station got my luggage registered and helped me in every imaginable way. The jour-

---

[1]   *The inside cover of the script contains the following note – not in the handwriting of the diarist:*
      Box 685. No.
      Road.
      Steenberg Bronkhorstspruit
      Lost 2 children on her farm & three here in the camp. One of the three was a married daughter Mrs Theunis Christoffel Botha she & her five children died here. Husband still fighting.
[2]   *"The end will surely be blessed."*
[3]   *In the original diary this whole script is written with a fountain pen. The words* and jolly *are crossed out in pencil.*

ney was quite uneventful, except that the train stopped quite suddenly once and we thought there was something wrong on the line, but it only turned out to be a herd of oxen. I believe we ran over one animal, or at least caught it on the cow-catcher.

There was no one to meet me at the Station because I was not expected by that train but one of the doctors saw me and asked me whether I was the "new lady help" (a question that tickled my fancy a good deal.) I answered "yes" comforting myself with the proverbs (?) "What's in a name?" and "A rose by any other name is sweet" or whatever it is, and he offered to escort me to the camp. On the way he pointed out various things to me and told me more or less what my duties would be. The camp is enormous. There are about 5 000 people in it[4] and I believe quite 1 000 cases of sickness. On an average three deaths daily. Dr H[amilton][5] told us this evening that

Johanna van Warmelo in her nurse's uniform

---

4   On 11 May 1901, one day before the diarist's arrival, the population of the Irene camp was 4118, of whom 968 were adult men, 1397 adult women and 1753 children. See report by N.J. Scholtz, the Commissioner of the Camp, to General Superintendent, Burgher Camps Department, Pretoria, 11 May 1901, in TAB, DBC (vol 3), Papers received: Burgher Camp Irene, 1901 April – 1902 Dec (unsorted file).

5   Dr Richard Hamilton completed his medical studies in London in 1895 and was admitted into South Africa as a medical practitioner in 1897. He practised in Johannesburg in 1899. He was one of the first medical doctors at the Irene Camp and seems, in spite of the diarist's negative comments about him (see entry on 1901-05-13) to have treated the camp inhabitants well. Thus Henrietta Armstrong commented in her diary on 1901-05-01: "We are sorry to hear that Doctor Hamilton is to be transferred to Volksrust. It's the work of the horrid [camp] commandant. Doctor does too much for the sick." See T. van Rensburg (ed.), *Camp diary of Henrietta E. C. Armstrong*, pp 76–77.

there have been 28 deaths since May 2nd. We walked up the "Main Road" through the camp to the top of the rise, where the hospital is, and then Miss Dürr[6] took charge of me and introduced me to the nurses. I know them all except two and the two English nurses who look after the hospital. We six Africanders have nothing to do with the hospital – we have to go from tent to tent and find out where sickness is and report to the doctor. Only serious cases are brought here – the others remain and are doctored in their own tents, where their relations help to nurse them. And we have no night nursing except in case of great emergency. Miss C[elliers] and I are to share a tent, which will be struck tomorrow. Tonight we are in an enormous marquee – one of the wards – which is very warm and comfortable. Alas, this luxury is only temporary and tomorrow night I shall be bitterly cold. Even now I am beginning to feel chilled and must make haste to finish writing. The nurses and doctors have their meals in a marquee like this. Supper consisted of cold roast beef, peach pickle, bread and "Stormjagers"[7] jam, tea and coffee. I made a very good meal and enjoyed the novelty of it all immensely – but tomorrow my work begins. One doctor (Dr Green)[8] seems very nice but I don't care about <u>my</u> baas,[9] Dr Hamilton. We have dubbed him One and Six – so in future you must know who I mean when I speak about 1/6. But now my hands are too cold – I must go to sleep.

May 13[th.] [1901]

The eventful first day is over and has been rather a success from one point of view – I can do more good than I expected but that is sad, for it means that there is more <u>need</u> than I thought. Alas, things are a thousand times worse in the camp than I ever imagined. Let me try and tell

6   Dürr, Sophia Margaretha Dorothea Elizabeth (1872–1953) was a daughter of Erich Johann Martyn Dürr and Maria Elizabeth Dürr. She never married. Sister of Mrs S.J. Celliers and of Mary Dürr (see diary entry on 1901-06-04). See T. van Rensburg (ed.), *Camp diary of Henrietta E. C. Armstrong*, pp 79 and 120.

7   *Stormjagers* is a Dutch word for dough cakes. It was made by dumping a piece of bread dough into hot fat and allowing it to cook until it attains a yellow-brown colour.

8   Dr Percy Andrew Green (1870–1957) was born in England and admitted into the South African Republic as a medical practitioner in 1895. See T. van Rensburg (ed.), *Camp diary of Henrietta E. C. Armstrong*, p 77.

9   my boss.

Rows of tents in Irene Concentration Camp

you what my work is. The camp has been divided into wards and the wards into rows of tents and the tents numbered. Now I have Rows 25, 26, 27, 28, and a short little one 29. Each row consists of about 30 tents so I have nearly 150 tents to inspect every day, and when at least every other tent has one or more patients you can imagine what a lot I have to do. I enquire at every tent whether anyone is ill and where there are patients I take down the row and number in my notebook, name and age of patient, nature of complaint etc. The serious cases I report to the doctor, but in little ailments I have to prescribe for myself – on my own responsibility – and my note-book today shows an array of diseases, fearful and wonderful to look upon. There is a small dispensary where the people can get milk, sago, maizena,[10] arrowroot, castor-oil, liniment, cough mixtures ect [sic] upon producing a written order signed by one of the nurses. We all have little slips of paper for the purpose and the number of orders I wrote today is astounding. The chemists will bless me. They are two second-class Hollanders, who snub the people and treat them badly and are all sweetness when we come there, so we have no chance of complaining, but I shall be even with them yet. The poor

---

[10]   In the original script maizena was spelt messina, but the diarist crossed this out in pencil and replaced it in pencil with the word maizena.

singing psalms and hymns – now and then I heard someone reading from the Bible or praying aloud – generally the youthful voice of some boy or girl, who is a little "geleerd"[36]. It is wonderful to see how patient and cheerful the poor things are. Sometimes when I wake at dawn I hear singing in the camp and late at night they sing and pray. On Sundays there is no end to the music and as they all sing together and half a dozen different hymns come floating across to us at the same time, the effect is something wonderful.

I wish I could remember all the names by which I have been called – nurse, *zuster*,[37] *tante*,[38] doctor, *nichtje*,[39] *mij ou sussie*,[40] and yesterday, to my great amusement, "*mij ou moedertje*"[41], by an old crony of at least 60.

Monday night. There has been a visitor in my camp tonight – the Angel of Death – the first time since my arrival. On my rounds this morning I found one of my patients – a boy of 12 looking very bad. The doctor saw him and we decided to move him to the hospital at once. I got a stretcher and some men and the poor laddie was taken to No 5 – the men's ward. His face looked terrible, all drawn with pain and with a deadly hue upon it. All day he lay there without moving or speaking and this evening the nurse went out for a moment to get him some milk food and when she came back he was dead. Failure of the heart, the doctor says. We thought he had a bad attack of malaria. I had to get a lantern and make my second night excursion to the camp – to tell his people, but this time I was accompanied by Miss F[indlay]. It was awful creeping into the cold dark tent with my sad tidings. The worst of it is that the poor boy has not a single relative here. He was with his father in the field some weeks ago, looking after cattle, and there was a fight somewhere near them and they ran hard to get away, but they were captured, he and his father and grandfather. The two men were sent to Bombay and he was brought here and was taken into an already over-crowded tent, by kind friends. His mother is in Pietersburg. His

---

36   "educated"
37   Sister.
38   Aunt.
39   Cousin.
40   My dear sister.
41   "my dear little mother"

name is Gert Bezuidenhout.[42] The woman who took him in is terribly cut up. When I told the news she just bent over her baby without a word and sobbed quietly. It was very sad. Afterwards they all came up to the hospital and we carried the body into the maternity Ward, which is empty just now, and there I helped them to swathe the boy. His face looks so sweet and restful in death – not a trace of pain left. My luck is turning now. I expect to hear tomorrow that little Susara is gone – she was all but gone when I was there late this afternoon. I told the doctor, but he said there was nothing to be done and it would be no use to go and see her.

H[essie] and I went to post some letters this afternoon, and in the office, when I was enquiring whether there was anything for me, a young Khaki said "Can't you cure fever, sister?" I thought he was trying to have some fun with me because of my red cross so I gave no answer, but then I looked into his face and saw that there was something wrong so I asked him what it was. He said he was in a burning fever and it was no use going to a doctor – he was only a common soldier and if Tommy dies it is easy enough to replace him etc, etc – all of which I know well enough to be the truth. I felt his pulse, his forehead was burning – so I took his temperature and was surprised to find it three degrees <u>below</u> normal. I told him to go to the soldiers' hospital and while I was talking an officer came in and the tommy hastily turned away, I whipped up my thermometer and disappeared. I don't want to get him into any trouble but Dr N[eethling] says I must take him some quinine pills tomorrow, so I shall make an excursion to the post for that purpose. I am always so sorry for these poor neglected tommies!

We then went for a walk to a little graveyard I noticed yesterday – a new one it seems. It is fenced in all round and the graves are in neat rows – over 100 of them, I counted. This day has been all death and the grave, and one needs a strong heart to sleep alone like this on such a dreary night. Is it not so very cold tonight but so horribly dreary and

---

[42] According to official records Gert P. Bezuidenhout (12 years) of Pietersburg died in the Irene Camp on 20 May 1901 of malaria. See T. van Rensburg (ed.), *Camp diary of Henrietta E. C. Armstrong*, p 129. See also TAB, DBC 62, Irene Camp Register of Residents, that mentions a Gert Bezuidenhout (12 years) that died on 21 May 1901 and is listed with people from the Pietersburg district.

the wind is enough to scare one's wits away. I must say I am nervous this evening. If the wind would blow a good old gale one would not mind but these long, deadly silences, with sudden, startling gusts terrify one. I wish I had a companion. There is one thing I am so afraid of. All around us there are great grass fires and I am sure if a heavy wind blew the sparks this way and set our grass on fire the tents would go too. The others laugh at me but I know only too well what these veld fires are on a windy night. Well, we are in God's hands and I must trust in Him and not yield to these foolish fears. My nerves are a bit unstrung with all the misery I have seen during the last eight days.

May 21st. [1901]

This morning when we were at breakfast Mrs A[rmstrong] came in – she had arrived from Pretoria and informed me that my mother was in my tent.

May 22nd. [1901]

So far I got yesterday and since then I have not had another chance to write. I don't know when last I had such days. Not one moment's rest and yet my work is only half done – that is what makes it so unsatisfactory. Now let me begin with yesterday. I flew to my tent, into the mother's arms and when I had done hugging her, I turned to find Aunt Clara, waiting to embrace me. What rejoicings there were in Klip Laar! I took them down to my ward and left them with some old friends while I went to see some patients. At about 11 we came up to my tent, where the mother produced some sandwiches and I got three cups of delicious tea and we had a fine old talk. It was perfectly lovely to hear some news and see familiar faces after what seems to me an endless exile. Then we went to the camp again – I to my patients, the two others on a trip of investigation. They came to my tent at about dinner time with marvellous tales – they seemed to know more about camp life than I do. Mama had some samples of sugar flour and coffee to sent to Stead. In the sugar was a whole lizard's head! They seemed much impressed by all the misery.

Sister W[alsh] invited them to dinner but they refused, preferring a simple lunch in my tent to an English dinner. It is not nice for us to mess with those creatures – every day I dislike it more. We often have Khakis to meals and we seven Africanders are getting heartily sick of it all. After dinner Dr N[eethling] came to my tent and I introduced him to my two relatives and we all sat here chatting until he had to go to work. Then I took my *"fermilie"*[43] to the graveyard and when we came back we had afternoon tea and at 4.30 Hessie and I walked to the Station with them. They brought me an enormous *koffer*[44] of things – flannel, clothing, food, medicine, oranges and I don't know what beside. Two letters from Line made me most happy – she is so glad about my undertaking and calls it "noble". Oh dear, if she only knew how little nobility there is about me! How worried and impatient I get! how I curse the English a thousand times a day! how I hate or loathe and despise them, ugh, the brutes and beasts – but I get quite crazy on this point – let me think of something else.

My poor little Susara[45] was dead when I arrived there yesterday morning – she coughed her last little breath out at 8 o'clock the night before, just after Gert Bezuidenhout died. I took Mama in to see the poor wee thing, with her pinched features, and she was horrified when I told her the child had looked just like that while she was living. That was my first death in the camp – (G[ert] B[ezuidenhout] was one of my patients but he died in hospital) – so I had to write out a report for the doctor. The poor mother had carried that little form in her arms for three months, and is so lonely now. Everywhere in the tents I see her – where sickness is, she is to be found – with her sweet, motherly, patient face.

When H[essie] and I were coming from the Station late that afternoon a woman rushed out to me – her boy was in great pain and she had been hunting all over the camp for me. I went in at once and found a boy of about 10, looking very bad – quite blue about the lips and moaning with pain. I rushed up to the Hospital and was lucky enough to find Dr G[reen] at once, but he did not seem over-pleased at being

---

43   "relatives"

44   suitcase.

45   Probably Susara M. Pretorius (3 years) of Boschfontein, Rustenburg, who according to official records died in the Irene Camp on 20 May 1901 of diarrhoea. See T. van Rensburg (ed.), *Camp diary of Henrietta E. C. Armstrong*, p 166.

asked to go into camp so late. I felt inclined to shake him. He was more annoyed still when I told him the mother would not hear of sending her boy to hospital and informed me he "took no interest" in such cases. He examined the boy and said it was pneumonia and advised me to put on a mustard plaster. I have never had anything to do with pneumonia and as the doctor was so unsympathetic I went to Mrs A[rmstrong] and got full instructions from her – she is never too tired, or worried to attend to anyone and yet she works all day and is suffering from indigestion. It was pitch dark when I had finished making my plaster and had trotted into camp with it and made my patient comfortable for the night. They had'nt [sic] even a candle and I had to give them one of my own. This morning I went to his first thing and was delighted to find him in little or no pain. The grateful mother said she would wash my feet for me – I could not help thinking it a rash promise – I am not fit to touch after walking about in the dust all day, and the water is so bitterly cold that one cannot often have a bath in these draughty tents. I generally have mine at midday, if I have time and there is no wind blowing. My nerves were so unstrung after all my adventures yesterday that I could not sleep – was awake half the night and imagined someone was in my tent – lit the candle once or twice and tried hard not to be foolish but it was no use, so I made up my mind to ask H[essie] to move into my tent today and there she lies opposite me – snoring peacefully. She has a very bad cold and we have been doctoring her with eucalyptus. She is a very nice girl and I am so pleased that Dr N[eethling] and the others are always so attentive and kind to her. The poor girl is a little deaf and generally sits perfectly silent while everyone else is jabbering around her. General conversation never reaches her – she only hears when she is addressed directly and then she is very quick. It is a great pity that such a charming girl should be so heavily handicapped. She is the essence of refinement and good taste – a perfect little lady in all she says and does. I am glad to have her for a companion and Mrs A[rmstrong] is very glad to have a spare tent – she wants it as a sort of store-room.

Tonight I hope to get some rest. I would have broken down soon if I had had to sleep alone. What is coming over me? I am as a rule the most fearless of girls – I never knew before what it meant to be nervous and here I find myself yielding to all sorts of foolish fancies. But one does see such dreadful things. One of my little girls had an enormous abscess at the back of her head and I had to bring her to the hospital to have it lanced. Today I had endless work in the camp. New milk orders have been issued (blue cards) and I had to go from tent to tent recalling the old ones and giving out the new. Then I had to make a note of the different cases of sickness for tomorrow's weekly report, and lastly Dr G[reen] asked us to find out exactly how many men, women and children we have in our wards, all this being in <u>addition</u> to our usual work of taking temperatures, prescribing medicines, writing orders for sago, rice, barley, arrowroot, etc etc. I found one of my patients with a bran[d] new son – arrived last night. There are a great many new arrivals expected, and alas, in most cases there is not a single little garment ready, and I have to supply them with material. I only got through two of my rows this morning and afternoon and towards dusk my voice was completely gone and I felt too tired to crawl up to the hospital. I can't understand what is the matter with my voice – it does not often play me such tricks.

Fancy, dear diary, what those cheeky Boers did in broad daylight at midday this morning. They coolly rode up to the *koppie*[46] to the right of the camp and drove off 500 head of cattle and a great many donkeys. I suppose Khaki feels rather like a donkey this evening. The Boers are all round us. Nothing else has reached me lately, in the shape of war news – we hear nothing here. I gave my Khaki patient in the post office some quinine pills yesterday. Of all the funny names I have, this is about the funniest – "*die middercijne*"[47]. I saw one little nipper nudging another this afternoon as I passed and heard him whisper "*Daar loop die middercijne*"[48]. I was awfully amused. But now I am too sleepy and tired to write more.

May 23rd. [1901]

My day has been rather satisfactory. I have got through an amazing lot of work – have my weekly report in order for the doctor, my census taken and all the milk tickets issued, besides having doctored dozens of sick people, and having spent the greater part of the day with a dying baby.

---

[46]   low hill.
[47]   "the medicine"
[48]   "There goes the medicine"

The poor little soul was just going when I left the camp and I could not stay with her because I must be in early, or I shall be laid up tomorrow. I have not been able to speak above a whisper all day – my voice is gone completely. My vocal chords are rather delicate and yesterday's strain on them was too much for me. Now I wonder whether I am in for a bad cold or what it is going to be. –

The Boers are sometimes very queer with their remedies. When I went to see the dying baby first they were just busy giving it a tablespoon-ful of warm dog's blood – and the poor dog was sitting outside with blood dripping from the wounded ear. I told them not to torment the child and yet when I came there again they were on the point of giving it a hot mustard footbath. I prevented them and gently told the parents that there was nothing more to be done. They were heart-broken, for this is their only little girl. There are more of my children looking very bad. This morning there was another new arrival – came into a tent where there are already eleven and where poverty, sickness and filth are reigning supreme. Oh, I wish no more children would be born while there is so much misery. A new nurse has arrived – Mrs Stiemens[49] from Pretoria. She is in Miss Malherbe's place. I am glad she has come – she has had some experience and looks a strong and healthy woman. She advises me to stay one month and no longer – she says we ought to go home and rest for a month and then come again. I shall see how I feel when I come to the end of my first month.

Visitors from Pretoria brought very good news today. They say every-thing is going splendidly in the field – a great many trains have been taken and our people are "*vol moed*"[50]. God grant it – God grant that an end may soon come to our troubles. It is quite true that the Boers took 500 head of cattle and donkeys in broad daylight yesterday and the best of it is that they belonged to an Erasmus[51] who <u>looted</u> all he possesses. He is one of those miserable "hands-uppers" who have only tried to profit as

---

49   Probably Rachel Jacoba (Kotie) Stiemens (neé Smit). She was married to Willem Johannes Stiemens. See T. van Rensburg (ed.), *Camp diary of Henrietta E.C. Armstrong*, p 90.

50   "full of courage"

51   Probably C.J. (Karel) Erasmus, who laid down arms on 18 June 1900 and subsequently remained on his farm. See diary entry on 1901-06-18 and also T. van Rensburg (ed.), *Camp diary of Henrietta E.C. Armstrong*, pp 75 and 90.

much as possible by the war, and never fought. Mrs A[rmstrong] wanted to buy one of his cows for a friend in Pretoria and he asked her £20. She told him it was too much and he need not be so independent with his cattle - the Boers would come and take them all one day and actually the Boers did! We are all so glad about it. They took a lot of sheep today and so it goes on always - Khaki simply can't keep his things from their roving fingers. A man was sent out today, from this camp, to the Boer lines - to bring as many hands-uppers as he can. He has been offered £10 a head. I hope the Boers will find him out and punish him - but just think how low England has fallen! She is trying every mortal thing to get the war to an end. A great many of the prisoners in Cape Town have been brought to their families here - we first thought it was on account of the plague, but Dr N[eethling] says it must be another dodge to

get the burgers to surrender. It won't help. Poor Miss Findlay is ill now - we think she is in for <u>measles</u>! - A woman who does my washing for me lost a husband and four children just before the war (fever) and four of her sons are prisoners, she does not know where, and she is here with three little ones - very delicate and <u>terribly</u> poor.[52]

Miss Findlay

May 24 [1901]. 4 o'clock.

The little Pietersen[53] baby died last night. I have not so very much work to do today and have been busy getting my own quarters tidy and comfortable. Last night at supper I

---

52   In her book *Het Concentratie-kamp van Iréne*, p 39 the diarist identifies this woman as Mrs Nel.
53   Probably Sofia Adriana Petronella Pieterse of Rooipoort, Pretoria, who was one year old when she died of measles in the Irene Camp on 24 May 1901. See T. van Rensburg (ed.), *Camp diary of Henrietta E.C. Armstrong*, p 165. See also TAB, DBC 62, Irene Camp Register of Residents 1901 Jan – 1902 Oct.

found some letters on my plate and a parcel of magazines from Pretoria – sender unknown – the address is written in an unfamiliar hand. I was furious with my Khaki patient (the one in the post office). He sent up my letters, with a note from himself, apologising for having kept them since the previous day and explaining that he had expected me to call for them myself. He wants to know whether I am on night duty that I have not been to the post again and informs me that he is much better "thank you" – only his cold is still very bad. The epistle is signed Harry Stokes! I can tell you I regretted having given him those quinine pills. I wonder if he thinks I am just a common Boer girl trying to get up a flirtation with him. I certainly am a Boer girl and am very proud of the fact – but not one of those who flirt with Tommies and that is what hurt my feelings. Surely even a common private can see that I am a lady!

Sister W[alsh] told me a joke. A new patient was brought into the hospital – a young man – and was placed on his side in a clean bed. He lay perfectly still all day and when he could endure it no longer he asked permission to turn on the other side – he would do his best not to untidy the bed! No wonder they are all so afraid of the hospital!

5.30 p.m. We have all just come back from the Station – a very jolly party – 5 nurses and Doctor Dandy (as we have nicknamed Dr N[eethling] because he is so spick and span and wore a fine buttonhole when he came here.) Our friends took some letters to deliver to friends in Pretoria. They are not allowed to do so but kindly smuggle them in for us. I have a spare half hour before supper so I shall tell you something interesting I heard from Dr Dandy a few days ago. He says that when the English were about to enter Pietersburg, a young Hollander – orderly to Gen Beyers – said he was not going to surrender and he was not going to run away – he would stay and see how many English he could shoot – so he hid himself in the long grass just beyond the town. The Australian Scouts entered the town on the other side and rode straight through, to find a place to camp in. When they reached the grass several bullets whistled through the air in quick succession, killing two horses and some soldiers. An officer gave the order to halt and rode forward alone crying out "Hands up, there". For answer he got a bullet through the head and fell down dead. The second officer then went forward and got a bullet through the groin – dead also, I believe. They then caught sight of the man and a shower of bullets rained on him, and then he stood up and wanted to surrender, poor fool, but of course there was no mercy for him. They all rushed upon him and transfixed him with their bayonets – made a pincushion of him, in fact – and carried him back to Town on the points of their bayonets. The first volley they fired upon him only carried away one of his little fingers.[54]

May 25 [1901]. 12 a.m.

Dear diary, there is untold dissatisfaction in Klip Laar today. First thing I saw this morning was that they were busy adding two rows of tents to my ward – 2½ – and I flattered myself that my protestations had had effect and these new tents were being struck for the use of my already over-crowded ward. Not so. I hear now that new people are coming from Rustenburg and that my tents of 15 and 19 and 20 inhabitants will have to remain as they are. Of course it is quite impossible for me to take all those rows in addition to what I had before so I am giving Row 25, the first in my ward, to Hessie. She has never had more than three rows and can easily manage another. She is quite willing but my patients in 25 are very dissatisfied and won't hear of my leaving them now that they are used to me. It certainly is a pity but what can one do? If I overwork myself there won't be anyone to look after them and as it is I have come home early because my voice was going again and I had two terrible fits of coughing in the camp, which exhausted me very much. Perhaps if I rest a little I shall be more fit for work this afternoon. And now I hear that Annie Rood is here – I shall be awfully glad to see her but it will mean a lot of talking again. She came to see me this morning but I was in the camp and she left word that she would come again towards dinner-time. My tent is swept and garnished and I have put on a clean apron and cuffs etc for her edification. How one does yearn for familiar faces in this land of exile! Perhaps she has brought me letters.

---

[54]   This incident is confirmed by G.R. Witton, *Scapegoats of the Empire. The story of the Bushveldt Carbineers*, p 43 who writes that the Hollander was a schoolmaster and that the officers who were killed were from Tasmania, Australia.

Sat[urday] night.

I had quite a lovely day with Annie and we finished up by going to the Station to see her off. She brought me no letters because she did not know she was coming until the last moment and the sweets she did bring for me she gave out in the camp. She says Fred and Con[nie] and Sara[h] are coming on Monday. There is news in the camp today. Gen. Pretorius[55] is lying quite near us with his commando and a kaffir brought in a letter to say that if we would send some waggons out they would give us plenty of nice dry wood for the women and they would supply with the best fat meat – because they have taken a lot of Erasmus' cattle. The cheek these boers have! It is quite amusing.

We are all very angry with the superintendent, Scholtz,[56] the biggest Jingo that ever lived. He makes the lives of our poor people a perfect burden to them and he has been trying for some time to work us out of the camp. The women and children have too many little comforts since the volunteer nurses set to work and it does not please his lordship, so this morning the doctor got a letter from him to the effect that the nurses are not to issue tickets for milk and medicines etc. in future and that no order will be carried out unless singed by one of the doctors. Of course it is quite impossible for the doctors to go through the whole camp to see where trifles are required, like a dose of castor-oil, a box of cough lozenges, a few quinine pills – they have their hands quite full with attending to serious cases, and we nurses might just as well go back to Pretoria if we are not allowed to be of some practical use in the camp. Scholtz "capped the climax" by saying that he must see the private supplies that are sent to us and he must know to whom we give them out. Now this is most absurd and I am quite sure he has no right to insist upon that. The things sent to us by friends are our own to distribute as we please but if his Jingoship insists upon this we are going to lead him such a life that he will be sorry he began with his nonsense. We are all going to make a list of the things we have received and rub it under

---

55   There was no General Pretorius in the forces of the South African Republic. The rumour was false.

56   N.J. Scholtz was the first superintendent of the Irene Concentration Camp from 8 February to 8 July 1901. He was originally from the Cape Colony and a British subject, but could speak Dutch. See T. van Rensburg, *Camp diary of Henrietta E.C. Armstrong*, p 63.

his nose wherever we find him – from Harmony so many oranges and tomatoes and eggs, from somewhere else so many candles and bars of soap – and so on – and Dr Green will send every order to him to be signed. I think Mr Scholtz will soon weary of it and leave us to do as we please.

We had Khaki visitors after tea, "Spoony" and a sergeant-major and we could not all run off at once so some of us remained in the marquée [sic] an hour or so. The sergeant was much concerned when I coughed once or twice and I said I was doctoring myself with butter-scotch, and to my surprise he offered to send me some tomorrow. Fancy, my having to receive sweets from a tommy! I feel so disgusted, especially when the other girls tease me. I shall never hear the end of the one in the post office.

One of my patients died this afternoon, of fever.[57]

May 26. [1901]

Although it is Sunday I have had a very busy day. I went through every tent in my ward, found three new cases of measles, a new baby – such a lovely little girl that had arrived at "*hoender-kraai*"[58] –, one poor little corpse and a few other strange "things". What does one not see on these morning rounds? If I were a good writer I would be able to publish a very interesting book on the subject, but as it is, I can only make a few notes for my own future use. We are all so pleased and excited because the Boers are at hand – a good deal of firing was heard this morning and Miss D[ürr] says she heard a few cannon shots in the night too. I know they often do fight in the moonlight, but I did not hear anything last night.

We have had wonderfully mild weather the last few days – quite warm at night but very windy and unpleasant during the day. While I write our tent is being crowded with women and girls from the camp, with orders for mealie-meal, soap and candles etc. We have a tent next door in which we keep our stores, and since that beauty Scholtz has made such stringent rules, we have taken to distributing private stores. It

---

57   Probably Marthinus J. Venter, 8 years, who died of malaria and was, according to the *Transvaal Government Gazette*, 10 July 1901, p 1132, the only death in Irene Camp on 1901-06-25.

58   "at first cock-crow"

means a lot of extra work for us and many are the "blessings" called down upon his smooth, sleek head. He is a great, fat fellow – positively shining with health and prosperity and he is so hard on the poor women and children that one longs to shake the brute. Oh, how I detest him, and yet one dares not say a word because he would think nothing of working us out. I think it is one of his ambitions to get rid of these volunteer nurses who ferret out everything that is wrong and who report all sorts of unpleasant cases. Yesterday the ration of meat was unusually bad – I opened some of the boiling pots and the steam that issued forth was positively sickening – anyone can see that it was diseased meat. And then the people do not get meat again before Wednesday – only twice a week. We were talking about the supply of rations last night and Dr G[reen] said it was barely "a living diet for a healthy adult". Just imagine delicate children living off ½ lb.[59] flour a day and nothing else – it is quite impossible, and many poor little ones are wasting away from want of proper nourishment.

The sisters Sophie and Mary Dürr, both voluntary nurses in the Irene Camp

I think we are going to have a storm – the sky is quite black in the west and I hear the rumblings of distant thunder. Rain would be a calamity in these "airy" tents and I have not a single umbrella or waterproof, wherewith to protect myself from the elements.

---

59   Approximately 225 grams.

Herbst[60] has just sent for me – woman seriously ill in Row 25.8. I must go at once.

May 27th.[1901]

While I write I hear an occasional cannon shot in the direction of the Magaliesberg. I have not done much work today because I expected Con[nie] and Sara[h] but to my great disappointment no one turned up and I am quite "off my stroke". I worked extra hard yesterday in order to be free today and now I have a good deal of spare time. Of course on my rounds this morning there were fewer cases than usual – they all seem to have recovered during the night. I had only one serious case to report to the doctor and three "new measles". Our great fun now-a-days is our dear Doctor Dandy – he keeps us all going. I never saw such a light-hearted, boyish, mischievous man and yet he can be so serious when it is necessary – he is an ideal doctor and we all like him and the patients adore him, one and all. There seems to be no end to his mad pranks when we are off duty and wherever he is to be found peals of laughter are heard. He has such an unusually hearty and frequent laugh. Some day when I have a little spare time I really must tell you about his tricks and nonsense – it is not fair that you should always see the shadowy side of our experiences, dear diary friend, – you will think this is a vale of tears and nothing else and I assure you we seven Boers manage to make our spare hours very pleasant – we all pull so well together, I shall be very sorry if an unsympathetic soul were to enter our charming circle. Mrs V[61] is coming today I think. I do hope she is nice.

Monday night.

Mrs V did not come, we think because it was a public holiday and all offices were closed in Town. I wish she would hurry up – Miss Findlay's ward is being much neglected, for none of us have time to attend to it. There have been more deaths than usual in the camp – some very sad cases. A woman called Ruttenberg[62] lost two children this morning

---

60   Not identified.
61   Mrs Maria Elizabeth Vlok (1877-1957), who replaced Mrs Armstrong as a voluntary nurse in the Irene Camp. See T. van Rensburg (ed.), *Camp diary of Henrietta E.C. Armstrong*, pp 96 and 107; J. Brandt-van Warmelo, *Het Concentratie-kamp van Iréne*, p 44.
62   She probaly refers to Antonie B. Ruitenberg (7 years) and Albertus Ruiten-

(measles) and one is dying. The first died a week ago and the fifth is also ill. Her husband is still fighting and knows nothing of the terrible news that is awaiting him. A Mrs Snyman[63] died today, a young woman (25) leaving three little children, whose father is also still in the field. The sad part of this story is that her sister Mrs Oosthuizen[64], a girl of twenty, died last week, leaving a six months old baby. Mrs A[rmstrong] tells me that she went to see the baby and found that the relations had trimmed its little bonnet with a frill of crape! Imagine a tiny morsel of humanity like that being decorated with crape, of all things. The doctor wants us to find out "for our amusement" how many children, living and dead, the women in our wards have ever had. He thinks this a good chance, not to be lost, of making up statistics – I think the result will be astonishing, for the Boer woman can bear children if she can do nothing else. I know of two cases where women have had seven children under nine years of age. This afternoon while we were at dinner a woman walked into the Maternity Ward from camp, and not five minutes afterwards we heard the baby yell, before a nurse or doctor could reach the marquee. The mother is very well this evening – temperature <u>normal</u>. We come across very curious things in a camp like this.

– Doctor Dandy is so good to the people – it really touches one's heart. This evening after supper he got up quietly and went to the camp to see a sick baby – something that Dr G[reen] would <u>never</u> do unless urgently requested. The child seems to be in great danger. We tease

berg (3 years), both of Pietpotgietersrust, who according to official sources both died on 27 May 1901; Johanna Hendrina Ruitenberg (6 years), who died on 9 May 1901; and Hendrik Ruitenberg (12 years) who died on 29 May 1901. See T. van Rensburg (ed.), *Camp diary of Henrietta E.C. Armstrong*, p 171. According to the list of deaths published in the *Transvaal Government Gazette* of 10 July 1901, p 1132, their surname was Rautenbach, not Ruitenberg. According to the handwritten Irene Camp register of Residents (TAB, DBC 62), Johanna Hendrika Ruitenberg (aged 32, of Potgietersrus), lost the following four of her six children in May 1901: Johanna Hendrika (5 years) on 10 May, Antonie Binneveld (7 years) on 27 May, Albertus (3 years) on 27 May and Hendrik (12 years) on 29 May.

63   Cornelia S. Snyman (25 years) of Rietvlei, Krugersdorp, died of pneumonia on 27 May 1901. See T. van Rensburg (ed.), *Camp diary of Henrietta E.C. Armstrong*, pp 92 & 174.

64   Johanna Helena Fredrica Oosthuizen (20 years) of Sterkfontein, Krugersdorp, died on 6 May 1901 of double pneumonia. See T. van Rensburg (ed.), *Camp diary of Henrietta E.C. Armstrong*, pp 81 & 161.

Miss F[indlay] about an old man in the camp and a few days ago Dandy wrote her a love-letter in his name, in a beautifully disguised hand. Last night I received a letter at table, signed by "Fred Spokes", asking me to come down to the post office. Of course I knew at once who the author of it was and now I am beginning to wonder whether that first letter from "Harry Stokes" did not perchance come from the same source. Dread thought! and I have been so frigid to my poor fever patient! But no, it is impossible – the first was genuine enough. I gave a sort of party in my tent this afternoon and invited the 6 Boers to come and eat preserved figs – a jar full that Mama sent me for <u>our</u> consumption, not for the public mess. I think they enjoyed themselves very much. Dandy seems quite at home amongst a lot of women.

May 28. [1901]

Firing heard again this morning. I feel miserable – a very bad cough and a cold in my head. One does not shake an ailment off easily in these thin tents. This morning my blankets and clothes were damp with dew, which seems to strike through everything. There is a good deal of sickness in my camp this morning – I have seven cases to report to the doctor. Miss Findlay is in a good deal of pain this morning and had a bad night. I hear Dandy next-door in her tent, cracking jokes and teasing Hessie. I never came across such a tease. There is no mercy for anyone who falls into his hands. H[essie] told me a few days ago that her head is so dirty that she can "plant mealies" on it and I was unwise enough to repeat it to him. Poor Hessie! She will never hear the end of it. He wants to send her mealies and wheat etc to sow for the use of the camp. But one does get very dirty here and it is not possible to have a bath every day – as to washing one's hair, I have not done it once since my arrival. I am getting so burnt that my own Mammie won't know me soon. Hessie saw me putting a little glycerine on my face and she said I must not do it – I would get "pitcher black", which was a polite way of saying that I am pitch black already. Some of my poor little babies are looking very ill this morning and I am very much afraid of another visit from the Angel of Death. They are so patient and sweet, the darlings – I do love the babies and oh, how my heart aches for them!

Bed. Klip Laar. May 30. [1901]

No entry since Tuesday and this is Thursday. How come it? Well, the fact is that I am ill in bed with a bad attack of influenza. All Tuesday I worked with a temperature of 101.4[65] and by the time evening came I was so ill that I had to go to bed early. The fever rose to 103[66] in the night and I had an awful time. Every inch of my body was aching and I coughed and sneezed my head ached and I just tossed about all night, so in the morning I decided to get up but stay in my tent and do no work. I dressed myself as usual and sent word to Dr G[reen] that I was not fit for work and after breakfast, which meal I made a pretence of eating in my tent, Dr Dandy came in to see me and while he was here, my mammie arrived, to my own great astonishment and delight, but I was too ill to entertain her and just lay looking at her and listening to all the news she had to tell. She was much concerned about my illness and begged me to go home with her, but I did not feel as if I could possibly undertake the journey.[67]

June 1st [1901]

My poor diary has been very much neglected but I am so weak and ill and miserable that it is quite an effort to hold my pen. I got up for a few hours yesterday afternoon and now I am up again but I am as weak as I usually am after an illness of many weeks. Quinsy does not even leave me in such a low state. I am ready to die of melancholy and depression. Dr Dandy says it is part of the Influenza and I think he will bring me a good tonic today. His medicines are excellent and have done me a great deal of good. Perhaps I am going home for a week or two – I am afraid nothing else will cure me, for one has no chance of recovery in these miserable tents. The wind is tearing in upon me now, a cold, dusty wind that makes everything grimy and aggravates my cough. To be ill in this place is certainly not the height of bliss – but enough about myself and

---

[65]   ± 38° C

[66]   ± 39° C

[67]   At 16:20 that same afternoon Dr Neethling telegraphically informed Mrs van Warmelo that her daughter was "decidedly better." See Telegram, Superintendent, Irene – Mrs van Warmelo, Harmony, 4:40 PM, 30 May 1901, in Archives of the *Nederduitsch Hervormde Kerk*, L IX/168, I, *Briewe van Mev v Warmelo aan haar kinders 1901-1905*, unsorted.

my sufferings – let me try to think of all the news we have heard lately. Yesterday Mrs Celliers came from Town, bringing us letters, parcels, sweets, cakes etc and a lot of news. Sir A. Milner has been appointed Viceroy of India, the peerage has been bestowed upon him and he has left South Africa for good; Lord Kitchener is going away and Sir Evelyn Wood is coming in his place[68]; the Boers are doing very well all over the country; 60 000 rebels are supposed to be fighting in the Colony; twenty-three young men escaped from Pretoria last week – procured horses and revolvers and rode through the guard in broad daylight (it is said that they stole old Rodda's[69] horses out of the stable – hooray!) de la Rey is said to have captured 8 cannon and it is a fact that the Boers have taken the rest of Erasmus' cattle – a great many horses and donkeys, even the black charger he was so fond of riding about the camp, was taken out of his stable. He has appealed to the British for protection now and I suppose they will give him a miserable little guard that the Boers can squash with one hand if they feel so inclined – the mighty England has no men to spare for protection of private property.

A terrible tragedy took place in Pretoria last week. That arch-traitor, Hendrik Schoeman, was sitting in his dining-room with three friends, his wife and two daughters when a bomb burst in their midst, killing him and one daughter and one or two friends and mortally wounding his wife and the other daughter. It appears that he had a bomb with a small crack in it and as the men sat smoking he blew out a match and stuck the charred remains in the crack, with the result that a terrific explosion took place, completely wrecking the house and smashing all the windows in the neighbourhood[70] – but oh, I am too utterly, hopelessly miserable to write.

---

68   All these rumours were false.

69   Probably either W.E. Rodda of the firm Rodda and Nottingham, carpenters, builders and contractors, of Pretorius Street, or T.J. Rodda, the manager of P. Henwood, Son, Soutter & Company, ironmongers and drapers of Church Street, since these are the only two Rodda's in Pretoria listed in *Longland's Pretoria Directory for 1899*, pp 109 & 163.

70   H.J. Schoeman, the former Republican general indeed died in Pretoria on 26 May 1901. The diarist's account of the circumstances of his death is more-or-less accurate. Schoeman and his one daughter died instantly and one of the visitors died a few days afterwards. The other victims of the explosions recovered. See J. Schoeman, *Generaal Hendrik Schoeman – was hy 'n verraaier?*, pp 214-215.

June 3rd. [1901]

I began this diary with one very good resolution - viz. to make an entry every day, but I should have said "in days of sickness excepted", for I have twice neglected this book - no, three times and if I go on feeling so weak I shall have to go home and there will be no diary at all - at least, not on the subject of an Irene camp. The day before yesterday, when I wrote the above words, was one of the most awful I have spent for a long time. The wind was tearing in at my door, bringing in volumes of fine, gritty dust that penetrated into everything and greatly aggravated my cough, making my poor sore throat perfectly raw.

General Hendrik Schoeman

All day I sat in an easy-chair, dozing occasionally and wishing myself at Harmony. On Sunday (yesterday) the weather was even worse than the day before, the wind being as fierce as ever and icy cold. The day was cheered by visitors, Connie, Sara[h], and Fred with many good things for us. I had to entertain them in bed part of the day, even Fred, for he could not sit outside and in the veld I suppose one can do all sorts of queer things that one would not do in Town. Fred is as good and thoughtful as ever. He brought me 2 tins of Marie biscuits, a large cake, butter-scotch, almond rock, Russian toffee, caramels and mixed sweets, a tin of cocoa, a parcel of rusks and some bovril. What an array! Of course we are all very glad to get these luxuries and I am sharing with other less fortunate ones. I got up in the middle of the day when it was a little warmer and made my tent presentable for the reception. Dr Dandy spent the greater part of the day with us and we were on the whole very happy, in spite of the terrific cold. The wind did not abate all day and I am sure the three Pretorians have gone home with the most awful impressions of Irene.

June 4th. [1901]

It seems impossible for me to get any "forrarder"[71] with this diary. Last night my hands were so frozen with cold that I had to leave off writing. It is nearly dinner-time now and I have just come "home" from my morning rounds – I must try and get some writing done now that it is warm. We have had lovely weather the last two days but the nights are terribly cold and consequently there is much sickness in the camp. Hessie found two children dead with measles in one of her tents yesterday and the third is dying, Prinsloos from[72] ___ Just fancy to lose three children in two days! To lose <u>one</u> seems to me terrible enough. I made friends with some of my new people this morning. My ward is very large now and I shall have my hands full but I don't mind as long as my health is good. I feel better this morning – stronger than yesterday, but my cough is still very bad. There is a change in our staff. Mrs Armstrong and Sophy Dürr have gone home and Mrs Vlok and Mary Dürr[73] are here in their place. I am not at all pleased at the change. I am afraid it is no improvement and it is a pity – we were all so happy together. They play cards of an evening in Mrs S[tiemen]s' tent and have no end of frivolity. We gave a farewell party in my tent on Sat[urday] evening for Mrs A[rmstrong] and Miss D[ürr] but they were all so rowdy that I was thankful when it

---

71   The diarist means that she is not making progress with the diary.

72   An open space follows – as if left open to fill in later. She probably refers to Anna Louisa Prinsloo (1 year) and Stephanus J. Prinsloo (5 years), both of Doorndraai, Waterberg, who both died of measles on 1901-06-03 and Gertruida J. Prinsloo of Doorndraai, Waterberg, who died of measles on 1901-06-08 in the Irene Camp. See T. van Rensburg (ed.), *Camp diary of Henrietta E.C. Armstrong*, p 167. According to the handwritten Irene Camp Register of Residents (TAB, DBC 62), Catharina Maria Prinsloo, aged 35, of Doorndraai in the Waterberg district, lost three of her five children in the camp, namely Stephanus Johannes (6 years) on 3 June 1901, Anna Louisa (12 years) also on 3 June and Gertruida Jacoba (3 years) on 8 June 1901. The mother and her other two children survived the war.

73   Maria Elizabeth Harreen Dürr (died 1960) was the sister of Sophie Dürr who has been mentioned previously in the diary. She initially worked for the Belgian ambulance in the Anglo-Boer War before becoming a voluntary nurse in Irene. See T. van Rensburg (ed.), *Camp diary of Henrietta E.C. Armstrong*, p 96.

was over, and the tent was in an awful state. Poor Hessie and I had to clear up when the others had gone at about 10 o'clock. When I was ill someone asked me what was the matter and I said I thought I was in for "peasles", and now they tell everyone Miss van Warmelo was very ill with "peasles". One gets teased a lot in this place.

There is a mad girl in my ward – about my own age. She lies on the bed, laughing and kicking up her heels and looks like a child of twelve. Poor little thing – I felt very sorry for her and promised to bring her some sweets. My basket contains many curious things when I go to camp of a morning – ½ doz[en] candles, a few bars of soap, a bottle of castor-oil, sweet oil, brandy, cod liver oil, cough lozenges, oranges, sweets, and a host of other things – and in my pocket I have a thermometer, this fountain pen, a pencil, milk tickets and two note-books – Weary and heavy-laden am I for I often have a blanket or some flannel to carry to this or that tent and my basket is very heavy. There are many trials in this camp life of ours and the worst is that with all our work we can do so little to relieve the distress around us. That is what I feel so much – my utter helplessness.

June 5th. [1901]

Such a wasted morning! Dr G[reen] told me not to go to the camp today until he had been through the hospital wards, as he wanted to go from tent to tent with me and make a thorough investigation. I told him I would be in Klip Laar where he promised to call for me when he was ready and here I have been sitting waiting most impatiently. I suppose he has a lot to do in the hospital. There were two deaths last night and I hear that six other cases are very bad. I have been reading that vile book "Pretoria from within, during the War" by the Rev Batts,[74] to while away the time, but it has made me so furious with its lies and abominations that I feel quite upset. The man took our burgers' oath for the express purpose of spying upon us and publishing a lot of lies. He was allowed to remain in the country when every other Englishman was put over the border and was shown every consideration by our people because they were taken in by his hypocrisy and believed him to be a warm sup-

---

[74]   H.J. Batts, *Pretoria from within during the War 1899-1900* (London, 1901).

porter of our cause and this book is their reward. I intend writing him a few lines to ask why he does not publish a copy of the oath he took – it would be most interesting to the public. But on this fair morning why should I dwell upon books and men like these? It is a most perfect day and my heart is full of memories as I sit in my quiet tent and gaze upon the strange scene before me – the camp with its hundreds of tents, the distant hills covered with thousands and thousands of grazing sheep. What is it today? The memorable fifth of June, the anniversary of the British entry into Pretoria, Fritz's birthday. My poor dear brother! Where is he today and what are the scenes that surround him on this, his twenty-third birthday? My darling boy, how I love and honour him for being where he is and how proud I am when I tell people that I have a brother still on commando! The feeling that he is still fated to give his life for our land and people, is with me as strong as ever. I cannot shake it off and every thought I send out to him is one great throb of pain.

– It is getting awfully late, nearly 11.30 – where can that doctor be? I am afraid it will be quite impossible for us to get through the whole of my ward this morning. I shall get out my writing materials and begin writing letters – perhaps that will fetch him. People always come when one is fairly settled down to some definite piece of work.

Evening. Dr Green came so late for me this morning that we only had time to see the serious cases before dinner. At first he was short and snappish – I think he was worried about the hospital – but after a while he seemed to get interested in his work and even cracked a few jokes with the patients. They are so tongue-tied in his presence, one can hardly get a word out of them and he loses his patience and frightens them more than ever by speaking brusquely.

June 6th. [1901]

I have had a hard day and am weary unto death this evening. When I got up this morning I made up my mind to go from tent to tent and find out as far as possible how many destitute families there are in my ward, whose relatives are still fighting. Fortunately the Clerk of the Weather favoured me and I set forth, heavily laden, but with a light heart and enjoying the sunshine and fresh air. When once I was fairly at work I got so interested in it that I went straight on for hours, and was amazed to find the rest of the staff at dinner when I arrived at the hospital, and the hands of the clock pointing to 1.30. I did not think it was later than about 12. I gave out a pile of blankets today or flannel and warm clothing – baize for petticoats, etc – all to women whose husbands are still in the field. They are without exception the most needy, for they are persecuted by the "hands-uppers" and get the worst rations and have to shift for themselves in the matter of wood and coal – in every imaginable way their lot is made far harder to bear than that of the h[ands-]u[ppers]'s wives and families. Oh, how we loathe those hands-uppers! More than Khakis and capitalists and anything else objectionable. They are insolent and lazy – traitors to their land and people. We had a discussion at table today on the subject and Dr G[reen] was furious because I said the hands-uppers get better rations than the others and I complained of the ration of meat that was given out yesterday. None of my people could use it and I see it all over my ward hanging on the tent ropes to dry in the sun. Such miserable stuff! Not fit for a dog to eat. And the milk was so watery today – no wonder the people complain and yet Dr G[reen] was very much vexed with me for remarking upon it, but I don't care. I shall speak my mind where it is necessary but I take care not to say too much because some enemy might work me out of the camp. But this morning I fairly lost my temper. I had been into a tent where an old woman told me with floods of tears that she had eleven sons and sons-in-law still in the field and I don't know how many brothers and other relatives.[75] The place was crowded with poor ragged children, sick and hungry and the misery was so apparent that I promised them as many blankets etc as I could spare and then I went my way. In the next tent I found some very poor people, whose relatives were also fighting, but I could not account for the presence of a great fat fellow who was sprawling on the bed, so I asked his mother what <u>he</u> was doing there. She gave no answer and then he said: "*Ik het lang genoeg geveg – ik het mij kom oôr-gee*"; *maar toen was die gort gaar!* "*Lang genoeg geveg!*"[76] I snorted with rage, "*dit is door zulkes zoo's jij dat die oorlog nog aan die gang is – dat onze arme vrouwen en kinders in kampen is en dood gaan van ellende. Als onze*

---

75   In her book *Het Concentratie-kamp van Iréne*, p 49, the diarist identifies this elderly woman as Mrs Prinsloo.

76   "I fought long enough – I came in to surrender myself"; but then the fat was in the fire! "Fought long enough!"

mans mooi samen gestaan het dan was die Engelsman lang al uitgegooi. Lang genoeg geveg! Umph!"[77] and I cought up my basket and flounced out of the tent. But afterwards I was sorry, or rather sore afraid of the consequences. Only once before had I forgotten myself and was priding myself on my great prudence and now I have spoilt it all. On that occasion I entered a tent and asked whether there was any sickness. The answer was no, all well, and I was just going out when a young hands-upper enquired with a most fetching smile whether sister would nurse him if he got ill. The sister's answer was short and very crushing, *"Ik pas nie een hands-upper op nie!"*[78] But I do, worse luck.

June 7th. [1901]

Yes, I was in a hands-upper tent this very morning. A man ran after me and took me to one of those large marquées [sic], swarming with vermin – I mean, men, – and there I found a fellow groaning with pain. I took his name and promised to send the doctor and then I fled looking neither to the right nor to the left. I was interrupted last night just as I was on the point of relating something very interesting. Dear diary, the Boers were in the camp the night before last. Six or seven of them paid a visit to our little apothecary, Dirkse,[79] and told him the latest war news and then they went to the railway station where they damaged the telegraph wires. Dirkse told me all about their visit yesterday afternoon, when I went to the dispensary to have a few prescriptions made up. They say de la Rey has had a terrible battle! Mrs Stiemens got a letter from Pretoria this morning in which this battle is mentioned. Heavy losses on both sides, they say. And they also say that nearly 100 men have escaped from Pretoria since I went away. ⁻ But I am much distressed about something. The Pretoria ladies who come every Friday –

June 8th. [1901]

I was interrupted as usual yesterday and must really try to get some writ-

---

[77] "it is because of people like you that the war is still going on – that our poor women and children are in camps and die of misery. If all our men stood together we would have thrown the English out long ago. Fought long enough! Ugh!"
[78] "I do not take care of any hands-upper!"
[79] No particulars on him could be traced.

ing done this evening although it is bitterly cold and I can hardly hold my pen. There is a piercing wind blowing that seems to cut one in two and I am dreading having to go to our tent from the marquée, which is comparatively warm. I have much news to tell – some of it very sad – but first let me finish with yesterday's experiences.

Camp scene in Irene

We were all looking forward to receiving letters and parcels as usual every Friday and to our disappointment the ladies arrived from Pretoria without anything. But when we heard the reason we were quite anxious. Miss Eloff told me that as she was getting into the train at Pretoria a little boy from Mrs Malan handed her some letters for us, which she put into her hand-bag. When she was in the train an officer came up to her and said, "You have letters in that bag". Poor girl, what could she do? She gave them all to him and was told to call for them at the Charge Office on her return from Irene, which means getting into hot water – or being reprimanded – according to the contents of the letters. I am quite sure there were some for me – one from Fred [Niemeyer], I suppose, and he writes such dreadfully indiscreet letters. Miss E[loff] promised to let me know how it passed off – we hastily arranged a little code at the Station when I went to see her off. When I came home from the Station a man ran after me and begged me to go into one of the large marquées, where a man was very ill. I went and found a "hands-upper" groaning in great pain – he seemed to be suffering from colic, so I went to look for a doctor – found Dandy, who immediately offered to go with me. He examined the man and said he had a stone in the bladder, so we came to the hospital and Dandy went back with an injection of morphia, which at least, gave the man a good night's rest. I suppose the stone will have to be removed. It was quite dark when I got to my tent and there I found more work. Someone in my ward was in great pain – a man called Prinsloo,[80] and he sent his son for a mustard poultice. I had to go and make that and go back to the camp to see my patient. And so it goes on all day. Our tents are always being stormed by all sorts and conditions of people with all sorts and conditions of complaints, and one has to be patient and considerate to all, in spite of weariness and ill-health. I am not feeling very bright today – had a little fever again and my throat is sore – but I daresay it is nothing. Dandy went to Pretoria on business this morning and will be back tomorrow by the first train. Miss Dürr is working in the hospital now because they were short of hands and we five have each taken over some of her rows in the camp, until someone from Pretoria comes to take her place. I have two rows of about 30 tents each and I have been worked to death the last two days and yet my own ward has been neglected. In her ward a little girl is dying of measles and this morning the mother, Mrs Wolmarans,[81] told me that her husband and two sons were still fighting. I told her how glad I was to hear it and

---

[80] Not identified. According to the handwritten Irene Camp Register of Residents (TAB, DBC 62) there were at least nine adult men with the surname Prinsloo with their families (including sons) in the camp at that time.

[81] According to official sources the only Wolmarans child that died in the Irene Camp was Cornelia P. Wolmarans (6 years) of Smitkop who passed away on 1901-06-17 of measles and bronchitis. See T. van Rensburg (ed.), *Camp diary of Henrietta E.C. Armstrong*, p 189. See also diary entry on 1901-06-17, where the diarist writes about the death of Mrs Wolmarans' little girl but calls her Jacoba Wolmarans. The handwritten Irene Camp Register of Residents (TAB, DBC 62) also mentions only one Wolmarans child that died in the Irene Camp, namely Cornelis Petrus (3 years). The mother was Johanna Christina Wolmarans (44 years) of Smitsdorp, who arrived in the camp on 26 April 1901 with her four children, including a daughter, Catharina Jacoba (10 years).

how I honoured her for being so brave under all her troubles and then she said she would not own any of her relatives who came to surrender and she told me how she had fled from Smitsdorp[82] with four little children, from the kaffirs; how she was exposed to heavy rains night and day and how they had to sleep under trees and bushes, for three days. This afternoon I went to see her little girl again and found the tent filled with weeping women and children. At first I thought the child was dead, but on entering I saw her lying on the bed as usual and then the poor mother told me her awful news. She says that soon after I left her this morning she received a letter saying that her husband and one son had fallen in one of the recent engagements. It was a terrible work trying to soothe the broken-hearted woman and I sat there sobbing with her, by the bedside of her dying child. I have not felt so utterly unnerved for a long time.

June 9th. [1901]

After yesterday's adventures I have had an unusually restful day. I could not finish writing last night because it was too cold so I did not mention the most exciting event of the day. We heard cannon firing in the direction of Johannesburg early in the morning, and towards 10 o'clock I noticed some "things" coming over the hills. We watched them and as I went from tent to tent I heard many strange remarks. Some thought they were Boers, others said they were prisoners and the general opinion was that they were Khakis. The last surmise proved to be the correct one and when they came nearer it was evident that they were Khakis, in full flight, judging by the way they came straggling in, in two and threes. All morning they came in, carts and waggons [sic], horses etc. and encamped on the hill opposite the camp – such a medley, in the greatest disorder apparently – and this morning at dawn they all disappeared again. There have been great fights all over the country – according to the rumours that reach us. I wish we could get some reliable news again. This morning Dandy came back from Pretoria – walked in while we were at breakfast, and said Annie Rood intended coming to Irene today, but as it was so windy he persuaded her to stay at home. I was

---

82   A hamlet that served as the administrative centre of the Soutpansberg Gold Fields, some 15 kilometres south of Pietersburg in the Northern Transvaal.

rather disappointed because I fully expected visitors today and Dandy was so serious that I never suspected anything and was surprised and delighted to find Annie and Miss Zeederberg[83] in my tent after breakfast. I chatted with them a little and then went to my ward, where I worked until dinner time, doing all my work, in order to be free in the afternoon. At 2.30 a whole party of us went for a walk in the Irene plantations, where we spent a most delight full [sic] afternoon. I have not enjoyed such a rest and recreation from my labours since I came here and it did me a world of good. We were a very happy party and I felt thankful and relieved to escape, if only for a few hours, from sickness and sorrow and Death. When we came back to the hospital we had tea and cake and sweets in Klip Laar and then we all went to the Station to see our visitors off. We came home quite late but I had a few neglected duties to perform so I went to the camp, with candles, milk and blankets. Hessie offered to go with me because it was so dark and then three young men, who work in the little shop that has been erected in the camp by Poynton Bros.,[84] and who sometimes pay us a visit, asked permission to carry my parcels, so the five of us set off on our strange errand. I went to see that poor Mrs Wolmarans and she told me some particulars of the terrible tidings that reached her yesterday. She says there is no doubt about her husband's death but the son may be some other Wolmarans. Her husband was with General Beyers and the man who wrote to tell the news, Potgieter, was a great friend of his and they were always together. Her little girl was not quite so bad this evening. Dr G[reen] seems to think there is just the shadow of a chance for her – but I am afraid not. I had a death in my ward this afternoon a girl of 12 or 14, Snyman.[85] She has been ailing a long time but she seemed to me half crazy – quite deaf and unable to say much – so when they told me she was worse, I did not report it to the doctor and, I am sorry to

---

83   Not identified.
84   In March 1901 a tender by Poynton Bros, a company based in Church Street West in Pretoria, to establish a shop selling general merchandise in the Irene camp, was accepted and soon afterwards this, the only shop in the camp, was opened for business. See J.L. Hattingh, *Die Irenekonsentrasiekamp*, p 145; and *Longland's Pretoria Directory for 1899*, p 34.
85   Catharina Aletta Snyman (13 years) of Kameelpoort, Pretoria. She died of measles and pneumonia. See T. van Rensburg (ed.), *Camp diary of Henrietta E.C. Armstrong*, p 174.

say, forgot all about it, and this morning I was much concerned to find her on the point of death. But for her it is a happy release.

June 10th. [1901]

Last night at about 10 o'clock when Hessie and I came to bed I suddenly heard the distant roar of cannon – <u>distinctly</u>. I told Hessie and we listened intently but of course she could hear nothing, but I heard it again and again, and we two sat looking at one another, too excited and restless to undress. We wondered what it was and what was going to happen, but after a while the sounds died away and only the wind was to be heard. But for me there was no rest and I lay awake for hours thinking over the events of the last two exciting years. There is no describing the sensations roused by the roar of cannon at night – I have never experienced anything like it and hope never to go through it again. We think an attempt was made to capture the cattle and sheep near Irene and that the Boers were beaten back. Miss F[indlay] says that while we were in the marquée [sic], before we came to bed, she distinctly heard several maxim volleys, as well as heavy cannon, and this morning the old man at the dispensary said he saw search-lights last night in the direction of the firing – out Johannesburg way. I have had a very hard day's work – did 60 tents in Miss Dürr's ward and 60 in my own before dinner and afterwards I went through the rest of my ward, but there are a great many new arrivals, to whom I have not been yet. They came this afternoon – I saw the poor things standing about, before the empty tents, with their boxes and bedding. I shall have more work to do than I can manage if someone does not come soon to take charge of Miss Dürr's ward. A great many prisoners passed through this afternoon on their way to Bombay. One of my poor old women rushed out of her tent and told me with tears that some of her relatives and friends had passed and were gone before she could see them.

Jun 11th. [1901]

What a glorious morning – what a perfect day! We had a little rain during the night and this morning the air is pure and sweet and fresh, and everything is so wonderfully serene that I can hardly believe this is Irene. I have been through about 60 tents and now it is 11.30 and I am sitting in my own tent waiting for Dr G[reen] who is going round my ward with me presently. I asked him to do so because there is a lot of sickness in my ward and I am rather anxious about some of my patients. While we were at breakfast this morning a boy died in the hospital, Gert Smit.[86] There have been a great many deaths lately. A new English nurse arrived this morning – a Mrs Fry.[87] She looks very nice and has a sweet voice and refined manners – rather a contrast to the other two. Last night when I came to bed I found our tent decorated with large advertisement pictures – a huge Bovril in crimson and white is hanging at the foot of my bed – the work of Dr Dandy while we were sitting in the marquée [sic]. There was also a tin of biscuits lying on my bed, which we appreciated very much. He is so funny sometimes – there are always peals of laughter in his neighbourhood. I think we would be very dreary without him – he is the only one who keeps us from moping when our day's work is done.

The Superintendent, Scholtz, wants to turn us out of our tents, which he says he requires for new arrivals. He will give us one of those large marquées [sic], but we are not all in favour of it, so I drew up a list of the conditions under which we consent to give up our privacy. Some of them were as follows: not more than six in the marquée [sic]; cocoa-nut matting on the floor; a table and lamp and curtains for a partition between the sleeping and sitting apartments. Then we want a separate bell-tent to use as store and bath-room. He was rather insolent – the great, mean Jingo, and said he would give us all the "sjam-bok"[88] in turn and afterwards he asked sarcastically whether we would not each like a whole marquée [sic]. I told him that no one had a right to turn us out of our tents and nothing would induce us to give them up, unless he promised to fulfil all our conditions. We have heard no more about it, so I don't know what he is going to do. He would give anything to get rid of us all.

What we have great difficulty with is in trying to induce people to send the serious cases up to the hospital. The Boers are all in mortal

---

86 According to official sources Gert Smit (4 years and 6 months) of Nylstroom died of whooping-cough. See T. van Rensburg (ed.), *Camp diary of Henrietta E.C. Armstrong*, p 172.

87 Sister Fry was a trained nurse who worked in the hospital under the supervision of Sister Walsh. See J.L. Hattingh, *Die Irenekonsentrasiekamp*, p 151.

88 "horsewhip"

dread of it and think that no one comes out of it alive – that the patients are starved to death, because we refuse to give typhoid patients solid food. Mrs Armstrong once had a typhoid patient in the camp and she never could understand his temperature, it was so erratic. He was at death's door for a long time but managed to pull through and when he had quite recovered, they told her <u>they</u> had saved his life by giving him meat and bread when she was not there. And the worst of it is that the relations and friends of patients in hospital smuggle food in when no one is looking. Sister W[alsh] showed me a few days ago, a dirty red handkerchief containing a few bits of tough meat; some sweets and <u>pastry</u>, which she found under the pillow of an enteric patient. Is it not terrible? One cannot help losing one's patience at the ignorance of some of these people and I am not at all surprised that most English doctors and nurses can't get on with them.

June 12th. [1901]

Today I have been here exactly one month and Hessie and I celebrated the event by going for a walk through the beautiful plantations, when our work was done this afternoon. We took some books, sweets and cakes (one <u>must</u> eat here at all hours of the day) and had a glorious half hour of perfect quiet. The sunset was magnificent and I enjoyed the beauty of nature to the full – one could have a lovely holiday here if there were no "refugees" and no misery. But I ought to go to sleep now – it is long past 11 and I have a lot to do tomorrow. We have a new doctor, Dr Woodriffe,[89] I think his name is. We are trying to find out what his position here is – is he coming in the place of "Oliver Twist" (Dr Green) or Dandy, or are we going to have <u>three</u> doctors? No one seems to know exactly and no one likes to ask.

June 13th. [1901]

Oh, I wish I could always be patient! I am so sorry whenever I have been sharp with any of our poor people and yet one cannot possibly know always whether cases are deserving or not. There are so many

---

[89]   George Borries Woodroffe (1869-1923) took over as medical doctor in Irene Concentration Camp from Dr Green. See T. van Rensburg (ed.), *Camp diary of Henrietta E.C. Armstrong,* p 100.

greedy people, who beg for all sorts of things and come with pitiful tales and often one cannot find out whether there is any truth in them. One cannot distribute groceries etc indiscriminately and yet I am so afraid of sending away empty someone who really requires my help. This morning I began work very early and managed to do three rows thoroughly before dinner, found one tent with eleven people down with measles and two or three other serious cases, which I reported to the doctor as "urgent". One girl had a temperature of 106.2[90] at which I was rather alarmed and yet, when I went there this afternoon, she was sitting up, drinking coffee and eating bread, just like any other mortal. Of course I bundled her back to bed at once, but I daresay I shall find her eating meat, or something equally good for fever, tomorrow. The amount of measles in my ward today is astonishing. This afternoon I finished off three more rows and came home when it was pitch dark. I suppose the fresh air agrees with me – at least, I don't get tired at all and must go to the camp again after supper, to see a dying child. And the way we eat! Hessie and I make three hearty meals every day and nibble at biscuits and sweets at all hours of the day. It seems as if we can never get enough to eat. Dandy presented me with a brooch, carved out of stone, representing faith, hope and charity and with my name "Joy" across it. It was done by one of the men in camp and is a beautiful little memento of my Irene experiences. We have all sorts of curios – silver rings made out of shillings by the prisoners who have returned from Green Point, ties, knives etc, etc. I am ordering a lot of things as I want to take some curios with me when I go to Europe.

We have someone in Miss Dürr's place now – Mrs Preller[91] – so I have only my own ward to attend to and consequently can do it far better. Dr Green is leaving tomorrow – now we know why a new doctor arrived upon the scenes so unexpectedly.

---

[90] ± 41.2° C

[91] Johanna Christina Preller (1878-1975) was the wife of the well-known historian Gustav Preller and daughter of Lieutenant-Colonel Henning Pretorius, who was the first head of the State Artillery of the South African Republic. Her grandmother on her father's side was Deborah Pretorius (born Retief), a daughter of the Great Trek leader Piet Retief. In later life she achieved national prominence as one of the three women who lay the foundation stone of the Voortrekker Monument in Pretoria. See T. van Rensburg (ed.), *Camp diary of Henrietta E.C. Armstrong*, p 98n.

June 14th. [1901]

Last night I went to the camp again after dark, with Miss Findlay for a companion, and when we came back we found some visitors – three young men from Poynton's "store" – and we all went down to the plantation, a party of ten, to see the teachers of the school. None of us knew where the house was and no one knew the countersign and we had no permit to go beyond the boundaries, so we prepared ourselves for adventures. When we came near the first outpost we were stopped by a "Halt! Who goes there?" "Friend",

Mrs Preller (Photo in later life)

we answered. "Advance and give the countersign", was the order and Dandy went forward and explained our difficulties to the man. He went into a tent to fetch the corporal and he allowed us to pass. But we could not find the house. The plantation was very dark and we enquired at two places but no one seemed to know where the cottage was in which the teachers lived. At last it struck someone that it was not in the plantation at all, but somewhere near the camp, where a small house had been seen lying amongst some trees, so off we set again and eventually found the place. It was 8.30 then and our hostesses had given us up and thought the Boers were coming when they heard us tramping round the house. We only stayed about half and hour and in coming back had more encounters with the sentries. One of them held his fixed bayonet on Dandy's breast because he was not able to give the countersign and was politely told to go to the dickens. When we got back to the hospital we were all very thirsty with the long tramps so Hessie and I went to the kitchen and made no less than 12 cups of cocoa. I used a tin of milk and half a tin of cocoa and worried rather over the extravagance of it, when so many poor people are without luxuries, but after all it seldom happens and we deserve something for our hard work.

Yesterday was one of my most trying days. I was on my feet from 7.30 a.m. till about 10.30 p.m. and only sat down to meals and had an hour's rest after dinner. This morning when I got up my ankles were so swollen that I could hardly walk, but I had to go to work as usual and the stiffness went over after a time. It is a wonder we don't get our feet and legs sore with all the trotting about over stones and rough ground. There are so sad cases that come under our notice now-a-days. It appears that Mrs Wolmarans' husband is dead, but the man they thought was her son, turns out to be another Wolmarans – Frederik, his name was. His widow is here and she has already lost two children at Irene.[92] Another woman received news of the death of her husband – he was run over by a waggon [sic], when he was taking a herd of cattle to some place of safety. A Mrs Drummond in the camp has lost four children within the last fortnight.[93] When one hears all these heart-rending accounts of suffering and death, one cannot help wondering why it all should be. I was feeling very bitter and rebellious last night as I was coming home in the dark, so weary and so sad, and then I passed a tent from whence issued the strains of a hymn. I stopped to listen and my ears caught this refrain – "*en het eind zal zeker zalig zijn*"[94], sung so sweetly and feelingly that the fount of my tears was opened and I sobbed out there in the cold and dark, tears of relief and resignation and hope. *En het eind zal zeker zalig zijn* – I must remember that and cling to it in days of darkness and doubt. "I cling to Thee – we cling to one another". That is the motto of the Irene Volunteer Nursing Staff and our badge is a simple spray of ivy. We are all to be seen wearing ivy and Hessie and I have even decorated our tent with long, trailing tendrils of the same. Over my bed on the tent walls, is a horse-shoe for luck, at the foot, my initials and when next we go to the plantation we are going to bring enough ivy to put "Klip Laar" in letters of green just opposite the entrance. As I sit here I am in a perfect bower – ivy all round me, creeping round the tent-pole, over the sides of the tent, round my looking-glass. The effect is exceedingly artistic and "Klip Laar" is the wonder and admiration of

---

[92]   No mention of those children could be found in official sources on the Irene Camp. See T. van Rensburg (ed.), *Camp diary of Henrietta E.C. Armstrong*, Appendix A.

[93]   The four children were Gertruida (2 years and 6 months) and Christina (9 months) who both died on 5 June, Anna (7 years and 6 months) who died on 9 June and John (4 years and 6 months) who died on 11 June. See T. van Rensburg (ed.), *Camp diary of Henrietta E.C. Armstrong*, p 140.

[94]   "The end will surely be blessed."

all. I wish the other girls would follow suit. If they don't, I think Hessie and I must make time some day to go to the plantation and get enough ivy for all the tents – it is great fun decorating them and it is done very quickly and I really think the trouble fully repaid by the effect. There is so little in our present lives that is lovely and refined that we ought to do what we can to keep ourselves from losing sight of the poetry of life. We have no music and we never had time to read so, if we don't care, we shall deteriorate altogether, although I must say I manage to discover a good deal of hidden poetry in some of the most distressing surroundings. That woman, for instance, ministering to the wants of <u>eleven</u> down with measles, two women and nine children in one tent. She has just recovered from measles herself and is still weak and now she is the only one of the family up and about and she has to nurse them <u>all</u>. And yet she never complains and has never once asked me for anything and I know they are frightfully poverty-stricken. I gave her candles, soap, blankets, barley, milk, castor-oil etc. etc. and she is very grateful for all I do for her and yet I have the greatest difficulty in finding out what she requires most. I wish I had a camera and could take a few snap-shots of these over-crowded tents – this one particular case is unique in its way. I can't help laughing when I go into it – I have to look for a bit of free ground to put my feet on and as to going to each patient in turn – it is an impossibility, there is no reaching some of them. I hope they will all recover. We had one very interesting case this afternoon. One of my patients, a young woman, Mrs Polderman,[95] has been going down to the dispensary lately to see Dr Neethling about an abscess that seemed to be forming under her tongue. He told her to come again when it was more developed, but yesterday and this morning she was in so much pain and so terribly exhausted by want of food that she was not fit to go to the dispensary. I found her in high fever this morning and suffering agonies. Her tongue was so stiff that she could hardly speak a word and she had not been able to take nourishment for two days and nights, so I offered to bring the doctor. When I saw him after dinner he said he remembered the case and thought he would have to give her

[95] Probably Anna Helena Polderman (26 years) of Wagendrift, Pretoria, who arrived in the Irene Camp on 6 May 1901 with her two sons, of whom one died on 22 August 1901. See TAB, DBC 62 Irene Camp Register of Residents.

chloroform as an operation was necessary. He thought it was not an abscess at all but a salt formation – called <u>calculus</u>[96] – something very rare. Dr G[reen] laughed at the idea and said it was nothing but an abscess. Well. I was just going, with two men and a stretcher, to bring her up to the hospital when someone came running up to say that a funny little stone had jumped out of her mouth and she was all right. The doctors wanted to see her so Dandy and Dr Woodriffe [sic] and I went to her at once and found her able to speak and swallow and in little or no pain. We examined the thing, an oblong, yellowish formation, the shape and size of a date-stone and very hard; the finest specimen, Dandy says, that he has seen outside of a museum. He asked to be allowed to keep it and is going to send it to the Edinburgh Museum. The doctors say I am very lucky in having had an experience of this sort, for one seldom come across it – not once in a lifetime as a rule. This is Dandy's second "calculus", and very proud he is of it.

Now we are all going to the station to see off our Pretoria visitors – our work is done for the day and this is our free afternoon; at least, we are free earlier on Fridays, because of the visitors who come regularly once a week. Dr Green is also leaving this afternoon.

June 15th. [1901]

This has been an unusually tiring day and I am more fit for bed than anything else, but I must make a few entries in this book of mine – it worries me when I miss even one day. Let me see, where did I leave off? We went to the Station, a large party of us, and gave Dr Green a hearty send-off. Now that he has gone we are all sorry. After all, he was not a bad fellow, though I used to get very impatient at his slowness and unpunctuality. He said something very gratifying when we bade him goodbye – thanked us all for our help and said he thought us "wonderful girls" for working so hard and doing so much good.[97]

---

[96] Calculus – a stone or concretion of minerals formed within the body. See *The Concise Oxford Dictionary of Current English*, Ninth Edition, Oxford, 1995.

[97] These were not vain words. In his "Medical Report on Refugee Camp, Irene" Dr Green wrote on 4 June 1901: "Six ladies from Pretoria who are voluntary workers visit in the Camp and live in tents. The Camp is divided into wards and each lady takes a ward and visits every tent in the morning and then reports to the Medical Officer on the serious cases, and does

- Miss Eloff told me that she went to the Charge Office for the letters and they were handed to her, unopened, by an officer, whose eyes twinkled mischievously and who told her "never to do so again". She promised and went on her way rejoicing. There were no letters for me. I got one from Mama last night in which she says she has been very bad with one of her attacks of bronchitis and she had no one to look after her, no one to bring her a cup of tea or a little soup and of course she missed me very much. I was awfully worried to think of her being ill but she is better again, so I need not go home just yet. I think it is a good thing she is learning to appreciate me a little – I am afraid my Mammie looks upon it as a matter of course that I should be tied to her apron strings and yet when I am with her she often talks as if she could do just as well without me. My feelings have so often been hurt on the subject of my "uselessness" that it is no wonder I can't tear myself away from a place where I know my services are required and where all I do is highly appreciated. Of course if Mama gets really ill I shall go to her at once even if I have to leave all my patients in the lurch. Charity begins at home and my first duty is there, of that there can be no doubt.

Last night late I went to see my most serious case, a young man called Engelbrecht[98], very bad with double pneumonia. His mother won't hear of having him removed to the hospital so we are trying to save him under most unfavourable circumstances. They have two tents, one for sleeping in and one "living-room" and I was horrified to hear that eight others shared the tent with him at night. I told the woman that if she wants to save him he must be alone with her and people are not to walk in at all hours of the day, so now the others sleep in their dining-room and they can consider themselves lucky that they have another place to go to. In most tents there are two, sometimes more, families. Poor anxious mother! I need not be afraid that she will disobey any of my orders. My slightest wish seems to be her law and she looks at me

what nursing for the sick she can. These ladies do their work well and it would be difficult and impossible for the present Medical Staff to do their work without them, as at present it is quite impossible for the Medical Officer to visit even the most serious cases more than once in two or three days, and in the meantime the ladies have to look after and report on the cases ..." See TAB, DBC (box 11), General Monthly Reports (Burgher Camps Department), 1901 May – Nov, unsorted files).
98   Not identified.

with worshipping eyes, full of gratitude, and I feel that days of weariness and sorrow are fully repaid by one single instance like this. And, thank God, there are <u>many</u> of them. But now there is an element in our harmonious circle – a note of discord – that troubles me. Two of us are inclined to be light and frivolous and their influence is having effect unfortunately. I shall not mention names – the staff is small and we hoped would remain select, but these two spoil everything. They want us continually to have sort of frivolity in the evenings and I am writing in our tent because the marquée [sic] is the scene of an uproarious game of cards. Last night we were all invited to the store by the three young men who act as "counter-jumpers". We all went – doctors and nurses – and I must say our hosts did all they could to make our evening pleasant but I felt miserably ashamed of myself and hoped no one would ever know I had been there. A vulgar-looking fellow sang comic songs and scraped a violin and another one recited a poem and then we all had cocoa and biscuits. At 8.30 one of the corporals hammered at the door and ordered silence, so the music came to an end to the great relief of some of us. Dandy was quiet and seemed depressed – he said afterwards that he was thinking of home. On our way back a policeman stopped us and wanted to know what we were doing out after nine, but allowed us to pass when he saw the doctors and our red crosses. I find I can go <u>anywhere</u> with the red X on my arm. So much for yesterday. I hope we shall not have more of that nonsense. We have come out here to work and our evenings must be used for rest or some profitable recreation. In consequence of this "dissipation" I find that I have not been getting enough sleep. Hessie and I feel tired every morning when we get up and we tire more quickly during the day than we used to. I suppose that is why today has tried me so much. I feel thoroughly "*bek af*"[99] tonight, but it has really been a very hard day. The first thing I heard was that one of my children had died during the night quite suddenly. I went to the tent at once and was terribly cut up to find that it was a little thing of two years, that has been suffering from fever and the worst of it is that the mother, Mrs Nel had lost a girl of 16 last week.[100] Her husband and

---

[99]   "down-hearted"
[100] Alleta Nel (16 years) died on 7 June and Barendina Fredrika Nel (2 years), of Loekasrus, Zoutpansberg, died on 15 June. See T. van Rensburg (ed.), *Camp diary of Henrietta E.C. Armstrong*, p 159.

two sons have been captured and she does not even know where they are, and four of her children are down with measles, one very bad.

A mother with her last surviving child, Irene

Of course I have done all I could to help her but the poor soul is in unspeakable distress – simply heart-rending. I took the doctor there but it was one of the saddest things I have ever seen – the tiny, silent form, lying wrapped up in a blanket on a coffer on one side of the tent, and on the other the four wailing, fretful children clamouring for water or milk and the poor demented mother in the midst of it all, grieving for the dead, anxious about the sick, torn with doubts about the fate of husband and sons. Oh God, oh God – and there are <u>thousands</u> of similar cases and there may be many more before this bitter strife comes to an end. I dare not on it all [sic] – especially this evening.

Dr Woodriffe [sic] had to be introduced to his patients this morning. I took him to about 8 serious cases, but there are a great many more for which we had no time. He had to go round with three of the other girls as well and has the hospital wards under his care. He is very nice indeed to the patients – very considerate and kind and seems to understand the people well. I hope he will go on like this. What I like about him is that he explains things to me and gives me many hints and directions and seems pleased when I ask him any questions. I shall learn a great deal from him. I worked until pitch dark today and even then I did not go near two whole rows – there was so much to do – such a lot of new cases. Nearly every tent has measles.

There was heavy firing heard in the Johannesburg direction yesterday at about 10 or 11 a.m. and in the evening the search-lights were playing all over the country and cattle and sheep were driven near the camp. The Boers are near us I suppose. There Mrs Vlok is calling me. It is her birthday and they are all in her tent eating and drinking and making merry. It seems unkind not to go – I shall just show myself for a little while and come to bed.

Sunday night. June 16th. [1901]

Five weeks at Irene today! Is it possible? How the weeks have flown and yet how <u>very</u> much have I not seen and learnt and suffered in that time. I did not think I would be able to stand a whole month and here I find myself over my time and most unwilling to go home. I wonder now how much longer the mother will be able to miss me. I have been working the greater part of this Sabbath, but this afternoon Miss F[indlay] and I managed to escape for an hour or two and we went to the plantation and roamed about there to our heart's content. How sweet and serene it was and how much good it did us. Visitors are not allowed to pick flowers on the estate but we were very naughty. We each gathered a bunch of violets and ferns and while we were busy an officer came strolling along – a dear old colonel – and he opened one of the conservatories for us and told us he would look another way while the pilfering was going on. On our way home we found Dandy sitting under the trees and I gave him a button-hole and he took us to some lovely secluded spots and was perfectly charming. I always like him so much when he is alone with one or two of us and in his serous moods. He is a little too frivolous when is with the two gay ones of our party. It was dark when I came home and I found a whole "commando" of men, women and children round Klip Laar, one for soap, another for candles, a third for cod-liver oil. The doctor told me that he had seen my poor little Dannie Cameron[101] and

---

[101]   Edward D.D. Cameron of Nylstroom (3 years) died on 17 June of measles and bronchitis. See T. van Rensburg (ed.), *Camp diary of Henrietta E.C. Armstrong,* p 135.

that he had told the parents that there was "no hope". I was so cut up to hear it that I went to them at once and found them all kneeling around the bed, praying and weeping. Poor souls, poor souls! How they adore the little fellow with his sweet face and winsome manners and what a little wreck he is! For the past few days he has been a little brighter and we were all so hopeful and suddenly this afternoon a change for the worse took place and I doubt whether he will live through the night. I took him some brandy and eggs and placed a few flowers in the wee, wasted hand. He was beyond speech but looked his thanks, my poor little favourite. May the Friend of our suffering little ones fold him close to His loving breast! And from there I went to the bedside of another dying child – Mrs Wolmarans's little girl. She has been ill 18 days and for a few days we had some hope, as in Dannie's case, but now she is going fast – going to the father who so nobly gave his life for land and people not ten days ago. One does not mind the <u>death</u> of these children, but oh, the suffering that goes before and the misery of the mothers! How our women have to endure in these days of desolation and bereavement – and they are so patient and resigned. It astonishes me and I marvel at it – each day it is a fresh revelation to me and I thank God for it. These women are the wives and mothers of Transvaal's lion-hearted men, who are in the field today against such fearful odds, in the face of so much privation and danger. I worship them – <u>they</u> are my heroes, my ideals, and some day I hope I shall have the chance of choosing a husband from their ranks.

Today I was in a tent, ministering to the wants of some poor sufferer, when I heard the sound of many footsteps passing. I went out to see what it was and this was the sight that met my eyes; a large coffin on a bier, carried by a six men – another large coffin, with the tiniest one I have ever seen, beside it – mother and child – another middle-sized one and lastly a child's coffin, five in all. And then came a crowd of people and some men carrying spades. My feelings were almost too much for me, for this goes on day after day and it is terrible to think of the wholesale extermination of our race, not only on the battle-field, but in camps, where women and children die of neglect and exposure.

June 17th. [1901]

The others are playing whist in the marquée [sic] and I have stolen away to the peace and solitude of my tent in order to write down the events of the day. I never write in my diary before the others because I always have to collect my thoughts – an impossibility when the others are laughing and joking around me. Besides I am so often plunged in the deepest melancholy and my eyes are so often blinded by tears while writing, that I prefer being alone. It does not matter when I am cheerful and have nothing sad to relate but generally my experiences are of the worst. Tonight my whole soul is filled with horror at something I heard this morning. A woman in my ward, Mrs ter Blanche, fled from the kaffirs not seven weeks ago, but she was overtaken by two fiends and what happened I cannot relate here – there are things, awful things in this life of ours, that one cannot speak about. She was in delicate health at the time and endured – oh God, what did she not endure? and at 4.30 this afternoon she gave birth to a lovely little baby girl.[102] I have been with her often during the last month but never a word did she tell me; she always sat there brooding, brooding and this morning an old woman told me the story and asked me to help the poor soul with a few necessaries. I have just come from there after seeing that she had everything for the night. She is doing better than anyone expected and I told her to get well for her dear husband's sake as well a for the sake of the children – this is the fourth, I believe, and her husband is still fighting. If the English would wipe the kaffirs off the face of the earth, it would be better than murdering their white brothers – but what is the use of talking of impossibilities – we must just try and be resigned to the inevitable.

My day began with two deaths, my poor little Dannie Cameron and Jacoba Wolmarans.[103] Dannie died soon after I left him last night – I went to see him this morning, poor little wasted face, so still and white,

---

[102]   In her book *Het Concentratie-kamp van Iréne*, p 72, the diarist recorded that the baby did not survive. The woman probably was Christina Catharina Terblanche (31 years) of Sterkfontein, Pietersburg. She arrived in the Irene Camp on 30 May 1901 with four children and on 1 July 1901 a fifth child named Hester Helena is recorded in the Camp Register. This child died on 3 September 1901. See TAB, DBC 62, Irene Camp Register of Residents.

[103]   See diary entry on 1901-06-08.

so unlike his usual cheeriness. What a child that was! and how everyone loved him! I had no time to go to Mrs Wolmarans this morning after we received the death notice, but late this evening I went down to her. She is subject to fits and I found her in one of them, the tent full of men and women, chafing her hands and feet. I quickly ran up to the hospital for brandy and the doctor went to her, but I do not know how she is now. Poor woman, while the child lived she bore up bravely, even under the blow of her husband's death, but now that the funeral is over and her arms empty, she breaks down and her life is despaired of. I always admired her strength and courage and her marvellous powers of endurance, but nearly three weeks of watching and weeping have been too much for her. One wonders what is to become of her fatherless little ones if she too is to be taken from them, but we must just trust them to the care of our Heavenly Father.

It is too cold to write in my tent so I must go to the marquee, but first let me tell you, dear diary, of some excitement we have had since yesterday. The Boers are quite close by and yesterday afternoon they captured about 400 horses just beyond the rise and they took a lot of donkeys and cattle. A boy of about 12 Bernard Steenekamp,[104] told me this morning that he was in the hollow yesterday afternoon, with a little nigger boy, watching about 50 donkeys and a great many more horses and cattle when two Boers rode up, one on Erasmus's beautiful black steed that was stolen out of the stable some time ago, and ordered the little nigger to drive the animals on to where <u>they</u> wanted them. The boy they said could go home and take their compliments to all the "*mooi nooiens*"[105] in the camp. Nigger returned late last night, weary and footsore. The other Boers, who stole the 400 horses, took the two fat and well-favoured horses from the kaffirs who were in charge, and sent them home with the news, on two lean and very ill-favoured beasts. v[an] d[er] Walt,[106] our "tiger", told me he saw them in the camp this morning. I think it great fun. This morning at about 12 am two heavy shots were fired – I thought from one of the forts, but the others say they were

---

104   Possibly Barend Steenkamp of Honingneskraal, Pretoria, who was 11 years old when he arrived in the Irene Camp with his mother and brothers on 2 March 1901. See TAB, DBC 62, Irene Camp Register of Residents.

105   "lovely girls"

106   Not identified.

dynamite explosions. I heard a few volleys of distant cannon at about dinner time – very heavy. And now for the marquée [sic].

June 18[th.] [1901]

been another of those busy, worrying days and I am not nearly through with my work yet. Miss F[indlay] and I are going after supper to visit a few of my most serious cases and take them some necessaries for the night. This morning I went through about 70 tents. In one of them I found a baby just dying[107] – there was a terrible scene. The poor mother lost all control over herself and her wails brought all the neighbours flocking in. It was terrible to see the poor little thing in its dying agonies, gasping for breath and rolling up its eyes, and we watched its struggles growing fainter and an infinite calm settling on the white little face. I was quite thankful when at last all was still and we closed its eyes and folded the chubby little arms on its breast. It was a very sudden death from bronchitis and the child was not at all wasted.

Camp scene in Irene

---

[107]   Not identified.

There is a girl of 10 in the same tent seriously ill with pleurisy and I am afraid all that excitement and commotion was bad for her, but of course I turned out all the inquisitive spectators at once. I took the doctor there late this afternoon and he looked very serious – I do hope she is not going to die, too, there are quite enough deaths coming on in my ward. It is terrible – I feel as if my nerves can't stand it much longer. Miss F[indlay] says I ought to go home for a rest and I agree with her – too much of this misery will break us down in the long run.

Hessie [Celliers] took it into her head to go home for a day this afternoon so I have promised to keep an eye on her ward. We took her to the Station – the whole lot of us – and parted from her as if she were leaving for good. When we came there we noticed that there was something unusual going on and were informed that Lord Kitchener was coming by the next train, on his way to Pretoria. First an armoured train came along with a lot of soldiers and after we had waited till we were tired, he came along in the state carriages. He was travelling in the passenger train, because the engine of the special train had an "accident", so Hessie had the honour of knowing that his lordship was travelling with her, at least not far from her. We were rather amused at the "accident" – it means that the Boers knew what train he was coming by and meddled with the line. They took the rest of Karel Erasmus's cattle and horses this morning – about 300 – so he is *"Kaal"* Erasmus[108] now and I am sure the name will stick to him for life.

June 19th. [1901]

How shall I collect my thoughts sufficiently to make my usual entries? I am getting half demented with all this work – it is enough to drive anyone crazy. Last night I wanted to go on writing but my tent was too cold and in the marquée [sic] there was too much noise. I did some sewing there and wrote one letter and then it was about 10.30 and we were all just thinking of going to bed when a shot rang out in the stillness of the night. Very much excited we all rushed out and listened. Another followed and another and the echoes vibrated in the vallies [sic] and from hill to hill and each shot seemed multiplied a hundred fold. We stood outside in breathless silence, and when two more shots followed, our

---

[108]   "Bare" Erasmus.

excitement and suspense knew no bounds. There is something very terrible about this midnight firing – it turns one's heart to stone and freezes the very blood in one's veins. The sounds came from the plantation and each shot sounded like a whole volley. We heard no more and went to bed after a time but none of us could sleep for excitement. Dr W[oodrooffe] told Dandy that sentries had been put in the plantation where they never had been before on account of the Boers coming in every night, and this morning I hear that they were actually busy breaking the door of a stable when they were fired upon. They fled without having achieved their object. I was awfully sorry that Hessie was away – partly because she will regret having missed it but chiefly because I was rather nervous about sleeping alone, especially as a large rat ran over me just as I was dropping off to sleep. I started up and at the same moment I heard a sharp "Halt! Who goes there?" just outside my tent. The answer "Friend" came quickly and then there was a conversation which I did not catch, but I heard the other girls calling out to one another and asking what was wrong so I shouted out to Miss Findlay for company and was glad to hear her friendly reply. My nerves are not what they were. I used to be the most fearless of mortals but this war has changed me completely. Perhaps I'll get all right again when the Angel of Peace settles on our poor land.

This morning I took the night nurse, Sister F[ry] to the estate. She has long been anxious to see it and I had promised her ever so long ago, but I was always too busy in the morning. We first went together to my most serious cases and then we went to fetch our rings. Mine is a lovely gold one with J.v.W.[109] on it and Irene. I have ordered about 10 for friends in Holland. After that we had a lovely stroll through the estate and picked some violets and ferns but were caught by the overseer unfortunately, who made us promise that it would never occur again. I said we would pick no more ferns but begged hard to be allowed some of the violets growing almost wild, so he said he thought the nurses might be privileged. He was quite polite about it, but looked annoyed. When we came to the hospital it was just 11, so I had two hours hard work before dinner and took Dr W[oodrooffe] to a few of my most serious cases. We rushed up just in time for a wash and while we were having

---

[109]   For Johanna van Warmelo.

our dinner a man came by to say that a child was bleeding himself to death – blood pouring from nose and mouth – so down we two went to camp again, without taking any rest. The poor little chap was lying back white and exhausted and before him, a sickening sight – a white blanket saturated with blood and covered with great lumps of it – solid clots – oh, I was horrified – but all danger was past and the doctor gave him some stimulant and prescribed something for him, and then, as we were in camp, we just went through my list. I had at least ten cases for him to see – three of them, alas, dangerous ones – all little children. One of them is a sister to the baby that died while I was with it yesterday and the mother's face as she questioned the doctor will haunt me for a long time. And she did not get much encouragement from him. He is a very good doctor and seems to know at a glance whether there is hope or not. I love going round with him. I learn so much from him and he is so awfully good to our people. When he thinks a case serious he instructs me to watch it particularly, to take the temperature two or three times daily and to report to him when there is the slightest change for the worse, and he explains things to me and gives me many useful hints. I was much pleased and touched by a little compliment he paid me this afternoon. He said that my ward was the best managed in the camp, that I always knew the name and age of the patient, the row and number and the nature of the disease. But that is because I am so careful and methodical in making notes – certainly not because I remember everything – that would be an utter impossibility, where there is so much to remember.

This life sharpens one's wits and teaches one to be quick and accurate – I live here, every moment of the day and if I had my wish I would remain here as long as my services are required. Ah Lord, how long will that be? Is there to be no end to this bitter, bitter struggle? It seems as if we cannot bear it any longer.

I am learning to love some of my patients so much that I cannot tear myself away from them, especially the little ones. They twine themselves round my heart and oh, how I suffer when they are taken away from us and how it hurts me to see them suffer! A few days ago I heard one say *"Hier is die dokter ze vrouw,"*[110] another one called me *"die dokter ze*

---

[110]   "Here is the doctor's wife"

Irene Camp: preparing dinner in front of a tent

meisie"[111] and another said *"Daar loop die rooie kruis."*[112] They have such funny ideas about us and look upon us as supernatural beings. I often think we do a great deal more good than we imagine, not only by bringing material help and comfort, but by our influence and example. How many of them look forward to our daily visit as the one bright ray of sunshine, how they watch for us and long for us during their hours of suffering and pain. If we do not keep up their standard of morality during these days of darkness and desolation, where will they not sink to? They are demoralizing and deteriorating in this camp life, with its filth and squalor and misery, to a heart-breaking extent and if we do not take pity on them, who will? When my little ones see me coming they fly to wash their grimy hands and faces – the news goes from tent to tent, one row up and the other row down, *"Hier kom die Zuster,"*[113] and I do my best to be always bright and smiling – my cuffs and collars and aprons must always be snowy white, my red cross very red and everything about me fresh and sweet, so that the memory of it can be with them for the rest of the day. But alas, alas, I am often impatient, especially when the mothers won't listen and keep the tents tightly closed so that no breath of wind can reach their poor, panting little ones, and when they refuse

---

[111]   "the doctor's girlfriend"
[112]   "There goes the red cross"
[113]   "Here comes the Sister"

to give the fever patients a drop of cold water and look horrified at the thought of washing a measles patient. And they are stubborn with the stubbornness of crass ignorance. We have many things to contend against but thank God, there are many compensations. Now I shall join the others in the marquée [sic].

"Harmony". Pretoria. June 20th. [1901]

Yes, dear Diary, don't look so surprised. I am at Harmony – actually though I can hardly realize the fact myself. But I am too tired to write – I shall tell you how it all came about when I am back at Irene tomorrow.

Tomorrow. June 21st [1901]. Irene Camp. "Klip Laar". Bed. 10.30 p.m.

Very sleepy and ded [sic] tired – too tired to spell wright [sic] – and cross and disappointed and worried and excited and sad. "Listen to my tail of woe". On yester-morn Hessie [Celliers] came back from Pretoria with the news that my Mammie was not at all well and that she wanted me home at once. As it was an utter impossibility to leave my ward without anyone in charge I made up my mind to do my work thoroughly and run over to Pretoria with the evening train, spend the night at home and come back with the first train next day. My plan was generally approved of, Dandy gave me a permit, which I took to Scholtz to sign and at 5 o'clock we were all at the station – the whole nursing staff, as if I were leaving for good. I had to have my permit signed by Capt Pitt,[114] who assured me that I would be allowed to go there and back on the same permit without any trouble. In the train the collector of passes took it from me and when I protested he said that a new law had come into force that very day and I would have to get my return permit at the Pass Office in Pretorius St[reet] the following morning. I was so angry I did not know what to say.

---

114 Probably Captain T.M.S. Pitt, who was, according to Savannah Publications, *Boer War Services of Military Officers of the British and Colonial Armies Imperial Yeomanry Mounted Infantry Local Units &cc 1899-1902 including Earlier Services*, pages unnumbered, a member of the British forces active in Transvaal from January to August 1901 and was the only Captain Pitt in the British forces in South Africa.

June 22nd. [1901]

So far I got last night and then my weary eye-lids closed over my weary eyes and I could <u>not</u> write – it was no use, I had to give it up, much as I regretted it. This evening there is quiet in the camp. Our gay ones have gone out and we three quiet ones – I won't mention names – are sitting in the marquée [sic] writing. Where was I last night? Oh yes, the guard took my return permit and left me chafing at the thought that I would not be able to come back by the first train. I told the man that I had to be on duty at 9 a.m. next morning and the officer who had signed my pass had promised that I would come back on it, so he said he would see the "superintendent" and when I got out at Pretoria he brought back my valuable slip of paper and said I may keep it "as a favour" be-cause I was a Red Cross nurse and had to be on duty at a certain time. So <u>that</u> little trouble ended well, and I was fortunate enough to get a cab and drove straight home. How the mother flew into my arms! and how glad we were to meet again! It was perfectly lovely and we talked "like a house on fire". The mother is nearly well again and has given me permission to stay another two or three weeks, but then I <u>must</u> go home for good. Mama had a great deal to tell me but as they are secrets of the utmost importance – dangerous secrets – I shall not mention them here. She is also making a note of things and some day I hope to get all those interesting facts from her. All I can tell you is this, our dear boy Fritz is safe and <u>very well</u> and things are going <u>extra</u> well with our men. I may not say how the news reached us. We have had letters from Dietlof. He is also in perfect health – in a fort at some place with an outlandish name.

When we had done talking Mama said we must go to Mrs Nieuwen-huis who intended leaving for Irene the next day, with a lot of goods for me. We set out walking slowly and talking all the time. They were much surprised to see me and Mrs N[ieuwenhuis] was glad to hear that we would travel together next day. From there we went to see Mrs P.M. Botha, who was leaving for the Colony and wanted some facts about the Irene camp from me. We spent a good hour with her and she told me many interesting things too, but they, too, must remain unwritten. We are living in such dangerous times that we cannot be careful enough. We took a cab home and sat talking till 12 o'clock, went to bed where we talked till about 2 o'clock – it seemed as if we could not get finished but at last we fell asleep from sheer exhaustion. It was so funny for me to be in a house again and I tried to play a little, but my fingers were so stiff and I could not play from memory, so I gave it up with a sigh of regret.

Next morning at the Station there was a regular gathering – about seven visitors for Irene and myself. Mrs N[ieuwenhuis] wanted me to take her all over my ward, so, dear diary, you can imagine my chagrin and consternation when I found I had forgotten my note-book at home. How I could have been so silly passes my comprehension. There I was unable to do any work – without my names and rows and numbers, without the serious cases, without a single note of the work I had done for the past six weeks and the notes I had made for future use. I could have cried with vexation, especially because there were so many tents I wanted particularly to take Mrs N[ieuwenhuis] to. It would have taken me a whole day to go through my ward systematically and find out where all my patients were, so I just worked "from memory" and took Mrs N[ieuwenhuis] to a few of the worst places. It is a blessing that I have such a good memory because I remembered all my most serious cases and some of the most destitute families. Mrs N[ieuwenhuis] was much impressed by all the misery she saw. At 12 o'clock I went to fetch Dandy to go round with me, while Mrs N[ieuwenhuis] went to my tent to wait for me. Dr W[oodrooffe] was down with an attack of Influenza so Dandy had to do his work. We saw about nine cases before dinner – Dandy is very particular and inquires minutely into every case – very systematically and thoroughly. He says my ward is terribly bad – there is more destitution and misery than in any other part of the camp. I know it and that is what makes my work so hard. Two of my rows are equal to about four of the others and I have more rows than anyone else, and now that there is so much sickness in my ward I feel that the work is really too much for me. The reason is that the Zoutpansberg people were cut off from the whole world for nearly a year before they were brought here and they are out of everything for a long time, many of them being without a thread of extra clothing; and then also most of them had to flee from the Kaffirs and they could not take anything with them and were brought here with nothing more than they had on their backs.

This morning I began work at 9 a.m. and at 1.30 p.m. I had only done three rows, i.e. nearly 90 tents. Dinner was over when I came here and the worst of it was that my ward was only half done and I had ten cases, of the morning's work alone, for the doctor to see. He went out first with Mrs V[lok] who said I must wait for him in my tent, she would not be away an hour. I waited and dear diary, will you believe it? She kept him until past 5 o'clock and I sat waiting impatiently – afraid to go away to finish my ward, because I expected him every moment. It was really very disheartening and it was nearly dark when he did arrive and he had to do his work in a hurry. There are several serious cases of pneumonia, that we want to be brought up to the hospital, but the parents won't hear of it. Then I have cases of bronchitis, typho malaria,[115] pleurisy and I don't know what beside, to say nothing of the measles and influenza. I was busy in the camp so late that supper was also nearly over when I came here and then I had to go <u>again</u>, to take anti-pyrine powders to a girl with a temperature of 106, and linen to the parents of a dying child. Poor little mite! this is their last and it was very dreadful to have to tell the mother that there was no hope. I put some fresh violets into the poor, wasted little hand and tried to soothe the parents, but it was hopeless. Someone was praying aloud when I came there and I stood outside listening with oh, such a mixture of feelings.

June 22nd. [1901]

Dear diary, we must part. The fates have decreed that I shall write in you no more and this evening I am going to make a dear little parcel of you and tie you up and – no, I won't tell you what I am going to do with you then. The fact is there are spies and mystery and treachery in the air. We are surrounded on all sides by intrigue and I have an idea that the eyes of the law are upon me and my doings particularly. Someone, who must be nameless, gave me a hint that I have an enemy here, who must also be nameless, and she unfortunately saw me writing last night and she asked me many innocent and friendly questions about my diary. And that after she had told an official in high circles that the nurses here were a lot of agitators and Mrs S[tiemens] and Miss v[an] W[armelo] were the worst! She is so sweet to me and yet I know

---

[115]   typho malaria – meaning not clear.

she hates the very sight of me and every word I say is snatched up and stored away for future use against me.

There are going to be "revolutions" in the camp. Scholtz, our Superintendent, wants to work us out and is trying to find something definite against us.

June 24. [1901]

I was writing in Miss F[indlay]'s tent last night and Dandy joined us and we sat talking until it was time for me to go to bed, so I did not do as much writing as I intended. Here I am again this evening. It is so peaceful in Miss F[indlay]'s tent – a regular haven of rest. I love coming here especially when the others are playing whist and making a noise in the marquée [sic]. I have made up my mind to fill this book before putting it in a place of safety, because I can't get another exercise book here and I don't know wherein to continue my diary, besides I am sure no one will come and search my papers yet. The time will come sure enough but not until I go away.

Camp scene in Irene

This has been a black letter day for me – three deaths in my ward – all children – and several more hopelessly bad. There is an appalling amount of sickness. I have never had so much to do before and as far as I know it will go on like this until my three weeks are over. Some days I long for a rest and think I can never stand this for another three weeks, but generally I wonder how I shall tear myself away from my work and my dear patients. But we are alarmed at the increase of mortality in the camp. When I came here first the average was about 12 and 15 a week and last week it was <u>27</u> and I am afraid it is going to be even higher this week. Seven more buried this afternoon and I believe two this morning. I was going to take Dr W[oodrooffe] to see a little girl late this afternoon when the mother sent word that the doctor need not come as the child was dead. I went there afterwards and found the little body lying on one side of the tent and four or five sick children huddled on the other – horrible to think that they must spend the night like that and yet, what can one do? There is no mortuary and if a child dies too late to be buried the same day, its body has to lie where it is all night. Another child, a boy of about 11, was brought from my ward to the hospital this morning at about 10 o'clock and he was dead by 12. The third death in my ward was her parents' last child and that was the saddest of all.

June 25th. [1901]

Miss F[indlay]'s tent again, which means lots of conversation and very little writing. I have had a never to be forgotten day of work and worry and heartache unspeakable. Somehow things tell on me more now than they did at first. I turned quite faint with misery this morning and had to support myself against a tent pole. Unfortunately it is another of the cases I cannot mention but there is no chance of my forgetting it. It has burnt itself into my heart for life. So many children are dying in my ward – three yesterday, three today and about a dozen more going. The responsibility is becoming more than I can bear, but I must not dwell on troubles this evening – I am too "blue" as it is. Cannon firing was heard in the direction of, I think Krugersdorp this morning at about 12.30 and yesterday we heard a heavy explosion in the direction of Johannesburg. Some say it was the blowing up of a bridge on the line but the general opinion is that some bad dynamite was purposely exploded at the Modderfontein Factory.

June 26th. [1901]

What shall I write tonight? It is almost impossible for me to put down my thoughts and feelings since I have the idea that this chronicle might fall into the hands of my enemies. It is a pity, because I have always had so much pleasure and satisfaction in taking this silent friend of mine into my confidence and now everything has been spoilt. Today has been full of trouble – more even than usual, which is saying a good deal. My poor little ones are dying off in dozens. There were no less than 10 deaths in the camp last night and tonight a great many are expected to take place.[116] Two of mine are sure to go tonight and I had to tell the mothers – one is such a lovely little baby of three months. It looks like a little corpse already and, thank God, does not seem to suffer much. There I hear the strains of *"het nieuwe Jerusalem"*[117] floating from the camp on the still evening air. How distinctly I can hear the words *"En het eind zal zeker zalig zijn"*[118] and how they comfort me! I shall never hear them in after years without thinking of Irene and its shadows.

It is such a glorious evening. The moon is shining brilliantly and everything is serene and peaceful. The others are playing cards in the marquée [sic] and Miss F[indlay] and I are together, as has become our wont of late, in her tent, which I have dubbed Pilgrims' Rest. I am glad the others have some recreation of an evening. It is good for them after the day of hard work and worry and helps to pass the long, monotonous evenings. Miss Dürr (Mary) has gone to Pretoria for the day and I asked her to take a letter to Mama. As it had to be censored first I took it to Mr Scholtz and asked him to read it. He said he did'nt [sic] want to read my letters and if I could assure him on my word of honour that there was nothing "treasonable" in it, he would put the censor's stamp on it. I did and he made me close it and oh, he was so affable! I wonder whether he knows that I know all that passed between him and Gen Maxwell – it is such a joke. I really must tell you, dear diary. Not long after my arrival here, when I was still new to everything, I was introduced to this Mr S[choltz] our "Commandant" and we began talking about the war. I did

---

116   Indeed, according to the official list of deaths in the *Transvaal Government Gazette*, 24 July 1901, p 1212, 13 deaths occurred in the Irene Camp on 26 June 1901.

117   "the new Jerusalem".

118   "And the end will surely be blessed".

not know him at all and made some rather unfortunate remarks. For instance he talked about the "base ingratitude" of these Boer women who have never even thanked him for two waggon-loads [sic] of fresh vegetables, that he was good enough to distribute amongst them. Of course I flared up and asked him whether he would be grateful for a few miserable vegetables after his home had been burnt and his farms demolished and his children taken to a camp to die of privation. This remark was repeated to the Governor as an instance of the mischief the volunteer nurses do at Irene in exciting ill-feeling and dissatisfaction, and all the comfort he got from the Governor was a quiet, "I quite agree with Miss van Warmelo". The Gov[ernor] repeated this to a friend of mine as a joke and she of course told me.

June 27. [1901]

I am going to make away with this book today. Last night I wanted to write many things still but Dandy joined us in "Pilgrims' Rest" and we talked until nearly 11 o'clock. He was in a very nice mood.

I went to bed last night feeling rather ill and tired and had a terrible fit of coughing – coughed all night and had a great pain on my chest – felt as if I was in for a serious illness. Today my temperature is 100 and I have been working hard all the time – we are just going to the plantation – D[andy,] F[indlay] and I. I think the walk will do me good. Last night at 12.30 I was suddenly startled by shots fired in quick succession quite close by – 5 or 7, I am not quite sure how many there were. The others were asleep and only three of us heard the reports.

6 p.m. Dandy and Miss F[indlay] and I have just come back from the estate. Brought home some lovely violets – the last. We were informed that no one would be allowed to pick flowers in future. Sister Fry is down with measles so we wanted some violets for her.

There is much sickness in the camp today. I have about 110 cases of measles alone to report tonight and some fearful and wonderful diseases, hitherto unknown to me – laryngitis, peritonitis, convulsions, paralytic strokes etc. Miss Durr has come back from Pretoria and says the mother intends coming to Irene tomorrow. I shall be glad. Had a letter from Edith [Goodwin] today. And now farewell, my friend. May we soon meet again under happier circumstances.

[Script V of Johanna van Warmelo's war diary is not with the other scripts in the archives of the *Nederduitsch Hervormde Kerk van Afrika* in Pretoria. It was impossible to locate it. However, it seems as if this script contains entries for only the period 29 June to 12 July 1901, and that those entries are not lengthy. In the diarist's book *Het Concentratie-kamp van Iréne*, she included lengthy excerpts from her diary from 12 May 1901. These excerpts were translated into Dutch by the diarist herself, with the assistance of her husband Louis Brandt. The excerpts do not end with the entry on 27 June, but continues up to 12 July 1901. These excerpts were almost certainly translated from Script V. What follows are translations of sections of the diary as published in Dutch for the period 29 June 1901 to 12 July 1901. (*Het Concentratie-kamp van Iréne*, pp 84-98):]

29 June [1901]

Yesterday no entries, but I was ill and tired and received a surprise visit from Mama. I stayed in my tent for most of the day. I longed to return home with Mama. To add to my misery Miss Celliers received a telegram to return to her home immediately. She hurriedly left with the afternoon train. A girl from the camp, Miss Grobler,[119] will replace her, both in the camp and in my tent, which deepens my dissatisfaction.

I have so much to tell you, dear Diary, of my work and my experiences, but my head is not quite clear lately and I seldom feel fit to write.

1 July [1901]

My health is not good and yesterday it was so bad, that I was absolutely fatigued by nightfall and not able to write. It was the end of the month and we had to hand out new milk tickets. I had to visit every tent in my ward and was making good progress when somebody brought the news that General Maxwell and Major Hoskins had arrived from Pretoria and the former wanted to see me. I showed them my ward; the two doctors, the two officers and me – a troop of five, which drew much curiosity and was watched with the greatest interest. The Governor asked

---

119   Probably Johanna Hendrina Grobler (20 years) who came from Pietersburg and arrived in the Irene Camp on 14 April with her mother, brother and sisters. See TAB, DBC 62, Irene Camp Register of Residents.

me to take him to some of my worst tents which I did, providing him with a dose of misery which he will not easily forget; but the contents of his comments made it difficult to fathom what he actually thought. He once asked why they do not wash themselves, and when I answered that they had no soap, he replied that I should order as much as they needed. He also said that he would talk to Scholtz and would inform him that I have to order food, clothing, bedspreads etcetera where it was necessary; – but when I told him that most of these items are usually not available, he made no comment.

I would now like to know what will be done to make life here more bearable. It cannot go on as it is right now. The two officers told me that I looked quite ill and advised me to go home to recuperate, but I answered that I was not ill but "tired of all the misery".

Irene Camp inhabitants and nurses with supplies donated to those who had nothing

2 July [1901]

Yesterday a wonderfully strange delivery took place in my ward: Miss Bodes gave birth to malformed twins – both still-born – two girls with heads as big as that of year old children and small, malformed limbs.

Unfortunately I was not called and missed the spectacle; but practically everybody else saw them and Miss Bodes says her tent looked like an exhibition throughout the day. The whole camp came to see the wretched little things. I found the calm way in which she spoke amazing. There she sat on the bed, breastfeeding her other little girl and nobody would guess that she had gone through such a horrible experience.

4 July [1901]

Yesterday I made no entries, since I went to Pretoria for urgent business and only returned this morning. The reason was that I can feel me health deteriorating and wanted to find someone to replace me, since my ward is suffering with me being in my present condition. My poor mother pleaded with me to stay in Pretoria, but it was report day and I had to go. It is no wonder that we become ill as a result of the food we get here: coffee, bread and meat, but no fruit and hardly ever vegetables, but our diet is superfluous compared to what the people in the camp are given.

At the Irene railway station I saw an elderly lady taking the dusty road towards the camp. I caught up with her and was delighted to hear that she had just arrived from England with a special permit of Lord Kitchener to visit various camps. Her name is Mrs Rendall-Harris [sic].[120] She seemed very sympathetic and interested in our work; I told her about it and we agreed to meet again later so that I can show her the worst cases in Irene. I then took up my rounds again and it was virtually hopeless since one falls far behind when absent even for only one day. Five deaths in the two rows that I visited after my return. There is enough work for 20 people. I was late for lunch and received only a cup of tea in the big tent, where I met Mrs Rendall-Harris again. She had been around with some of the English elements and had been shown the best side of the camp only. I now showed her my ward and opened her eyes to the real state of affairs. She listened to everything I said while tears flowed down her cheeks.

---

[120]   Mrs Helen Harris was the wife of Prof Rendel Harris of Cambridge, England. Lord Kitchener gave her permission to visit the concentration camps as a representative of the pro-Boer women in England. She visited Irene Concentration Camp on 4 July 1901. See T. van Rensburg (ed.), *Camp diary of Henrietta E.C. Armstrong*, p 100.

After our return to the big tent she began compiling a list of the items most urgently needed. While we were busy with this, Mr Scholtz entered the tent. A long discussion followed during which it became clear that Mrs Harris lacked moral fibre, since she hesitated to report on what she really saw, while he brushed aside the suffering of the people. I attempted to set things in their true light, but he became angry and said: "The people here would have been quite content, had they not been stirred up from Pretoria." With that he stared at me, and I answered with silent contempt. We are used to be called "agitators" and "political agents"; that is the unfortunate fate of all people who work for their fatherland with passionate love, and we have to bear this in silence, as the women here have to bear poverty, humiliation, insults and illness.

It was with regret that I left Mrs Harris and returned to the camp to finish my rounds. I found numerous dying children; their mothers pleaded with me with tears in their eyes to fetch the doctor. I promised that I would, and by half past four went looking for him, but nobody knew where he was. After lunch he napped until 4 o'clock, drank a cup of tea and then disappeared. Nobody knew where he was. It was growing dark. My children were dying due to a lack of medicine. No wonder that my feelings for Dr W[oodrooffe] were dark and bitter.

Somebody then told me that he was near the chemist. I met him in that direction and he then followed me to my ward. After treating the most urgent cases, he left again. Subsequently I found a baby who had just died – having succumbed without any medicine to relieve his last hours of agony.

5 July [1901]

It is half past eleven and I attempt to write in bed, but it is too cold. My day was satisfactory since the doctor was friendly to me after the previous day's events. There were some tragic deaths and illness as usual. The women who lost her still-born twins yesterday also lost her only son. My observation is that once there is a death in a family, it is usually the beginning of a series of deaths in that family.

6 July [1901]

I managed to do a surprising amount of work today. When I think of all the patients I visited today; the number of temperatures I took; the orders that I wrote out, and had countersigned by the doctor, for milk, medicine, candles, soap, rice, etcetera; the complaints I had to listen to; the words of sympathy, of hope, of encouragement and of reprimand that I uttered, I cannot but wonder how I managed everything.

I gave a camp-stretcher to a woman who had to lie on the bare ground and numerous mattresses which Mrs Domela Nieuwenhuis sent us, to people who were in great need.

7 July [1901]

There are now only three serious cases in my ward. This morning a small boy died and his mother asked me for white linen to make a shroud. She has had a bitter time. Soon after my arrival here, she had lost her only daughter and now one of her sons. She has only one son left. Fortunately he seems strong and healthy.

Since it is Sunday, Miss Grobler and I went for a walk to the farm Iréne at sunset. When we returned we found the gate locked. There is now a barbed wire fence around the whole camp and at a certain hour all the gates are closed and locked. We were cut off from our home, and did not know what to do, but fortunately an officer on horseback arrived and arranged with a guard to open the gate for us.

It was late by the time we reached the hospital, but I had to go to the camp. I had a small bunch of violets for one of my patients, a lovely little girl, who will probably pass away tonight. Poor Betsy! She has been ill for a long time – first malaria, which drained her strength, then typhus and now pneumonia, to which she has no resistance. I love this little girl as if she is my own sister. She always seems happy, always smiling, never complaining. She was so glad when I gave her the flowers, which she pressed to her face, while muttering a few words of thanks. And now she is going to the Friend of friends and her poor mother is too down-hearted to give her any help. For two months now I have been in contact with the deathly sorrow of bereaved mothers and I have often wondered how they managed to cope, since it is so ghastly to witness their distress.

The Irene Camp water pump

8 July [1901]

When I started working this morning, I was told that our beloved Betsy had passed away last night. I immediately visited the poor, bereaved mother. The soulless body lay in one corner of the tent, and I gazed at it with great sorrow. She has now been taken from this impure place to the home of her Father. The expression on her face was one of never-ending rest.

9 July [1901]

Yesterday I had no more time to write and even now I have hardly a free minute, since I am handing out the last supplies and saying my farewells. My whole ward knows that I am leaving and I have to listen to numerous complaints. It makes me sad to leave all my friends here in this camp. This morning a lovely child of two months in my ward passed away. The little corpse seemed so clean and white that I felt nothing of the fear that usually fills me when I see a dead body.

"Harmony", Pretoria, 12 July [1901]

Home, home, beloved place, after an exile of a full two months! My previous entry was on the 9th. I left Iréne [sic] on the 10th and will never forget the agony. Dandy felt ill and looked awful and the other girls were all but happy. When I did my round with my successor, Miss Westmaas, we found five dying children and so many cases of illness that I felt bad to leave my ward in such a state, especially since Miss Westmaas has no experience and is only 18 years old.

When I arrived home, Mamma told me that Dr Kendal-Franks[121] [sic] was going to Iréne [sic] the next day and wanted to see my ward. I went to the Portuguese consul, Cinatti, where Dr Franks was lodged, and offered to give him a list of my worst tents. Everybody immediately said that it would be better if I accompany Dr Franks. We agreed to meet each other at the station at eight o'clock the next morning.

How the people stared at me when they saw me walking to the hospital with a gentleman "in khaki". I introduced him to the matron and to Dr Neethling and left him with them, since he first wanted to see the hospital, dispensary and supplies. That kept him busy the whole morning. After lunch we went to my ward, where I showed him my worst tents which had lately become so notorious. He was, as are everybody, struck by the poverty and suffering of the people and promised to use his influence to improve matters. In one tent two children of Mrs Oosthuizen were dying. At her urgent request we entered and Dr Franks examined them, but there was nothing he could do. What would be the outcome of his visit? Will something be done to lessen this horrible death rate? I fear nothing. Nothing has come of any of this lightning, superficial visits. Dr Franks has already alluded to the dirtiness of the people, instead of going to the root of the problem, namely bad and insufficient food, insufficient clothing, exposure to the winter cold and other hardships of camp life. We took the 3.36 train back to Pretoria, which means that Dr Franks spent less than five hours in Iréne [sic] to examine that camp.

---

121   Dr Kendal Franks was a British military surgeon who visited the Irene Camp in July 1901 and subsequently compiled a report which, in the diarist's opinion, did not truly reflect the sad state of affairs in the camp. See J. Brandt-Van Warmelo, *Het Concentratie-kamp van Iréne*, p 105. R. & N. Musiker, Franks, Sir Kendal Matthew St John, in *DSAB* V, pp 277-278.

Part 4

"Love on one side, war on the other" – Pretoria, 13 July to 31 December 1901

[Script VI]

"Harmony". Pretoria.
July 13th 1901

This is a very nice exercise book - I am quite charmed with it - so charmed that I got two. Well, I hope the war will be over long before this one is full, and before I begin the next I hope I shall know something definite about my own future plans. Where was I last night? Busy with Gen Maxwell's interview with me. He asked me how things were at Irene and I told him that some improvements had been made, but that there was still a good deal of bad management, viz. great delay in getting in fresh supplies of stores and medical comforts. He wanted to know why the doctors did not report such things to him, so I said Dr Franks would see him and tell him all about his visit. He also asked how we liked the new Superintendent[1] and seemed amused at my answer, "Mr Scholtz bullied us but I think we are going to bully this new man – he looks so small and sickly and afraid!" The Governor looked as if he thought we were never satisfied. He told me that Mr S[choltz] was going round the country to visit all the camps and report to him and, seeing the dissatisfaction on my face he asked whether I thought he would do it well. "No", I answered, "I think I'll do it better. Will you let me go round to Belfast, Vereeniging, Middelburg, Potchefstroom etc and send you my report?" "Yes, you may go". I could hardly believe my ears and yet he was in earnest. So many people have tried to get permission

---

[1] G.F. Esselen was the second superintendent of the Irene Concentration Camp from 9 July 1901 to 5 February 1902. See T van Rensburg (ed.), *Camp diary of Henrietta E.C. Armstrong*, p 98n.

280

to visit the other camps and they always met with a direct refusal, and even now I can't understand why I should be so favoured. It is certainly not because I am in Khaki's good graces or because I flatter him and close my eyes to his many faults. No indeed, I speak out my mind on all occasions – I tell them exactly how I find things and very often they have to listen to unpleasant home-truths from me. And now I intend going from camp to camp as soon as I have rested thoroughly. It will be very interesting and I have no doubt will do me a lot of good. I spoke in jest when I asked to be allowed to go, but the General took me quite seriously. I am afraid Scholtz's report and mine will not bear the slightest resemblance.

From the Gov[ernmen]t Buildings Johanna Grobler[2] and I went to the post and did some shopping and came home quite late – I was very tired. We made music again because J[ohanna] longed so much to play before she left for Irene. She is very musical and plays very well indeed, considering the few advantages she has had. She is quite a superior kind of girl and has had far more education than most Boer girls. She left early next morning and my Mammie and I found ourselves alone again. The former is fortunately nearly well now – the latter is quite well, thank you, and oh, so glad to be at home and out of all that misery. Now the reaction is setting in and I feel utterly disinclined to exert myself and yet I have no intention of yielding to this fit of laziness. Only yesterday I refused to do anything, but just coddled myself. There was a meeting of our Vocal Society in the morning. They sent word that I must be at Hollenbachs' at 12 o'clock to attend it and I sent word that if they could not come and hold it here they would have to do without me, and that terrified them all so much that they came over to Harmony in a great hurry and we had our meeting here. A great deal of business was transacted and we intend giving an invitation concert soon – no Khakis – but more of this anon.

In the afternoon I had visitors – Henriette Aubert and Mrs Fockens and towards sun-down Mr Cinatti came to see us. He told me that the Governor, Major Hoskins and all the consuls were going to spend the day at Irene – today – and he wanted a list of my worst tents from me.

---

2   Probably the girl from the Irene camp – see diary entries on 1901-06-29 and 1901-07-07.

Those poor tents of mine are becoming quite notorious. I sent a letter
to Miss Findlay with him asking her to show him round. The Governor invited the whole diplomatic Corp [sic] to lunch with him at Irene.
What excitement there will be and <u>why</u> did I leave my little round tent
at Irene? Mr C[inatti] told us all sorts of news but I can't remember
everything. One report was that the Basutos were rising against the English and they had taken one of the "refugee" camps, killing the soldiers
and transferring the women and children to their own country where
they supplied them with milk, meat and mealies in plenty. What an
absurd story and yet we enjoyed it so much that we have been telling it
to everyone.

Fritz was quite well on the 29ᵗʰ June and sent his love to us – never
mind <u>how</u>, you always want to know too much, dear diary. I will tell
you some very wonderful tales when the war is over, and the terrors of
Martial Law no longer hang over us. Last night when I had done writing
I had a lovely warm bath and crept into bed, where I slept like an infant
until nearly 7 o'clock this morning. This seems a trifling event to record,
but you must live in a tent for many weeks without such luxuries as hot
baths and then you will agree with me that it is <u>not</u> such a trifle after all.
Tomorrow I am going to wash my hair – Sunday or no Sunday. I won't
go to church but just sit under the trees and think – I require a whole
peaceful morning for all the thinking that has to be done.

Pretorius Street, Pretoria at the time of the Anglo-Boer War,
with a cab on the right

I went to Town after breakfast to do some necessary shopping, spent the whole morning there and went to have dinner with Oom Paul M[aré]. They were all glad to see me after my long absence and had many questions to ask and we talked and told one another all the things we had heard and experienced. What exciting, stirring times we are living in! Every person we see has his own story of death and danger, misery, plotting, scheming, to tell – every one has a different opinion to give on the many thrilling events of the day. How we learn to know and love one another, to appreciate the good qualities, to deplore the faults of our own people. I always get sad unto death when we get on to the subject of the faithlessness and treachery of some Africanders. How can anyone be so base, so utterly without any feeling of patriotism at a time like this? It is the saddest problem to me.

I find Pretoria much changed. Most of our old friends have gone away and the only people we seem to associate with now are the consuls and their families. I don't really mind – I am looking forward to a perfectly restful time, no pleasure, no gaities – at least only the kind I appreciate most, such as music and reading. I mean to practice hard every day. Someone I know is passionately fond of music and I am sure he would be very much disappointed if I cannot play or sing to him and oh "my one talent" has been so cruelly neglected during the last two years. How now about my fine plans for studying music when the war is over? Recent events have changed everything for me. I still hope to go to Europe – now more than ever – but how can I go to Germany or Switzerland when he[3] is in Holland. I shall have to go and stay somewhere near him – in Groningen perhaps, where I can see him often and get to know him before I bind myself by any promises. The prospect is very inviting and already I see myself in a cosy room at some pension or other, with a piano and lots of music, and a frequent visitor in the shape of a very tall and distinguished-looking young man, who loves me to desperation and woos me so ardently that I must yield – vain dreams! Is the future ever as we picture it to ourselves? I must not build all sorts of castles – I must live in the Present only and leave my future in Higher Hands than mine. Only I do so long for human love and sympathy – when will they be mine?

---

[3]   Louis Brandt.

I am sitting alone in the dining-room. Mama has gone to bed early and I am alone - my thoughts have travelled far. I have been in Holland for many months and have just discovered that I love "someone" and cannot do without him. I must tell him so. Where is he? Let me get the map of the Netherlands. Dear me, Groningen lies right away in the north, far from every other place I know. How lovely! Now I shall have him all to myself - no friends, no relatives, nothing but - one another! Let me look at his photo again. It is lying beside me - it always does now-a-days, whenever I find myself alone. I am trying to read that face, to fathom it to the very depths - how impossible! It is a perfectly sealed book to me. I know absolutely nothing of what lies beneath that calm exterior. Shall I ever know? Can a reserved man like L[ouis] B[randt] ever lay bare the secrets of his heart and reveal himself - his true self - to an "uncivilized Boer girl" like me? Will he not always feel the difference between us - in our education, our up-bringing, our views, our thoughts and feelings? I am sure he does not regard me at all in the light of an uneducated person and yet in many things he must find me wanting - it is quite unavoidable, and may be the cause of much disappointment and misery. The more I think of the great risk he runs the more I marvel at it, and yet I am sure he did not act impulsively - that face looks too strong and decided. What a fine face! He does not know how much he has helped me by sending me this photo - and that reminds me - he wants one from me. The one in nurses' uniform is not a true likeness and the one in visiting-dress has a silly smile - I can't bear it. I think I shall have another made, specially for him. That's an idea!

Hessie [Celliers] was here this afternoon - dear girl, I was so glad to see her again. She says she is longing to go back to Irene - well, I don't, not just yet, and perhaps never again.

Sunday. July 14th. [1901]

My day of laziness has been quite as satisfactory as I expected. Breakfast in bed, up at ten, washed my hair and sat in the sun like a pussy-cat, blinking my eyes and drowsily thinking, for all the world like one who had nothing better to do in life than indulge in day-dreams. After dinner, another nap and then I dressed myself for the afternoon - with an effort, I must admit, for one gets more indolent the more one yields to it. We had a lot of visitors, Mrs Fockens, three uncles and three young men. Mrs F[ockens] <u>may</u> go round the camps with me – I asked her to think it over and she promised to do so. I must have a chaperone and the mother won't go and so I must find some married woman, who has no home ties. Anna [Fockens] is the very one, only I am not sure if she is strong enough. She says the consuls did not see Dr Neethling yesterday – neither was Miss Findlay to be seen, in fact, it was all most unsatisfactory. I suppose they only were introduced to the English crowd and only saw the most favourable side of the camp. It is a shame and I must hear tomorrow what Mr Nieuwenhuis says about it. I am going to see them tomorrow. From tomorrow I am going to be very energetic – no more day-dreams and naps. I feel thoroughly rested.

There was some war news today – part of Maraisdorp[4] – in the Colony – has been burnt down by the Boers, at least all the homes of the English, I suppose by way of vengeance for the burning of <u>our</u> homes.

Oom Pieter says he struck an English officer in the Club the other day. It came about his way. Capt Somebody or other was talking to another officer about the Boer women and girls and saying all sorts of dreadful things about them, so Oom P[ieter] went up to him and said he would paddy-whacks him if he said it again, and he actually repeated it all, and when he had done Oom P[ieter] gave him a few knocks that he won't forget in a hurry – The best of it is that the fellow instantly apologised and when Oom P[ieter] went home a little later he found him waiting outside and a second apology was gone through. The man has no spirit if he can't uphold his own statements.

Now that I am at home again I don't know what to write in my diary. For two months I have never been at a loss and now I find myself without news of any description. I can write about myself, but one rather hesitates before putting down, in black and white, one's inmost thoughts, especially when there is always the chance that one's private correspondence may have to be examined. No one is safe under Martial Law. Any moment a gentleman in Khaki may march into the house and demand the keys of our desks and writing-tables – it has happened, not once, but dozens of times, to my friends. And yet, if I do not make

---

4   Since the war re-named Hofmeyr. This news was, as so many rumours in Pretoria were, false.

a confidant of this book and unburden my mind occasionally, how am I to get through the time? how can I be happy or satisfied during the next two months of suspense and longing, without some outlet to my overburdened heart? I think I shall just risk it. It will do me a lot of good and even if this book is destined to fall into the hands of strangers what can it matter to me what they think of the confessions of a girl?

Now that I know that L[ouis] B[randt] loves me, now that I may allow myself to think of him as a lover, as my future husband perhaps, I find my thoughts dwelling on him continually, and it is most trying, most tantalising that I know so little of him and that so much time must elapse before I can know more about him. He is one of the most reserved men – I saw that at first glance and often experienced a feeling of chilled disappointment when talking to him. Tonight I am so depressed and nervous – so afraid that after all I have made a mistake and that he will find out his mistake in speaking on so slight an acquaintance as ours is.

Tonight I am very glad I did not quite bind myself when I wrote that impulsive letter, and yet I do not regret it either. Things would have been very different if I had carried out my previous plan of sending Marie a few calm, indifferent words – that might be taken as words of discouragement or as a slight concession, just as he chose. I wanted to wind myself up into a rage with him for slights, fancied or real, in the past, and instead of that I found myself writing a sweet and joyful epistle! Good gracious, now that I come to think of it I am a very contradictory woman, full of moods and tenses, swayed this way and that by melting sunshine, a blue sky, softly dazzling white clouds. I must have been under some strange influence when I wrote that letter and sometimes it gives me quite a shock to think of it, but generally if fills me with the deepest peace. If I only knew how he will receive it – I cannot wait so long, oh no, I cannot and yet, I must. Now I know something of the uncertainty he went through. I wonder when he found out that I was the woman he loved. Does it not seem strange for a man to propose after a nearly four years' separation and that after such a very slight acquaintance! The correspondence between us has been of the most casual. Sometimes I kept him waiting many months for an answer to his last letter and sometimes he kept me waiting, and, strange to say, this last was more frequently the case. When his photo came I wondered what he meant by sending it and then some sentences in his letters made me suspicious and yet I could not understand some of his actions. In the letter of March he describes his new home and dwells upon his loneliness. He says his cat and dog are good friends but that is not all a man wants – later on he says he must just wait and be patient until I or my photo arrives. Now that might mean anything. He had very many chances of writing to me and seldom made use of them. How am I to understand him? Well, now it is my turn to wait and be patient. Time goes so fast in these eventful days of ours that I shall get a letter from him before I expect it, not doubt – unless the mail has got lost or the Governor "forgot" to send my letter. By this mail I am writing again – by every mail, I promised in my last, so that he need not wait so long again. I shall write and tell him all about myself and my doings, my homelife, my friends and studies and recreations, my experiences of the war and at Irene; but until I have heard from him direct I shall not again touch upon the subject of the understanding between us. What an [sic] unique correspondence ours will be! I must say I think the whole thing rather romantic and interesting and, if it were not going to be so one-sided for the next two months, I would quite enjoy the prospect.

July 15th. [1901]

This morning immediately after breakfast I went to see Mr Cinatti to hear how the consuls' visit to Irene had passed off. He says there can be no doubt that things have much improved during the last few months, but still the misery is very great and all the consuls agree that the sights they saw were very sad. They had a grand lunch at the Station and spent a lot of their time in inspecting the camp and hospital, but they could not get hold of anyone they wanted to see particularly. Mr C[inatti] asked three of four times after Miss Findlay and they all wanted to see Dr Neethling, but they were put off until it was too late. I wonder what that means. When they were coming home Gen Maxwell asked Mr C[inatti] what his opinion was about the camp and his answer was, "General, your tiffin was a beauty, but your camp is very sad". He tells me that very soon there will be no milk for the camp – there is none to be had anywhere at the Coast and the supply here has almost run out. What a prospect that is! All those poor, ailing little ones will die for want of nourishment if they get no milk. Hundreds of them live on that and nothing else.

I also went to see the Dutch consul. He was in, but Mrs N[ieuwenhuis] had gone to Town to buy barley, rice and candles for Irene. He told me much the same about their visit and asked me to let him know exactly what the weekly death-rate was while I was there, as he is sending a report to Holland and wants as many facts as possible. The high mortality is something so alarming that that is the one point on which we are all "agitating" – to use Scholtz's favourite expression. I must write and ask Dandy the figures – I did not make notes all the time I was there.

From the Dutch Consulate I went to see Mrs Bosman about her recent visit to Potchefstroom. She is our clergyman's wife and a very good and energetic woman. She says it took the Governor three weeks to make up his mind whether he would allow her to go or not and even then she had no end of trouble. But she has come back safe and sound and read the report to me that she is about to send in to him. To my mind it is not half strong enough judging by the state of affairs as she told them to me. She says people are literally dying of starvation in the Potchefstroom camp, not because they don't get enough to eat but because what they do get is not fit for consumption. One woman told her that she had not received meat for ten days, and the next day, when she went to see her again, she saw a piece of mutton lying outside in the sun, so she asked the woman why she complained of not getting meat if she did not use it when it came. For answer the woman fetched it and asked her to examine it – it was diseased! They try to make soup of it but the children bring it up whenever they try to eat it. Very few of the people use the coffee and sugar they get and when she asked them what they live on, the answer was, "Flour and water". One woman told her in dry-eyed misery that she had lost two children and they had died of hunger. And this is what I am going to! Yes, for I have definitely decided today to go round the camps on a tour of inspection and that as soon as possible. It will be a very hard task and my heart fails me when I think of it, but I suppose just as I received sufficient strength to minister to the wants of our sick and dying at Irene, I shall be helped and strengthened in this new undertaking. I may be able to do a great deal of good by it. Mrs B[osman] says the camp is clean and sanitary arrangements good but – and these are the words she uses in her report – "only the strong-est can survive, on the rations served out to them". She had heard of my intention of visiting some of the other camps and begged me to go to Middelburg, Belfast and Balmoral as soon as possible. I asked her to go with me but she does not feel much inclined and advised me to get Mrs Stiemens – she has just come back from Irene and is very anxious to be-gin work somewhere else. She would be far better than Anna F[ockens] – she is strong and healthy, cheerful and sympathetic and very good company. I must go and see her tomorrow – oh no, then I have to go to Philipp's lucheon party – well, then on Wednesday.

Mr C[inatti] told me that de Wet passed the Springs at 3.30 p.m. on Saturday and when I asked him "whither bound?" he said, "de Wet is not a gentleman who gives notice of his arrival or departure, or informs anyone of the direction he is about to follow", and so it is. De Wet is one of the most independent of mortals, bless his brave heart!

This afternoon I had another nap after dinner – I confess it with shame and regret. It seems as if the "reaction" has set in, never to depart no more – I don't know what has come over me. Later on I went to see Aunt Clara, who is ill with Influenza and then I walked home through the Park. I find time enough now, in these solitary walks, for reflection and, needless to say, my thoughts turn persistently into one channel. Sometimes they are golden – glorified by the prospect of my future, as it appears when I think that I shall learn to love <u>him</u>, but sometimes they are so sad, so sad – usually when I dwell upon past misunderstandings or disappointments. Or is it because my whole life, my every thought and feeling, has been tinged with melancholy by what I have gone through? If L[ouis Brandt] knew how <u>much</u> love I shall want to make up for the past, will he still be ready to give it to me? I shall not be satisfied with a portion or with half of his love, I shall want <u>all,</u> when once I have given <u>my</u> all. I must make him understand this.

July 16th.

This morning's luncheon party has passed off most successfully and I am quite charmed with Mr Gordon. Let me try and remember some of the "true news" I heard this morning. The English have evacuated Pi-etersburg; the Boers have taken Middelburg and partially destroyed it;

fighting has been going on round Johannesburg for the last three days; French is going with a mighty force to sweep the Colony and expects to startle the whole country soon; Steyn was surprised and surrounded with 27 men one dark night – he escaped with four men, in his stockinged feet – the other 23 have arrived in Pretoria and will be sent away soon[5]; at Vredefort and Parijs in the Free State a lot of fighting has taken place and those two small places have also been partially destroyed by the Boers. This, and a great deal more, was repeated to me in high glee this morning. I enjoyed myself immensely. My dear, good friend Consul C[inatti] was there with Cèléste, Mr Gordon, Mr Philipp, our host and yours truly. We talked war talk and politics all the time and were in perfect sympathy with one another. Of course I was questioned a good deal on the subject of camp life at Irene and had to tell all my experiences. Mr G[ordon] gave me permission to send a letter to L[ouis]. I told him it was a personal letter and contained nothing about the war and he said it would be all right. I don't think he was quite pleased that it was not about the war – he looked as if he felt inclined to say he would send any mortal thing for me. One good thing is I may close the letters I write to L[ouis]. I am sure he guessed that it was a love affair, he looked so knowing. Bother the war! bother censors and consuls and Martial Law! Why can't I have the pleasure of a free, unreserved correspondence with this strange unfamiliar sweetheart of mine? But I suppose this romance is only in keeping with the rest of my eventful life – it would be curious indeed if the love affair of my life were to run smoothly – I would not trust it at all. Now it is in keeping with the rest of my wonderful history. I think I ought to write a book some day when I am an old woman and the vicissitudes of life have come to an end – we shall see. Perhaps by that time I shall have something better and more interesting to do. I sometimes wonder whether this daily chronicle is not a great waste of time. Of course I think everyone ought to make notes of events and a diary is an excellent thing for everyone, but not the way I keep it. I make too much of trifles and dwell too long on my own private thoughts

---

[5]   On 11 July 1901 virtually the whole government of the Orange Free State was captured by a British unit near Reitz in the Free State. President Steyn managed to escape on the back of a horse, leaving his coat and hat behind. See N.J. van der Merwe, *Marthinus Theunis Steyn, 'n lewensbeskrywing* II, pp 20–24.

and feelings and that is where the waste of time comes in. To keep a diary improves one's style and strengthens one's memory, besides being a splendid thing for future reference, but what is gained by writing down all passing emotions? The only good it does me is that I find some outlet for my overburdened heart – some companionship in this silent confidant of mine – but is that worth the risk I run of having my most sacred thoughts scanned and perhaps ridiculed by some profane person in the shape of an officer or some one authorised to see the military laws carried out. They do not say "by your leave" when they come and search our papers. Oh no, they march into a house and order you to sit down where you are while they ransack every drawer and shelf, roll up carpets and examine curtains etc. I hope nothing of the sort will ever happen at Harmony – I think the mother would go into a fit. Well, I am going to bed. It is late for I have been busy all evening with one of my long family letters, destined to be smuggled through – never mind how! Oh, we are very smart – quite too smart for Khaki. Some day I'll tell you all about our plots and schemes and conspiracies. I know enough to fill a three volume novel.

July 17th. [1901]

If I knew enough last night to fill a three volume novel I wonder a how many novels I could fill tonight? This sounds rather funny but my head is in a whirl with all the events of today and I don't feel as if I can form a single rational, readable sentence. Let me begin at the beginning. I went to Town early because I had a lot to do and I had to attend one of our vocal society meetings at 12 o'clock. I went to see Mrs Nieuwenhuis first and found her hard at work with bales of flannel and warm dresses for our poor little ones in the camps. She is a marvellous woman, so energetic, so sympathetic and true – I never leave her without feelings of great respect and admiration. There I met one of the Dutch nurses – Sister van P[6] – who was brought into Town some months ago between armed tommies, as a suspected spy. They thought she was a man in woman's dress and kept her a prisoner – even now she cannot get out, although she has done all she could to be allowed to go back to the Boers. About ten days ago she got permission to go to one of the con-

---

[6]   Not identified.

centration camps. They wanted to send her to the Irene hospital but she refuses to work for money and prefers being in the camp, so I think she will go to some other camp – as they have enough help at Irene now.

Everyone is full of the latest news – the evacuation of Pietersburg, the withdrawal of troops from all parts of the Transvaal to send reinforcements to the [Cape] Colony. There are 6 000 Boers lying round Johannesburg at this moment, Kaalfontein Station has been blown up, Florida destroyed and I don't know what besides. Everyone is full of new hope and courage and there is a suppressed excitement in the air that makes itself felt wherever one goes. I went to see Miss Eloff and found them all very sad about our President's poor old wife. She lost a daughter about a month ago and has fretted herself into a dangerous state of health – her heart is so weak that she may fall down dead any moment and she is not left alone one second. Poor old soul! I do hope she will last until her husband can come back to her again – it would be a dreadful thing if she were to die now. But they are very anxious about her and I am afraid we may expect the worst any moment.

At our vocal Soc[iety] meeting it was decided that we are to give an invitation concert as soon as possible. I have to go to the Governor tomorrow to get the required permit.

I came home late – past our dinner-hour and was just practising a little at about 3.30 when a visitor was announced – a Mr Botha[7] – a funny little man who was crippled by lighting on commando. He had most important business with us – I can tear the very hair out of my head that I may not write down all about it – it would be too dangerous. When he left us I went to see Mrs Gilfillan[8] to show her a letter I had received from E[dith Goodwin]. The poor girl is in ill-health and wants to come to us for a change but, because I may be going away any moment, we can't take her in. There are other reasons too but I can't mention them here. Mrs G[ilfillan] who is related to the Goodwins said E[dith] would

---

[7]   Willem J. Botha, a burgher from Pretoria who was hit by lightning at Pietershoogte on the Natal front early in the war and subsequently suffered from headaches and was at times unable to walk. He was a stranger to the diarist and her mother before July 1901. See J. Brandt, *Die Kappie Kommando*, p 132.

[8]   The wife of either J.C. or W.H. Gilfillan, who both lived in Celliers Street, Sunnyside. See *Longland's Pretoria Directory for 1899*, p 131.

be most welcome so I hope she will soon come. Then I took an extract from the "Times Weekly" to Consul C[inatti]. It was cut out of the paper – but (as usual) a few copies came through and one of them reached our hands – shall I say "as usual" again? Towards dusk the mother and I went to see Mrs JC[9] in connection with Mr B[otha]'s important business – oh dear, how hard it is to write when one has to write in riddles! She gave me a very interesting letter from her husband to read. It was dated June 29th and contains news from several relatives and friends. In it he mentions Fritz v[an] Warmelo, who sends much love to us. The letter was evidently sent through one of our prisoners, for J[an] C[elliers] says "an English gentleman, who is soon leaving us" promised to post it in Krugersdorp. It was censored, as most letters are, and something it contained

Willem Botha (Little B)

was evidently not to Mr Censor's taste, for he scribbled over it in thick ink and very impolitely wrote over it "We are soldiers of the king and we'll fight for England's glory, to the bitter end". Three other lines were rendered quite illegible in the same way but we can't make out what is written over them. I think it very rude of Mr Censor to make such a mess of other people's correspondence. J[an] C[elliers] writes that all is well with him and his comrades – that they have been marvellously strengthened from above and he urges his wife to be brave and patient. It is a very beautiful letter and did my heart a lot of good.

I hear that Kitchener went to Johannesburg and asked de Wet, who was in the near neighbourhood, to come and talk to him and our dauntless general's answer was "I don't want to talk – I want to fight". They are sick and tired of all the fruitless conferences. Kitchener is not going to England, but straight to India. General Littleton[10] takes his place.[11]

---

9   Probably Mrs J. Celliers.
10   Must be Lyttelton. See Harrington, A.L., Lyttelton, Sir Neville Gerald, in *DSAB* IV, p 334.
11   The diarist is wrong. Kitchener was not replaced.

July 18th. [1901]

An eventful day – very eventful. I must remember this date. My memory is fairly good, so I shall just store away in my brain all the interesting things I saw and heard and did today. Other events can be recorded here. I went to see Mrs Stiemens to ask whether she would go with me to the different camps – she consented with pleasure. Then I went to the Gov[ernment] Buildings to ask Gen Maxwell about permits etc. The German Consul[12] was with him and I had to wait some time and when I was at last shown in his lordship seemed in anything but a good humour. He shook hands and greeted me with a curt "Well, what is the matter with you now?" "That is very unkind of you General" I answered. "Why?" he demanded. "Oh, because that sounds as if I trouble you every day". "Well", he said, smiling slightly, "what can I do for you?" "That's better", I answered cheerfully and straightway plunged into business. He gave me permission to go, with Mrs S[tiemens] as chaperone, to any of the camps, except those in the north and Potchefstroom – he told me why I had better not go to P[otchefstroom] but I can't remember what the reason was. I said I was willing to run all sorts of risks and he made some remark about a charge of dynamite under the train not being exactly pleasant, also that there would probably be no accommodation for us at the camps etc but I was not going to be frightened by any of these suggestions. We made a great mistake in talking politics – somehow we always do and I am always sorry afterwards. It aggravates me beyond endurance and yet there is a certain irresistible fascination about it. He told me all about Pres. Steyn's narrow escape – how he slept in Reitz, a small, deserted village in the Free State, with 27 men; how they stabled their horses and made themselves generally comfortable; how they were surrounded and surprised at dead of night by the English who took all the horses before the alarm was given; how Steyn escaped on a small pony that was standing unnoticed in the back yard; and how all the others were captured. The Pres. must have fled into the wide world in nothing but a shirt because all his clothes were left behind him – even his boots! And his pockets were ransacked and a good many letters and documents found. Some of the men captured are – Generals Cronjé (the Second) Wessels and Fraser and a lot of

---

12   Baron Ostmann.

other very well known, important men.[13] This is a great joy to the English, but I think they forget it in the chagrin at the President's escape. Major Hoskins sat and looked from one to the other while we argued, with an amused smile that tickled me very much. I rejoiced openly and blessed the "small, unnoticed pony" and expressed great admiration for the brave Steyn – the Gen. said he could not understand how anyone could admire a man who had been the ruin of his country etc. etc. I have never known the Gen. so quarrelsome and unkind – as a rule we get on very well, but this morning there was something radically wrong with him. I suppose things are going <u>very</u> bad outside – we have every reason to think so. The poor General would have been even more out of temper had he known where I had just come from, where I was just going to, what I had done and what and whom I had seen. Some day I hope I shall have the extreme pleasure of telling him all about it. But now I must write some letters for Holland.[14]

---

13   See diary entry on 16 July 1901, p 290. The captured men included Generals Andries Cronjé (a Free State general) and Jan Wessels, Pieter Steyn (the brother of the President), State Secretary T. Brain as well as Gordon Fraser, the President's brother-in-law and private secretary. See C.R. de Wet, *Die stryd tussen Boer en Brit. Die herinneringe van die Boere-generaal C.R. de Wet*, pp 239–240; N.J. van der Merwe, *Marthinus Theunis Steyn, 'n lewensbeskrywing* II, pp 20–24.

14   In her book *The Petticoat Commando*, pp 158–164, the diarist revealed what the interesting things were that she saw and heard and did that day, which she would have loved to tell General Maxwell about. It actually began the previous day, when Willie Botha told the Van Warmelo ladies that two spies had arrived in town, were staying with Mrs Hendrina Joubert and wanted to see Mrs van Warmelo. At nine o'clock on the morning of 18 July the diarist and her mother met the spies. They were Captain J.J. Naudé and his private secretary, Greyling. They had some reports with them which they wanted Mrs van Warmelo to forward to President Kruger in Europe. In addition they were looking for a sample of dynamite that had been smuggled to Pretoria from Europe via Delagoa Bay (today Maputo).

     The diarist herself volunteered to fetch the dynamite for them from a secret venue in Pretoria. She went on her bicycle and made sure that she was not followed. At the destination a brown paper parcel and a brief note containing instructions on how to mix dynamite was handed to her. The parcel contained a bottle of yellowish powder – ostensibly a remedy for colic – as well as a pot of paste that was supposedly to be a salve for chapped hands. Mixed together correctly, the two substances would make up approximately half a kilogram of dynamite.

     The diarist was cycling back across Church Square to Mrs Joubert's

July 19th. [1901]

This evening my diary has to be neglected. I have been a prisoner in the house all day with sore throat and have no news to tell. My throat is not really very bad but it was an awful day, cold and windy and we were afraid I might be in for an attack of quinsy so I just took extra care of myself. Mama went to Town this morning and I had some visitors – H[essie] C[elliers] our friend Mr B[otha] with his little walking stick, Mrs Morice and Mrs Struben.[15] Hessie came to tell me how very bad things are in the "refugee" camp here[16] – That whole families have been without tents, living under the open sky night and day, and that they have to pay for the medicine they get. I want to go and see for myself tomorrow. I sat sewing all day and since I left Irene I have not had such a day of rest and meditation. When a woman is sewing she can do no end of thinking and I found myself dwelling on anything but the war and its horrors and miseries – I thought today of L[ouis] and the wonderful way in which we were brought together and the more wonderful way in which he made known his love for me. My own path seems quite clear to me now. I am learning to love him too and this is no school-girl's fancy, but the lasting, true love of a woman, fully matured. Its embers have been slumbering in my heart for nearly four years and needed but a word from him to fan it into a blaze. That word came and took me completely by surprise and left me at first too surprised to realize it but now I have had time to think and all I can say is – I love him, I love him. With these sweet words in my heart and on my lips I want to go to bed – they have been ringing in my ears – the very air seems filled with their melody.

---

house with the parcel under her skirt when she decided to use the opportunity to visit the Military Governor in connection with her proposed visit to the concentration camps. That was how it happened that she entered Maxwell's office with dynamite in her possession. The visit went off well, as described in the diary, and the diarist afterwards proceeded to Mrs Joubert's house with the dynamite, promises of more dynamite to come and instructions on how to mix it. That evening the spies left Pretoria with their mission accomplished. See G.D. Scholtz, *In Doodsgevaar. Die oorlogservarings van kapt. J.J. Naudé*, p 138.

15   Not identified.
16   Probably the Vanderhovensdrif Concentration Camp which was situated on the eastern side of the Apies River north-east of the city centre. See P.J. Greyling, *Pretoria and the Anglo-Boer War*, p 82.

July 20th. [1901]

This evening again I must neglect my diary. I have a long letter to write to W[illiam] S[tead] – someone who is leaving for Europe will take it tomorrow.

Letters from Holland brought us very bad news today. Poor Uncle Henri[17] is dying – he has cancer of the stomach. He must be dead now for the letters are fully three weeks old. It is terribly sad – a man of 54 cut off in all his strength like that. There was also a long letter from L[ouis]. What a strange man he is! He knows that by this time I must have received Marie's communication and yet he says no word about it. His letter is cool and friendly – just as usual – not a hint of anything warmer. It makes me quite anxious and I sometimes wonder if Marie did not make a huge mistake – misunderstood him perhaps! And then my letter to him! Good gracious, I get cold as ice at the bare thought – but what nonsense this is. Still I am in a most difficult position and I think the best thing I can do is to write and tell him that after having thought the matter over carefully I have come to the conclusion that I ought not to write to him again until I have heard from him. Shall I? And go for five or six weeks without sending him a line? I must think about it.

July 22nd [1901]

My last entry was on the 20th. That is because I did not find a single spare moment yesterday. I sat writing from breakfast until dinner time without lifting my head and felt very much pleased with the result of my labours – never mind what they were. And in the afternoon we had a stream of visitors and in the evening I wrote again until Mr B[odde] came to fetch – and then it was too late to tackle my diary and I was sick of pen and ink.

Colonel St. Clair brought me a letter from Dietlof, dated June 5th.[18]

---

[17]   H.A.N. van Warmelo, a notary who lived in Woudenberg in the Netherlands. He was a brother of the diarist's father. See Archives of the *Nederduitsch Hervormde Kerk van Afrika,* Pretoria, L.E. Brandt Collection, IX/165, file titled *Briewe aan Ds en Mevr L.E. Brandt 1892–1911,* unsorted, various letters from Tante Coos to the diarist.

[18]   The original letter is in the Archives of the *Nederduitsch Hervormde Kerk van Afrika,* Pretoria, L.E. Brandt Collection, IX/168, file 3, titled *Briewe*

Dear diary, we are very sad about our President's wife. The poor old lady passed away on the evening of the 20th and was buried yesterday afternoon. We only heard of her death when the funeral was over. Her poor, poor husband! how terrible for him to lose her now when he is so far from home and everything is in such a dreadful state! She died of misery and nothing else – the events of the last two years have been too much for her. It would not surprise me at all if he died too, now that his dear wife has gone. They were so devoted to one another and this separation has been such a cruel trial to them both.

President Paul and Mrs Gezina Kruger

War news there is none and I find myself quite at a loss what to write in this book. Sometime this week I may be going to Middelburg and then I shall have plenty to write about. Mr B[odde] left for Europe this morning. He took a photo from me to L[ouis] to be posted on the Continent. I did not think it quite safe to send it by post from here – there are too many risks, and I should like him to get it in good order.

---

van die kinders Van Warmelo aan mekaar, 1885–1928, unsorted. In his letter he attempts to convey to her the dreariness of his imprisonment in Ahmedwagar Fort, India, and his longing to do something worthwhile for the duration of his detention.

July 23rd. [1901]

Went to the dressmaker – am having a close-fitting costume made of men's serge – a very pretty, dark blue – not quite navy. I am badly in want of a winter dress. Uncle Paul was here this afternoon – brought a very interesting document for us to read. No war news reaches us and I am longing to be on "active service" again. Home life does not suit me at all when there is so much to be done elsewhere.

July 24th. [1901]

Went to Cinatti late this afternoon where I found a very pleasant and sympathetic little gathering – three consuls – C[inatti], N[ieuwenhuis] and A[ubert] – the three warmest pro-Boers. They were discussing the concentration camps and welcomed me with open arms – for am I not an authority on the subject, in a small way? They are filled with horror at the ever-increasing mortality and think the appearance of scurvy in the camps the beginning of great misery. To my surprise I hear that (my) Oom Paul's document of yesterday is public property – it is a copy of two important letters that passed between Burgers[19] [sic] and Steyn – we have them elsewhere. They were discovered at Reitz in the pockets of the clothes Pres Steyn left behind him in his hurried flight and have been published in the Gov[ernmen]t Gazette.[20] I only hope the English also found a copy of the resolution passed by our generals – that will take the shine out of their unholy rejoicings, but of course they will keep a thing of that sort strictly private. I have more to write about but don't feel inclined this evening.

19   Acting President Schalk Burger of the South African Republic. See J.M. Schoeman, Burger, Schalk Willem, in *DSAB* II, pp 106–108.

20   It was not published in the Transvaal *Government Gazette* which was issued in Pretoria. The letter from Burger to Steyn was dated 10 May 1901 and contained suggestions that the governments of the two republics should meet to discuss ways to end the war. The letter included a depressing report on the battle-worthiness of the republican forces in the Transvaal. Steyn answered that he was extremely disappointed with the stance of the Transvaal government and expressed his sincere belief that the Republics should continue fighting. The two governments eventually met at Waterval near Standerton in the south-east of the South African Republic (Transvaal) on 20 June 1901 and decided to go on with the war. This decision was made known to all the fighting burghers. See C.R. de Wet, *Die Stryd Tussen Boer en Brit,* pp 231–233 & 238.

July 25th. [1901]

I can't understand what has come over me – I am so utterly listless when I take up this book, so disinclined to write that I generally content myself with a few uninteresting lines. But it is no use forcing oneself to write and I decline to make an effort. Went to Town this morning, fitted on my new dress, went to Dobbie with Fred, where I had a delicious cup of tea and some cake, went to Mrs Nieuwenhuis and talked politics till 1 o'clock, flew home for dinner and after dinner went to see how the sick children not far from us, in tents, were getting on. Spent the whole afternoon with them – poor souls! It reminded me of Irene and its woes. That was my programme for the day – I am a regular butterfly since I came home and it is high time I set to work again. Met Dr Woodrooffe in Town this morning. He says the sick last week at Irene numbered 100 less and the deaths 10 less – a great improvement. The sight of him made me want to go back to my people at Irene.

July 27. [1901]

I have not found out yet what is wrong with me that the fluency of my pen has so completely deserted me. Even writing a simple letter is a great effort and last night the sight of this book made me feel inclined to flee from the house, so I wisely refrained from making any entry. But tonight I really <u>must</u> – it is no use yielding to this fit of laziness. I have not been lazy "all round" – it is only that I want to get away from my own thoughts and from everything that reminds me of my own personal experiences – the reason is this. I don't know <u>how</u> I am going to get through the next five or six weeks. Until I hear direct from L[ouis] my life is an intolerable burden. I must frankly confess now that I would give anything to be able to recall that impulsive letter of mine. It seemed all right at the time but now my only thought is – What <u>will</u> he think of me? How will he take it? and my only wish is now, that I had written through Marie, as he did. Not that I regret the contents of my letter but I am thoroughly ashamed of myself for having written at all. What will he think of it? It worries me night and day and is making me so unsettled and irritable that I don't know myself. Well, it is no use making myself wretched over what cannot be undone – I must just wait, I must be patient, only it is hard now that I have found out that I – shall I say it again? – love him, love him, love him. But I must not make too many confessions. This behaviour of mine may be such a disappointment to him that he gradually may lose all his love for me – and there I am again! He has never said he loved me and he did not ask me to marry him – all he wanted was a friendly correspondence and there I wrote to him as if I were answering an offer of marriage! It is scandalous. Oh dear, oh dear – shall I <u>never</u> learn? But it is no use – I must just wait – I must try and forget this miserable business.

My neglected yesterday – where was I, what did I do? Turned out the dining-room in the morning – a nice hard work that gives one no time for thought – darned some stockings – a mechanical bit of drudgery, that leaves only too much time for unwelcome suggestions and misgivings; went to vocal rehearsal in the afternoon and sang "like a bird". What did dear Mrs Uggla[21] often say to me? *Als Johanna eenmaal liebt, zal haar mooie stem in een paar dagen ontwikkelen!*[22] I used to laugh at the idea but now I begin to think she was right, as she always is. My voice yesterday was full and rich and clear as a bell – only once or twice I had to be silent because there was a tremor caused by the emotion. I felt at singing again and hearing that divine 23rd Psalm by Schubert – one of the finest productions under the sun, for a chorus of female voices. I have seldom enjoyed a rehearsal so much as yesterday's – there was a pleasant <u>tone</u> and full sympathy between the members.

This morning I turned out our bedroom – I seem to have a mania for cleaning up lately – anything for active work!

This aft[ernoon] I went to see the Governor about our permits for Middelburg. He was very charming and affable this afternoon, to make up for his last discourteous reception, and said I could go as soon as I pleased, only he impressed it on me that he expected a full report of all I had seen in the camps. I am going to travel at Gov[ernmen]t expense and for that reason I am supposed to send in reports. He made me understand that he refuses all other people who come to him with the same request – I am an exception. Of course Mrs Bosman can get

---

[21]   Probably the wife of Ch. Uggla who worked for the NZASM, lived in Celliers Street, quite close to Harmony and is the only Uggla listed in *Longland's Pretoria Directory for 1899*, pp 172 & 212. Spelled Uggea on p 172.

[22]   If Johanna falls in love, her pretty voice will develop within a few days.

permits, but with difficulty and he is very dissatisfied with her because she got permission to go to Potchefstroom, sent him in a meagre few lines and did not go near him again. He says I must not do "like so" – I must pay him a visit when I come home, so that he can cross-question me, I suppose.

He began with politics again but I declined repeatedly to give my opinion, and <u>yet</u> I was drawn into argument. He asked me whether I did not think the Boers ought really to give in now and I flared out with – "Why does'nt [sic] England give in? Why does everyone say the Boers ought to give in? We are fighting for our own and England is fighting for what belongs to another – why should'nt [sic] she give in?" He looked thoughtful a moment and then said, "I suppose it is a matter of *Eendracht maakt macht*[23] – or whatever you call it". I repeated his words and said I failed to see the connection. "Well", he said, "is'nt [sic] Might Right all the world over?" "No indeed!" I protested vehemently, "Might is Right in England and your motto is an apt one, but <u>ours</u> is Unity is Strength! In our land Might is <u>not</u> Right". He seemed much surprised to hear that <u>that</u> was the translation of *Eendracht maakt Macht* and it seems very strange that he should have been so misinformed – I am sure it has been done purposely.

July 28th. [1901]

I was too sleepy last night to continue writing. When I was in the Gov[ernmen]t Buildings, my old friend from Irene, Mrs Rendel-Harris, called here with Mrs Bosman and Mrs Malan. The three ladies have got permission to go to Middelburg tomorrow to inspect the camp and Mama and I are presently going to give them some messages for friends of ours at M[iddelburg]. It is a lovely moonlight night, but very cold – the walk will be delightful. The mail brought us only a postcard today, saying that Oom Henri is sinking rapidly. By this time it must all be over. Not a word from Marie or — anyone else but that is only to be expected.

Gustav F[ichardt] was here this afternoon and we had nothing but war-talk from 3.30 till 5.30. It is an exhaustless topic and we <u>never</u> tire of it – and it is interesting to hear the different tales different people have

---

[23] Literally "unity makes strength" – the slogan on the coat of arms of the South African Republic.

to tell. He was at Mrs Kruger's funeral and says it was very largely attended. An English band was playing waltz and other music in Burger's Park all the time! That speaks volumes for the tact and good feeling of our most noble foe. The very day after the funeral, when Mama went to see the bereaved relatives, the house[24] was in the hands of six detectives and a waggon [sic] was standing before the door, waiting to carry off all the President's private correspondence. There was no question of respect and consideration for the relations in the house.

As far as we know there is no war-news.

July 29[th.] [1901]

Today there is. Consul C[inatti] told me this afternoon that Bremersdorp[25] was taken by the Boers, many prisoners made and 420 000 rounds of ammunition captured. B[remersdorp] is the capital of Swaziland. This is very good news, especially about the ammunition. Even children are becoming rabid little Boers in these thrilling days of ours – I heard something funny about Mrs C[inatti]'s little son – a tiny chap of 5 years. He and his mother were both ill, lying side by side in the same bed, and every time she closed her eyes he said, "*Mammie, maak oop jou oogen*"[26], and at last she turned her face from his persistent little lordship – but then he implored again, "*Mammie, maak oop jou oogen, Mammie kijk naar mij – ik is noch nie een Engelschman nie.*"[27] It is very amusing and one wonders where children get their ideas from. I know many who will never accept Queen's money and always ask for "*Oom Paul se kop*"[28] in exchange.

– We had a letter from Dietlof this morning through Col St. Clair. He writes that we must get a written order from Gen Maxwell that he is to be treated as an officer, not only now, but on his return voyage, as he can't stand the food the burgers get, and no well-educated, refined man can endure the life they have to lead. He is treated as an officer

---

24 President Kruger's house in Church Street was, after the death of his wife Gezina on 20 July 1901, taken over by the South African Constabulary. See W.J. de Kock, *Die Krügerhuis Pretoria. 'n Aandenkingsbrosjure*, p 45.
25 Today called Manzini, in Swaziland.
26 "Mother, open your eyes."
27 "Mother, open your eyes. Mother look at me – after all I am not an Englishman yet."
28 "Uncle Paul's head" – a coin with Kruger's head on it.

now but only as a favour on account of the position he held here in the Gov[ernmen]t Service, but when he is sent home that comes to an end and so he wants us to intercede for him. I shall take his letter to the Governor when I go and fetch our permits on Wednesday. Had a visit from Little B[29] this afternoon. That generally means something interesting but today there was nothing unusual.[30]

July 31[st.] [1901]

Last night, I could not write and this evening I am so thoroughly *"bek-af"*[31] that I don't know what to do with myself. After trotting about all afternoon getting permits and passports and letters of introduction, buying necessaries for the journey to Middelburg, arranging about the clothing, blankets and foodstuffs I have to take for the camp people I come home late and cross and tired to find a letter from the Governor that "for very good reasons he has changed his mind and has cancelled all my permits" – that and no more; curt, decided and without a word of apology or regret.[32] What on earth can it mean? He begs me to return

---

[29]   W.J. Botha – see diary entry on 1901-07-17, p 292.

[30]   In her book *The Petticoat Commando*, pp 187–188, the diarist recorded that Botha brought them extremely disturbing news that day. He revealed to them that in some mysterious way he had received a note from Gordon Fraser, the brother-in-law of President Steyn, who was at that time a prisoner of war in the Rest Camp in Pretoria. In this note the men of the Secret Service were implored to warn President Steyn and General de Wet that one of their prominent officials was actually a traitor who was paid by the enemy to betray their plans before they could be carried out. Fraser's fears seems to have been unfounded. The editor is not aware of any traitor among Steyn's officials.

[31]   "down-hearted"

[32]   The original letter is in the Archives of the *Nederduitsch Hervormde Kerk van Afrika*, Pretoria, L.E. Brandt Collection, IX/187, titled *Algemene korrespondensie 1901–1931 (J. Brandt)*, J.G. Maxwell – J. van Warmelo, 31 July 1901:
"Dear Miss van Warmelo
"Since this afternoon when you came for your permits to go to Middelburg, I have come to the conclusion that it will be better for you not to go. I have allowed Mrs Harris and Mrs Bosman to go & this will be sufficient. I have very good reasons for changing my mind and I therefore beg you will return the permits to me as I have cancelled them.
"Yours truly,
"J.G. Maxwell.
"P.S. Anything you want to send up for the children if you send them to

the papers he gave me this afternoon so I shall trot down to his highness with them and ask "what the dickens" it all means. I am really awfully put out about it and simply cannot understand it. There is mischief brewing sure enough and I could give anything to know what it is. I am too tired and worried to write any more. Had letters from Lady Lily[33] and Mrs Maritz Botha.[34] Yesterday from Mr Bodde that he had arrived safely at Durban.

August 2[nd.] [1901]

No entry yesterday and now it is late and I am tired, but I must make a few notes. Went to Mr C[inatti] yesterday morning and gravely laid the Governor's letter before him. He was furious as I expected and said it was only another proof of the terrible state the camps are in and then he said I must write the Governor a polite and sarcastic little note thanking him for helping me out of a difficulty, as it was really impossible for me to go to the camps and I only got my permits because I had already placed by services at his disposal and I did not think I ought to break my promise (a shot in the eye for the General, who thinks so little of breaking his!) but, I could not go and tell a lot of lies, so I only laughed at my dear, funny old friend, who gets so furious with Khaki that he does not know what to do with himself. Then I went to tell Mrs N[ieuwenhuis] not to pack the things I had to take and there I had to show them the mysterious document too and to listen to their expressions of wrath and disgust. I had a private conversation with Mr N[ieuwenhuis] – very interesting but too – too – private to be mentioned here. He gave me more reasonable advice, so I went to the General and presented him with his letters of introduction etc. We talked for a long time and I asked him whether he could tell me what his reasons were for this sudden change of mind. Oh yes, he could and did but the one was more lame and insignificant than the other. I told him it was a great pity he did not think of these things before making promises he could not keep and it was not fair to me to let me make all sorts of preparations and go

---

me I will see that they are sent up & delivered."

33   Not identified.
34   The original letter can be found in Archives of the *Nederduitsch Hervormde Kerk van Afrika,* Pretoria, L.E. Brandt Collection, IX/168, file 6, titled *Briewe aan Mev van Warmelo, 1878–1915,* unsorted.

to all sorts of expense and then put me off at the last moment, and what do you think he said in self defence? "I was weak". There was nothing for me but to go home after that. Weak indeed! He talks as if I pleaded so hard to go that he had to yield – and as a matter of fact he took up seriously a suggestion that I made more in fun than anything else.

August 3rd. [1901]

I am so much absorbed in "Hilda van Suylenburg"[35] that I don't find time for this poor diary. But what a delight it is to indulge in the luxury of reading once more! Now that my "tour" has fallen through I have much leisure and I am devoting a little of it to music and literature. I cannot go back to Irene until the concert is over and shall make the utmost of this unexpected rest. After hearing for many years about this new woman book I have at last got hold of it and think it very fine indeed. – There are many rumours afloat – that the Basutos are rising in earnest now; that much fighting is taking place in the Colony – in Durbanville, Piquetberg etc; that the Boers have blown up an important bridge, Nel's Poort, I think and a great many other things, that I can't remember just now.

This morning between 10 and 11 a.m. we were startled by heavy firing quite close by in the Johannesburg direction. The pom-poms sounded so near that I was sure they were from the fort but they must have been just behind the hills. It is the first time I have heard pom-poms so distinctly. A great many cattle and sheep were driven into Town – for safety, I suppose – thousands and thousands of the poor beasts, lowing and bellowing and kicking up such a dust! My heart is always very sore for these poor animals. It was bad enough in summer, when food was plentiful, but now that there is not a single blade of green grass and very little water and one wonders <u>how</u> they manage to exist. The European mail has been delayed this week on account of the blown-up bridge.

August 4th [1901] [Sunday]

Dietlof's 29th birthday. This morning's European mail brought us news of Uncle Henri's death. He died on the 6th July at the age of 54 – comparatively quite young. Poor uncle, poor Tante Coos! It is a terrible

---

35   Author not identified.

blow to her – they were so passionately devoted to one another. Their court-ship was quite a romantic affair. They loved one another for many, many years before they became engaged. He was a poor notary, not in a position to marry and too honourable to bind a girl to him for an indefinite period and she spent all the best years of her life in waiting for him, until at last he earned enough money to support a wife. <u>Then</u> he pro-posed to her and they were married and lived very happily. They had no chil-dren. I shall miss him very much when I go to Holland. He was the image of my dear father and his voice and eyes and

Henri van Warmelo, a brother of the diarists father, in his youth

manners reminded me every moment of our dear sainted father, whose memory is growing more and more precious as the years go by.

This morning in church Mr B[osman] alluded several times to the Middelburg camp and its miseries. Things must be <u>very</u> bad. His text was "*Troost, troost mijn volk,*"[36] and his sermon most impressive and touching in its deep sorrow. If ever we needed "*troost*" it is now. Mama and I went to Oom P[aul] for dinner and spent a few pleasant hours with them, in celebration of our dear prisoner's birthday. Heard no fresh war news, although we talked war all the time. Come home at 3.30 in order to receive our usual Sunday visitors – G[ustav] and A[rchie] turned up, but no one else, and they had no news to tell us either. My poor old diary will never get full at this rate but I can't <u>invent</u> news, can I? Mr McFadyn[37] went to Cape Town yesterday and took a small parcel from us to Line – a ring, curios, <u>etc</u> (this last is very comprehensive, a great deal more than anyone can imagine is contained in that single word "etc".)

---

36   "Consolation, consolation my people"
37   Probably W.A. Macfadyen, English lecturer at the State Gymnasium, who is the only Macfadyen mentioned in *Longland's Pretoria Directory for 1899*, p 149.

August 5th [1901] [Monday]

Visit from Mr B[otha] – full account to be found elsewhere.[38] Stormy meeting held this afternoon after vocal rehearsal. We had an extra rehearsal on account of the approaching concert and then I protested against some things our conductor[39] has been doing. He is a very good musician but he wants to domineer over us all and we are not going to allow it. We had a private meeting – only "*het bestuur*"[40], because the members have nothing to do with the case – and I told him plainly that if he thinks he is going to get English people and Khakis and things in our society while the war is in full swing he is much mistaken – and that is just what he has been trying to do gradually. Music has nothing to do with politics under ordinary circumstances but while we are in this bitter struggle he cannot expect us to sing with and be friendly to our country's enemies, and as all the honorary members as well as the "working" members are heart and soul anti-English, he ought, out of consideration for us, to leave things as they are and not try to introduce the "foreign element" while our feelings are so hot. I am quite willing to admit that when the war is over and the English are the victors, we shall <u>have</u> to mix with them – but oh, heavens don't let's talk or think about such horrible, blood-curdling eventualities. Then I shall flee from this dear land of mine. I shall seek fresh pastures in foreign countries, I don't think I <u>could</u> live here under the English yoke. But of course this is all rubbish. We are <u>not</u> going to lose our independence.

---

[38] In *The Petticoat Commando*, p 189, the diarist recorded that Botha visited them early on the morning of 4 August and informed them that on the previous night five spies had reached the town in safety. The five spies found it tough to approach the town, since the searchlights persistently followed them, but eventually managed to creep through the barbed-wire fence and entered the town safely. They then seperated, each going to his own destination. One of the spies was, however, followed by three detectives. When he entered the house where he intended to stay, the detectives closed in. Two guarded the front and the third one the back door. The young spy became aware of this situation. He decided to flee for his life and rushed through the back door. The detective attempted to stop him, but the spy fired on him at point blank range and then fled under the cover of darkness. This spy managed to escape, but the British authorities subsequently implimented stricter vigilance. The diarist referred to the shooting of the detective again later on in her entry on 1901-08-05.

[39] Probably Ten Brink.

[40] "the committee"

- There is some excitement in Town. An English detective was shot on Sat[urday] night (3rd inst[ant]) and died of his wounds at noon to-day.[41] Three of them were on the track of one of our spies and two stood at the front door of the house he entered, while the third guarded the back door. The spy rushed out there and gave the man two shots – escaping into the wide world. No one has seen him since. I hope he managed to get out to our people safely.

August 6[th.] [1901]

de Wet is reported to have been killed. What, again! You may well be surprised, dear diary. I don't know how many times he has been killed and wounded and captured. Consul C[inatti] told us that Bremersdorp was taken by the Swazies and that the Boers followed – that is the latest version. Oh yes, and de Wet has taken a lot of money again £800 000 – after or before he was killed, I don't know which – in the Free State.

This was told us by Little B[otha] whose news is generally fairly reliable. It appears that he stopped a train with his usual "cool cheek" and when the driver pleaded hard for a great many tins containing young trees, which he said was private property, de Wet said that he particularly wanted those tins as the English had burnt all his beautiful trees and it was about time he planted some fresh ones. He ordered the Tommies to carry them away, some distance from the line, and then he said the tins were too heavy, they must take out the trees – and lo and behold each tin was found to contain a smaller one full of money! de Wet pretended to be very much surprised and so pleased that he gave the Tommies each £2 and sent them back to the train. I give this story for what it is worth. As far as I know there is nothing else in circulation today. Our life is going on as usual only there is a feeling of unrest in the air. We are in a state of nervous dread, as if some great thing is about to happen and we are very anxious because we do not hear from Line. Her last letter is dated July 15th and she usually writes regularly every six days. There must be something seriously wrong. The mother will try and send a wire.

---

[41]   In *Die Kappie Kommando*, p 185, the diarist wrote that the detective, Moodie, was not actually killed but seriously wounded and survived.

August 7[th.] [1901]

There has been a lot of excitement all over the Town. I hear that fighting took place near the barbed wire fence round Pretoria last night and that a policeman was shot. One thing is certain that a great many houses were searched for spies "and things" last night.

August 8[th.] [1901]

Today the British Government has issued a fearful and wonderful proclamation.[42] I have not read it yet but I am told that it is to the effect that unless all burgers surrender before the 15th inst[ant] their properties will be confiscated and our officers banished for life. Did you ever? But they quite forgot to add that the officers must first be captured before they can be banished. As to confiscation – well, I am not afraid. I think that the men who are still fighting are influenced by higher motives than England bargains for. To them the loss of worldly possessions has no terrors, and all material considerations sink to insignificance before the loss of independence, freedom, liberty and everything else dear to the heart of a true-born Transvaler. Some of our people are in great depression over this proclamation and fear that many hundreds of fighting burgers will surrender on account of it but I say no, no, a thousand times <u>No</u>! Let me tell how I have argued the matter out to myself. To-night I have a feeling of exaltation. I feel as if the final test has come, the crisis, the turning-point in our eventful career. We have long said that our nation is being sifted – tried by fire. Well, the enemy has done what it could to induce our men to be false to their national instincts. It has taken our wives and children and ruined our homes; it was sure that <u>that</u> would force our men to surrender, but it was most bitterly mistaken. Then it said "I shall deprive them of the small portion of land for which they are fighting," but the Boer's answer was, "Dost thou then believe that we value our worldly goods above wife and children? If the woes thou broughtest on our hearts' treasures, failed to bring us to our desolate homes and at they feet in supplication, dost thou believe that

---

42   Published in Transvaal *Government Gazette Extraordinary*, III/78, 7 August 1901, p 1261. This proclamation was called a paper bomb by the Boers and the State Secretary of the South African Republic, F.W. Reitz, wrote a brilliant satire ridiculing it. See F.W. Reitz, *Oorlogs en andere gedichten*, pp 10–11.

the threat of confiscation of our land will have more weight with us? No, by the God who made us, we shall <u>never</u> yield". And the few who are too weak to fight against this last supreme test – what of them? Their surrender will weaken our forces to a certain extent but what of that? We want our men to be influenced by the purest and noblest motives in this struggle for independence and all who are unable to resist this last temptation (for it <u>is</u> a temptation to leave the thorny path of virtue for the ease and comfort of the "broad way" that leadeth to destruction) are quite welcome to desert the ranks of the fighting few. The time has now come for only our <u>best</u> to remain in the field. May God give them courage and strength. Oh, if I were a man tonight I would glory in the great sacrifice; wife, children, home and now <u>land</u>, gone! – nothing but my trusty Mauser[43] and my weary steed – no helper, no comforter, but the God of my fathers – may these thoughts fill every breast tonight. But I am only a woman, helpless against the sorrows of my people and it is a sad woman I am this night when I think of what I heard today. Rev B[osman] told me that the misery at the Middelburg camp is beyond all description. There were <u>503</u> deaths during the month of July[44] – that fact alone speaks volumes. I am thinking seriously of asking the Governor to let met go for a month to Middelburg instead of Irene, to work in the camp. There is far more need and he can't refuse it if I promise to "be good". I must think about it. And now for a little music to drive away the shadows.

August 10th. [1901]

It is Henry's[45] birthday today. We shall not forget it soon because it has been rather an eventful day to us. After a long and alarming silence we received a letter from Line (written in pencil on account of illness) through the American Consul. And this afternoon we received a parcel from her through a Mr Horn,[46] an English officer. She sent me a lovely

---

[43] The majority of Boers were armed with German 7mm Mauser rifles when the war broke out in October 1899. See J.H. Breytenbach, *Die Geskiedenis van die Tweede Vryheidsoorlog* I, pp 84–85.

[44] According to the table of statistics compiled by J.C. Otto (*Die konsentrasiekampe*, p 172) a total of 404 deaths occurred in the Middelburg camp in July 1901.

[45] Probably Henry Cloete, the brother in law of the diarist.

[46] Not identified.

bracelet and two warm silk spencers, and the mother two blouses. We have also heard news today that has made us very happy, but I can't tell you what it is. This afternoon I went to see how Mrs M[47] was and found a large gathering there – at tennis. I had to stay a few minutes for decency's sake and an officer told me that there was going to be peace in September and when I expressed my surprise, he said, "only they don't know what year". He says Kitchener told someone the war would be over in September and the man asked innocently "But what year, sir?" K[itchener] was furious. I don't think he is the right one to go to with frivolous remarks.

August 11th. [1901]

Sunday. Church this morning and after the service we sang to the empty benches – the H girls[48] and I. It was too glorious for anything – they say my voice was wonderfully sweet and rich. Visitors this afternoon. D.B.[49] told us in confidence that our house is being closely watched and advised us to get rid of all dangerous papers. I think I shall have to take this book away and begin another and then just be more careful in what I put down.

[Entry in the diarist's "Love diary" – back part of script VIII]
Harmony. Pretoria. S[outh] A[frican] R[epublic]. August 11th 1901

This to be my "love-diary" – something quite new and owing its existence to the war, for have we not been told in confidence today that our house is being closely watched and that our private papers may be examined any moment? It is a fact, and there I am with my confessions of love in black and white in another book! What am I to do? Get rid of the tell tale diary and begin a new one? I think I can't do better. This one is being written in lemon-juice and will never betray my secrets, and some day when the war is over I shall just iron out these pages and lo, all shall be clear and distinct for perusal – that is to say if I ever want to read all my nonsense over. I am keeping this diary more with the idea of relieving my feelings occasionally. That is my motive – not because I think my love experiences worth immor-

---

47   Probably Mrs Morice.
48   Not identified.
49   Not identified.

talising. When one is as much in love as I am it is very hard to keep it to oneself, and when the object beloved[50] is thousands of miles away and does not even know he is beloved, it makes things ever so much worse.

This glorious Sabbath! It has been a white, white day to me and I have never been so light-headed and *"levens lustig"*[51] during the war as I was today. I had arranged to sing with some friends after the service in the empty church and we took a lot of music and first sang Mendelssohn's[52] glorious duet "Ich harrete des Herrn" and then I was implored to sing some solos, which I did gladly, for in what way can one better express joy and love and thankfulness than by singing out from a full heart. My voice sounded very beautiful in my own ears but I thought it was because I was so happy but after the first solo they clamoured for another and I sang on and on, my voice seeming to gain in volume and purity as I went on. Afterwards the girls told me that they had never heard me sing like that before and I remembered how often Mrs Uggla had told me that when I <u>love</u> my voice would develope [sic] And now I love and I just want to sing all day. Strange that even in these dreadful days of our[s] love can have such an effect! I did not think I could <u>ever</u> be happy again and yet in the midst of death and danger and oh! such desolation I am filled with a mysterious exaltation, and I only get miserable when I think how far he is and how long it may be before we meet again. I have made up my mind to one thing. I am not going to tell him I love him until I have seen him and judged for myself if I love <u>him</u> or an ideal I have formed from my remembrance of him. It would be a very reckless thing to bind myself <u>now</u> – we <u>must</u> first meet and learn to know one another. Besides it would not be fair to him. I must give him a chance of knowing me thoroughly before he binds himself. When he has seen me again and <u>still</u> wants to marry me, it will be time enough to tell him I love him. If I tell him so now he is bound to marry me – he is a man of honour and will never break a girl's heart – but I shall not give him a chance of ruining his own life's happiness. To me the thought that he wants to marry <u>me</u> is most wonderful. Why <u>me</u>, a poor little Boer girl, when there are thousands of good and beautiful and rich and clever girls in Holland who would require but one word from him, to bring them to his feet? For my love is all a man should be. He is not only very good but he is over six feet and strong and healthy, and his appearance is strikingly distinguished

---

50   Louis Brandt.
51   Exuberant.
52   Felix Mendelssohn (1809–1847), famous German composer.

and aristocratic. Of very good family, refined, noble, cultured – but there my knowledge of him ends. I don't know whether he is clever and I am sure he is not rich but these considerations are nothing to me – all I want is a good husband and that he will be. I like his name so much – Lou Brandt. Everything has been saying it to me today – in music, in the very ticking of the house-clock I hear the words Lou Brandt – Lou Brandt. Fancy, to have gone through 25 years of life and such eventful years as mine have been and never to have loved until now. In all my love-affairs I have never yet been touched by the breath of passion – I have been moved by feelings of pity, respect or deep affection, but love never! I always knew that there was a passionate nature slumbering beneath this calm exterior but I did not know the depths of love and tenderness of which I am capable. He will find out some day. I shall open my rich treasure and pour it into his heart. I shall stagger him with the infinite, the boundless love of which a woman is capable after she has passed the years of silly, sentimental school-girl attachments. Three whole weeks must pass before I can receive that first letter of his – three weeks! How shall I live through them? An even then the question is whether he received my letter in due time – whether there was no hitch anywhere. How am I to contain myself if the mail comes and there is nothing from him? How am I to bear the disappointment? Well, I am just going to fill my life with many interests and I am not going to be too sure that the 1ˢᵗ Sept[ember] will bring a letter – I think I must expect it a week later – on my dear father's birthday Sept[ember] 8ᵗʰ. But how am I going to get through the time before I can go to him? It may be months – it may be years before this war comes to an end and God knows my duty is here even if I feel drawn to him by the powerful chords of love and human sympathy. My love, my love, may God soon bring us together, before we lose the freshness of our youth! Goodnight, dear heart – pray for me ever as I pray for thee.

August 12ᵗʰ· [1901]

There is silence in the Town – no rumours are afloat as far as I know – not an atom of news from the front reaches us. I was informed today, by one who knows, that the women and children are going to be moved to the coast, in order to be nearer provisions. What next! And the war will be over in September!

The following story was also related to me. When Mrs de Wet (our de W[et]'s wife) was moved from her home in the Free State to Johannesburg, an officer stood talking to her in a friendly manner – just before she left her home. Of course it interested him to be so near <u>Mrs</u> de W[et] seeing how impossible it was to get near <u>Mr</u>. He told her that her husband was completely surrounded and would soon be captured, and then taking some eggs one by one from a basket that stood near him, he formed a circle and placed one in the middle. "This is de Wet", he said, "how is he going to get out?" She shrugged her shoulders and began talking of something else, gradually drawing his attention to some engravings on the wall, and as soon as his back was turned, she quietly pocketed the egg. "Hulloa!" he exclaimed presently, "where's that egg?" "Where's de Wet?" she retorted.

Mrs De Wet and her children in Johannesburg

Bravo, Mrs Station Master – I think you were very smart if the story be true. But one hears so many funny anecdotes that spring from some imaginative brain or other – I never believe anything I hear now. A war like this makes one very sceptical.

Mrs Bosman says the Governor told her he was very sorry he had to withdraw my permits, because he was afraid I would never forgive him and he likes me so much and enjoys talking to me, etc and now he supposess I won't go and see him any more. How is one to understand his behaviour? He is a regular weather-cock. Mama had to go and see him this morning about a young Dutch doctor who is anxious to come up from the Colony to work in one of the camps. Line wrote about him and begged me to go to the Gov[ernor] and ask him to wire at once, but I declined the honour and sent the mother who was received most cordially and had her request instantly granted. So it appears that "the clouds are rolling bye Johnnie" - I hope so; it is dreadful to be on the black list and to have a sword hanging over one's head.

[Entry in the diarist's "Secret diary", written using lemon juice and not ink - front part of script VIII]

August 17th 1901. Harmony. Pretoria.

The following official despatch was brought us a few days ago from our generals by spies.

Afloop onderzoek der gevangene "handsuppers" door Veldcornet Baden-horst by Zandspruit. Op Donderdag laatsleden werden op de plaats van H. van Groneveld naam onduidelyk geschreven ter dood veroordeeld G. Brits C. Brits P. Brits O. Brits vier zoons van G.B[rits]. Hendrik Kock en Martiens Brits tot 20 gezel slagen en vogelvry verklaard F. Kock, L. Joubert, L. Kock elk 25 geeselslagen en vogelvry verklaard. Zekere D.G. Oosthuizen werd staatsgetuige gemaakt. In gevecht laatst leden Maandag sneuvelde F. Kock, zijn zoon Lodewyk werd gewond. De vonnissen zijn laatstleden Vrydag voltrokken.[53]

Ermelo 30 Juli 1901. Oorlogsbericht

Omtrent de Zwazie Expeditie werd de volgende berichten ontvangen. Gen[eraal Tobias] Smuts en Ermelo commando namen 10 wagens waarvan vyf beladen: - 15 000 patronen, 1 hand maxim, 50 geweren

---

[53]   "Outcome of investigation of detained "handsuppers" by Field Cornet Badenhorst at Zandspruit. Last Thursday, on the farm of H. van Groneveld name not clearly written the following were sentenced to death G. Brits, C. Brits, P. Brits, O. Brits four sons of G. B[rits]. Hendrik Kock and Martiens Brits each 20 lashes and outlawed. F. Kock, L. Joubert, L. Kock each 25 lashes and outlawed. One D.G. Oosthuizen becomes state witness. In a skirmish last Monday F. Kock killed in action, his son Lodewyk wounded. The sentences carried out last Friday." This report could not be confirmed by other sources.

ongeveer 400 beesten, 50 paarden. M. Joubert die zich onder de roovers (Engelschen) bevond werd dood geschoten, terwyl Jan Tosen 10 geselslagen en £25 boeten, kreeg. In het gevecht sneuvelde 18 roovers en werden gewond 37 gevangen genomen. Aan onze zyde gewond A. Cameron, vleeschwond aan been J. Roos, P. Retief. 5 of 6 Kaffirs zijn doogeschoten. Bremersdorp is in assh gelegd als zynde een schuilplaats voor de roovers".[54]

This despatch reached us yesterday.[55]

August 19ᵗʰ· [1901]

For a whole week no entries! The fact is I have had no end of writing work to do and every day, when that was done, I felt disinclined to make my usual notes. Besides there was nothing particular to write down – only rumours one more wild and extravagant than the other.[56] For about

---

[54]   "Ermelo 30 July 1901. War report. The following reports were received on the Swazi expedition. General [Tobias] Smuts and Ermelo commando captured 10 wagons of which five were loaded: – 15 000 rounds of ammunition, 1 hand maxim, 50 rifles about 400 cattle, 50 horses. M. Joubert who was with the thieves (English) was shot, while Jan Tosen was given 25 lashes and fined £25. In the fight 18 thieves were killed and 37 wounded were captured. On our side A. Cameron flesh wound leg, J. Roos, P. Retief. 5 or 6 Blacks were shot. Bremersdorp was burned down since it is a shelter for thieves."

[55]   General Tobias Smuts did indeed burn down Bremersdorp (later renamed Manzini) in Swaziland on 21 July 1901. Commandant-General Louis Botha sent Smuts there after receiving complaints from the Swazi Queen Regent Labotsibeni concerning the conduct of an irregular British unit called Steinaecker's Horse, who allegedly looted Swazi homesteads. See P.G. Cloete, *The Anglo-Boer War*, p 254.

[56]   Actually there were exciting developments to write about, which the diarist briefly alludes to in her secret diary entry on 1901-08-22 and later on revealed in more detail in her book *The Petticoat Commando*, pp 205–212. In that book she records that:
"[On 15 August Willie Botha walked] up the garden path of Harmony, wearing that air of happy mystery so familiar to his fellow-workers.
"The spies had come at last, not the Captain [Naudé] himself, but his secretary, Mr Greyling, with two other men named [Jan] Nel and [Willie] Els ... They ... were staying with Mrs Joubert ...
"Mr Botha ... told [Mrs van Warmelo and her daughter] ... that these men had been sent to procure a copy of the secret railway time-table, an official book containing full detailed information on the military trains ...
"Mrs van Warmelo promised to do her best, but gave her visitor little hope of success. [The Van Warmelo ladies spent the rest of that morning]

ten days we were told most persistently that Kimberley had been taken by the Boers, and now it seems to be a fact, only one does not know how much to believe of the ornaments attached to the story. Dame Rumours says for instance that diamonds were taken to the value of £25 000; that the Gov[ernmen]t Buildings and all great warehouses etc have been destroyed as well as more than half of the private dwellings; that de Beers and another mine were blown up; that damage was done to the value of between 8 and 11 million sterling; and that (and this is the best of it all) that de la Rey borrowed the cannon from the English, with which he cleared his way to Kimberley. It is said that he dressed himself or one of his staff as an English officer and went with some Boers dressed as tommies to ask the officer in command of some troops to lend him his

---

in seeing different people, trusted friends, on the subject ... [They were everywhere] met with the same objections. Most people had never heard of this time-table, and those who knew of its existence, were convinced that it would be quite impossible to get a sight of it, as it was in the hands of officials only...

[Suddenly they thought of someone who could help them – a person only referred to as D. They met him near Church Square. He was not very positive:] 'I know the book exists, but I have never seen it ... If by any chance I am able to procure a copy, you will find it under your front door between 5 and 6 o'clock [this evening].'

"Well satisfied, the two ladies ... went to Mrs Joubert's house to tell the spies that there was just a chance that ... [they would procure the time-table] ... Whether she found the time-table at Harmony or not, Hansie promised to come back that evening, with the European and Colonial newspaper cuttings, so eagerly sought after by the men on commando.

"Arrived at Harmony at about 5:15. Hansie could conceal her impatience no longer, but, running up the garden path, she threw open the front door with a flourish, and behold, a small flat parcel on the floor, a book wrapped carelessly in a bit of white paper! The secret time-table! ... [With on the slate-coloured cover an instruction in thick red letters:] *For the use of officers and officials only...*

[Hansie immediately took the time-table to Mrs Joubert's house, where she handed it to Greyling] "with strict injunctions not to mention her name on commando, for it was a well-known fact that there were traitors in the field, who lost no opportunity of conveying information to the British. She did not tell him how the book had come into her possession...

"They parted in fun and high good-humor, but Hansie's heart was wrung with many a pang, and many a deep and earnest prayer for their protection was sent up by her that night."

This history is also briefly related in G.D. Scholtz, *In Doodsgevaar. Die Oorlogservarings van Kapt. J.J. Naudé*, p 146.

Maxim Nordenfeld as there were some Boers near – he would return it within the next few hours – but when it did not come the officer went with his men to fetch it and was kept away by his own cannon! And so de la Rey marched into Kimberley with 500 men, being followed afterwards by his whole force of 5 000. So the story goes.

In short I shall try to tell the other news. Carolina, Bethal and Bremersdorp have been destroyed; the Boers were 3 days in possession of Wellington; Morley's Scout have been completely smashed up; Gen Botha is somewhere on the Eastern line; one of our commandants came in (so Khaki says) with 100 men and surrendered on the last proclamation! There is so much to tell that I don't think I shall go on – my other and more important writing claims all my time and attention now.

<u>Evening</u>. Hessie [Celliers] has come in from Irene and has just been here. She told me a lot of news. One night they heard a lot of firing close by and heard next day that a poor donkey who refused to Halt! and who did not say who went there was shot dead. He was buried with military honours and some time later his brother met his end in the same manner. Capt Morley[57] is dead – died of wounds received when his scouts (all <u>Boers</u> drilled by him) were routed. Capt Hunt[58] also dead. Capt Morley is only badly wounded (<u>Later</u>.)

[Entry in the diarist's "Love diary" – back part of script VIII]
August 20[th.] [1901]

A letter from my love – he calls me his dear Johanna, for the first time and oh, how the blood rushes to my face and how fast my heart beat! And how happy I am because now I know it is all right and his answer to my letter will be what I expect. Dear heart, I am learning to love you more and more every day and it will be quite a task to keep my secrets from you but in that respect my duty is quite clear to me. I <u>cannot</u> bind him until he has seen me and asked me again – it would be most unfair to him even if he thinks

---

[57]   Captain R.W. Morley, a British officer who commanded a "joiner" unit called Morley's Scouts. See A.M. Grundlingh, *Die "Hendsoppers" en "Joiners". Die rasionaal en verskynsel van verraad,* pp 227–233. No evidence that Morley was wounded could be found.

[58]   Captain P.F. Hunt of the Bushveldt Carbineers was killed in a skirmish on 6 August 1901. See A.M. Davey (ed.), *Breaker Morant and the Bushveldt Carbineers,* pp xx–xxi.

he loves me now and is sure of himself. I am not going to take advantage of the difficulties that are in his way and I shall never give him the chance to regret his rashness. He must remain free until he can see me and judge for him self whether I am "worthy". Of course I know I am not worthy but never mind I shall not tell him if he does not find out for himself. He need never know for I am sure I shall "grow good" by his side. But how am I going to be merely friendly to him for an indefinite period? how stay the torrent of love words that rush to my lips whenever I take up the pen to write to him? I shall require all my self control if I want to be true to my convictions. This book must be my confidant until I am free to confide in a warm living human heart. When will that time come? The years are slipping past and I am getting old, with all my cravings for love and sympathy unsatisfied – and a woman at my age has strong desires and many unsatisfied longings unless she can shower her heart's treasure of love on some worthy object. And he is worthy – thank God I know as surely as womanly instinct can tell anything that he is good and that his life has been as pure as any girl's. And I have always wanted to marry a pure man. Perhaps that is why my 25th birthday will find me still in single blessedness – I was never sure of anyone. But my faith in him is absolutely perfect. My Lou, if you only guessed one tenth of the love and longing of my heart tonight. Just those few words from you have made me realize what you are to me.

Do you know, dear, that I was very sad when your letter came. Let me tell you all about it. I once had a sweetheart – just after I met you – a German aristocrat, an officer – just as straight and tall and distinguished as you are but much handsomer – a regular Adonis Apollo. Never has anyone loved me so madly. He met me one evening at the Middelbergs'[59] musical reception and heard me sing and fell in love with me then and there. I doubt whether even you can ever love me as he did – it was something too sweet and wonderful and intoxicating. I had never know anything like it before and was in great danger of being carried away by it, especially as everyone – relatives and friends – urged me to encourage him. Everyone knew because he could not have hidden his feelings anymore than the sun can hide

---

[59]   Middelberg, Gerrit Adriaan Arnold was an engineer and director of the Nederlandsch Zuid-Afrikaansche Spoorwegmaatskappij (NZASM) (Dutch South African Railway Company). He and his wife Leopoldina lived in the ZASM house in Market Street (later renamed Paul Kruger Street) where they held weekly musical evenings. See Spies, F.J. du Toit, Middelberg, Gerrit Adriaan Arnold, in *DSAB* II, pp 473–474.

his light. When I was in the room he had eyes and ears for no one else, he was ever at my side, he met me wherever he could and called here as often as possible and very nearly intoxicated this poor little country girl with his passion. And he was good, an honest upright man with a wonderful history that made his love for me more incomprehensible still, and the respect and tenderness he showed me were enough to turn any girl's brain.

But something kept me back. Were your prayers even <u>then</u> hovering over me dear Love? What was it that gave me the strength and courage to be cool and reserved to my ardent lover under <u>all</u> circumstances. To this very day I cannot tell but I think your image filled my breast even then. He was not a Christian but that could not have kept me from loving him though it certainly would have kept me from marrying him – there was something else that kept me unmoved under his warmest words and the reserve on my part only inflamed him more and made him more determined to win me but it at least kept him from declaring himself for many months. I hoped to avoid that altogether but it was not to be and when I told him gently and pityingly (for my own heart was full of sorrow) that it could never be and that I am a woman of character and my <u>no</u> means <u>no</u> he straightened himself like the brave soldier he is and took it as a death blow with white lips firmly set and great drops of perspiration on his drawn brow. Dearest, I think I suffered nearly as much as he did for I hate to give anyone pain. When the dreadful ordeal was past he took my hand gently and asked whether I had not even friendship to give him. With a great sob in my throat I promised him that for life and tonight he needs it. Oh, my friend, he wants it so badly and where can I find him? He left Pretoria after my refusal because he could not remain near me and became officer in command of the Johannes-burg Fort. That was just before the war and when war was declared he was one of the first to go to the front, he, an *Uitlander*,[60] with no ties and duties here, and for nearly two years he has been in the field, always in the thick of every battle, with his brave artillery and now, oh God, he has been cruelly wounded. He was riding ahead of thirty-five of his men when a maxim was turned on him. He has lost one arm and got one shot through the shoulder and another through the leg. His men were also terribly mauled about but he got the full brunt of it. And now that beautiful body is maimed for life and he is a helpless cripple! Oh, it is too dreadful. May God reward him for his loyalty and faithfulness! I am so proud of him now, Lou, and so proud

---

[60]   Outlander/foreigner.

that he used to love me, as proud as he is of his wounds tonight I am sure. We are trying to find out where he is.[61] Goodnight, dear Love, goodnight, only two weeks more before I get your letter!

Aug: 22nd. [1901]

It seems to have become the rule now that "gaps" should appear in my diary. I am very sorry but have been frightfully busy. Am getting sick of pen and ink – have so <u>much</u> writing to do always. The news of Kimberley seems to be true – Mafeking has been burnt, Stellenbosch in our hands – also Hanover, according to some people. Great hauls have been made

One of Line's daughters with a doll that was used for smuggling

in Machadodorp where our people took clothing, food and ammunition. Posters are up all over the Town announcing that if the Boers do not surrender before the 15th Sept[ember] a proclamation will be issued that peace will be declared and all men caught in the field after that will be shot as rebels. What next! I suppose they will officially announce to the Powers that the Republics have been annexed and if they accept it, it will really be a fact. I also hear that some time ago a Reuter's cable in one of the Natal papers told of an offer of intervention from the Dutch Queen to Pres Kruger, if he would be satisfied with the Suzerainty and his answer was No! We think she must be supported by the great

61   Perhaps Captain von Wichmann (or Weichmann), who was of German descent and with whom the diarist was acquainted. She wrote him a letter while he was serving with the State Artillery on the Natal front in the early stages of the war to which he answered sending greetings to her mother. See Archives of the *Nederduitsch Hervormde Kerk van Afrika*, Pretoria, L.E. Brandt Collection, IX/168, file 6, titled *Briewe aan mev Van Warmelo, 1878–1915*, unsorted, F. von Wichmann – J. van Warmelo, Opper Tugela, 1900-01-28.

Powers or she would not dare to offer anything like that and the President knows he is going to get absolute independence or he would not have refused such a good offer. But I am not even sure about it, and very few people seem to know anything about it. - Mrs M left on the 20th inst[ant] with three dolls for Line's children.[62]

---

[62]   In her book, *The Petticoat Commando*, pp 58–60, the diarist supplies detail that adds significance to this simple bit of information:
"The next adventure was with a charming lady, who we shall call 'the English lady'. She was so *very* English. (If the truth were known, she was not really English, but Cape Colonial, and, as is often the case, more English than the English themselves, and more loyal to the Queen).
"She [was planning to leave for England when she] unwisely said to a friend of Hansie's ... that she would take good care not to convey letters or parcels for the Van Warmelos... because she was quite sure they 'smuggled', or, if she did consent to take anything, she would examine it thoroughly and destroy whatever it contained of a doubtful character.
"When this reached Hansie's ears she made up her mind that 'the English lady' and no other, would be her next messenger to Alphen. She ... deliberated long with her mother. At last she was sent to town to buy three medium-size dolls.
"It did not matter what kind of dolls they were, but they had to have hollow porcelain heads, and they were bought from one man only, an indispensable fellow-conspirator in one of the principal stores in Church Street.
"When she came home with the dolls her mother seemed pretty well satisfied with the heads; they looked fairly roomy from the outside, and so they were found to be when one of them had been carefully steamed until the glue melted and the head dropped off.
"Hansie had been writing, without lifting her head, while her mother prepared the doll. The sheets of paper, rolled up into pellets, were then forced through the slender neck, and the dolls weighed to see if the difference in weight were noticeable. It was not. The head was glued on again, a blue cross was marked on the body, and the dolls were neatly wrapped in a brown-paper parcel.
"'The English lady' soon after came to pay her farewell call. After the usual formalities had been exchanged she remarked that she hoped to visit Alphen soon after her arrival in Cape Town.
"Mrs van Warmelo was charmed and delighted, and asked whether she would be good enough to take a parcel of three dolls for Mrs Cloete's little daughters.
"There was just one moment's hesitation, then 'the English lady rapidly made up her mind.' 'Yes, with pleasure, but I must have the parcel tomorrow, because my trunks have to be closed and sent on ahead.'
"Mrs van Warmelo turned to her daughter in grave consultation. 'Let me see, it is too late now, the shops will be closed, but you can perhaps go to town on your bicycle early to-morrow to buy the dolls and have them sent straight to Mrs.-'s house'.

We had a visit on Tuesday from two English ladies - Quakers - who have come to inspect the camps and alleviate misery wherever they can.[63] They brought a letter of introduction from L[ine] and are coming to spend tomorrow morning with us.

Two of our men were shot yesterday - two mere boys - caught going out with documents and I think food etc to our people.[64] Khaki is becoming very strict, which shows that he is very uneasy. My own private opinion is that Khaki is at his last gasp and next month we shall have the extreme felicity of parting from him.

[Entry in the diarist's "Secret diary", written using lemon juice and not ink - front part of script VIII]

August 22nd [1901]

I hear that our three spies[65] had quite an escape after I parted with them on the evening of the 15th. They drove in a cab as far as the wire fence that encloses Pretoria with a friend who always goes with them to see them "safely off the premises". He had a pass but they had none (every man has to carry a residential pass and may be asked by every policeman to produce it). Just as they neared the fence the searchlight from one of the forts was turned full on them, making broad daylight of the darkness of the night. They were so terrified that one ordered the cabby

---

"'Yes mother, I'll do that with pleasure, but I won't have them sent. I'll take them to her myself to be quite sure that she will have them before twelve o'clock.'

"The next morning Hansie took the dolls to her fellow-conspirator behind the counter and had them made up into an unmistakably *professional*-looking parcel, tied and sealed with the label of the shop.

"Thus were the suspicions of 'the English lady' lulled to rest. For her comfort, should this ever reach her eye, I may say that there were no dangerous communications in the doll's head, and should she feel resentful at having been outwitted, she should have known better than to *dare* one of her country-women under martial law."

63   Anna Hogg of Dublin and Annie Frances Taylor of London. Both belonged to the Society of Friends (the Quakers). See R. van Reenen (ed.), *Emily Hobhouse Boer War letters*, p 457n. See diary entry on 1901-10-08.

64   The one was Reiner Christiaan Upton (1867–1901) who was found guilty of espionage for the Boers on 13 August 1901 and executed on 22 August 1901. See T van Rensburg (ed.), *Camp diary of Henrietta E.C. Armstrong*, p 111 and also S.B. Spies, *Methods of Barbarism?*, p 72.

65   Greyling, Nel and Els – see footnote 56 on p 317.

to turn to the right and another to the left but fortunately he ignored them and boldly rode straight on, thus disarming the Tommies of any suspicions they may have had at seeing a cab so near the fence at night. A whole crowd of soldiers were standing near some corrugated iron buildings, laughing and talking and looking at the cab. Fortunately the light was soon turned in another direction and the three men descended with their parcels and took leave of vdW.[66] They were soon in the deep furrow along which they creep until they reach the fence, and cautiously wending their way to friends and liberty when someone came running after them and shouting to them to stop. It was v[an] d[er] W[esthuizen] with a parcel they had left in the cab! That was a very risky thing to do and nine men out of ten would have let the parcel be. The cabby is a relative of one of the spies and in the whole secret so he comes in very useful. Greefling[67] said he would probably come to town again on the 10th Sept[ember]. I hope to see them again – it is most interesting and relieves the dreariness of our lives. No one can understand how refreshing it is to meet men who come straight from our commandoes especially when one is in the hands of the enemy and one only receives war news from one side. We know that these spies at least bring in reliable information.

Aug[ust] 24th [1901]

I am not feeling very well and have been playing an invalid's part for a day or two. My "tummie" is out of order, dear diary, and tomorrow I am going to have the pleasure of taking a dose of castor-oil, which reminds me of childhood's days and its desperate struggles whenever that most painful task was forced upon me.

There is no news as far as I know – at least all I have heard is that Khaki has been getting paddywhacks at Bronkhorstspruit. Capt Morley is not dead, but badly wounded through the stomach. – Our vocal society has decided to give an invitation concert on Sept[ember] 6th and I have to go to the Governor to get a permit. – We had a terrific duststorm this afternoon and now some rain is falling. It is a dreary, windy night and I am in a bad fit of the blues – perhaps because I am not feeling well. I shall go and make a little music – that might cheer me up a

---

66   Van der Westhuysen, the cab driver who is referred to as "a friend" earlier in this entry.
67   Greyling.

little. Am learning a lovely Italian song and a few new ones by a Swedish composer, Lass_on (not Lass_en).

Aug[ust] 25th [1901]

No mail delivered yet and I am so impatient. Next week I can get an answer to my letter to L[ouis] – the time has flown, after all. There is a rumour that our old President is dead. Of course we don't believe it. Mrs Louis Botha visited the Queen of Holland. The Queen went personally to Hilversum to condole with our Pres when his wife died, and every flag in the Netherlands was hanging half-mast, even over the palace. The Queen is the pluckiest, bravest, fair-minded-est, little woman that ever lived and I do not wonder at the pride and adoration of her people.

We had a <u>terrific</u> hailstorm this afternoon and heavy downpour of rain afterwards. Hailstones the size of big almonds (in their shells). Lots of damage done in the garden, but the world looks quite new now – after all these many months, dry and dusty, such a storm clears the atmosphere and cleanses all the griminess of the long winter months. We are thankful for the rain. Now the grass will grow and our commandos will have plenty of food for their horses. – Not well enough to write more.

August 26th. [1901]

A long day of coddling and playing the invalid. This is my third day at home but tomorrow I hope to be all right again. I have just been reading and darning stockings all day and weeping copiously from sheer depression and anguish and unrest of soul. This last "employment" is most unusual with me and has frightened me into believing that some great calamity is about to befall us. My mammie went to Town this afternoon and I sat in the empty, silent house fighting against the fears that came creeping upon me. I worked feverishly, but my eyes were blinded by tears – I took up a book and tried to read, but my whole body was shaken by a tempest of sobs, so I had to yield and let nature have its way with me. Strange, for one as calm and self-controlled as I am. Of course the mother noticed it at once and wanted to know what it was all about, but she said very little and lets me go my ways when there is something unusual with me. One thing is certain – our mammie never <u>prys</u> into her childrens' secrets.

This evening I have read a most beautiful book - "Het Zusje" by Henri Borel. It is a sequel to one I read a few weeks ago. It is not a book one can discuss lightly - nor do I feel myself able to "review" it this evening - it has entered deep into my soul and its influence will be with me for the rest of my life, of that I am quite sure.

August 27th. [1901]

"Playing the invalid" has become a serious business with me. Dear diary, I have a touch of dysentry and look and feel a perfect ghost. May it soon be over and may it not lead to some serious illness - typhoid or anything similar! I am particularly anxious to keep well until the concert is over and then I am more anxious than ever to be well, for have I not today been informed that I must get ready to go back to Irene towards the 7th Sept[ember]. It will only be for a month and the mother has half consented to let me go, if she can get someone to sleep here while I am away. Went to Town this afternoon in spite of feeling very weak - or rather because I felt so ill and had an idea the walk would do me good. Went to Munro[68] and had another photo taken because no one likes the first - this time in walking dress with straw hat on. I suppose you think me a vain, frivolous creature but it is for him and I want it to be a good likeness. From there I went to ask Gen Maxwell for the permits to hold our concert (noticed with amusement that the urchin wrote under my name "nature of business: - permission to have a consort"). Governor was engaged but Major Hoskins gave it to me and then we sat talking and I asked him whether he thought Dietlof would be allowed to go away from Ahmednagar[69] to some other place, because he could not stand life in a fort and the heat and confinement were giving him slight attacks of congestion of the brain - an old complaint of his. He said if we wrote and told D[ietlof] to place himself in the hands of the medical officer he might be allowed more freedom - long walks and better food - but he did not think he would be sent anywhere else. Had a letter from the dear boy today again - he is a good correspondent.

---

68   J.C. Munro, a photographer in Market Street (today Paul Kruger Street). See *Longland's Pretoria Directory for 1899*, p 155.

69   The prisoner-of-war camp in India where Dietlof van Warmelo was a captive. See D.S. van Warmelo, *Mijn commando en Guerilla-commandoleven*, p 214.

August 31st. [1901]

Dear diary, it is four days since last I wrote in you and I can thank God all the days of my life that I am writing again so soon. I had an idea my days were numbered and I really have been very ill. This sharp attack of dysentery has left me quite a wreck. I am, oh, so weak and <u>so</u> hungry now and they won't let me eat! Yesterday I tried to read but had to put away the book because it said "she brought him a cup of tea and a host slice of brown buttered toast" and then it spoke about sardines and soft-boiled eggs until I flung the book into a corner and stared at it in moody silence. This morning the mother consented to give me a little tea and brown toast (without butter) because I would not rest until I got it and for my lunch I had chicken-broth and a biscuit and now I am already wondering what the next thing will be.

Riek H[70] has been awfully sweet and attentive and Mrs Nieuwenhuis came to see me and Uncle Paul and Aunt C[lara] and on Thursday we had a long visit from Little B. I lay on the sofa while he told us all the news he could think of and cheered me immensely. There has been a great fight. We captured 27 officers and 2 000 men and I think 5 cannon. I forget where this is supposed to have happened. The men were released but the officers are to be kept prisoners until the 15th Sept[ember] so that we can see what England's next move is to be. If they shoot any of our men as "rebels" those officers will be shot down one by one like dogs. If England is going to begin anything of that sort after the 15th (and it seems to be the general opinion) this will be "war" no longer but "murder" on both sides and I know which side will suffer most. Now I must go and rest a while.

<u>Evening.</u> A glorious moon rising; sweet, pure fresh air, with a summery-evening feeling about it and in my heart the sweetest music. For why? Because <u>the</u> letter has come – most unexpectedly – and has made a red letter day of this sweet spring day – no, not <u>red</u>, a pure white, dazzlingly, bewilderingly sweet day and evening and night – a day never to be forgotten as long as I live – of renewed and slowly returning health, of chicken-broth and biscuits, of purple hyacinths, pale green ferns, snowy frezias [sic] with yellow hearts and intoxicating scents, of beautiful books arousing the thoughts of beauty and holiness slumbering in my

---

[70]   Not identified.

breast and lastly, in the deepening twilight, in the hush and solemnity of evening, his letter – the first love-letter from my love. Oh, it was almost too much for me in my present weak state. How secure he is in his faith, how he trusts God in everything! How sweet and good and noble he is! I am only just beginning to realize it and to feel my own unworthiness. He wants me to come to him – oh, how my heart bounded at the thought and how I had to struggle with my own longing and impatience – to resist this temptation to leave home and mother and brothers, friends, country and people for him. If everything here were peaceful I would go but now I dare not think of it. My duty is here and here I shall stay even if I knew that he would get impatient and refuse to wait, and marry someone else. It would break my heart, for at 25 one does not get over things as easily as at 17, but I would have to do it. But he will never change. He tells me that seven years ago he broke off an engagement. So he too has had to go through that mill – I know what it means and how much suffering and humiliation there is in those few simple words. This makes me so much surer of him, for no one makes the same mistake twice – at least not people who are thoughtful and earnest and who take the lessons of life to heart. I am going to write to him this very evening although the mail only left yesterday and a whole week must pass before the letter goes. This is the Queen of Holland's birthday. How strange and sweet and lucky!

September 1st [1901]

Sunday. This has been one of the most perfect spring days I have ever enjoyed – I shall never forget it – but now I am off to bed. I have been behaving myself like an ordinary mortal today and feel rather tired now. Never closed my eyes last night, strange to say! There was a big military funeral this afternoon – some Lieut Col who was killed on the Pieters-burg line when a provision train was taken by the Boers.[71]

---

[71] On 31 August 1901 Republican scouts under command of Jack Hindon derailed a British military train between Waterval and Hammanskraal north of Pretoria. When the troops on the train refused to surrender, the Boers opened fire. The British casualties amounted to about 40 men, of whom one officer, namely Lieutenant-Colonel C.F.S. Vandeleur, 13 men, one civilian and two black men were killed. The Boers seized ammunition, dynamite and food supplies. See P.G. Cloete, *The Anglo-Boer War*, pp 261–262.

[Entry in the diarist's "Love diary":]
September 1ˢᵗ [1901]

This has been such a golden and glorious spring day and I have been so intensely happy that I must write in my "love diary" tonight. Love on one side, war on the other. Between them I am developing into quite an interesting creature. One thing is certain, my character is being fully matured in these days of stress. Why has today been so sweet to me? Because I have received my dear Love's first letter and I have been quite intoxicated with my own bliss. Last evening it came. I only expected it today but the mail was delivered earlier than usual for my express benefit. I was crazy with joy last night. I could not sleep but lay on my back staring into the gloom, thinking, thinking, praying, smiling, sighing, praising alternately, all through the night. And this is a sensible woman of 25 with a world of sorrow and suffering behind her and perhaps a future more heavily laden still with the woes of mankind. But you see, dear love-diary, in all my many rich and varied experiences I have never loved before – strange as it may seem. It is a fact and I have often heard and read that if you "take it" at a mature age you "take it" very badly indeed. It seems to be the truth. My love wants me to go to him as soon as ever I can. He does not say he loves me, he does not ask me to marry me [sic] all he shows me is that he wants me and that he does not know how to wait for me. I am so delighted that he says I gave him no encouragement and even sometimes took away the hope he had. That is just as it should be after he treated me so badly long ago: But now I am going to make up for everything and dear diary, you have no idea how charming and refreshing and sweet it is to say all sorts of nice encouraging little things to a man who is'nt [sic] engaged to you, but to whom you fully intend engaging yourself some day. My love has been engaged before. That was quite a little slap in my face just at first but now I am satisfied. It has done him no harm and if he learnt as much by it as I did by my own unlucky engagement, we can both be very thankful for it. He says he is "very happy". That is a good deal from such a reserved man.

[Entry in the diarist's "Secret diary", written using lemon juice].
September 1ˢᵗ 1901.

Quite a long time has passed since last I made "private" notes. My mind has been much occupied with other things but now I have some news to tell. I think I mentioned in some other book that v[an] N[ikkelen] Kuyper and two others were in a fix and Mama was asked to conceal them. She refused, for she has orders from Naudé[72] to have dealings with him and Gr[eyling][73] and [Little] B only – not to expose herself by taking in other spies. Well, I begged her to take pity on these men but (most fortunately) She would not hear of it. The men were concealed by other friends and after some days escaped safely to their nest in the S[churve] Bergen.[74] We had nearly forgotten them when news reached us of their capture last week, Kock,[75] Botha,[76] Kuyper and two others. They were brought into Town and their trial is in full swing. Yesterday Mama came home with appalling news, Kuyper had turned King's evidence and was giving away his comrades one after the other. The cad, traitor, hound, mean sneak, coward, ugh! I want to go into a fit when I think of him. To save his own precious skin he is betraying the good friends who risked their all in giving him shelter. Five Hollanders have been betrayed and of the men who were with him, two will be shot on evidence he gave against them. But that is not all. He is even going out of his way to give information unasked. He has told the English how the spies come in and out, when they come, where they take refuge! O God, I cannot bear to think that there are such people in the world. The enemy has put a strong guard at the place (near the Lunatic Asylum)[77] and now I don't know how N[audé] and G[reyling] are to come in again. The English had not the faintest suspicion on that spot and are now in their glory over this valuable infor-mation. My blood runs cold when I think what an escape we had. Such a fellow would have told that we had harboured him and then we would have been "in for it". In this way we may still be betrayed some day but I hope not. Then we shall have no more chances of doing good apart

---

72 Captain J.J. (Koos) Naudé. See J.P. Brits, Naudé, Jacobus Johannes, in *DSAB* III, p 652.

73 Naudé's private secretary. See J. Brandt, *Die Kappiekommando of Boerev-roue in geheime diens,* p 46.

74 Skurweberg – a hilly area west of Pretoria.

75 Not identified

76 A Boer spy Willie Botha – not Little B. G.D. Scholtz wrote about this inci-dent that two spies were captured by the British when they attempted to enter Pretoria. When told that they were to be executed, they revealed the names of members of the Secret Service of the Boers whom they knew. The British subsequently arrested James Gilliland, Botha and Christiaan Hattingh. See *In Doodsgevaar. Die Oorlogservarings van Kapt. J.J. Naudé,* p 165. A search of British military records in the National Archives in Pre-toria revealed no evidence on this incident.

77 On the western side of Pretoria.

from all the misery that may be inflicted on us. That timetable[78] alone is enough to bring us "to the stake".

It is working wonders judging by the numbers of trains that are flying into the air now. Last week three – all heavily laden with provisions. One had a lot of Khakis on board and the poor things were awfully mauled about. I don't know how many were killed and wounded and when the Boers stormed the wreck, some of the unhurt Khakis showing fight and were terribly cut about. A Lieutenant-Colonel[79] was buried this afternoon with military honours. I heard strains of the funeral march and wondered what it meant and was told the whole story by Gustav [Fichardt]. This happened on the Pietersburg line. The great loss of life in connection with these trains preys on my heart since we had a hand in it. I feel as if we are helping to murder and yet our commandoes are depending on the taking of those trains. They get their food, clothing and ammunition from them, in fact the continuation of the war depends on the number of trains they take. We had [a] hand in sending out the dynamite and fuse etc wherewith to blow them up and now through us they know what time it has to be done. But I fear the English will soon change their time table at this rate but then we must just get hold of the new one too to send out.

September 2nd. [1901]

When that officer was killed the Boers made a great haul. The train was laden with provisions and thousands of pounds were taken in money – all the salaries of officers and men and officials. Thirty-seven men were killed and wounded. It happened 15 miles this side of Pietersburg and the Boers had waited eight days for that train. First came two trucks laden with Tommies, then the engine, then more trucks and another engine and then all the provision-trucks and carriages. The Boers were very smart. They laid the detonaters and fastened a string to them which a hidden Boer pulled as soon as the first two trucks were safely over, so that the engine was wrecked. Then they stormed the train and fought until 37 Tommies were killed and wounded and the rest surrendered. One whole truck contained nothing but "drink" – I hope our men won't misbehave themselves when they get hold of it. Lieut

---

78 The railway time-table that the diarist and her mother procured for the Republican spies – see footnote 56 on p 234.
79 Vandeleur. See footnote 71 on p 329.

Colonel Vandelier[80] (or something) was in a carriage with three women and some children and when the explosion took place he put his head out of the window saying "I want to see if there are any Boers about". The next moment he drew back suddenly and told the women to get under the benches and while he was speaking a bullet went through his heart and he fell at their feet dead. One of the women was wounded, and afterwards a boer walked into the carriage and told them the fighting was over and they were out of all danger. Rumour says that he then and there stooped down and pulled off the dead man's boots and took his watch etc., but I don't believe it. – de Wet has been up to all sorts of mischief in the Colony, for a notice is up in Town that the Rev Murray[81] has been sent out to beseech our Napoleon to withdraw his commandos from the Colony. How silly the English are sometimes! None of us knew where de Wet was and we were beginning to worry over his strange silence and now they "give the show away" themselves. He is burning farms and ruining homesteads there as they have done here. Apr 27 1902: This was not true.[82]

[Entry in the diarist's "Secret diary", written using lemon juice:]
September 2nd. [1901]
More revelations! That hound Kuyper has given away about 15 people in Town and he has even told the English by whom he was met outside – Greefling,[83] Otto[84] and one other. No one knows all the names of the people who have been betrayed. Ours may be one of them! and I very much fear that the J's[85] and Little B have been given away. I trotted to

---

80   Vandeleur.
81   The Reverend Charles Murray of Graaff-Reinet planned this peace mission himself. He and the Rev J.F. Botha of Richmond indeed met both Pres. Steyn and Gen. De Wet on 9 Sep 1901. They failed in their endeavour, since Steyn said he would only recall the Republican commandos from the Cape Colony if the full independence of the Republics were guaranteed. De Wet added that arrangements were being made to send even more commandos into the Cape Colony. See A.M. Grundlingh, Die "Hendsoppers" en "Joiners". Die rasionaal en verskynsel van verraad, pp 138–139.
82   This sentence was later inserted by the diarist, probably on the indicated date.
83   Greyling.
84   Not identified.
85   Probably Mrs Hendrina Joubert, wife of the late Commandant General Piet Joubert and their son Jan Joubert (J.J.).

Town this morning to see the latter but found no one at home. I was very eager to know whether they are safe so far because Little B told Mama that on Friday evening he was coming home when he met a man he knows, Pullen Preller,[86] with a girl. The moon was shining brilliantly and just as he had passed them he heard Pullen say: "This man has also been given away". He went home in a great fright and told his wife and the two poor souls never closed their eyes. The worst of it is we shall not know who is on the list. The English will not say a word to the betrayed but just watch them unseen and unsuspected. We are all making up our minds to be extra prudent in future but we are living on a burning volcano. The tension is very great. The only man Kuyper has not betrayed is his brother-in-law, Delfos,[87] who harboured him. He was supported by three of his comrades so it appears that they made up their minds beforehand to betray all. It makes me very sad to think that there are such base people in the world. If Greefling [sic] mentioned our names to them it is all up with us. He would sooner die than bring us into trouble but these young men live in an atmosphere of danger – Death is their daily bread – and they have become quite reckless. He may have told these men in a confidential moment that I was with him just before he went out of Pretoria and – dread thought! – that I had brought him a t[ime] t[able]! *Dan is die gort gaar!*[88] There are great events in the air! We shall hear of wonderful things soon.

Received Line's first lemon communication today! Things are "fine" in the Colony, she says we must let our generals know that something is brewing in Europe and they must try and hold out another six months.

September 3ʳᵈ· [1901]

This evening I am writing for the mail and have no time for this book – besides there is nothing particular to tell.

[Entry in the diarist's "Secret diary", written using lemon juice:]
September 3ʳᵈ [1901]

Great excitement again today. J.J.[89] came to us this morning quite early

---

86   Not identified.
87   Cornelis Frederik Delfos (1868 – 1933), who is regarded as the pioneer of South Africa's iron and steel industry, was married to Johanna van Nikkelen Kuyper. See W.P. van R. van Oudsthoorn, Delfos, Cornelis Frederik, in *DSAB II*, pp 170–171.
88   Then the fat will be in the fire.
89   Jan Joubert, a son of the late Commandant-General Piet Joubert and his

with the news that there were four spies in Town and two were going out again tonight – if we had anything of importance to send now was our chance. One of them is a boy of about nineteen, Erasmus – Mrs J[oubert]'s adopted child.[90] His parents were both killed by lightning when he was a child and the J[oubert]'s took him. He has been in the field all along and this is his first visit. He arrived last Sunday evening and when asked by them "what the Dickens" he wanted here in the heart of danger he said he had come to see how they were all getting on (!!) and to get some clothing and horse-shoe nails etc. They came through Skinner's Court[91] and did not see a single Tommy and had heard nothing of Kuyper's treachery. J.J. wanted all sorts of European and Colonial news to send out so this afternoon we took him a packet of cuttings that friends have been collecting for us for this very purpose. Mama also sent a match-box with a false bottom, underneath which was a letter for Greefling [sic] – a tiny, closely written letter containing some information and warnings to be very careful. This boy will see him and tell him that the road is guarded and that they must by no means come in the way they always do, also that his name has been betrayed by Kuyper. At first they were angry with this reckless boy but now we see how useful he may be and I think it is a great blessing there is someone who is going to warn the others. J.J. hunted all over the town for nails but could not get them. The stores only sell them to black-smiths and military etc and the blacksmiths wanted to know why he could not bring his horses to them to be shod. He did not ask at any stores because it would look too suspicious and so Erasmus has had to depart without these articles. We were there at 5.30 and at 6 he was to leave. Mrs M[92] was going to drive out with him a far as she could. We did not see him because it is not safe to have to do with too many of these spies. Since that Kuyper business everyone is extra careful.

September 7[th.] [1901]

On the 4th inst[ant] I had no time to write, on the 5th we had final rehearsal, when the mother and I were escorted home in a terrific dust

---

wife Hendrina. Joubert was seriously wounded in the Battle of Nooitgedacht in December 1900 and spent the rest of the war in Pretoria. See G.D. Scholtz, *In Doodsgevaar. Die Oorlogservarings van Kapt. J.J. Naudé,* p 136.

90 Probably L. Erasmus. See J. Brandt, *Die Kappie Kommando,* p 259.
91 On the western side of the town.
92 Probably Mrs Malan, the daughter of Mrs Joubert and step-sister of Erasmus.

storm by G[ustav] F[ichardt] at 9.30, and he had to tear home on his bicycle in order to be in before 10 o'clock, and last night the concert came off. So it comes that I have made no entries. On Thursday I went to see the Rev B[osman] to tell of my intention of going back to Irene next week. He told me that he had received a letter from the English Gov[ernor] asking him to call up a church meeting and to propose that the church should act the part of peace-maker. He read his answer to Gen Maxwell to me, in which he absolutely declines to have anything to do with the matter and gives as reason that he cannot act without the *Voorzitter*,[93] who is absent, or without the Vice-voorzitter, Dr Ackermann,[94] who is seriously ill; also that he cannot be expected to break the oath of neutrality and several other very good reasons. He had to choose his words carefully so as to not to offend too much by refusing. To my amazement I heard in Town that day that the English had commandeerd seven of our "leading townsmen" to travel backwards or forwards on the trains to protect them from the Boers. They tried the same dodge long ago – in the beginning of the occupation – but it was a failure. The men chosen are Beckett,[95] Rood,[96] Brugman,[97] Vorster,[98] Bell,[99] Smit[100] and another. I don't know whether

---

93   Chairman.
94   D.P. Ackermann, minister of the Dutch Reformed Congregation of Wakkerstroom, was the deputy chairman of the Synod of the Dutch Reformed Church in Transvaal. See De Villiers, D.W., Ackermannn, Daniël Petrus, in *DSAB* V, p 2.
95   Probably T.W. Beckett, a prominent businessman and owner of Merton Keep, a residence in Arcadia. See *Longland's Pretoria Directory for 1899*, p 115.
96   Probably Karel Rood, owner of Parkzicht, a residence in Maré Street. See *Longland's Pretoria Directory for 1899*, p 163.
97   Probably the son-in-law of General Koos de la Rey, Dr J.L. Brugman.
98   Probably Swart Barend Vorster, former member of the First Volksraad. See *Longland's Pretoria Directory for 1899*, p 174.
99   Probably P.W.T. Bell, the director of the State Printing Office. He is the only Bell listed in *Longland's Pretoria Directory for 1899*, p 115.
100 Probably J.S. Smit, the former Railway Commissioner. According to A.M. Grundlingh, *Die "Hendsoppers" en "Joiners". Die rasionaal en verskynsel van verraad*, p 184, only Vorster, Brugman, M. de Villiers and I. Haarhoff were actually forced to go back and forth with the trains between Pietersburg and Pretoria. J.S. Smit successfully protested against participation in the process.

they are going. Some are trying to get out of it and say they cannot possibly break the oath of neutrality by assisting the English – which is an excellent reason for refusing to do anything of that sort. Of course the Boers would not worry their heads about these men if they have made up their minds to take this or that train, and that is what makes this action so ridiculous. England has indeed come to a sorry pass if she has to resort to such measures. There is plenty of other news but I can't remember it all. For three days there were no Cape mails and the European mail has also been delayed – that means, of course, line destroyed somewhere.

– The Kuyper[101] trial continues and I heard today that 20 people are one the list now. Whether our name appears I cannot tell, and we shall not know just at first. Everyone thinks Khaki will keep the names very close and watch all suspected people until they have "proof positive". Otto[102] has been captured too – the man who was supposed to have shot the detective. He says Louw[103] shot him and not he (Otto) and that Louw was mortally wounded in one of the recent engagements (got four bullets) and when he was dying he told Otto that he had shot the detective. I wonder whether Otto says it to remove suspicion from himself – very likely that is how it is – and while there are no proofs he can at least not be condemned to death. We think that two of the prisoners will be shot and the rest sent away. Mrs A.F.[104] was on the list to be sent away and someone told us and asked us to warn her, which we did yesterday, and now I hear that our mutual friend CDC[105] interceded for her and "averted the catastrophe".

I wonder whether anyone will be kind enough to intercede for us if ever we get into a similar scrape.

– Our concert last night was a great success. To begin with, there were no Khakis, incredible as it may seem. Then the music was lovely, the refreshments plentiful and very good, the decorations extremely artistic and lastly there was a friendly, cheerful, homely tone about the whole

---

101   The trial of the spies in which G.J.E. van Nikkelen Kuyper gave evidence against his former comrades.
102   Not identified.
103   Not identified.
104   Probably Mrs Anna Fockens.
105   Probably Consul Demetrio Cinatti.

gathering which is quite unusual with public places of amusement. The girls were all in white or cream and looked perfectly charming and each one wore a spray of flowers, presented by *"Den Directeur."*[106] I suppose there were some English spies present, as there always are everywhere, but they did not see or hear anything that had to do with politics, except the conspicuous absence of the Khaki colour, a fact which speaks volumes for the patriotic sentiments of our society. I quite enjoyed myself and everyone says I looked "lovely". I wore cream silk and chiffon and lace and a beautiful garnet pendant.

This morning at 11 o'clock we all assembled in the Hall, in our evening finery, to have our photo taken on the decorated platform grouped round ten Brink, who was seated before the lovely black Bechstein grand. I hope the photos will be a success. Then we divided equally amongst us what remained of the refreshments and came home laden with cakes etc like a lot of school children. Now our frivolities are at an end and we are going to set to work seriously to study some new things – at least, the others are. I am going to study other kinds of things at Irene – patience, perseverance, endurance and Heaven knows what besides. I don't know what has come over me but this time I dread the thought of Irene. Perhaps it is the prospect of the great heat, against which I cannot stand, but the fact remains that I would give anything to get out of it. It would be easy enough because Mama wishes me to stay, but they want me there and I feel that my duty is to go.

September 8th [1901]

Mama has been ailing for some days and is not at all well – in fact she feels so ill that I have been obliged to give up the idea of going to Irene. She simply dreads the thought of losing me, even for a month and as I am all she has, I suppose I must stay with her if she wants me. It was with a great effort that I made up my mind to stay, perhaps because it is so much pleasanter at home and I was afraid of being influenced by thoughts of home comforts and luxuries. I have sent H[essie] C[elliers] word that she must get ready at once to go in my place – she can be spared from home and is eager to go. But now I mean to go in for hard work and make the most of my time at home. I shall practice "like a

---

106   The Director.

house on fire" and do a lot of good reading and devote as much time as I can to works of charity. I am certainly not going to waste my time.

I have had a lovely day. R[iek] H.[107] spent the morning with me and we sat under the trees, sewing and talking and enjoying the great beauty and infinite peace of dear Harmony, and this afternoon we had a crowd of visitors and I had to entertain them alone because the mother could not appear. For the fun of the thing I shall mention all the names here: – Consul Cinatti and Cèléste, Baroness Pitner,[108] Consuéla Minnaar, Mr and Mrs Leliveld, Sophie Dürr and her sister, Fred and Gustav and afterwards Riek again with a message to the effect that I was requested to go round tomorrow afternoon with Mrs Eloff, President of our Vocal Society, to thank some of the people who helped us with our concert. Mr Cinatti told me privately that the Boers had had a great victory. Three commandos attacked the English at Lake Chrissie, between Ermelo and Carolina and "squashed" them completely, taking no end of stores and ammunition. Lake Chrissie was a sort of depot of the English.

Today is the anniversary of my dear father's birthday. I wonder whether our boys remembered it – Dietlof in India, Willem in Holland and Fritz in the field.

For continuation see the second book like this.

---

[107]   Not identified.
[108]   Wife of the Austrian Consul-General in the South African Republic.

[Script VII]

"Harmony". Pretoria, S.A.R. Sept[ember] 9th 1901.

My old dairy and I parted company this afternoon in a strange and unexpected manner and now I have to begin a bran[d] new one. The poor thing was'nt [sic] even old – it was in the prime of its life – only just half full and there it is this evening far from its beloved mistress. She is trying to console herself with a new confidant but cannot help thinking regretfully of the old. I have all sorts of confessions to make and find myself absolutely tongue-tied, because if I am not very careful I shall have to part with this book too, before it suits my convenience. It has been an eventful day. –

Tomorrow I shall write down some of my experiences but now I must go to bed. Mama is ill and was examined by Dr Clara Weiss[109] today, who advises her to keep very quiet indeed. Consequently I have had to give up the idea of going back to Irene – it would be very unnatural to leave home and nurse strangers when my own mother requires my services.

[Entry in the diarist's "Secret diary", written using lemon juice:]
September 9th 1901.

Such a morning as I have had! We are in great danger and I am writing this before taking it to a place of safety. Every paper in the house is [sentence unfinished. Followed by open space of about 2 centimeters in the script]

There I lost my place – Dr Weiss came to see Mama and I had to go to her and now I don't know where I am. That is the worst of this kind of ink!

I believe I was just saying that we have removed every document and paper out of this house to some place of safety. I am afraid this book must go too – it is very incriminating – that is if ever Khaki gets hold of it and sees a few words and subjects it to the heat necessary to bring out

---

109   In the early phases of the war Dr Clara Weiss was a medical doctor with the Klerksdorp section of the Transvaal Red Cross. See A.P. Smit & L. Maré (eds), *Die beleg van Mafeking. Dagboek van Abraham Stafleu*, p 65n.

what I have written. Well, let me be quick about telling my story. This morning before breakfast a girl came in a great state of mind to tell us that Little B was arrested last night at 8 o'clock by two detectives. Poor dear little man, so he too is on the list of the betrayed! I dressed and went to Town at once after making a hasty meal as Mrs B[otha] wanted to see one of us and the mother is not well enough to go out. I first went to AC[110] and he advised me get rid of all incriminating papers at <u>once</u>. He told me that Fritz Krause who took the oath of allegiance and is in the English service in England has been betrayed and is being sent out to S[outh] Africa to be tried for high treason.[111] He was working for us all the time and the AC thinks that Kuyper and that set gave him away. Then I saw the young men who have been helping us DB[112] and F[red] N[iemeyer] and G[ustav] F[ichardt] and told them that our fellow-conspirators had been arrested. We were all in a highly excited state and DB told me "in confidence" that we are sure to go over the border after the 15th. Well, the mother and I are packing! And I drew every penny of our money out of the bank this morning – saw the manager myself and told him Mama had a large sum to pay and she required all the money we had in the bank. He fortunately asked no questions and helped me himself to pack the bundle of banknotes into my hand bag. If the English hear of it they will know at once that we are on the alert but I hope the manager won't mention it.

Now where was I again – another interruption! I went to Fred [Niemeyer] to leave the notes in his safe while I went to make a most dangerous visit. I went to see our poor persecuted little friend Mrs B[otha] who is in very delicate health and was trying hard to be brave and unconcerned. She told me how it all came about. It appears that the man Otto, with whom her husband has always worked and who was caught some time ago, was condemned to death. He was very brave and staunch about

---

[110] Not identified.

[111] F.E.T. (Fritz) Krause (1868–1959) was a lawyer and state prosecutor in the South African Republic before the Anglo-Boer War. As special commandant of the Witwatersrand he had to surrender Johannesburg to Lord Roberts in 1900. Subsequently he was allowed by the British authorities to stay in the city. In 1901 he was allowed to go to Britian, where he was indeed charged with high treason. Eventually, early in 1902, he was sentenced to two years imprisonment for 'incitement to murder'. After serving his sentence he returned to South Africa where he ended his career at a high age as a respected senior judge. See J.N.R. van Rhyn, Krause, Frederik (Frits) Edward Traugott, in *DSAB* III, pp 479–480.

[112] Not identified.

refusing to betray anyone but when he heard the death sentence and was offered a pardon if he mentioned the names of some of the people he knew were in communication with our generals, his heart failed him and he gave away Little B. Mr Liebenberg[113] and will you believe it? <u>his own</u> sweetheart Miss du Plessis,[114] who is in the Pretoria Goal at this very moment with three other women who were arrested. Does it not seem incredible that a man can become such a craven-heart at the thought of Death? My brain refuses to grasp it. What other persons he has betrayed we do not know. He has saved his life but at the ruin of his own soul – his honour. From my heart I pity him.

Last night Little B and his wife were sitting under the verandah at about 8 o'clock when two detectives arrived on bicycles and produced a warrant for his arrest. They searched the house and took home every paper they could lay hands on but fortunately he had been prudent enough to remove all serious things previously. That is a great blessing for without proofs they can do absolutely nothing. He promised his wife that he would never betray a friend – that they could shoot him before they got any information out of him, and she told him she would rather never see him again than know him to be a <u>traitor</u>. She is a brave and true woman.

It was dangerous for me to be seen there and I soon went away, for the house is being closely watched and I am sure a detective followed me home and took my address. I went to Fred [Niemeyer] to get my hand bag and then hastily jumped into a cab in the hope of escaping any followers but men on bicycles can go anywhere and there were several travelling along my way. Mrs Louw, mother of the young man who shot the Detective and who is reported to have been killed in action afterwards, is also betraying people right and left. If women are beginning to talk too, I am afraid we are done for. I wonder whether <u>I</u> would betray anyone if I were starved and ill-treated and threatened with death. I don't think so! It may seem a conceited thing to say but for the life of me I cannot imagine myself giving away a friend for the sake of saving my own skin. It does not seem possible and <u>no</u> van Warmelo would do it.

September 10th [1901] [Secret diary]

The cordon is drawing in round us and I feel tonight as if there is no way of escape for us, look where I may. This morning I went to Town

---

113   Not identified.
114   Miss Lottie du Plessis.

again to see what news I could fish up. What I heard staggered me. JJ was also arrested with Little B. I cannot realize the awful calamity that has befallen us all. I heard particulars this morning from Rev B[osman]. He tells me that Otto stood the trial bravely and refused absolutely to betray a single friend. He was put into a cell by himself and on Saturday evening at 10 o'clock they read his death sentence to him by way of giving him something pleasant to think of during the long hours of the night, and then they casually remarked that his life would be spared if he mentioned the names of some of the men who are in communication with the spies. Poor boy! I can so well imagine his struggles that night and how he wrestled with himself before he made up his mind to save himself at the cost of his honour. On Sunday morning he gave the names required of him – six men, Liebenberg, J. Joubert, Willem Botha (our Little B), Franz Smit, Els and Hattingh,[115] and three or four women of whose names I am not aware except that of his sweetheart, Lottie du Plessis. If he had been a dead man tonight I would have honoured his memory all my life, but what is he now. A Traitor, oh God, a traitor to his land, his people and his love – and a <u>coward</u>! And the worst of it is, he would not have been shot. He is under age and there were no proofs against him and he could under no circumstances have been shot. But he saw no one and had no advisers and had to fight his temptations by himself. What grieves me to the very heart is to think that Krause[116] and his companion[117] gave their lives for <u>this</u> – two noble men, heroes, who would have been spared if they had chosen to betray their friends. They held the fate of all these men in the hollow of their hand and yet they remained staunch and true to the very end. Not a word escaped their lips and they met death bravely and undauntingly as any man of honour would. The men who were caught on Sunday are all trustworthy – except Els. Rev B[osman] told me this morning that he would not be surprised if Els turned King's Evidence and then it is all up with us. He is

---

[115]   Gert Els and Christiaan P. Hattingh. Els was a shoemaker and the father of the Boer spy Willie Els. Hattingh was the Chief Caretaker of the Government Buildings in Pretoria and a deacon in the Dutch Reformed Church. He never actually left Pretoria but worked for the Secret Service Commission within the city until he was captured. See J. Brandt, *Die Kappie Kommando*, pp 126, 132 & 174–181; G.D. Scholtz, *In Doodsgevaar. Die Oorlogservarings van Kapt. J.J. Naudé*, pp 52, 133.

[116]   Adolf Krause. See J. Brandt, *Die Kappie Kommando*, pp 220–226.

[117]   Venter. See J. Brandt, *Die Kappie Kommando*, pp 224–225.

father of the young spy[118] I met at J's[119] on the 15th Aug[ust] and is the only man we never felt quite sure of. Of course we are in a great state of nervousness and dread and Mama, who is not at all well, is worrying herself terribly.

Yesterday we removed every incriminating paper from this house so that in case of an unexpected arrest we may at least not have proofs of our guilt in the house. That is the advice we have received from all our friends. Of course this book is enough to bring us into the greatest trouble but I doubt whether Khaki will worry his head about what appears to be a blank exercise-book. If he were to take this thing home and put it into an oven to "cook" he will be much astonished at the result.

Commandant-General Piet Joubert and Mrs Hendriena Joubert with their son Jan (J.J.) a few years before the war

Fred told me this afternoon that he saw Mrs J[oubert]'s carriage standing before the Military Governor's office. I wonder whether the poor old lady went to plead for her son. To think that our Com[mandant] Generaal's [sic] wife should be in such serious trouble today! We can be thankful that the poor old man did not live to see this day. The general opinion is that Little B will be sentenced to death – if they find proofs I am sure he will, but then please God, I shall be granted courage enough to save his life by betraying my own share in his doings. If I promise to give away one person if they will spare his life I am quite ready to confess my own "sins", even if they shoot me – but I shall never give away anyone else – oh dear me, no, diary mine. Never, never, never!![120]

---

118   Willie Els. See J. Brandt, *Die Kappie Kommando*, p 228.
119   The Jouberts. See footnote 56 on pp 317–318.
120   In the original script the third 'never' underlined twice.

September 11th. [1901]

Mama is still ill and I have been too busy to write. I shall tell the latest news briefly – President McKinley[121] is dead. Lord Milner is in Johannesburg and Lord Kitchener went over to see him this morning. Now we are all looking out in great anxiety and expectation to further developments. The fateful 15th is fast approaching – I wonder what it will bring us. We must be patient.

[Entry in the diarist's "Secret diary", written using lemon juice:]
September 11th. [1901]

This morning I went to see JJ's sister, Mrs Malan, to hear the details of his arrest. It was not advisable to go to his own house as the chances were that it was being closely watched. She was ill – influenza and worry and anxiety, but I saw her and she told me everything. Poor old Jannie [Joubert] is in the Rest Camp.[122] On Sunday night the Provost Marshall [sic] himself and another officer "called" and declared their intention of searching the house. He wanted to know where the ammunition was! Imagine the consternation! Jannie said he knew of no ammunition except a box full of cartridges standing on the loft that had been lying about the house and which they collected when the English took Pretoria. He took them up to the loft and showed them the box and they said he must appear the next morning before the P[rovost] M[arshal] to give a satisfactory explanation. They found no documents in the house except an old heliographic chart which the Com Gen used to use long ago in Kaffir wars. J[annie] went next morning and had to give an account of himself. It does not seem to have been quite satisfactory, for Khaki sent him to prison. He was very independent and absolutely refused to take the oath of neutrality which he has hitherto escaped, strange to say. His mother went to the Governor and I believe he has promised to release her son on condition that he "signs parole". They have been treated with great kindness and courtesy and the English evidently have not the faintest suspicion of the real state of affairs. I asked Mrs M[alan] what she would do if Naudé and Greefling [sic] arrived tonight and she coolly

---

[121]   President McKinley of the United States was shot by an anarchist on 1901-09-06 and died a few days later.

[122]   *Arrest* Camp, the diarist calls it in her book *The Petticoat Commando*, p 249.

answered *"Ik zal hulle herberg"*[123] so <u>her</u> brave spirit has evidently not been daunted by these events. Of course she is by no means sure that the English <u>don't</u> know <u>all</u>. This leniency may be only a blind. Even our names may be known – in fact we expect detectives here any moment. While Mama is ill they can at least not send us away but we may be kept prisoners at Harmony until she is well enough to "travel".

September 12th [1901] [Secret diary]

Copy of letter:- *10 Sept[ember] 1901*

Aan Zyn Hoog Ed Den Staats President

Europa

Hoog Ed. Heer.

Daar wij in zoo zwakke kennis zijn is deze U.H.E. misschien een verrassing. Als Hoofd van Speciale Diensten (werken) onder onze Ed. Gest. Comdt. Generaal heb ik de gelegenheid U.H.E. deze korte rapport te maken.

Aangezien of door afwezigheid onzes Com. Gen. is het mij onmogelijk hem te zien doch met onze H.Ed. Waarnemende President Burger thans in dist. Ermelo geef ik U.H. Ed. de vaste vertrouwen dat het hem nog wel gaat. Verder met al onze andere commandos hier in Hooge Veld zoowel in andere gedeelten van Transvaal en O.V.S. gaat het zeer goed en staan nog vast. In de Kaap Kolonie gaat het ook nog goed volgens onze laatste rapport, dan heeft de vyand in de nabyheid van Cradock een groote verlies en iederen dag worden onze commandos grooter en grooter door burgers die nog steeds aansluiten. Onze vyand heeft nu hunne handen vol en voeren nu hunne troepen naar Basutoland en K. Kolonie alwaar zij zich net zoo noodig heeft als in Transvaal en O.V.S. en verder wordt door den vijand alle pogingen aangewend ons onze wapenen neer te laten liggen. Wy hebben onze vertrouwen in den Aller Hoogsten Die onze zaken iederen dag voor ons lichter maakt. Het is U.H.E. misschien bekend dat al onze vrouwen op verschillende plaatsen, dorpen enz[ovoorts], in kampen geplaatst zijn en volgens laatste rapport uit Pretoria dan gaat het met onze arme vrouwen treurig en ellendig. Er zijn ook vele sterfgevallen. Onze plaatsen, huizen en veld zijn geheel afgebrand and vernietigd doch aan paarden, kleeding and voedsel hebben wij nog geen gebrek. Alhoewel velen van ons getal is afgegaan stryden wy nu nog dapper voor onze zaak en kosten Engeland nog iedereendag

---

[123] "I will accomodate them."

levens voor hun onrechtvaardige en onheilige zaak. Wy wenschen U.H.E.
gezondheid en gespaard leven toe en bevelen U in de handen van den
Allerhoogsten opdat U.H.E. uw dapper volkje in een Vrije Republiek eens
weder mocht ontmoeten, hetzy over dagen of over jaren. Het spyt my
dat het niet raadzaam is mijne naam te mogen noemen en blyf met
Hoogachting Uw Eds.

Dienst w. Dienaar

Hoofd Speciale Werken der Z.A.R. ten Velden. [124]

---

[124] "10 Sept 1901
To his Excellency the State President
Europe
Your Excellency
Since we have so little information this will probably be a surprise to Your
Excellency. As the Chief of Special Services (works) under our Comman-
dant General I use the opportunity to make this brief report.
On account of or because of the absence of our Commandant General
it is impossible for me to see him but with our Acting President Burger
presently in the Ermelo district I can assure you that he is well. Indeed all
is well with all our other commando's here on the Highveld as well as in
other parts of Transvaal and the Orange Free State and they stand firmly.
In the Cape Colony all is similarly well according to our last report, the
enemy suffered a major loss near Cradock and our commando's grow in
numbers each day with more burghers joining. Our enemy is fully occupied and are sending troops to Basutoland and the Cape Colony where
they are needed as much as in the Transvaal and the Orange Free State
and furthermore the enemy attempts to convince us to lay down arms.
We trust in the Almighty who makes issues more bearable for us every
day. Your Excellency is probably aware that all our women are placed
in camps in various places and towns and according to the last report
from Pretoria the poor women are in a pitiful and wretched state. There
are numerous deaths. Our farms, houses and veld has been torched and
demolished but we have sufficient horses, clothing and food. Even though
our numbers have dwindled, we are still fighting gallantly for our cause
and costing England lives for their unjust and unholy cause. We wish you
health and may your life be spared and may you remain in the hands of
the Almighty and meet your brave people again in a Free Republic, either
within days or within years. I regret that it would be unwise to mention my
name and remain Your Excellency's Willing Servant
Chief of Special Services of the South African Republic in the Veld.

Copy of letter to the Committee of Spies in Pretoria:-
Sept[ember] 10th 1901.

De Wel Ed. Heeren H.E.B.B.[125]

Wel Ed. Heeren.

Door Gods goedheid ben ik nog in staat om Uw Ed. Heeren rapport te maken dat alles hier met ons zoowel met al onze andere commandos nog wel gaat. In myn plaats zend ik u myne Luitenant en verzoek ik U Ed. beleefd om hem te voorzien met alle rapporten bizonderheden omtrent alles. Door omstandigheden ben ik verhinderd om zelf in te komen. Ik moet Zn Ed. Gest. den Com. Gen. persoonlijk zien, doch bij andere keer wensch ik u zelf te zien. Ik verzoek ook s.v.p. dat U Ed. my rapporteren waar mijne vrouw is en alles omtrent haar. Ingesloten vindt U Ed. rapport aan Staats President Europa. Is het mogelijk dat u of andere van U Ed. deze Rapport kan weg zenden of doen zenden. Verder heb ik niets te rapporteeren. Met ons allen gaat het goed en mijn innige verzoek aan U Ed. is om uwe werk getrouw voort te zetten, alles zal recht komen. Wij vertrouwen op God van wien wij onze verlossing verwachten en zullen vast staan tot dat die verlossing komen zal. U Ed. kan deze Luitenant vertrouwen met eenig geheim of wat ook. Ik zend hem in mijn plaats omdat hy vertrouwbaar is met eenig geheim. Verder verzoek ik U Ed. de heer P.J. Grevelink[126] *die laatst by U Ed. was, verder in geen geval te vertrouwen al heeft hij eenig document door my geteekend of wat ook. Vertrouw hem niet en [ ]*[127] *hem by de Engelschen.*

Hoogachtend en met heilwenschen heb ik de eer te zijn U Ed. dw. dr J.K.L.[128]

Hoofd Speciale Werken ten Velden.[129]

---

[125]   C.P. Hattingh, G. Els, W.J. Botha and Willie Bosch. The latter was cripple. See J. Brandt, *The Petticoat Commando*, pp 136, 211 & 216.

[126]   Probably Naudé's former secretary, P.J. Greyling.

[127]   Space left open in original.

[128]   Naudé was the Chief of Special Works. Not clear what J.K.L. means.

[129]   September 10th 1901.
Excellencies H.E.B.B.
Your Excellencies
By the grace of God I still am in a position to report to you that all is well with us and also with the other commando's. In my place I am sending you my Lieutenant and request you politely to provide all reports and details regarding everything to him. Circumstances make it impossible for me to come personally. I have to meet the Commandant General personally but on another occasion I will meet you myself. I humbly request you

September 13th [1901]

The following "it is saids" I give for what they are worth: –
(1) that General Botha is in Town to negotiate,
(2) that he is Lord Kitchener's guest,
(3) that Pres McK[inley] is not dead but badly shot,
(4) that spies are in Town and that that is why the streets are being so closely watched,
(5) that T[jaart] Kruger (son of our Pres) has surrendered with three men (this will surely break the backs of our fighting burgers),
(6) that Gen Lucas Meyer has been shot by Louis Botha because he wanted to come and surrender with his whole commando, and so on, and so on.

Mama is still ill and I have had no time for anything, so I don't know how much truth there is in the above rumours. Yesterday was a particularly busy and eventful day and in the evening Mr B[130] called and I was almost too tired to entertain him. Letter and postcard from Dietlof today.

[Entry in the diarist's "Secret diary", written using lemon juice:]
September 13th. [1901]

I managed to make copies of the above reports yesterday – Sept[ember] 12th 1901 which I shall always remember as one of the most eventful days of my life. Now that my work is done and I have an hour to spare I really must write down my experiences of yesterday. In the morning at

---

to report to me where my wife is and news regarding her. Enclosed please find a report for the State President in Europe. Is it possible that you or somebody you know can send this report on. I have nothing else to report. We are all well and my earnest wish is that you will keep doing your duty with devotion, everything will be fine. We trust in God from whom we expect salvation and will stand firmly until salvation arrives. Your Excellencies can trust this Lieutenant with a secret or whatever. I am sending him in my place since he can be trusted with any secret. Furthermore I request you not to trust P.J. Grevelink who visited you previously, even if he has documents signed by me or whatever. Do not trust him and [open space] him with the English. With due respect and benediction I have the honour to be your obedient servant J.K.L.
Chief Special Works in the Veld.

[130]   Not identified.

about 10.30 Mrs M[alan] came flying over with Miss M[131] – J.J's sweetheart with the exciting news that three spies were in Town and if we had anything to send out we must get it ready immediately. In a few hurried words they told us how these men had come in at the utmost peril of their lives. There were four of them, Nel[132] and [Willie] Els,[133] with whom I have had dealings, Ferrol[134] and van Wijk.[135] They came from the High Veld and had not received warning of all that had taken place – the betrayal of the Committee of Spies in Town and of the road through which the spies always enter the Town. They have gone to and fro for months without seeing a single tommy but on Wed[nesday] evening when they reached the wire fence they were unexpectedly met by a regular storm of bullets. One of them hastily gave the order to retreat and they ran round Pretoria over the railway line, round the koppies and hills and entered the Town from the opposite side. When they came together again one of them was missing! Young Els has disappeared and no one knows whether he was killed or wounded or taken or whether he ran with them and fell into some hole or other breaking his leg perhaps. Who knows where he is at this moment. The three came in torn and bleeding and had to slink through the streets avoiding the electric lamps until they reached Mrs M[alan]'s house. There they heard to their horror that the Committee was in the hands of the enemy, that J.J. was in the Rest Camp and that his house had been searched and was under suspicion so that they could not possibly shelter there. No one knew what to do with them but afterwards they were stowed away in the waggon [sic] house of Mrs David Malan.[136] There they lay closely packed in one small waggon! [sic] Mrs M[alan] brought us the reports and asked us to try and send away the one to the President.[137] The other one, for the Committee had to be destroyed. Miss M[alan] had all these documents with a number of private letters in the bosom of her dress. What horrified us beyond measure was the warning from Naudé, Captain of the Spies, that Grevelink is not

131   Miss Malan, the fiancé of Jannie Joubert. See J. Brandt, *The Petticoat Commando*, p 252.
132   Jan Nel, see footnote 56, p 317.
133   The son of the spy G. Els.
134   Probably Lieutenant Farrell, who was a trusted comrade of Captain Naudé and often acted as commander of the Special Service Corps when Naudé was absent. See G.D. Scholtz, *In Doodsgevaar. Die Oorlogservarings van Kapt. J.J. Naudé,* pp 129 & 131.
135   Not identified.
136   Not identified.
137   Letter dated 1909-09-10 – see secret diary entry on 1909-09-12.

to be trusted. He is the man to whom I gave the lb. [pound] dynamite and worst of all, <u>he</u> received that railway time-table from my hands! They will try and keep him on commando but if he escapes from there and comes to inform the English – it is all up with me. This news upset us terribly (I thought his name was Greeflink and that is how I have always spelt it). I promised Mrs M[alan] that I would go to her house at dusk with anything we may have to send out and she left the two reports with me. As soon as she was gone I hurriedly made copies of them in lemon juice in this book "for fun". After dinner C[onsul] C[inatti] came and I told him that we were in greater danger than ever. He advised us to leave the country immediately at which I laughed him to scorn. Then two ladies called and told me that the Town was in a great state of excitement – armed Tommies were marching up and down the streets, peering into every cab and carriage, stopping every man for his residential pass. The lower part of the Town and west of Market St[reet] were cut off and no one was allowed to go backwards or forwards. The general opinion was that there were spies in Town and Khaki knew of it and every house was being searched systematically. I controlled myself with difficulty – it was such a temptation to say "there <u>are</u> spies in Town". As soon as they were gone I got myself ready to go when Fred [Niemeyer] arrived. I told him at once that I was in trouble and that may be I would require his help. From him I heard that Louis Botha was in Town "to negotiate" and that that had a good deal to do with the prevailing excitement.[138] We walked to the park together and sat down in one of the sheltered corners and then I unfolded a scheme to him, that had been slowly forming in my mind all day. I wanted to borrow three mens' residential passes to give to the spies. I myself would walk through the streets with them and escort them as far as the fence and then I would come back alone and return the three passes. Fred looked at me with admiration and said I was a plucky little girl but he thought the whole thing too utterly risky. I was determined and asked him whether he thought G[ustav] F[ichardt] and DB[139] would lend their passes to me. I did not ask him for his own – somehow I felt <u>that</u> would be all right if it came to the push. He offered to go to his rooms and see the "fellows" while I went to tell the spies to wait – I was to meet him at his gate as soon as I had seen the men. He went off in one direction and I in another and when I got there I was told

---

[138] Botha was not in Pretoria at that time, but in the south-east of the Republic.
[139] Not identified.

by Mrs M[alan] that they were nearly ready to leave but they would wait if I could get passes for them. There was no time to lose. I rushed to Fred's rooms and met him just coming out with G[ustav] and DB. "Fred", I panted, "be quick, they are in a great hurry". He drew me aside gently and said "They refuse to lend their passes". "Refuse!" I echoed and nearly staggered back. "O, God, and this means life or death to those men. They cannot appear on the street tonight without passes". "You can't blame them, Joy, it is a great thing to ask". "Fred", I said solemnly, "you once said I must come to you if ever I find myself in any trouble. Now I come. Help me". And then he promised to do his best. He called the other men and told them to think. They were very silent and very serious, perhaps ashamed of themselves, especially when Fred drew his pass from his pocket and placed it in my hands. Of course I gave it back to him at once. One pass was no good to me and I could not let my friend run any useless risks. We were standing in the garden all the time talking in broken whispers so Fred said I must come into his room to avoid suspicion. It would be all right – there were three men and he would draw the blinds and lock the door. I did not like it quite but there was no help for it and I had the sense not to allow Mrs Grundy[140] to interfere with me at such a critical moment, so I went in and there Fred rummaged in a drawer until he came upon a document signed by J. Weston Major, Ass[istant] to Mil[ilitary] Governor. Then for the next twenty minutes there was a great rush and scramble. B and Fred gummed and glued and typed and forged while G[ustav] F[ichardt] sat on the bed watching in silence and I rocked to and fro in nervous dread in the easy chair Fred had placed me in. I shall never forget that half hour as long as I live. It seemed an eternity and I just prayed that we may be ready in time. I never lifted my head because I did not like to look round the room – no one spoke and all I was aware of was a maddening longing to flee from the room. Once I suggested going to tell the men to wait but Fred said he would soon be ready. Then the supreme moment came. Fred had to forge the Major's signature and he threw himself back, pressing his throbbing temples and trying to calm himself for the dangerous task. First he tried it on another slip of paper. That went beautifully so he nerved himself with a desperate effort and wrote on the document. We

---

140   Mrs Grundy was a character in a Thomas Morton play, *Speed the Plough* – she was the personification of prudish behaviour or propriety – usually in a negative way. By the mid 19th Century Mrs Grundy was established in the public imagination, see *Mrs Grundy,* http://en.wikipedia.org/wiki/Mrs_Grundy, accessed on 24 July 2007.

closed our eyes and turned away, sick with suspense. If he made a mess of that signature all was lost. Bravo! Hurrah!! Magnificent!!! In a moment all was confusion. The deed was done and on the closest examination one could not detect the difference between the original and the forgery. Then under it in bold strokes, the full date and we were ready. I sent Gustav home in a cab to reassure the mother and to tell her I would soon be home – I shook hands with B and thanked him for his help and arm in arm Fred and I went to the house. He could not come in so we parted at the gate and I promised to fetch him afterwards in his room so that he could see me home. It was 7 o'clock then and everyone else was at supper. Mrs M[alan] met me, wringing her hands and crying, "Where have you been so long? Why did'nt [sic] you come a minute sooner? They've gone!" But then I felt inclined to lay me down and die. Fortunately there was'nt [sic] time for that. I immediately made up my mind to run after them, asked what direction they had taken and ran like the wind, Mrs M[alan] shouting after me, "When you see four men, call "Jasper"". In passing Fred's place I stopped a moment at the open gate and calling out "Fred" I ran on again without looking round to see if he had heard, but he was fortunately on the look out for me and soon caught me up and together we ran and ran until I was thoroughly exhausted. When we were some distance from the new Sunnyside bridge we saw four figures just crossing it under the electric light. "You must run again Joy", he said and putting his arm round me he literally carried me along. Alas! the four figures proved to be four Kaffirs coming towards us and with a broken sob I realized that our efforts were in vain. It was no use running then. The streets in Sunnyside are not lit and we could not see ten yards ahead of us so we sauntered slowly and sadly home, my good friend soothing and comforting me with the assurance he felt that they must have got out safely. A brilliant meteor flashing across the heavens just then seemed to confirm his hopeful words, at any rate, I resigned myself to the inevitable and commended the lives of our three heroes into the hands of our Father in Heaven. Mama was in a great state when I came home and very thankful that I was still alive. The document I have before me now – a tangible proof of the reality of yesterday's experiences and an interesting memento of the same. I always knew that Fred was clever but last night he surpassed himself.

Sept[ember] 14th [1901] [Secret diary]

We feel as if some great event is about to take place. Tomorrow will be that long-looked-forward-to day the 15th Sept[ember]. Being Sunday we do not think anything unusual will happen but I wonder what Monday will bring us. There are 6 000 troops in Pretoria and I have been told on good authority that the Generals Botha, Beyers, de la Rey and Ben Viljoen are lying quite close to Pretoria with large commandos – otherside Wonderboom, I hear. Perhaps Khaki expects an attack. Botha <u>was</u> here[141] but went out again at once I think and is now supposed to be waiting outside for further developments. But it is no use writing about the "situation". No one knows anything about it and we have only to wait and be patient. I feel as if we are soon to be out of our troubles. Let me tell what I know of the fate of our three spies. V[an] d[er] W[esthuysen] escorted them through the Town and Sunnyside and over the railway line where he left them. They were then not far from the wire fence and out of the worst danger, so we have every reason to believe that they have escaped with their lives, especially as v[an] d[er] W[esthuysen] heard no firing at all and as far as we know no men were arrested that night. Of course we know nothing of the fate of young Els. Consul C[inatti] told me this evening that the Consuls' report on the camps was published <u>in full</u> in London! This is a great thing for us. I read that report – it was magnificent and will make a great sensation all over the world.

[Entry in the diarist's "Love diary":]
September 14th [1901]

As this is written in "white ink" I cannot refer to what I have already written – nor can I find out when last I made an entry. My heart is very sore this evening. Two mails have arrived without a word from my Love – two whole weeks have passed since I received his first love-letter and since then – silence! What can it mean? I do not for one moment doubt that he has written regularly – it is not neglect on his part – oh no, it is our arch-enemy, the Englishman. I told Lou to write through Consul C[inatti] which is really not allowed but he is a good friend and is always ready to help us. Now I am quite sure his letters were opened and of course they would keep the enclosures from ever reaching me. Even a love-letter! I wish I could be quite sure that he did not write about the war but I am afraid he may have said something and then it would bring Mr C[inatti] into great trouble. Well, I must just hope for the best.

---

141   The diarist is wrong – Botha was not in Pretoria at that time.

September 16th. [1901]

I ought to make entries every evening but we are so unsettled and nervous that I am not fit for anything. There is such a strained feeling, such
suspense that it is almost more than we can bear. Everyone was looking
out eagerly to the 15th inst[ant]. Why, I don't know, but everyone of
us expected great and startling events and when the wonderful day fell
on a Sunday, we all said "tomorrow, tomorrow." And now it is already
the close of "tomorrow", a wild and stormy evening, with heavy rain,
unceasing flashes of lightning and roaring thunder – but nothing else. A
good deal of fighting seems to be taking place but no news reaches us, at
least, nothing definite. They say that Boxburg [sic] has been laid in ruins
but I have heard the same story so often that I may be pardoned for
becoming rather sceptical on that point. Only the Government Buildings are supposed to be standing. What I know for a fact is that Pres
McKinley died of his wounds yesterday. Also that four of our generals
are lying just otherside Wonderboom with strong commandos – Botha,
de la Rey, Beyers and Ben Viljoen. What the object is of this concentration of forces round the capital, no one seems to know exactly, and
Khaki is, to use an expression I heard this afternoon, "in the deuce of a
funk." They seem to expect an attack on the Town – at least there are
quite 6 000 troops in Pretoria and everyone is very much on the alert.
Some say that the Boers have thirty-seven English officers as prisoners
and have threatened to shoot them all without mercy if any harm comes
to the twenty political prisoners (Hollanders) whose trial has been caus-
ing so much excitement. Others think the Boers are going to sweep
through the town to release all the men who are caught here. My own
opinion is that they are just lying near to show how strong they still are
and to dare the English to attack them.

Now that the 15th and 16th have passed without excitement we are
looking out to Wednesday the 18th inst[ant]. On Wednesdays the *Government Gazette* is always issued and generally the Proclamations come
out at the same time. Now we expect something very wonderful in the
way of proclamations and I have even seen someone who says he has
read it, strange as it may seem. He says that is contains some passing
strange clauses, one of them being, that all families having husbands, fathers, sons or brothers on commando will have to go in camps in Natal

– or leave S[outh] Africa at their own expense, if the prospect of camp life does not seem inviting enough. Then we shall have to go for has Mama not a son, and I a brother on commando? I sincerely hope so, if he has not long been lying in a soldier's grave. Yes, I hope so – even with the rain beating down pitilessly on all unprotected mortals, and the wind howling fiercely and the elements raging in merciless fury. Rather be out there in the naked veld, my brother, than in ease and luxury at home, and rather in an unknown, neglected grave in all the pride and strength and beauty of your young manhood than faithless to *"land en volk."*[142] But may God have mercy on us all! When the English have proved to us that we have a son and brother fighting still we shall pack up our belongings and go. We have begun already in a small way but the appalling question rises "What is to become of Harmony?" Someone told me today that no one will be allowed to let their houses as the English are purposely clearing the towns in order to make room for their own returning refugees. Well, I am not going to worry until the evil hour comes – we shall have more than enough to think about then. Another clause in the Proclamation is that all men must take the oath of allegiance to the British Crown or leave the country. This may be true. I am sure England has come to such a pass that nothing under the sun is too mean and low and sneakish for her to do.

September 18th. [1901]

When one is sad and tired it is not easy to keep a diary, and I am both this evening and yet very anxious to make a few entries because I have been spending this day in the Irene Camp and have much to tell. But first I must finish with yesterday. We heard a lot of news. The night before, I saw four rockets rise and burst one after the other in the direction of the asylum, and we wondered who was feeling gay enough to indulge in fireworks, but yesterday we heard that they were alarm signals from the English. There was an attack and the fighting lasted many hours, far into the night. All the towns-people heard rifle-firing, but we are too far away. Khaki was in a great state and thought the Boers were coming to take the Town, but they were only frightening our friends a little. But the Town was in great excitement next day and the number of rumours we heard was astounding.

---

142   "country and people."

M.F. told us good news from the Colony – reliable information received from – I may not say whom. The Boers had taken Mossel Bay and kept it for three hours. The people escaped in boats and on rafts and nearly went crazy with terror, until a gun-boat came to the rescue and shelled the Boers until they retreated, taking with them every mortal thing they wanted. All over the Colony the rebels are rising and even in Natal Dundee is supposed to have been taken. But the best news of all is an awful disaster the English had at Belfast. There were about nine block-houses. The English occupied five and left the other four vacant and the Boers found it out, so in the dead of night they quietly took possession and began blazing into the air to attract the enemy, who immediately sent soldiers from the full forts, to man the empty ones. They were allowed to reach within 30 y[ar]ds when the Boers opened fire and shot them so badly that they rushed back to their comrades, who thought they were Boers beaten back and shot to pieces what was left on them. Then a commando lying on the other side attacked them unexpectedly and between the two fires there was nothing left and the Boers were in possession of all the forts. They must have found a lovely lot of ammunition. I am no soldier and certainly not a strategist, so I am not sure whether there is any sense in the above incoherent description.

I made up my mind suddenly to go to Irene for the day, so I went to get a permit. Mr S[143] (the Sup[erin]t[endent] of Burger Camps) looked "amused" when I came in, which rather aggravated me until I remembered that he must know me quite well by reputation as "the agitator". His look plainly said that he did not think my appearance dangerous and he asked politely what I wanted to go to Irene for. "For pleasure", I answered shortly, which took him so much by surprise that he began writing my pass-port without another word, for he is used to many pretexts from people anxious to visit the camp – sick relatives, business etc and no one is really allowed to go without a good reason. Then I had to go to the Gov[ernment] B[ui]ld[ing]s to get it signed by the Governor, who was engaged, so I had to come back for it two hours later. They are so awfully busy in the gov[ernment] offices that one can get nothing done. Gen Maxwell made no objection to my going to Irene, strange to say, so I got up early this morning and was just going to dress when it began to rain and M[ama] would not hear of my going out, but fortu-

---

[143]   Probably N.J. Scholtz.

nately I saw a bit of blue sky half an hour afterwards and determined to make a rush for it. I have never in my life dressed in such a hurry and I literally tore up to the Station, arriving there just in time. Found Mr A.P.[144] who sat in the same carriage and chatted amicably, telling me all the news I had heard before and a great deal more. He was on his way to J[o]h[anne]sburg and we agreed to travel back by the same train.

At Irene I found doctors and nurses in great confusion and excitement and everywhere I saw signs of some change going on – tents were being taken down, women were packing their few belongings – and then I heard, what I could hardly persuade myself to believe, that since the day before, all families of fighting men were being removed to Natal. I was only too soon forced to believe what they told me. My friends advised me to go to the Station at 2 p.m. if I wanted to see any of my old patients – in camp I would find very few as most had left the day before and the Pietersburgers had long ago been sent back to Zoutpansberg. I simply dreaded going into the camp and made up my mind to wait till after dinner and then go to the Station with all the nurses. In the meantime I talked to Dandy and to anyone who had a few moments to spare. They were all very busy and I felt like a fish out of water but managed to do a lot of talking and to tell them all he latest news. The doctors were writing certificates for patients unfit to be moved, and the nurses were preparing little necessaries for them to take with them for the road; milk for the tender little ones about to undertake a long journey in open coal trucks, warm clothing and anything else they could lay hands on. I heard some dreadful stories from them, of how the people were turned out of their tents by force when they refused to go, how some received only half an hour's notice and had their belongings thrown on trolleys, how many had six and eight loaves in the oven and not a morsel of food to take with them, and how they were bullied and buffeted and frightened to death, poor ignorant souls, by the assurance that they were going over the big sea-water and would never come back again. Not one of them knew what their destination was and it was pitiful to see their distress, and many were weeping and some were cursing and showing a brave, undaunted front. I went early to the Station and saw there one of the saddest sights imaginable. The train was getting up

---

[144]   Probably A. Philipp.

steam and I counted about 24 trucks, heavily laden with coal, wood, furniture and bedding and these poor mortals closely packed in dozens and dozens – women, children and tiny, wailing infants. I ran up and down the platform, along the train, shaking hands and uttering words of encouragement and hope. Many of them burst into tears when they saw me and sobbing, held my hands, but most of them were all smiles and so glad to be able to bid me goodbye. It was strange and sad meeting and stirred me to the depths of my heart, for I have lived and suffered with these people and love and know them well. I told them not to believe that they were being sent out of the country and urged them to be brave and strong for the sake of the men who are in the field today. But my heart sank for I could see signs of an approaching storm and I knew they would be drenched and frozen before night came. And so it is. The storm is raging and a prefect deluge is over us and they must be in it too, without a thread of dry clothing, not a drop of anything hot to drink and many of them without a morsel of food. But I shall never forget the spirit they showed as the train moved off. They waved handkerchiefs, aprons, *kappies*,[145] sunshades wildly and shouted goodbye and hurrah to us. I was quite carried away with enthusiasm and shouted and waved with the rest. "Put that in your pipe and smoke it" I muttered as I passed a few lounging Khakis, but if the bravery of their victims annoyed them they did not let us see it. So this is what England means to do! Punish helpless women and children because they cannot get hold of the fighting men! It is too cruel and inhuman and fills my whole soul with contempt and loathing unspeakable.

September 22nd [1901]

Line's birthday, which we celebrated by dining with the Maré family. I am not writing very regularly lately – perhaps because there are so many rumours that I don't know what to believe. What I know for a fact is that Gen Botha is in Natal, doing great things. Dundee, Newcastle and Greytown have been taken. At Newcastle the English got a terrible beating, lost some cannon, over 2 000 mules, food and ammunition enough to last us a year. Their number of killed and wounded was very great. Gen

---

[145]   Bonnets.

Maxwell told Mr DN[146] that "it was a hard knock". In the Colony things are going finer than ever and I have an idea that the English are beginning to realize how utterly hopeless the case is for them. The dreaded proclamation has not been issued yet and we think is has been withdrawn altogether, because [Lord] Milner sees he has gone too far already. But of course we don't know – it <u>may</u> still come out and we are just quietly going on with our preparations. Lady Maxwell has come back

Little B's wife has a daughter – the first child after twelve years of married life – and the poor father is in jail. They are gong to ask permission to take the baby to him – I hope they will get it.

Mrs N[147] also has a baby – a son – in one of the Natal camps. We must try and let her husband know. – It worries me that for three whole weeks I have received no letter from Lou[is Brandt]. I am sure he has written regularly, but the letters have gone astray and I simply cannot understand how. I am thinking seriously of going to see the Post master about them tomorrow. I have every reason to think they have been withheld purposely.

September 24th. [1901]

I was to have spent the evening at H[essie]'s but am kept at home by a very bad cold. My misfortunes seem never to come to an end. During the last few months I have had Influenza, Dysentery, Colds, back-aches, heart-aches, head-aches. Shall I <u>ever</u> be free from care? Tonight the military band is playing in the park – there is a fancy fair on – and it makes one feel perfectly desperate.

The English say Louis Botha is surrounded by 20 000 men and can only escape "by road to Zululand". It stands to reason that he <u>will</u> escape that way. There are many reports about again about that wonderful proclamation that is coming out. Tomorrow, some say, when the *Gov[ernment] Gazette* comes out. What change will it bring into our lives I wonder. – JJ is going to be sent away. His mother was here this morning. There is to be no trial and we are much relieved to hear that B[otha], H[attingh], E[lls], B[otha], K[lock] and others are no longer in

---

146 Probably F.G. Domela Nieuwenhuis, Consul-General for the Netherlands in Pretoria.

147 Possibly Mrs Naudé, wife of Captain J.J. Naudé. See secret diary entry on 1901-12-21.

jail, but have been moved to the Rest Camp, from where they are going to be transported "to the ends of the earth."

September 26th. [1901]

Last night we heard that Mr Maritz-Botha[148] had been captured, so this morning we went to Town to try and get permission to see him. The new proclamation came out yesterday but in no way affects us and for the present at least we are in no danger of being sent away, but some of our friends will suffer very much by this last "whereas"[149]. Mr M[aritz-]B[otha] was captured about ten days ago as far as we can make out – at least, soon after the 15th – and so he has been "banished for life". It amuses us very much for the English always forget to say "if we win", just as they forgot to say in the proclamation that all officers will be banished for life "if we catch them". Major Hoskins told us that he thought Mr M[aritz-]B[otha] had already left and soon after we left the Gov[ernment] B[ui]ld[in]gs someone told us that about 200 prisoners had just passed on their way from the Rest Camp to the railway station. We tore up at once and asked to see Captain Hudson,[150] who was in charge of the prisoners. He was right at the end of the platform and we walked towards him all along the line of trucks filled with our poor men. I said goodbye to them in passing but an armed Tommy pounced on us at once and ordered us off the platform and only allowed us to pass on when I said I wanted to speak to Captain H[udson]. He was very courteous indeed but firmly refused to allow us to speak to any of the prisoners, so Mama wrote a few words on an enveloped and asked him to give it to Mr [Maritz-]B[otha] with a photo of his wife and children which she had received from Cape Town some weeks ago, and he promised to do so and advised us to "get into the shade", which amused me very much, for "the shade" was not within speaking distance of the train and I saw at

148 Probably the husband of Mrs P. Maritz-Botha, a close friend of the Van Warmelo ladies.
149 In official proclamations the British usually made superfluous use of the expression "whereas".
150 Probably Captain H. Hudson of the 3rd Battalion Shropshire Light Infantry, who was active in Transvaal from September 1901. See Savannah Publications, *Boer War Services of Military Officers of the British and Colonial Armies Imperial Yeomanry Mounted Infantry Local Units &cc 1899–1902 including Earlier Services*, pages unnumbered.

once that he wanted to get rid of us, so we went away with a few regretful glances to the men, who could have told us so much war news and would so highly have appreciated a few friendly, farewell words from us. It is a most sad and depressing sight and affected me nearly as much as the sight of the train load of women and children at Irene.

We also saw Mrs Little B this morning with her lovely baby girl, of which she is as proud as proud can be. Her husband is in the Rest Camp now and far more comfortable. The poor fellow nearly died in his awful cell and had to have a doctor, who said another two days of that life would have put an end to him. - Then we went to see JJ. He comes home every day at 11 o'clock with a Khaki, who sits in the little front parlour, and keeps an eye on him to and from the camp, while he entertains visitors in the drawing-room. He told us all sorts of news and seems rather to enjoy his camp life. A prisoner told him that he saw one of the van Warmelos a month ago (Fritz of course as he is the only one) with Izak [sic] Celliers[151] and some others - on their way to the Colony, if you please. They were in perfect health but he says they have every reason to think that Jan Celliers has been killed.[152] I don't quite understand the whole thing but it appears that they were suddenly attacked by the enemy and scattered and when they came together again they found one grave (someone buried by the enemy) and two bodies of their comrades which they buried. J[an] C[elliers] was not with them and they thought he had escaped to some other commando but two prisoners meeting one another in the Rest Camp (of the routed party) discussed the whole thing and one asked the other (Preller)[153] whether J[an] C[elliers] had been with him and he was amazed and said they all thought he was with the others. Then Preller said that when he was taken he was the English burying someone and was refused permission to see the body so he did not know who it was. I am afraid there is no doubt about its being poor J[an] C[elliers] and then may God have mercy on his wife! We dare not tell her until we have more certainty and in the meantime it is horrible to meet her and be as usual knowing of the shadow hanging over her.

---

[151]   Should be Isaac Celliers.
[152]   Jan Celliers survived the war.
[153]   Not identified.

October 1st [1901]

With the new month I am making many new resolutions. I have filled my fountain pen afresh with the intention of writing regularly in this neglected diary of mine (the pen writes thick on this smooth paper but is so convenient for me when writing in the garden). I get up before the sun now and go to bed early – take a nap at midday also to make up for the early rising. Jim wakes me and as I am very lazy and love my morning sleep, he has orders to stand before the window and knock until he sees the blind go up. I would be lacking in moral courage indeed if I went back to bed again after that. This small paradise of ours is so absolutely perfect at sun-rise and so gloriously peaceful and serene that it does not seem as if anything could go wrong on a day begin thoughtfully in its stillness and beauty. I am going to plan my mornings very carefully. The very first duty will be the gathering and arranging of the flowers while the dew is still on them and then comes an hour's reading and meditation – then my housework while it is still fresh and cool for active work and after breakfast sewing and practising etc. This last I have made my mind up to – my music must not be given up. My voice has become so full and strong lately that singing is no end of a joy, and I mean to go in properly for music – singing and playing. I think my heart won't ache so often at the waste of all these precious years, if I try and make up for that now.

Just lately I must admit I have been yielding very much to the demoralizing influences of war, but now I mean to fight and overcome them. There is someone else to think of now and I must not disappoint him. I had a letter from him on the 28th Sept[ember], the first one in four weeks – through Mr C[inatti]. I was much troubled to hear that he has not been receiving my letters, and believe that the same man who kept back his all those weeks has been keeping mine. Last week I went to complain to the P[ost] M[aster] but he said he had nothing to do with it and referred me to the head Censor, Major W.[154] I explained how it was that my letters were addressed c/o Mr C[inatti] and he assured me emphatically that the consul's letters were never opened. I could see that he was not trying to deceive me, but afterwards he sent for another censor Mr v[an] d[er] S[puy][155] and that man lied – I saw it in his eyes besides he turned to me when he heard Mr C[inatti]'s name and asked

---

[154]   Not identified
[155]   Van der Spuy. See diary entry on 1901-10-19, p 380.

"Are you Miss v[an] W[armelo]?" and then I heard him say in an undertone that he had found out that the consul forwarded letters under cover. He glanced several times at me with a meaning smile, which I could not understand, but this I know – he kept back those letters and no one else, and now he is sorry for me and lets my correspondence pass – at least the very next mail brought me Lou[is Brandt]'s letter in which he complains that he does not hear from me. It worries me very much.

There is no news that I know of. The man Broeksma[156] was shot in J[o]h[anne]sburg yesterday for incriminating documents found in his house, in connection with the Krause case. Nine young girls in Maraisburg C[ape] C[olony] were sentenced to one month's imprisonment for warmly welcoming and encouraging the "rebels" when they took the Town.[157] Oh, mighty Britain, great has been thy fall! In the Eastern Province the Boers are burning farms wholesale and the "loyals" are asking protection from the English, who are just as helpless and raging as themselves – B[otha] H[atting] E[ls] B.K.[158] and JJ were tried last week and may be released, for there is no evidence against them forthcoming. They are merely being regarded as prisoners of war. Little B was allowed to go home with a Khaki guard for two hours to be present at the baptism. He was nearly crazy with joy and his wife says he kissed the baby's feet and went on at a rate, while she wept for very joy. Poor souls! The Khaki became confidential afterwards and told him that on the 11th inst[ant] peace would be proclaimed and the English would leave the land. The Powers had intervened! He was an Irishman, so that accounts for the wildness of this tale.

Mrs JC[elliers] and her brother spent last evening with us and I was so haunted by the thought that she may be a widow that I could hardly speak to her – and she was so bright and cheerful and so pleased when she heard that Fritz and the others had gone to the Colony. She took it for granted her husband was with them, although we tried to impress

---

156 Cornelius Broeksma, an ex-public prosecutor in the government of the South African Republic, was executed in Johannesburg on 1901-09-30 on charges of breaking his oath of neutrality and high treason. See R. Kruger, *Good-Bye Dolly Gray. A history of the Boer War*, pp 435–436.

157 Seven young girls between the ages of 15 and 19, as well as a Mrs Brooks, were sentenced to 30 days imprisonment. They were also accused of urging the Cape Rebels to continue fighting against the British. See C.J. Scheepers Strydom, *Kaapland en die Tweede Vryheidsoorlog*, pp 135–136.

158 Not identified.

it on her that our informer had not mentioned his name. I think it is a shame to keep her in ignorance but M[ama] won't hear of telling her of the rumour.

Thursday. October 3rd 1901.

The Chronicle gives the following, the Globe inserting the poem annexed: –

"Is this a Birthday?" – Pope
Christian de Wet's Birthday.
The Invisible Man – H.G. Wells.
Who can report of him? – Shakespeare.
I think there be six Richmonds in the field – Shakespeare
'E 'asn't got no papers of 'is own,
'E 'asn't got no medals nor rewards,
So we must certify the skill 'e's shown – Kipling.
'E's a daisy, 'e's a ducky, 'e's a lamb!
'E's a india-rubber idiot on the spree,
'E's the only thing that doesn't give a damn
For a regiment of British infantree! – Kipling.
There's a lean fellow beats all conquerors – Thomas Dekker.
How shall we rank thee upon glory's page,
Thou more than soldier? – Moore.
The Boer in charge – Rider Haggard.
I honour him even out of your report – Shakespeare.
Most elusive, most tiresome, most Christian de Wet.
Today is a day that we must not forget;
Our obvious duty we can but obey,
So here's "Many happy returns of the day"
Its' dull for you spending it out on the veldt,
No sweet, sugared cake, and no ices to melt
In your mouth, not a drop, I am sure, of champagne,
No butler to fill up your tumbler again.
So come, Sir, we pray you, and taste of the best,
Where a Kitchener waits on your every behest,
Where, if you but seek British outpost and trench,
You'll have at your service a chef that is French.

· · · · · · · · ·

I spent last evening with the Essers, so could not make any entries. In the morning we were told that Louis Botha has issued a proclamation in which he declares every Britisher under arms to be an outlaw and orders his men to shoot them as such, wherever they find them. It seemed incredible but when trusted friends told me they had <u>read</u> it, and promised me a typed copy I had to believe it. We told everyone the story and discussed it in great excitement all over the Town and lo, at eventide I am informed that the proclamation was an invention of Broeksma's for which he was shot! I have again made up my mind to believe nobody and nothing – not even the evidence of my own senses.

We had an adventure at Harmony last Sunday that I forgot to relate. Mr [Horace] Dely[159] came to take out some honey, the bees got angry and attacked a beautiful mare, stinging her so frightfully that she was dead next morning. The Tommies were driven out of their tents and sat all morning far away on the hillside – homeless and miserable – we could hardly show ourselves and every passer-by was attacked until about noon when they quieted down again. Yesterday the sergeant major came to tell us that Major Poore, Provost Marshall [sic], requested us to remove the hives immediately. Mama had the one nearest the camp taken to the bottom of the garden but the others are going to remain where they are. It was foolish in the extreme to put up a smithy so near the bees and now they expect us to take them away.

Friday. Oct[ober] 4th [1901].

No news. Vocal rehearsal today.

Saturday. October 5th [1901].

Last night I had a vision. I cannot call it a dream – it was too vivid and impressive. I though I was leaning from the casement of my bed-chamber, watching the rays of the setting sun. Suddenly the rays seemed to take shape and I called my mother to see the strange apparition – the form of an angel-woman, robed in white, majestic, tall, divinely beautiful – bearing in one hand a scroll of manuscript, waving aloft in the other our flag – our *Vierkleur* – in the soft and dazzling hues of the rainbow. She spoke. Words of peace and victory fell like music from

---

[159]   See J. Brandt, *Die Kappie Kommando*, p 285.

her lips, and then in awed and hushed silence we listened to ill tidings she brought us, concerning my beloved sister. Her infinite tenderness and compassion stirred my soul to its depths and holding out my arms to her I cried, "O God, O God, O God!" and then we watched her fade away and all that remained were the rays of the setting sun. I woke, quivering in every nerve with emotion, and in the morning I told Mama the whole thing. She was quite impressed and looked quite as if she expected soon to hear bad news from Line, mixed with the good news of "peace with honour". I was so full of this dream or revelation that when I opened "Daily Light" I wondered whether my portion would in any way have reference to the angel-woman of my dreams. My amazement knew no bounds when I read the opening words for October 5th. "Write the vision, and make it plain upon tables, that he may run that readeth it. For the vision is yet for an appointed time, but at the end it shall speak, and not lie; though it tarry, wait for it; because it will surely come, it will not tarry." Hab[akkuk] 2 [versus] 2 [&] 3. Afterwards it says "Oh, that thou wouldst rend the heavens, that thou wouldst come down!" In fact the whole of my daily reading was on the subject of visions, which has so deeply impressed me that I have been able to think of nothing else. Tonight I feel as if we are on the verge of great things.

Sunday morning. Oct[ober] 6th [1901]

This morning I don't. It is not possible to conceive great and stirring events in the calm serenity of such a day. I am lying under Harmony's pear trees, simply revelling in the beauty of nature; Carlo, the Faithful, lazily stretched at my feet, the "Meditations" of Marcus Aurelius open beside me, and, best of all, my own meditations to fall back on when other things fail me. Harmony is so sweet, so beautiful. I have never appreciated it as much as I do this Spring – Heaven only knows why, when my heart is so troubled and tempest-tossed. I think as we grow older we become more oblivious to the events around us, we are not swayed this way and that by every passing emotion, we dwell more securely within ourselves. It is so with me. I find my temper growing daily more equable, my mind less likely to be disturbed by outside events and yet, I do not become callous nor indifferent. My sympathies have become more subtle during the last two years, my individuality more pronounced, my perceptions keener, to say nothing of the development of my sense of justice and the abnormal growth of my love of fatherland. The last has almost become a ruling passion, but I do not regret it, neither do I consider that it is going too far. If I say that I would gladly lay down my life for my country, it is no exaggeration – it would even be a joy to me to sacrifice this beautiful young life of mine, with its fair promises for the future, if I knew that by doing so I could save "*land en volk*". I am only looking out for the chance – who knows if it does not come to me one of these days. Just now I am leading an ideal life, but it would not satisfy me long. With returning health I find myself longing for "active service" again and yet I know there is no chance of going back to Irene during the trying summer months. Besides, Mama is not at all in good health and is so evidently distressed at the thought of my leaving home again, that I have been obliged to give up the idea. This early rising gives me plenty of leisure and I am taking up music again, with renewed vigour. There is a certain duty I owe a certain Somebody and for his sake as well as my own, I am trying to improve myself. I wonder what he is do-ing this minute – probably expounding the scriptures to his little flock. I wish he were here to expound them to his little girl instead – I am sure she would appreciate it more than the flock does. I long and long more intensely every day to be with him – to get to know him as I ought to before I promise to marry him. Perhaps the time is nearer at hand than we think. And now this fountain pen of mine is exhausted and I must need stop writing.

Tuesday evening. Oct[ober] 8th. [1901]

Torrents of rain, flashes of lightning, peals of thunder and howling wind – a tempestuous night that makes us think with terror of our thousands and thousands of women and tender little ones exposed to all the fury of the elements, and of our burgers in the open field without so much as a tent under which to take shelter. At times like these all our sorrows come crowding upon us in overwhelming, crushing force. When the sun shines we do not realize to the full the desolation of our land, but on a night like this! – God knows it is almost more than we can bear. There seems to have been a lot of fighting all over the country. Red Cross trains are passing to and fro on the Eastern Line – we watch them daily - and yesterday Gen M[axwell] told CM[160] that the Boers had attacked a British Camp near Rustenburg, killing and wounding 27 officers. Col Kekewich[161] who was in command is reported dead. The Boers gave up the camp again - I suppose when reinforcements came - and the English buried sixty Boer dead. So they say - so do I not believe. In a battle near Krugersdorp 15 officers were killed. They say Botha is "completely hemmed in". Persistent rumours are afloat about Kitchener's departure - some say he had a difference with Milner and has gone for good - that Kelly-Kenny is in his place temporarily and that Littleton[162] is on his way to take over the command. The stories one hears are many and marvellous. I quote them just because I would have nothing at all to write if I only had to write what I know to be true. I saw Miss Findlay from Irene yesterday (our "Fairy") and she told me a lot about the present state of the camp. The average number of deaths is fifteen weekly - quite bad enough, but an improvement on what it was while I was there. Mrs Bosman has received a letter informing her that in future the services of the six volunteer nurses will be dispensed with, and we are all furious about it, but quite helpless. What can we do? We have been expecting this for some time because the English long ago realized what a mistake they made in permitting red-hot Boers like ourselves into one of these "hidden death-camps". We have not only been the means of saving many valuable lives, but we have made the lot of those helpless victims endurable to a certain extent - two unpardonable sins - for has not the first impeded the process of extermination and the second strengthened the women in their determination to endure camp life for years rather than induce their men to surrender? We volunteers were their only earthly refuge and consolation - without us they are entirely at the mercy of their jailers and I dare not think what they will have to suffer now. We "agitated" when the food was unfit for consumption, we "agitated" when they required clothing and blankets, we collected for them - we had friends, money, influence all of which

---

160 Probably Consuela Minnaar.
161 Colonel R.G. Kekewich, who was active in the Western-Transvaal at that time. He survived the war. See S.B. Spies, Kekewich, Robert George, in *DSAB* II, pp 360–361.
162 Probably Lieutenant-General Sir T. Kelly-Kenny and General N.G. Lyttleton. The rumour was false.

we placed at their disposal. With our watchful eye upon them no great wrong could be permitted long, but now, there is not a living soul left to care what becomes of them. They can stand by one another, but they are all helpless, ignorant creatures and it breaks my heart that their one ray of comfort should have been taken from them. Of course, no reason is given for this act of inhumanity but we know. We have written and made up reports, we can prove that our statements are <u>facts</u>, we have made known to the world the real state of affairs in these camps and our noble foe can endure this exposure no longer. What good is it for them to appoint and send out commissions of enquiry, who go from camp to camp making the most superficial observations and then write glowing accounts of the ease and comfort, aye the <u>luxury</u> of the "refugees" – when these accounts are contradicted and exposed in all their black falsehood, by a staff of loyal true-hearted workers? I see in the "CapeTimes" that Miss Hogge and Miss Taylor[163] express every satisfaction at the state of the camps and suggest that "English trained nurses replace the Dutch volunteers". Oh the treachery of these people who come out "all for love, you know", and sit in our drawing-room, drinking our tea and listening with tears of pity to our accounts of the misery we have come into personal contact with, and then publish their expressions of satisfaction. Satisfaction at <u>what</u>? At the sight of starving little children, of worn-out, suffering women, of poverty, filth, degrada-tion, where once abounded milk and honey, happy homes, peace and prosperity! Do they not realize that it is England's greed of gold that has brought us to such a pass? Are they <u>still</u> so blind and puffed-up with arrogance and pride that they do not see the great injustice of it all? It reminds me of what D[164] ... told me when I was at Irene last. He says he managed to get hold of Dr Kendall-Franks' [sic][165] report on Irene and read in it that "Miss van Warmelo's ward was rather bad and he saw some very poverty-stricken families there, but most of the state-ments made by her were <u>untrue</u>!" – and that is the man who flattered me and called me an angel and told me how highly he respected me for the noble work I was doing. He did not give me a chance to prove my statements and then he gives me the lie in an official report, after having

---

163   See diary entry on 1901-08-22.
164   Probably Dandy (Dr A.C. Neethling).
165   Should be Kendal Franks. See diary entry on 1901-07-13.

asked oh, so sweetly, whether he may make use of my name. I was at Irene for two months and he for one solitary day and yet he knows a great deal more about it than I do. – Now I have let off some steam in the above tirade and feel a little better. The storm outside has also abated somewhat so I think I shall go and make sweet music. Had a letter and photo from Lou by last mail.

Friday. Oct[ober] 11ᵗʰ· [1901]

Yesterday was our President's birthday – a very wet and gloomy one – but I celebrated it all the same by going to ten Brink's concert. Fred came in a cab to fetch me and we enjoyed ourselves very much indeed. This is the first public performance I have been to since the Khakis came here and I was pleased to see so few of them, and those were in an evening suit of dark blue, so that they were not "Khakis" at all. Major H[oskins] was there and bowed to me oh, so friendly-like, wondering perhaps what had brought me out of my shell. The music was beautiful and I was charmed with the soprano, Mrs E[166] who was a vision of loveliness and sang with feeling and fervour, in a full, rich voice, clear and sweet as a silver bell. The tenor, a German, was also very good, and ten Brink played both violin and piano in his usual masterly manner. I went behind the scenes during the interval and asked ten Brink to introduce me to the two vocalists for I was quite in love with the sweetness and beauty of Mrs E's happy little face. She and I had a nice chat about music – but enough about this concert. Fancy, dedicating more than a page to a little recreation! But there is nothing else to write about. We hear no news. Today it is two whole years since Martial Law was proclaimed and God knows that peace seems farther off than ever. Two years! Can anyone conceive such a calamity? Who had any idea that this war could last so long. I gave the whole thing six months from beginning to end and felt quite aggrieved when it went over that time. Now I am beyond feeling aggrieved or despairing or elated at anything that may take place. – We are having a great deal of rain and I am afraid we are in for a very wet season. Our poor men in the field! Our poor little children and suffering women in the camps! May God have pity on them all and soon restore to our troubled land – peace with honour!

---

166   Not identified.

October 14th. Monday. [1901]

Things have been so quiet that I have had nothing to write, but today something reached my ears that I really must make a note of – something that concerns me personally. The C[inatti]'s tell me that a letter has been published in the *Westminster Gazette* on the subject of the camp at Irene and all the world and wife says – "it was written by Miss v[an] W[armelo] and she is packing her trunks for immediate departure." This is a great piece of news to the lady in question and I assure you, dear diary, she is as calm and settled as can be. Baron P[itner][167] told them it was a very sharp letter and there is no doubt whatever as to its origin and as he goes often to the Governor I suppose he heard the news there. The letter contains many of my own expressions about "agitators" etc. Now I wonder what it all means and of course I cannot tell until I see the letter myself. Someone has promised to bring me a copy of the *Gazette* tomorrow and then I can judge for myself whether anyone has been making public use of my expressions and experiences. The whole thing is a mystery to me.[168] I begin to doubt whether I shall long be left here in peace, for Khaki has a right under Martial Law to send anyone away on suspicion – proofs are not always necessary. I wish they would leave me alone – I was actually told that Major Hoskins said at a dinner at the Governor's one night that Miss v[an] W[armelo] was the whole cause of the exclusion of Khakis at the concert given by our vocal society last month. That is most unfair. We girls are all to blame (?) – the whole twenty-three of us, for there is not one of our girls who would consent to sing to Khakis during the war. ten Brink asked us to assist him at his last concert and we all refused – without exception – and Major H[oskins] must credit me with a good deal more influence than I possess if he thinks that I swayed the whole society. He can bring me into trouble by making such statements and I have a good mind to go and take him to task for it.

The third and last bit of news about myself is that Consul Gordon

---

372

has been passing my correspondence. So "people say". Now it is quite true that Mr Gordon has allowed me to have my letters addressed to his care, as several other consuls have done, but they were always open and never contained a word about the war. It would be base indeed to abuse his kindness and we were always particularly careful not to write anything "treasonable", just as we always were when poor, dear Mr Hay passed our letters. Not for worlds would I have got him into trouble and I think I am far too loyal to my friends and too honourable to betray the confidences of anyone who was good enough to do me an act of kindness. There was a time that no letters reached us at all except those sent through the consuls. Mr Hay was in this respect the most obliging and courteous of men. But now we do not even send a harmless letter through Mr G[ordon] because the posts are fairly regular, and the consuls tell us that all their correspondence is secretly examined, even official despatches – no matter how they are sealed. It seems impossible and yet it is done, by a process which was explained to me by ____. Red-hot, very sharp knives are slipped under the sealing-wax and then the rest opened by steam. Afterwards the seals are heated underneath and put on so cleverly that no one can see that the letters have been tampered with.

– So much war news is afloat but I am sure of nothing; Beyers attacked a camp at P[iet] P[otgieters] Rust and took it,[169] with a lot of food and ammunition; our "leading townsmen" are "travelling" again at Government expense and even Mr de Wildt[170] was commandeered to go on the trains for the protection of Khaki's life and property, but Mr Domela N[ieuwenhuis] protested – I have not heard the result but I don't see what right they have to commandeer the Vice-Consul of the Netherlands or any other "neutral" person. Mighty England has come to such a pass that she has to put men on the trains at the point of the bayonet, to protect the goods! Ha, ha! I am immensely amused at the

---

[169] On 1 October 1901 Beyers' men captured a British camp on the farm Pruisen, south of Potgietersrus. See G.D. Scholtz, *Generaal Christiaan Frederik Beyers 1869–1914,* p 80.

[170] Probably Mauritz Edgar de Wildt, a civil engineer who grew up in Holland but emigrated to the South African Republic in 1888. He worked for the Dutch South African Railway Company but was not deported to Holland when the British forces occupied Pretoria in June 1900. See J. Ploeger, De Wildt, Mauritz Edgar, in *DSAB* V, pp 196–197.

idea of de Wet allowing a train to pass untouched because it contains a leading townsman.

Today we heard heavy cannon firing in the Magaliesberg direction.

J. Joubert, Botha, Hattingh, Els, etc, etc were all sent away this morning – even the Rev Goddefroy[171] – in fact there has been a regular clearance in the Rest Camp. The Irene Volunteers came back last week – dismissed for ever from their field of labour in the camps. "Fairy"[172] came to see me last night and had a lot to tell me about Irene as it is now.

October 16th [1901]. Wednesday.

Cannon firing is to be heard daily. The Boers are again in possession of Skurveberg. Our brave general, Scheepers,[173] has been captured. Kitchener of Khartoum is back again. The Dutch Consul and family are leaving soon – for a holiday. Mr de Wildt has been excused from "travelling."[174] The families of B[otha] H[attingh] E[ls] etc have been sent away to camps in Natal. The Essers went to Europe this morning – Philipp leaves next week. Sarel Eloff[175] and Hans Malan[176] are reported to have died in captivity. I am still supposed to be sitting on my boxes – The above news "in brief" I give for what it is worth.

I have also been told that war has been declared between England and Abyssinia (don't know how to spell it) and that Russia is backing A[byssinia]. Too good to be true, dear diary – I don't believe any more extravagant tales. Such an event would be our salvation, so I trust it is not a false report.

---

[171] Goddefroy was captured in June 1901 and sent as prisoner of war to India. See *DSAB* III, pp 337–338. See also diary entry on 1901-03-27.

[172] Miss Findlay.

[173] Commandant (not General) Gideon Scheepers surrendered himself to the British forces in the Cape Colony on 1909-10-10 when forced by bad health to seek medical assistance. He was shot by a British firing squad on 1902-01-18. See G.S. Preller (ed.), *Scheepers se dagboek en die stryd in Kaapland*, pp 73–77.

[174] He was exempted apparently on the representations of the Netherlands diplomatic representative that he was acting as vice-consul at the embassy. See S.B. Spies, *Methods of Barbarism?*, p 243.

[175] Grandson of President Kruger. The rumour was false.

[176] Not identified.

October 18th [1901] Friday.

Dear diary, I have no end of writing to do – in fact for the next week at least you must expect nothing but neglect from me. I shall only enter the most important events – if there are any to enter. There is no war news to relate now. The English shot Com Lotter[177] as a rebel, and I believe seven others – or two were hanged, I was told. Mr C[inatti] said to me "Never mind, my dear little sing – it means the rising of 120 other Colonials" and he is right. If Khaki only knew that he is cutting his own throat by these severe measures. Mr C[inatti] is very funny. He takes a great interest in that letter in the *Westminster Budget* [sic] and wants to find out who the writer was. He put a riddle to me: – "What is dis? It is small and oblong and white and was laid by a hen", to which I answered innocently "An egg". "Are you sure?" "Yes". "Well", he said, "we are just as sure that Miss v[an] W[armelo] wrote that letter". He has taken to calling me his "dear little sing" now, to everyone's amusement. Yesterday Mama and I had a most charming and entertaining visitor, Dr Pontsma,[178] who has permission from Lord Kitchener to go to the Boers as Red Cross doctor. He left Pretoria this morning for Kroonstad and was accompanied by an American assistant, Mr Spruce.[179] Dr P[outsma] saw Line often at Wynberg and told us all the news about her and the children and Alphen.

We killed a big snake in Jim's room yesterday and I "arranged" the corpse neatly on the step of the front verandah, hiding the mutilated head under the violet plants. It looked wonderfully lifelike and gruesome and each visitor in turn announced his or her arrival by jumps and shrieks, to the delight of a certain naughty little "sing" who was peeping through the blinds.

Our vocal society gave its first *"gezellige avond"*[180] last night – great

---

177 Commandant Johannes Cornelius (Hans) Lötter (1875–1901) was indeed shot by a British firing squad in Middelburg in the Cape Colony on a charge of being a Cape Rebel fighting on the Republican side. See A. van den Hoek, Lötter, Johannes Cornelius, in *DSAB* V, pp 462–463.

178 Probably Hessel Jacob Poutsma who came to South Africa from Holland in 1899 as war correspondent but joined a Dutch ambulance. He later on organized his own ambulance to assist the Republican forces. See C.R. Ould, Poutsma, Hessel Jacob, in *DSAB* I, pp 672–673. See also secret diary entry on 1901-10-18.

179 Not identified.

180 conversation evening.

success, much fun, music good, bad and indifferent, refreshments excellent.

[Entry in the diarist's "Secret diary", written using lemon juice:]
October 18th 1901. Friday.

I have been a long time in making new entries and now there is so much to tell that I don't know where to begin. Some weeks ago I took it upon myself to appoint a new committee of spies – in place of the men who were betrayed and who have now been sent to Bermuda. This time I thought we shall try women so I appointed my own Mammie President, I appointed myself Secretary and I appointed three other women Mrs Honey,[181] Mrs Malan and Mrs Armstrong, three of the finest women in Pretoria.

On the 15th inst[ant] we held our first meeting at Harmony, with closed doors and a plentiful supply of cocoa and biscuits to soothe the throats worn with speech. The Secretary sat at the head of the table strewn with a great many imposing-looking but valueless and harmless documents, and in a solemn voice unfolded her plans to an attentive and respectful audience. Everyone falling in with the suggestions the Sec[retary] read aloud an oath by which they all bound themselves to sacred secrecy and promised to strain every nerve to be of assistance to "our brothers in the field". The idea is this:– the dauntless Five are to collect reliable information, newspaper cuttings of European news etc to send out with the spies; to harbour said spies in some place of safety; to receive and dispatch official reports from our Generals to the Pres[ident] and Dr Leyds; and to provide as far as they can for the things required by the generals. A dangerous and difficult task indeed! We are bound by oath not to betray to a living soul that such a Committee exists – there is only one other person who knows – a certain friend of mine, who must be nameless, who will type everything for me so that no one ever takes out a scrap of my writing – and then of course the Captain of the S[pecial] Services[182] will have to know as he works through us. In about a

---

181   Probably the wife of J.H.K. Honey, who in 1899 worked for the Customs department of the South African Republic. See *Longland's Pretoria directory for 1899*, p 136. However, in the recollections of Miss E.G. Honey, who was a daughter of the Mrs Honey who was involved in spying activities for the Republican forces, there is no mention of a Mr Honey. See National Archives, Pretoria, TAB, A932, Interview with Miss Dollie Honey.

182   Captain J.J. (Koos) Naudé.

fortnight he is coming again and then we shall explain our duties to him, as well as the secret cipher and the key to be used in future. I am in communication with Dr Leyds and hope to be able to show our people many valuable services – that is to say if I don't get notice to leave the country soon – I am in daily dread of it because of an article in the Westminster Budget [sic] which I am supposed to have written – but my "public diary" treats on this subject so I shall go on to other things. The young man, Els, who was lost, has come out safely at one of the commandos. This bit of news gave us great satisfaction. (I hear cannon firing in the J[o]h[anne]sburg direction.) And now for the news.

For a long time Line's letters has been full of a certain Dr P[outsma] who was anxious to join the Boers – he brought very important news from the President. She wrote this in lemon of course and we were wondering how on earth he would manage to get through the English lines. He has gone to Delagoa Bay where he was waiting for an opportunity to join Botha. Yesterday morning to our amazement he presented himself at Harmony, cool as cucumber, bold as brass, and unfolded to us a tale as strange as strange can be. He had been arrested in L[ourenco] M[arques] on suspicion of smuggling through ammunition to the Boers (as a matter of fact he was guilty and our men are now in possession of five million bran [sic] new Mauser cartridges.) After three weeks in durance vile, no incriminating evidence being forthcoming he was allowed to write an application to Lord K[itchener] for permission to go to the Boers as Red Cross doctor. I read a copy of it. In it he offers to take despatches or proclamations to the Boers in return for the permission to go. In the mean time he had made friends with an American Mr Spruce, a great Boer friend (apparently!) who was anxious to go with him as assistant. He said all right, knowing full well that there was foul play; that the man was not Spruce at all; and that he was nothing more nor less than an English spy. But Dr P[outsma] was deaf and dumb and blind and did not see the great rolls of banknotes in his hand and was not at all surprised at his influence and his great zeal. They arrived here and Spruce had to be introduced to the English and permission had to be got for him to go too and enquiries and investigations had to be made – all as a sort of blind that Dr P[outsma] should not suspect that S[pruce] was their agent and they knew all about him.

Oct[ober] 19ᵗʰ· [1901] [Secret diary]

Was interrupted yesterday and now I am quite off my stroke. Dr P[outsma] more than suspects that there is some foul plot to assassinate or poison de Wet or Steyn to whom he is going and that this Spruce is the tool so he has made a clever plan. He is not going straight to de Wet, but will join the first small commando he comes across and will secretly give the officer in command a note, in which he asks to be immediately arrested with his assistant, as spies – to be separated from him, handcuffed in spite of struggles and protestations and to be kept in custody for a day or two. Then Spruce is to be shot as a spy and Dr P[outsma] goes where he has to be. If this comes off well it is a very clever plan.

He stayed with us all day and told us so much about his experiences of the war that my head reels with the remembrance of it all, and in the afternoon he went back to the hotel promising to come and say good-bye next day. Within an hour he was back here again with the news that he was leaving at once. This amazed us beyond measure, for we had told him he would not be allowed to go for many days – perhaps weeks and he could make up his mind to being put off and delayed again and again, as the English always do with everybody. The best of it is that he takes neither report nor proclamation – only a little letter to the generals in which the authorities announce their great generosity in allowing a doctor to go to the Boers. Of course this confirms all suspicions of foul play and I am dumb with astonishment at their utter stupidity and foolishness. Why all this haste in getting him away? Why do they not make use of him in return for the service rendered to him? Fools, fools! Do they imagine that he is too blind and innocent and confiding not to see through their treachery? As if they are so anxious to provide the Boers with doctors because they love them so much – feel so sorry for them! I wonder where he is now and how the very dangerous game he is playing has terminated. Spruce has cash unlimited and his mission is "to offer intervention from America on certain conditions!" Ha! Ha! How we laughed at it and how seriously Dr P[outsma] asked him to say no more – he was quite satisfied that his mission was a good one and if he didn't mind he would rather hear no state secrets – as Red Cross doctor it was better for him to know as little as possible etc etc. So these two men are scheming and plotting against one another and I know who will come off best. Dr P[outsma] has a marvellous character and if ever a man can talk of a thrilling history he can. When war was declared he came out with the ambulance from Holland, worked here in the hospitals and afterwards went with the field ambulance. He went everywhere with Steyn and de Wet until one fine day he got typhoid and was taken prisoner in some town or other. The way he got ill is quite wonderful. He and Pres Steyn had to cross a river so they stripped, put their clothes on a waggon [sic] that was going round in order to get over an easier way and swam across. The river was full – turbulent and muddy and they were thankful when they reached the other side, but – no waggon [sic] was forthcoming and for five or six hours they were in the broiling sun without a shred of clothing and no shelter. The sand was so hot that they could not touch it and after a while the[y] began to get parched with thirst and in desperation when they could no longer restrain themselves, the[y] drank some of the filthy water. Next day the doctor was raving with delirium and had to be taken to a hospital. After ten weeks of dangerous illness he got leave to go to Holland where he saw all his friends, Dr Leyds, President [Kruger], spent a whole day with Stead, saw Morley,[183] Labouchere,[184] etc had a glorious sea voyage and came back well and strong, with a "mission" – like Mr Spruce. He told us what it was. In Cape Town he saw Line almost daily and they tried every way of communicating with Botha but in vain, so at last he made up his mind to apply for leave to go back to the Boers. No one was more astonished than he was when his request was granted and he of course at once suspected treachery. He has promised to let us know by Naudé how his adventure comes off.

We asked him where de Wet was and he looked so mysterious and important that we worried him until at last he said, "de Wet is de Wet no longer" and no more could we get out of him, so de W[et] is evidently going under some other name. This is a secret I shall guard with my life if necessary. He told us how they were chased for four or six weeks night and day by Knox;[185] how they escaped sometimes when no escape seemed possible and even de W[et] gave up all for lost; how they took trains laden with every imaginable luxury and comfort; how once a train contained 3 000 pairs of riding breeches and all along the line hundreds of Boers could be seen pulling off their old "breeks" and proudly putting on the new; how an old Boer caught up a bottle of champagne and made off with it on the approach of the rescue armoured train and how

---

[183]   John Morley was a liberal British politician and outspoken critic of his government's war policy in South Africa – in other words a pro-Boer. See T. Pakenham, *The Boer War*, p 465.

[184]   Labouchere was a radical British politician, founder of the newspaper *Truth* and supporter of the Boer cause in the war. See R.J. Hind, Labouchere, Henry Du Pré, in *DSAB* III, pp 492–493.

[185]   Probably Major-General C.E. Knox.

a bullet went ping! through it and how angry he was at the loss of the beloved liquor; how sometimes after a fierce battle there was not a man killed or wounded – nothing for him to do, and how the burgers stand side by side through every peril and hardship. The man is so full of admiration and respect for the Boers, so passionate and hot-blooded at the cruelty and treachery of England, so full of enthusiasm, so convinced of our triumph in the end that contact with him is bracing and invigorating. I think he is a wonderful character and oh, I hope he will be successful. He has brought a splendid suit of clothes for Steyn – fine and strong with boots and gaiters and everything belonging to an outfit. He is tall and broad too and passed them as his own.

But now I really must write to Stead and Dr Leyds – a fine opportunity for smuggling letters through next week!

[Last entry in the diarist's "Love diary":]
October 19th [1901]

My poor little love diary is a hopeless failure because I have nothing to tell and just one disappointment after the other. Oh, it is dreadful not to get his letters. That horrible fellow that renegade, van der Spuy,[186] hates me and keeps back all Lou's letters. The wretch! and I am so helpless. I can prove nothing and he has my entire correspondence in his hands. The worst of it is he keeps back some letters I send to Lou so that L[ou] does not know that he must not write care of Mr C[inatti]. What am I to do? If I were not out of favour in high circles I would go to Gen Maxwell and ask him to interfere but I have sinned grievously against Khaki and may have to leave the country soon, but never mind! Then I'll go straight to my love. Oh! I am longing desperately for him – every day it gets worse. When will all this misery end? It seems as if I am never to be happy in this world of ours but I am keeping up my courage. Does he not always urge me to be brave and strong? I will.

October 21st 1901. Monday.

This is L[ouis Brandt]'s birthday – his 29th, I believe, and I celebrated the event by playing tennis at the Niemeyers'. There were a good many people and I enjoyed myself very much and played fairly well considering that it is years since last I touched a racquet. I mean to go in for it

---

[186]   A censor – see entry on 1901-10-01, p 363.

regularly now. I wonder how L[ou] has spent the day – hope I shall be with him when his next birthday comes along – I am beginning to feel very miserable at this prolonged separation. Four weeks hence I shall be twenty-five years old – a regular old maid. – "Fairy" told me this afternoon that Dr N[eethling] had left Irene and had received permission to go to his parents in the Colony. Now we shall probably lose sight of one another altogether. So goes it in this world of ours – friendships are formed only to be broken – "change and decay" in all around I see, people drift apart and no one seems to care. I wish I did not care so much. I am not thinking of Dandy now, oh no, but of someone else. Never mind!

Dr P[outsma] told the mother that he attended that arch traitor Eddie Cooper when he was wounded, and the cheek of the man is really worth remembering. He had £60 with him which he gave to the doctor, coolly asking him to send it to his wife. The officer in command heard of it and of course immediately took possession of it, dividing it between the twelve Boers who had captured him. *Goed zoo!*[187]

This morning my cousin, Ignatius Maré,[188] was here and he told me that he saw about 120 Zoutpansbergers joining the English – taking the oath of allegiance, donning the Khaki and going out armed as cattle rangers, scouts etc. They were under his own Veldcornet Briel,[189] with his two sons and I[gnatius] knows them all intimately. Some of then in passing him said "good morning", but his answer was "*Hi kona.*"[190] The treachery and faithlessness of our own people will be the ruin of us and that is why this war doesn't come to an end.

October 23rd [1901] Wednesday.

A perfect deluge all day, but now all is serene again. Yesterday morning Mr C[inatti] brought me a letter from Lou after all and asked me to take it to the censor. I did so in the afternoon and asked the man to censor the letters in future before putting them in Mr C[inatti]'s box as it would save me a lot of trouble. He said something about "irregular

---

[187] Well done!
[188] Probably a son of Paul and Clara Maré.
[189] Field Cornet A.Z.A. Briel of the Soutpansberg Commando. See A. Grundlingh, *Die "Hendsoppers" en "Joiners"*, pp 21 & 254.
[190] "Oh no".

proceedings" and gave me no answer when I accused him pointblank of having opened the previous letter and kept it back because it contained news he did not intend should reach me. I could see by his face that this was the case but what can one do? Soon afterwards Mr D.N.[191] told me that Gen M[axwell] had said to him that one of the consuls was passing letters under cover. This surprised me very much. So! even the General knows of this? I thought and straightaway informed my Portuguese friend – fortunately for he was not unprepared for the complications that followed. He had occasion to pay the Governor a business visit this morning and just as he was leaving, Gen M[axwell] handed him Lou's letter and asked him how it came to be addressed to his care. I could not help laughing at Mr C[inatti]'s recital of what followed. He waved his arms and stamped his feet, called it "one big dirty trick" and a "prying trap" and demanded an explanation. How did one letter addressed to him come not in his hands but in the General's hands? What meant it all? What impudent impertinence was this? The Governor told him the censor had sent the letter to Lord Kitchener (here poor old C[inatti] nearly went into a fit) and he had sent it to the Gov[ernor] requesting him to investigate the matter, but when he heard Mr C[inatti]'s version of the story and how often I had been to the censor about these very letters, he made light of it and agreed with Mr C[inatti] that such a censor deserved thirty days hard labour. But now the question is – shall I be allowed to get those letters? To think that my correspondence has been brought under the august Kitchener's notice!

Philipp came to say goodbye this afternoon – is leaving tomorrow. I have been very busy indeed helping DN with their preparations – the sale takes place tomorrow and I have been helping yesterday and this morning to get the house in order. On my way home I had an adventure. I was driving slowly in a cab when I saw coming from the opposite direction our poor political prisoners, about 20 of them in convict garb with arrows and PG in large letters all over them and guarded by five or six armed Tommies. I thought my heart would burst with rage and pity and as luck would have it I passed them just on the bridge – so near that I could almost touch them. On the impulse of the moment I leant out of the cab and cried out to them *"Dag, burgers van Transvaal.*

---

[191]   Probably Domela Nieuwenhuis.

Hou goeie moed – verlossing is nabij!"[192] The cab swept past and all I am conscious of is a few bewildered stares, open-mouthed amazement from my cabby, who turned round to see if his fare had gone out of her mind, and my own loudly-beating heart. There was no response from the men – a few sullen, despairing faces is all I remember, and of course the guards were too much taken aback to stop me, but when I came home I told the cabby to wait while I ran to the house to fetch some money. To my surprise I found an officer on horseback standing near the cab under one of our willow trees when I came back with the money. He stood still for some time, watching me, and then rode away in silence, leaving me to wonder what it meant. I am afraid there is trouble in store for me. Not a soul is allowed even to greet the prisoners and there I actually made them a small speech! Mama was horrified when I told her and says I had better pack up and be ready for immediate departure.

October 25th. [1901] Friday.

Yesterday the sale of D[omela] N[ieuwenhuis'] furniture took place and I officiated in the dining-room as detective in plain clothes. I kept a watchful eye on the silver spoons and other small articles of value and enjoyed the novelty of it all immensely. There were a good many people – all sorts and conditions, Jews and Gentiles, the former predominating and Mrs N[ieuwenhuis] tells me their belongings fetched nearly £500, which was very good indeed, considering the hard times. I bought ½ doz[en] beautiful crystal fruit dishes for £1.

Today I lunched in the Grand Hotel with them and then went to a reception held in their honour at the Vice Consul's, where they were presented with parting presents and addresses. Mr N[ieuwenhuis] got a magnificent bronze group, a painting by Oerder[193] and an album of Transvaal views with the names, artistically arranged, of the givers. Mrs N[ieuwenhuis] got a massive nugget brooch. Speeches were made,

---

[192] Good day, burghers of the Transvaal. Do not falter now – salvation is near.

[193] Frans David Oerder (1867–1944) was a renowned painter who lived in Pretoria. He fought in the Republican forces for virtually the entire duration of the war. See K. Kempff, Oerder, Frans David, in *DSAB* IV, pp 418–420.

toasts etc, eating, drinking, laughing, chatting – not a bit like war. The rooms were most beautifully decorated with palms and roses – one of the finest displays I have ever seen in Pretoria. And now we have wished our friends God-speed and they too must pass out of our lives, like everyone else – for a time at least. How and when and where shall we meet again? Oh, I cannot bear to think of all that may, and probably will, befall us before our country is at rest and we are free to go away and forget all the misery of the past.

This morning Mama and I met our poor prisoners again and we nodded again and again and waved to them. Some of them nodded slightly in response, one or two touched their hats furtively and a few smiled in a friendly way. Now I shall always be on the look-out for them.

I saw the censor again today and he says he sent Lou's letter to the head censor and he sent it on to Lord Kitchener. There are rumours about of much fighting.

October 25th. [1901] Saturday.[194]

Letters from Europe – two from Lou, one that came by today's mail and the one that "has been recovered from the Commander in Chief" – to use the censor's own words. I must write and thank the censor for forwarding it and yet I feel so mad with him for this cheek yesterday in saying he always enjoys reading my letters – they fully repay him for his trouble! Wretched man! how can I write to my friends when I know he is looking out for my letters. Lou's don't contain any war news, that is one thing certain.

There seems to be a lot of fighting – we heard cannon firing this morning in the Irene direction and I quite forgot to tell you, dear diary, that on the night of the 22nd inst[ant] at about ten o'clock, the mother and I were startled by hearing heavy firing in the Magaliesberg direction. We went out under the verandah to listen and distinctly heard about a dozen heavy cannon shots. It is gruesome listening to that sort of music at night. Fritz's comrade, Franz Lottering,[195] who was once reported killed, has been captured and is now in the Rest Camp, where we hope

---

194   Should be 26 October.
195   There are numerous references to the close ties between Lottering and the Van Warmelo brothers in Dietlof van Warmelo's book *Mijn commando en guerilla-commando leven,* eg on pp 47, 51 & 52.

to pay him a visit tomorrow. He will perhaps be able to tell us news of our beloved boy.

This is one of the most beautiful evenings imaginable. The moon is as brilliant as it only can be in tropical countries, the air crisp and cold, everything most serene, making it difficult for us to realize that we are in the heart of such a fierce and bloody war. When, oh <u>when</u> will it end? That is the one cry on our lips and in our hearts, morning, noon and night, and some days it is enough to drive one mad. Try as I do I cannot always be strong and brave and cheerful, and I shall remember the week that is past as one of the darkest and most desolate I have ever had the misfortune to live through. Thank God! the worst is over now and I am beginning the new week with new faith and courage.

October 30th. [1901] Wednesday.

This is the second anniversary of the battle of Modderspruit. I have made no entries the last few days. Landdrost Schutte[196] has been captured with about 90 men, but as he is not a fighting man and has just been trying to save some cattle from the enemy, it does not mean much loss to us. de la Rey is reported to have got a beating from Methuen – I don't believe it!

We were not allowed to see F[ranz] L[ottering] but a friend saw him and he told her that Fritz fought at Tarkastad.

A violent storm is raging – I can't write tonight, dear diary – you must please forgive me. *Ik is bedroef.*[197]

November 2nd [1901]. Saturday.

I am getting very lax about my diary, partly because I have so much other writing to do, but chiefly I think because the rumours one hears are so very vague and unreliable. That a great deal of fighting is taking place is evident, for the ambulance trains with their sad burdens, pass and re-pass on the Eastern line, and solitary locomotives fly past all day sometimes with only a truck, laden with workmen and implements to repair the damaged line. The Boers have taken Rustenburg and Warm Baths – but I believe went away again. We hear the distant roar of can-

---

196   Landdrost (Magistrate) C.E. Schutte lived in Potgieter Street, Pretoria, before the war. See *Longland's Pretoria Directory for 1899*, p 165.

197   I feel sad.

non almost daily and the town is full of officers and men. Major Wol-marans[198] was taken a few days ago with, they say, 70 men, but I am sure there were not so many. Gen Buller has been dismissed on half pay for a speech he made,[199] which is said to have had a demoralizing effect on the British troops here. Poor old Buller! if he had only known that that is the fate of every Englishman who speaks the truth! Kitchener of Khartoum looks glum when I meet him on the bridge and his cap is going more and more into his eyes. His life is not a bed of roses either.

Someone says we took seven or eight cannon the other day but where and how no one seems to know. A Cape paper says "the Boers are at the City gates!" Bravo, Boers, you are certainly getting on.[200] Our friends B[otha] H[attingh] E[lls] J[oubert] etc who have been at Ladysmith all this time, have now been sent to Bombay. I hope they will go to Dietlof's fort and tell him all the news. Brugman and the others who have to travel all over the country to protect the trains have been ordered away again. They got the order about a week ago, but every time they arrived at the Station, they were informed that the train was not leaving that day (Boers ahead!) but now I believe they have actually gone. Someone who went away more than a week ago has not come back yet and has never been heard of since. His relatives are very anxious and don't know whether he has been blown up or captured by the Boers. This forcing of leading townsmen to travel against their wishes is one of the meanest actions of all England's mean actions in this war. They first force burgers of our state to take the oath of neutrality and then they force them to break that oath by protecting the property of the enemy. Our noble foe! I never told you, dear diary, that at Irene they have a wire (barbed) enclosure,containing a small tent, in which the women are shut up whenever they do not behave, i.e. when they complain of the rations or call the handsuppers names or "spread sedition" in any way.

The other day a poor woman was too ill to wash her sheet in the

---

198   Major J.F. Wolmarans of the State Artillery was captured near Ermelo on 1901-11-01 and sent to St Helena as prisoner-of-war. See J. Ploeger, Wolmarans, Jan Francois, in *DSAB* III, p 852.

199   Buller was indeed relieved of his command and placed on half pay after a speech he made in England on 1901-10-10. See S.B. Spies, Buller, Sir Redvers Henry, in *DSAB* II, pp 99–101.

200   Even though the diarist sounds skeptical, this was not far-fetched.

river so she washed it in her tent, and that brute Esselen shut her up for a whole night in this "kraal", with a coolie woman and two or three kaffirs! This awful degradation and indignity so filled us with horror that Mrs J[oubert] wrote to the Governor, protesting against it, and his answer was that it was necessary, for sanitary purposes to make an example of her, and the case was exaggerated (as usual) for the woman was supplied with a chair to sit on! Not a word about the kaffirs! The nurses that have been sent to Irene now are a terrible lot – barmaids and worse! the "things" that were put over the border by our government before the war. According to the *Gazette*, the mortality in the camps, continues to be something appalling. I dare not think of these victims of the war – it breaks one's heart, especially on a wild and stormy night, such as we have so often had lately.

Khaki has never been so much on the alert as now. Houses are being searched all over the town, men are stopped for their residential passes at every street corner and the other evening even women were stopped and held in the street until an officer came to question them. The two M[innaar] girls were kept a whole hour in the pouring rain! Only we two quiet old ladies are left in peace – our house has never been searched and we live in peace and security. Well, they can search Harmony till they are blue in the face but never a scrap of writing will they find. This uninteresting chronicle contains nothing incriminating, but I don't think they will enjoy reading its contempt and dislike for all things English. We are somewhat in favour again in high circles – our letters are no longer censored (at least not under Martial Law, but I am not such a donkey as to think they are not opened by steam, which is much worse, as it makes one feel easier about writing and one is inclined to say things better left unsaid. No, dear M.R.,[201] I am on my guard against you – the "Agitator" is not half as simple and confiding as she looks!)

Mama had a letter from Gen Maxwell a few days ago, saying that in answer to enquiries he made about Dietlof he has received news from Bombay that D[ietlof] is in good health "and the best lawn tennis player in the camp". He asked her to send him a written statement as to D[ietlof]'s "social standing" here, which he would forward to the officials in the fort so that he could be treated as an officer.[202] Now was'nt

---

[201]   Not clear what she means.

[202]   J.G. Maxwell – Mrs van Warmelo, Pretoria, 28.10.1900 (date should be

[sic] that kind and thoughtful of the General? Of course the mother answered immediately, giving him full particulars. – I hear that Lady Maxwell is down with dysentery.

Dietlof van Warmelo, standing the furthest right, and other Boer prisoner-of-war tennis players in India

Today's mail brought me such a dear letter from my Lou. I am getting very much in love with him and wonder how I am to get through the time that must elapse before we can meet, but we have both made up our minds to be patient and brave and now that a regular correspondence has been at last established I think we shall manage to live on letters (and thoughts) until it pleases the Lord to bring us together. I think we are going to be very, <u>very</u> happy in the future. He is so good that I cannot help being good with him and even the thought of him makes me long to be all he <u>thinks</u> I am. May God help me never, never to disappoint him!

28 October 1901), Archives of the *Nederduitsch Hervormde Kerk van Afrika,* Pretoria, L.E. Brandt Collection, IX/168, file 6, *Briewe aan Mev van Warmelo 1878–1915,* unsorted.

November 4th [1901]. Monday.

Yesterday afternoon a deluge of rain such as we are not likely to forget in a hurry. Rev B[osman] visited Irene and says the misery there is indescribable. The tents are always saturated and the people who have no mattrasses or bedsteads have to sleep on the wet ground, and they are literally dying of starvation – the food is so bad. The Gov[ernmen]t Gazette shows an appalling list of dead. For the month of Sept[ember] in all the camps 1 223 and in the Standerton camp alone during the first ten days of October 108 deaths, of whom 84 were children under 8 years. The women are in such a frightfully low state that they can take any illness[203] – they ought all to be living in luxury if they are to be saved – oh, no I dare not think of it tonight, I am <u>so</u> miserable.

Even the glorious news we have had fails to cheer me up. The English have had three terrible reverses during the last few days. In one Col Benson was mortally wounded[204] – was buried here yesterday. I read the English official report this evening at C[inatti]'s and it speaks of "heavy losses" (marvellous admission!) and the capture of two guns by the Boers, who were 1 000 strong, under Louis Botha. Ten officers are reported killed, about 15 wounded and between 300 and 400 men killed and wounded. Ben Viljoen, de la Rey, and Beyers are fighting all over the place, in fact the Boers seem to be suddenly and mysteriously endowed with fresh energy and courage. Emissaries have been sent to Botha from the Colony asking for officers, as there are plenty of good fighting men and very few officers. I fancy this request will be instantly complied with. Boers have been in Wellington, and in Natal no end of fighting is taking place. All this is very encouraging to us and yet we can be pardoned if we are weighed down by a sense of depression at the untold misery around us. *Ik is* <u>weer</u> *bedroef en zal maar eindigen.*[205]

---

203 The diarist probably means that the women could not withstand any illness.

204 Commandant General Louis Botha led the Boer attack on a British column commanded by Lieutenant-Colonel Benson at Bakenlaagte, about 30 kilometres north-west of Bethal, on 30 October 1901. The Boers, numbering about 1 200, overran their adversaries. They captured two field guns in the process, but did not follow up their success. The British losses amount to 67, including Benson, killed, 164 wounded and 120 captured. The Boer losses were less than 100 in all. See P.G. Cloete, *The Anglo-Boer War a chonology*, pp 274–275.

205 I feel sad <u>again</u> and will have to end.

November 5th [1901]. Tuesday.

Some children with blackened faces have been carrying a fearful and wonderful Guy Fawkes about the streets today – to my great amusement. Otherwise no one seems to have noticed this memorable day, but we had some more good news by way of celebration. Mr C[inatti] read another official despatch to me – fierce fighting at Bronkhorstspruit for the last three days, the cannon are stuck in the river beyond reach of Boer or Briton, but as reinforcements are being sent they hoped soon to beat back the Boers. A large convoy was captured near Rustenburg – by the Boers, of course – they have no large convoys to <u>be</u> captured. Louis Botha is reported to have been killed at the battle of Brugspruit but as he has been killed so often and died of enteric once I am sure he will soon be all right again. I met a whole column of English riding down Church Street – four abreast – dirty and tired, evidently having travelled from far. The officers also looked very weary and disreputable. A little later I saw about a dozen trolleys, laden with women and children and their few miserable belongings, being driven to the Station, from where they left this evening for the Natal camp. They are the families of our fighting men and received notice yesterday to pack up and go. Mrs Nel[206] came to say goodbye to us – a splendid woman, whose husband and two sons have been in the field since the beginning of the war. One boy is 16 and the other 14 and their brave mother thanks God that they are where duty calls. I was impressed by the resolute way she said that she would rather hear that her husband had fallen in action that that he had surrendered. That is exactly how I feel about Fritz. Does it not seem rather an exaggeration? and yet it is a fact – on my word of honour – rather a free-born Transvaal burger in heaven that a traitor to land and people. I call these handsuppers <u>traitors.</u>

November 8th [1901]. Friday. 10 o'clock p.m.

And this terrific storm has been raging for hours! It seems incredible. While I write the roar of thunder never breaks off, peal after peal, crash after crash, vivid, dazzling flashes of lightning, torrents of rain, mixed with hail, and a howling wind. Such a night is never to be forgotten. One is impressed by its magnificence, by its awful grandeur and yet I think

---

206   Not identified.

one would go mad if it had to last any length of time. I want to go mad with the thought of our thousands and thousands of women and tender little children exposed to all this fury. Where is the God of pity tonight? Surely not in our desolate land, not in our ruined, blackened homes – not in <u>South Africa</u>!

The fourth storm within a few hours is just approaching, the one more violent than the other, and this one threatens to surpass all the others. The Lord hath turned His face in wrath from us – the hand of the Lord is laid heavily upon us, His ear is deaf to our cries and supplications. – I cannot write. My soul is crushed by the sorrow, sin and suffering around me, my head is aching from the fury and violence of the storm. My poor mother, who is terribly nervous in these storms of ours, is lying stretched on one sofa. I shall rest a few minutes on the other and compose myself before I continue writing.

Now I feel better (10.30) but it has been a great struggle. The reason why I am so hopeless, so despairing is that today I heard of the terrible mortality in the camps. Enteric has become a regular epidemic and is carrying off young and old. I don't see <u>how</u> we are going to continue this war. That most accursed nation, the English, is exterminating our women and children because their husbands and sons and fathers refuse to bow to the yoke of tyranny, because they are determined to fight for land and liberty as long as they have an atom of strength left. But "vengeance is mine" saith the Lord, and verily it seems as if England is about to receive her punishment. The British man-of-war "Terrible"[207] has gone down with all on board – many hundreds of men on their way home after an absence of over two years. It is a horrible tragedy and one would be a fiend indeed to rejoice in <u>such</u> a national disaster. We know no particulars yet.

A furious battle at Springs, where hundreds of English were killed and wounded, has been added to their misfortunes of the last ten days. The Boers have never before fought as they are fighting now.

But now I am going to bed to try and sleep off this nervous restlessness, this misery – oh God it is more than I can bear. Have pity on us, Oh Lord and make an end to our troubles. Lord we look to <u>Thee</u> for deliverance. Feb[ruary] 23 1902. We never heard the truth about the *Terrible.*[208]

---

[207]   Another false rumour.
[208]   This sentence was obviously inserted into the diary on the date indicated.

November 10th [1901]. Sunday night.

Last night a terrific storm raged – tonight it is the same, and this is the third night in succession that we have gone through this terrible – this awful misery. I think I suffer more than the women under canvas, on their account, not on my own certainly, for in my sheltered home I am safe from the fury of the elements. Last night when the whole house was shaking and peals of thunder crashed over head, I wanted to write, but changed my mind because I was afraid of again betraying thoughts of doubt and despair. It was wicked of me to say such things but sometimes I am nearly out of my mind with misery. Tonight the storm is quite as bad, accompanied by heavy wind and hail, but, though utterly sad, I am not in despair and I feel inclined to write down the news brought me by today's mail. I had a long letter from L[ouis Brandt], and I was very sad indeed to hear of his dear Grandmother's death. My poor Lou! He evidently feels it terribly and I know they were all passionately devoted to the dear old lady, who was one of the sweetest and best of women. I am just going to write to him to comfort him and this letter will be a very important one, for he asks me to bind myself to him definitely and I have decided to do so. It is a weighty step to take and God knows how utterly unworthy I feel of a man like Lou, but I have long prayed for guidance and it seems to me clear enough that we are destined for one another. So tonight in this fearful storm, with a heart filled with the desolation of land, the woes of people and the blackness of the future, I am going to write the words that will bind me for ever to Lou Brandt. Strange betrothal strange sequel to a stormy life! But perhaps my days of calm and peace are not very far off.

November 15th [1901]. Friday.

Five days since my last entry but I have really been too busy to write. I have been gardening, dressmaking, cooking, house cleaning, practising, and last but not least, I have been writing love-letters. The last named is an occupation I feel tempted to continue to the exclusion of all other pleasures and duties. There is so much I want to tell my love I could write to him for hours and then it is very hard to know that what ought to be sacred between us only, will be examined by an outsider. Of course I am very careful in what I write and my letters certainly do not contain many terms of endearment but it is bad enough that they are read by an outsider at all.

I have just gone through a most unpleasant experience with someone else and I think it is high time my engagement was made public. It gives me great pain to bring trouble into the lives of good and honest young men, like – – , men I admire and respect and whose friendship I long to keep. And yet I have found out that friendship and unrequited love do not go well together, and if I dread these "unpleasant experiences", it is more because I know they mean the loss of good friends, than because of the pain they give both parties. This sounds rather selfish and heartless but I mean it well. Pain is good for us and I am sure it does these young men no harm to be in love with someone they respect highly. An honest love affair is one of the best lessons of life and does more towards keeping a man in the strait and narrow path of virtue than anything else. Please don't be deceived by this philosophy, dear diary; it only shows how much I feel the events of the past few days and how very sad I am for the sake of that most chivalrous and honourable young man, G[ustav]...F[ichardt]...

There is no war news. All we know is that there must be trouble on the Eastern line, for we see daily passing, armoured trains, ambulance waggons, Khakis, cannon, horses etc. and endless stream backwards and forwards. The Buffs[209] are reported to have surrendered to Louis Botha. Lastly, there is talk of peace proposals again – Kitchener and Schalk Burger are supposed to have met, but as I saw the former this afternoon near the bridge, I don't know what to believe. After the terrific storms the weather is most glorious, each day seems clearer, purer, fresher than the last, and I have been revelling in nature, beautiful nature. – The house is being painted and new benches and tables have been made for the summer house, but these last have still to be painted and I have volunteered my services, for am I not giving a birthday party on Monday and do I not want the summer house to be in perfect order? I do. I shall be twenty-five on the 18th inst[ant] and very likely this will be my last birthday at home, so I want to have a few relatives and friends round me to celebrate the event – war or no war.

---

[209]   2nd Seaforth Highlanders regiment. See Savannah Publications, *Boer War Services of Military Officers of the British and Colonial Armies Imperial Yeomanry Mounted Infantry Local Units &cc 1899–1902 including Earlier Services*, pages unnumbered.

November 18th [1901]. Monday.

I have had such a lovely birthday. Got up at 5 and arranged great bunches of flowers for the summer house, though the weather was very threatening and we feared that the whole thing was going to be a failure, but towards midday it cleared up and we had a glorious afternoon, cool and fresh and yet sunny. Now that we have brought in every thing and our visitors are safely home again, the rain is coming down in torrents and thunder and lightning are the order of the night. I had a few lovely presents and wore the mother's, a charming frock of flowered muslin. [sic] It has been a happy day in spite of the war.

I think the Boers wanted to get into Pretoria to congratulate me because we heard cannon firing in the J[o]h[anne]sburg direction several times this morning. I told Oom Paul the best thing he could wish for me is that I may be twenty-four next birthday. I don't like it a bit that I am getting so old.

Have just written a long letter to my beloved. Love letters are my only joy now. There is no war news that I know of.

November 21st [1901]. Thursday.

They say that de Wet is in Kroonstad with 4 000 men and that he fought for three days; also that there has been another big battle somewhere near Springs; that J[o]h[anne]sburg is going to be made the capital and lots of other news that I don't consider worthy of being repeated. – On the night of the 19th we had one of the most terrific storms. – I have no time to write more. The mail leaves tomorrow and I am not nearly through with my weekly correspondence.

November 23rd [1901]. Saturday.

It seems a waste of time to write in this diary when I have nothing to tell. It has been a most uneventful week as far as we are concerned. Today's mail brought me my usual letter from Lou, but it did not contain anything particular. He wants me to go to Holland at once, foolish boy. If he only knew how utterly impossible that is and how gladly I would go if I could! – The town is very full of officers and men, which always mean something – I wish we could hear some news. Red Cross trains have been flying up and down the Eastern line and there are vague rumours of big battles all over the country but not a scrap of reliable information is allowed to reach us. I am going to practise and try and forget the war and all this misery and unsettledness – it is enough to drive one mad. Sometimes, like tonight, I feel it more than usual.

November 26th [1901]. Tuesday.

Although my diary makes a very poor show just now, it is not because I have been lazy but I have had such a lot of other writing to do. And I have had no definite news to tell but now there are rumours afloat of terrible disasters to the English. A great battle against Botha is supposed to have been fought on the 22nd inst[ant] near Silverton, and it is said that Brugspruit was <u>nothing</u> to it. In the Free State also a lot of fighting seems to be going on. de Wet is evidently becoming alarmingly active again.

I went to the Governor this afternoon to get a permit for RH[210] to give a children's concert next month. Major H[oskins] attended to me as the General was engaged and when I asked whether he thought I would be allowed to visit Irene he said I could try but he did not think there was much chance. The condition of the camps becomes daily more terrible and I had some information from DB[211] this afternoon that fills me with horror. I am going to get <u>facts</u> and publish them if I can. One thing is certain – something <u>must</u> be done and I am no longer going to look on with folded arms. Mrs H,[212] who has just visited Irene with our old general's wife, says the misery there is indescribable. The people get no soap, no candles, and their rations are daily becoming worse. One woman told how her baby died in the night and she was in the dark all night with its little corpse – not a candle to light up the darkness and misery. Of, it is too terrible. I shall go to the Governor again, but see him I <u>must</u>, even if I am to be punished for my persistency. They think they have crushed all the energy out of us bit we'll show them that there is plenty of spirit and determination left – I want to be able to do our poor sufferers some good – but how?

---

210   Probably Riek H.
211   Not identified.
212   Probably Mrs Honey.

November 29th [1901]. Friday.

Everyone is now speaking of "peace" and everyone seems to expect it within the next few months. Someone, who is as a rule very cautious, told us this morning that he is expecting startling developments from day to day and he would not be a bit surprised if the war got settled in a most unexpected manner. There must be something brewing in Europe but what can it be? Dr Leyds has gone to Berlin and Austria is said to have appealed to the powers for intervention. One hears the most wonderful stories and there are many people who fully believe that not a shot will be fired in South Africa after December 16th. Oh, may God grant it! It is indeed time the war came to an end, if only for the sake of our poor women and children. We got a lot of statistics of the camps this morning and my heart stood still when I read of the terrible mortality. The calculations prove that after a little more than three years the whole population will be exterminated at this rate. I have the papers in a place of safety and will say no more about them here. I know what use to make of them. Kitchener is said to be very much against these camps but of course he has to obey orders. Downing Street will have a big account to settle when the day of reckoning comes, believe me.

Of the recent fights we have heard no particulars, which shows that the English came off second best.

I am busy making preparations for the announcement of my engagement – making up a list of names etc. The event will take place in January, I hope, and in the meantime I am informing a few intimate friends by letters. Had congratulations from E[213] today – the sweetest letter she has ever written to me. I will send it to him.

December 2nd [1901]. Monday.

A day of great lassitude and weariness – I suppose on account of the enervating heat. We have been expecting rain or a great thunder storm again, but it passed off and all is oppressively serene. To me these days are most trying – I simply cannot stand heat, and I have so much to do and may not indulge in idleness. There is a good deal of "talk" again but no reliable information. A train load of Khakis and cannon went out on the Eastern line yesterday afternoon, and in the morning

---

[213]   Probably Edith Goodwin.

an ambulance train, so there is something wrong – or right! Someone told me today that the enemy got a severe beating last week. It is supposed to have happened in this way. One of our despatch riders came suddenly upon a British patrol. He immediately tore his reports into shreds, and scattering them to the winds, he tore away for dear life. Of course the English picked up the fragments and laboriously put them together and read that de Wet was in a tight corner and badly in need of reinforcements, would de la Rey come to such and such a place with the utmost speed? Imagine the delight of our simple and guileless foe! They instantly prepared for departure – going to catch de Wet, you know – and got such a warm reception from him that they did not know what to do with themselves. I give this story for what it is worth and it has caused my great satisfaction merely to repeat it. There is no reason why I should not believe it – it is just like de Wet.

Well, I am much too tired to write more this evening – Line wrote today expressing her joy and satisfaction at the news of my engagement. It seems like a dream to me – not a bit real – and it is very sad for us to be betrothed under such circumstances but perhaps our happiness will come soon.

December 3rd [1901]. Tuesday.

In connection with several arrests made in Johannesburg some time ago, four men were shot yesterday and seven were to have been shot today.[214] This is merely a repetition of the Cordua case – there never was any plot at all, but go on, England! Nothing can be better for our cause that this and the concentration camps and the hanging of "rebels".

The incredible news has reached us of a rupture between Queen W[ilhelmina] and her husband. Someone who read the announcement at the Gov[ernmen]t Buildings today told us that she has appealed for a divorce – that her husband used violence towards her and this caused the miscarriage she had some time ago.[215] Great Heaven, the world seems to be just one huge inferno – I simply cannot and will not believe

---

[214] Apparently the shooting of these men did not take place. See diary entry on 8 December 1901.

[215] Partly true. They were not divorced, but did not live together like husband and wife. However, there is no evidence that he ever acted violently towards her.

this awful story until I know it to be proved beyond a shadow of doubt
– it is too utterly monstrous to be true.

[Entry in the diarist's "Secret diary", written using lemon juice:]
Harmony. December 6th 1901.

I should very much like to fill this book and take it to some place of
safety but we have no more adventures to relate. Since those spies were
fired on and barely escaped with their lives in September none of our
friends have been in Town. We know that spies have been here but they
are not "in our set" and probably know nothing about us. If we could
only get hold of one of them to send out a message to Louis Botha.
Here this Ladies' Committee is sitting twirling its thumbs and unable
to do a single thing. It is such a great pity for I am now in direct communication with Dr Leyds and can send him a message by every mail
– through the White Envelope of course. And yet I don't know. Perhaps it
is just as well that we have nothing important to communicate just now.
Mama and I are in a terrible state of anxiety. A White Envelope, written
Nov[ember] 8th to Line has never reached her! The letter contained nothing about the war and should have been allowed to pass but Line never
received it and we can't make out what has become of it. The censors
may have discovered our secret and may be waiting to catch up some
more – something of greater importance – for the last contained only a
little war news. I sent another envelope containing a few Christmas cards
from J[o]h[anne]sburg (Mr G[ordon] posted it for me) asking her to let
us know immediately when she receives the missing letter. She is on the
black list and her correspondence is being closely watched. Aunt v E[216]
writes to us that she got a letter from Line which was written <u>before</u>
M[artial] L[aw] was proclaimed in Cape Town in which she tells Aunt v
E that she is going to send her a code to use when M[artial] L[aw] was
proclaimed. The censors kept this letter back until M[artial] L[aw] reigned
supreme, opened it, marked those passages with two crosses and sent
it to Aunt v E. The code never reached her of course and now we are
so afraid that Line sent it in the same way <u>before</u> Martial Law and that
without her knowledge and that she is making use of it and the censors
are catching up all her bits of information! She will go on writing and
they will keep back Aunt v E's letters so that L[ine] will never know that
she receives nothing. Fortunately one of our Italian gardeners, Pera,[217]

---

216   Probably Nellie van Eeden, sister of the diarist's late father.
217   Not identified.

went to Cape Town a day or two ago and we smuggled a letter through for L[ine] with him – in a matchbox with a false bottom! He is to deliver it personally to Mrs K[218] who will send it to L[ine] – or give it, as sending is not safe. Pera was quite game for any amount of mischief, to my great delight. If he can't find Mrs K he said he would "fire" the matchbox.

What alarms us so much is the thought that Line's code was the white envelope and that that is the reason why my last went astray! Great Heavens! Then we are done for and the sooner we pack our traps and go the better for us. I am becoming quite reckless in my anxiety and am for sending her a white envelope every day until we hear whether she receives them or not. Tomorrow the European mail will be delivered and if I receive a W[hite] E[nvelope] from Lou I will know that our secret is not yet discovered. I have had two from him containing no war news of any importance but the last two mails, there was no W[hite] E[nvelope] – perhaps because I warned him to be extremely careful and use it only in cases of emergency! I dare not send him another W[hite] E[nvelope] until I know if it is quite safe, and it is a great pity because I have some very important statistics of the camps to send Dr Leyds and Stead.

I shall see what news we get and relate them here as soon as possible. I want to get this most dangerous book out of the way. Last mail I found lying in our box a parcel addressed to Mrs Wentword Box 56. I was on the point of throwing it back when I saw the postmark – Tunbridge Wells and knew at once that it came from Mrs B[219] and was meant for us. Took it home and found that magnificent book Peace or War in SA by Methuen.[220] It is splendid and is now going round to all our friends. Oh, Mr Censor!

December 8[th] [1901]. Sunday.

It is not true that those men in J[o]h[anne]sburg were shot – I believe two others were condemned but no one seems to know whether the sentence was executed. The latest war news is the capture of two convoys by the Boers – an enormous one of 120 waggons [sic] at Pienaar's River and a smaller one in the Middelburg district. Today I heard that Botha is surrounded by twenty columns and cannot possibly escape. The old, old story! de Wet is supposed to be somewhere not very far from Pretoria. Badenhorst's commando has had a serious reverse ac-

---

[218]   Not identified.
[219]   Mrs Bodde. See J. Brandt, *Die Kappiekommando*, pp 170–171.
[220]   A.M.S. Methuen, *Peace or war in South Africa* (London, 1901).

cording to Khaki and 103 men were captured but B[adenhorst] himself escaped. That arch traitor Jan Celliers,[221] that renegade, that Judas Boer and every other name that is sweet and lovely, went out with his hands-up commando of 300 men, assisted by over 3 000 Khakis and dealt our people this heavy blow. Amongst the prisoners young Westmaas[222] and Gregan[223], two boys who escaped from Pretoria one night about six months ago. Gregan had taken the oath of neutrality so we don't know what his fate will be, but Westmaas was under sixteen when the English took Pretoria and did not take any oath, so he will merely be sent away as prisoner of war. His father was sent to Pietersburg last week to "protect the train" and at one of the stations he saw a number of our prisoners and one of them called to him asking if he were Mr W[estmaas] from Pretoria. He said "yes" and then the man told him that he had seen his son a few days before and he was quite well. This was the first news his parents had heard from him since his brave and clever escape from Martial Law and it is curious that he should have been captured almost immediately afterwards.

– Now I think that is all the news I have collected since Tuesday. We are much disappointed that the European mail has not yet arrived but there has been a slight accident to the "Dunottar Castle", and I am not even sure that we shall get our letters tomorrow. I wonder what I shall hear from Lou.

Went to church this morning, but the heat was something terrible and we are all feeling quite knocked up with it. The minister was not up to much and I found my thoughts wandering into all sorts of unholy channels.

Dear Lou, forgive me for calling you "unholy". I have not had much joy from you lately – my thoughts are always so sad and oh, these long-

---

221   This Jan Celliers was the former Republican Commandant J.G. Celliers who recruited Boers for the National Scouts, which actively supported the British army. See A. Grundlingh, *Die "Hendsoppers" en "Joiners"*, p 248.

222   In her diary entry on 1901-12-28 the diarist hints that young Westmaas' name was Frans. He was probably the son of C. Westmaas, of whom a son, according to the commissioner of police, 'absconded' from Pretoria. See S.B. Spies, *Methods of Barbarism?*, p 242.

223   Probably a member of the family of W.J. Gregan, a bookkeeper who lived in Troye Street, Sunnyside, close to Harmony. See *Longland's Pretoria Directory for 1899*, p 133.

ings are so hard to bear. People are not all quite nice about this engagement. They don't think I can care much about a man who is a perfect stranger to <u>them</u>, but never mind, we'll show them that we know what we are doing.

Dietlof van Warmelo, in centre holding a book, with the debating society in a prisoner of war camp in India

December 9th [1901] Monday.

Very unpleasant news from Dietlof. He says an order has come from headquarters (viz. Pretoria) that he is no longer to be treated as an officer. My poor brother is now with the riff-raff and I am going straight to the Governor tomorrow to ask what the reason of this strange new departure is. It is shameful. He has all along been treated as an officer, but one day we asked for a little more freedom for him, as his health was not good, and the result is that they have withdrawn the few privileges he had as officer. Of course Major Poore is at the bottom of this and I should like to wring his long, thin neck. He is so hard on our prisoners always and is nothing but an unfeeling brute. Everyone hates him and I suppose the Governor will refer me to him tomorrow – a most delightful prospect truly. I have never yet had an interview with him and always hoped I would escape him – oh yes, we did once have the honour of seeing him under our roof, on the memorable occasion that he walked into our drawing-room with a pipe! Mama has had more dealings with him and says he is so discourteous and abrupt. We'll see tomorrow.

– We are very sad this evening. Things are not going so well with us. The English have captured over 300 of our best fighting men during the last week and the horrible part of it is that these victories have been achieved solely through the assistance of our own burgers – men like "General" Jan Celliers and Andries Cronje[224] – own brother to our Paardeberg hero. Be brave and courageous, my sad heart. "Darkest before dawn", and when all seems lost deliverance will come. Now is the time for us to trust in Him Who has been with us during the last two wonderful years.

December 13th [1901] Friday.

I have been too miserable to write in my diary. Things were looking very black and everyone was so depressed and despondent and I even heard some of our bravest supporters say that if this went on much longer the Boers could not win. Of course I have been wretched and melancholy too but never in despair, thank God for that.

The captures effected by the Judas-Boers caused all this hopelessness but now a sudden change has taken place. I mentioned the fact that the last European mail had been delayed, and it is not here yet, although the next one is due this evening. It now appears that there has been no accident at all but that Mr Censor is at the bottom of the mischief, for in the leading article of today's "*Natal Witness*",[225] that most Jingo paper, the public is informed that last week's mail brought no magazine or paper that did not betray growing dissatisfaction with the Ministry. England is returning to sanity and the public is beginning to realize that it is being dragged to a precipice etc. etc. The article is headed "Mutterings and Growlings" and every word betrays unrest and anxiety, distrust of the Government, bitter rebellion against the heavy and ever increasing taxation and determination to come to the truth, to face facts in all their nakedness and no longer to be duped by capitalists

---

[224]   A.P.J. (Andries) Cronjé – brother of Generaal Piet Cronjé who on 27 February 1900 surrendered to the British at Paardeberg, was active as a National Scout and recruited a Scout unit consisting of a few hundred former burghers. See A. Grundlingh, *Die "Hendsoppers" en "Joiners"*, pp 254–258.

[225]   Mutterings and Growlings, *Natal Witness*, 13 December 1901, leading article.

and stubborn, wrong-headed statesmen. Never have I read such sentiments in the *"Natal Witness."* We are like new creatures this evening
and I am half crazy with a sudden, new hope that the end of the war
is not far off. I have always had hope that the Boers would win but I
was afraid that it would be some years perhaps before our victory was
assured, but now there is growing up in my breast a strong belief that
things <u>cannot</u> go on like this much longer. Everyone says there is to be
an armistice from Dec[ember] 15th until the end of the year. God grant
it! Those days, those memory-laden anniversaries will be easier to live
through if we can have the blest assurance that for a time at least there is
no bloodshed in our land. Peace in our poor, persecuted land! Peace, if
only for two short weeks – oh, may God grant us this one boon!

I went last Wednesday to see about Dietlof, and as I expected, Major
Hoskins referred me to the Provost Marshall [sic]. I knew the Governor
had nothing to do with this wretched business. I told Major H[oskins]
I hated going to the P[rovost] [Marshal]'s office so he gave me a sort of
letter of recommendation, which made things easier for me and saved
me the trouble of waiting for an indefinite length of time. To my relief
I was conducted to the presence of an officer who treated me with the
utmost courtesy and consideration, and I did not even catch a glimpse
of the obnoxious P[rovost] M[arshal].

I think this man must be Capt Bonham,[226] of whom I have heard
only good reports. He promised to investigate the matter and to let me
know what the result is, but I have not heard from him since. He did
not seem to think there was any chance of D[ietlof]'s being treated as an
officer, because we have no proofs that he was one, and *Krijgscommis-
saris*[227] is not a "leader" but I have an idea they will make an exception,
because he has been treated as officer for six months.

[Entry in the diarist's "Secret diary", written using lemon juice:]
Dec 19th 1901

It is a wonder the events of the last few days have not unsettled my rea-

---

226   Probably W. Bonham of the Essex Regiment, who was (as a lieutenant)
appointed to the staff of the Commissioner of Police in Pretoria in June
1900. See Transvaal *Government Gazette Extraordinary,* 1/2, 16 June
1900, p 9.
227   War Commissioner.

son. Perhaps they have – I really could not say whether I am sane or not but I shall try to relate those event with some show of sanity. I have only a few minutes to spare. Other duties are awaiting me, viz. my duties as "secretary" to Captain N[audé] head of our Gov[ernmen]t Secret Service. Now this sounds rather as if I am off my head but I assure you the above statement is a fact. At this very moment Capt N[audé] is sitting under our trees in the summer house and what is more he has slept two nights under our roof and has partaken of five meals at our table. Astounding revelations! Harmony become a refuge for spies! I can hardly realize it.

Captain J.J. (Koos) Naudé

Now let me begin at the very beginning with my narrative so as to miss no detail. Since that very memorable 12th Sept[ember] we have had no news from outside – three full months no one came in on account of the great danger, but on the morning of the 17th inst[ant], at break of day, three travellers entered our town – stained, torn, weary, and passed through the guards and were respectfully saluted by all, which mystery I will explain presently. It is a mystery, for no one is allowed to be abroad before 6 am and then such suspicious-looking characters. That very day M[ama] and I spoke of N[audé], said we thought he would never come again, regretted the appearance of the young moon, which means no spies in Pretoria and wondered how we were going to communicate with Gen Botha in future. At 8 o'clock that night Flip[228] came in suddenly to say that two ladies were looking for Harmony, they were at the front gate. I went out at once and found them coming up the garden path, told them I was Miss v[an] W[armelo]. What did they want?

Evening.
I had to break off suddenly and don't know where I was. The men have

---

[228] The diarist explains in her entry on 1902-01-26 who Flip(pie) was.

just gone and we had had <u>such</u> a time – but this will come presently. I think I was telling of the two mysterious women who said two men wanted to see Mrs v[an] W[armelo]. I said ["]Why don't they come to the house? You can't expect my mother to go and meet them at the gate." "Oh yes, she must, she knows them, they will tell her themselves what they want." Well, I fetched the mother and whispered to her to be on her guard – they were either spies or the English were setting a trap for us. We all walked to the gate together and then one of the girls said she would go on ahead and fetch them – they were not at the gate, they were waiting near the wire fence. This made me rather suspicious, especially when we waited and waited and no one came.

Harmony's front gate

The girl had disappeared altogether and in the meantime I was trying to pump the other one but could get nothing out of her. M[ama] went back to the house and girl no 2 said she would go and look for no 1 leaving me standing at the gate with my own reflections. After endless waiting I saw something coming and as the mother joined me just then we went forward to meet them. My heart stood still when a tall English officer advanced – helmet on, revolvers etc. and saluted us in the moonlight, but when he stretched out his hand and whispered "Capt N[audé]" I understood it all and grasped his hand warmly whispering "Welcome." Then all was serene. He introduced his corporal Venter,[229] took leave of the ladies and the four of us sauntered up to the house talking freely and loudly as we passed the sergeant's tin "villa". The good man was calmly sitting inside, smoking and reading, little thinking that his arch enemies were within a stone's throw of his house. I was wild with excitement. We did not talk much when once we were inside but flew about the house, made fire and soon had the kettle boiling, made cocoa, fried ham and eggs and soon had a fine repast spread out before them, cold plum pudding, rusks, bread, butter jam etc. Poor things how they fell to! They were so weary, so stiff, so utterly done for that they could hardly sit up straight. After their meal they stretched out on the sofas, supremely content with their pipes and we sat beside them talking, talking till nearly midnight. How can a pen ever describe their thrilling adventures, their hairbreath escapes, their hardships, privations, fatigue? Oh God, my heart was so full sometimes that I could have burst into tears. I could have given my life for those men, so brave, so strong and calm, facing death a thousand times without flinching, looking their troubles philosophically in the face, trusting implicitly in their God. The faith of N[audé] is sublime – there is no other word for it.

Tonight I am so worn out with sleeplessness and anxiety that I can hardly hold my pen but by degrees I hope to write down some of the things I heard – even if it takes me some days. It is quite worth the trouble.

Dec[ember] 20th [1901] [Secret diary]

After a good rest I feel a bit more settled. Where was I? We talked that night and listened to their wonderful stories of death and danger. They had come into Town at dawn that morning – three of them. N[audé] as officer and V[enter] and B[rinckmann] as Boers in Khaki. They did not know our house and had no idea where to go, actually walked through Harmony's grounds – across the main road, over Sunnyside bridge, and hid themselves in the thick poplar bush beside the river. Three kaffir police sprang up and saluted N[audé] respectfully as he passed – but for his uniform the men would have been done for. B[rinckmann] went to his

---

229   This visit to Pretoria by Naudé and the Boer spies Venter and Brinckmann is described in detail in G.D. Scholtz, *In Doodsgevaar,* pp 180–191. See also J. Brandt, *Die Kappie Kommando,* pp 290–323.

relations at Arcadia and promised to send someone to escort N[audé] and V[enter] to Harmony in the evening. When night fell he sent his sister and V[enter]'s to their hiding-place and the four of them marched about Sunnyside through the Tommies camps past General M[axwell]'s house and the War Office until they at last came upon the unsuspecting Flippie, who volunteered to show them the way. The two men had a terrible day in the bush, lying in one position as flat as possible in the awful heat, without food and nothing but a little filthy water in a hole nearby to drink. They were thankful, I can tell you, to reach this haven of refuge and to be welcomed by such friends. I could have given my life for them but instead of that we had to cook for them and make their beds and carry water for them and do all in our power to make them comfortable. Later on I'll tell all the news we got out of them. Of course the mother and I hardly closed our eyes that night and every time Carlo barked we jumped with fright and in the morning we were up early but somehow then all my fears had vanished and I felt as if I had been harbouring spies all my life. We had to bring baths in for them as quietly as possible and wash their dishes ourselves so as not to rouse the suspicions of our watchful Flippie, and Jim too is very cute. At 10 o'clock I flew to Town on my bicycle to tell people who had to come to see N[audé]. For many reasons I shall not mention a single name.

I went to V[enter]'s relations to say they were on no account to visit him at Harmony – he would go to them that night. I got a splendid suit of clothes for him from somebody, so that he could go out as a gentleman, sewed on his buttons, gave him ties and studs and a new sailor hat – I believe he had on clothing belonging to six different people. N[audé] had to keep on his Khaki so we could only provide him with clean underclothing. The unmistakeable smell of commando pervaded our erstwhile peaceful abode. We fed them and coddled them and they just let us do with them exactly what we pleased. Poor souls! I suppose the sight of a woman was perfect bliss to them. In the afternoon we had quite a crowd of people – in fact I was horrified! Mrs M[alan] and H[oney] and A[rmstrong]. Mr N[iemeyer] and F[ichardt] and G[230] and A[231] and in the evening Mr B.[232] I thought the visitors would never end – casual callers dropped in and while I entertained them in the drawing room M[ama] kept the others quiet in the dining room. Mrs M[alan]

---

[230]   Not identified.
[231]   Not identified.
[232]   Not identified.

got a list of things that N[audé] wanted and promised to bring them next day. In the evening V[enter] walked boldly away to his own house where he stayed for the night and following day. He has been five times in Pretoria and nine times in J[o]h[anne]sburg. This was N[audé]'s 25th visit to Pretoria!! Next day M[ama] gave N[audé] a suit of F[ritz]'s clothing to wear and from that moment he walked freely about the house and garden and sat under the trees, while his uniform and helmet lay buried in the secret hiding place in our room. We were quite easy then and told the servants we had a visitor for the day. Mrs M[alan] brought what they wanted – boots, hats, clothing, soap, matches, salt etc etc and the mother packed and arranged things for the evening's departure. V[enter] was to call for him at about 7 p.m. but he did not come till about 8 and we were getting quite nervous with the thought of his possible fate. Imagine our horror when we found B[rinckmann] waiting under the six willows with <u>four</u> girls and another man. We nearly got a fit! Coming to see them off, if you please. B[rinckmann]'s three sisters and Venter's one and a sweetheart. It made my blood run cold to think that all these people know that we kept the spies – it is not fair of them to be so indiscreet. They parted from them there and we said goodbye to N[audé] here because he was going to follow afterwards and meet the others in bush. He actually kissed us! (I hope my Lou won't mind.) v[an] d[er] W[esthuysen] went with them to help with the carrying of their heavy parcels through the bush and this afternoon he told me that when they came to the drift they found guards and had to lie down and wait, then B[rinckmann] borrowed v[an] d[er] W[esthuysen]'s residential pass and walked on ahead to see if the coast was clear, but came back and said it was not possible to get through – v[an] d[er] W[esthuysen] must go home as they would lie in the bush until the moon went down. He had to go back so we don't know how they managed. God only knows how they do manage. They had on two or three riding-breeches under the top suit ever so many shirts and coats and each one carried a bag of necessaries. I strapped the smallest of them over my shoulders and found the weight more than I could bear. How then do they manage to walk through thick forests, creep through barbed wire fences, climb walls and sometimes creep on all fours for many hundreds of yards! It is a mystery to me and yet they do if often. N[audé] says food is plentiful – good meat and more than they know what to do with – fruit that they find on the farms, plenty of fresh milk, but mealies are getting scarce. Clothing <u>very</u> scarce, ammunition so-so. They take all they want from the enemy, they strip their prisoners and give them their old rags in exchange. Horses good, especially in the High Veld. Latest reports from Colony excellent. There everything is plentiful and Colonists join daily in hundreds. No sickness to speak of on commando. Surrenderers are things of the past – the men are thoroughly sifted by this time and will stand to the last – he says they can still afford to lose 1 000 of the weak minded ones. Men full of hope and courage – very cheerful in spite of untold sufferings. They get chased about for days – sometimes without any rest and have to endure hunger and fatigue but often they have quite a jolly time. N[audé] gave a concert on President's birthday! And when they get to a farm where a few girls are still to be found, they take them out riding and driving! God bless them – our brave lion-hearted heroes. God bless them! When these men related their experiences in a simple, unaffected way, perfectly natural and straightforward I often felt the tears rising in my eyes and my heart swelling with emotion and a passionate love and pity, tenderness and respect. Their faith in God is sublime and puts us to shame...

Later
My dearest Love, you see I have filled this little book and I want to direct the last words to you. I have been absorbed in other things, my Love, and you have only been present in my thoughts as some sweet vague blessing to dwell upon afterwards. Now the reaction is setting in and I find myself going back to you and for this evening at least I want to put all excitement from me and think of you only. I wrote to you today – with a mighty effort. Just an ordinary letter when my heart was bursting with its burden. When shall I tell you all there is to tell? When will you hold me in those strong young arms of yours where I so often, often long to be? Oh may God bring us together very soon my own dear Love – I cannot live without you any longer. I am a woman and a passionate one and I want you every moment of my life.

December 20ᵗʰ [1901]. Friday.

Just a week this evening since my last entry. Disgraceful is it not? But oh, I have been so busy and am even now too tired to write - still I shall give the latest news briefly. Our brave general Kritzinger[233] has been captured and will probably be hanged as a rebel. This is very bad news

---

[233] General P.H. (Pieter) Kritzinger was indeed captured by British forces at Hanover in the Cape Colony on 1901-12-16. See P.G. Cloete, *The Anglo-Boer War a chronology*, pp 283–284.

and we feel it dreadfully but never mind! If they kill him the colonials will be so mad that hundreds will rise to avenge him. Bad news No.2 is that the English are publicly arming the natives against us. Last Monday (or Tuesday) about 50 of them received guns and ammunition on the Market Square and marched through the principal streets, out of the Town. This I have heard from people who <u>saw</u> them, one of them being an Englishman, to use his own words "a Britisher to the backbone". Of course we knew all along that it was being done, but the English always denied it, but now they no longer conceal the fact, on the contrary, they are publishing it to the gaze of the astonished world and I am just wondering what measures that world will take with regard to this new barbarity. Is it possible that England can do whatever she pleases, that she can break every mortal law of civilization with impunity? Is there no help for us in heaven or on earth? Oh God, it seems too cruel, too unjust, that we should be persecuted and tortured in this way, for defending <u>our own</u>. The arming of natives is a most serious affair. People talk of hell let loose in S[outh] A[frica] – it is <u>nothing</u> to what it will be if blacks are provided with arms. I shudder at the mere thought. A proclamation has come out to the effect that "coloured men" who have proffessions or trades need no longer carry passes, only they must have a card of exemption! This is the beginning of what we have [been] fearing all along and I don't know what the consequences will be. I dare not think of the future – if the war does not end soon things will go badly with us all. Tonight I feel perfectly desperate.

Have not yet heard from the P[rovost] M[arshal] what D[ietlof]'s fate is to be. His last letter had half a page torn out by the censor!

[Last entry in the diarist's "Secret diary", written using lemon juice:]
Harmony. Dec[ember] 21st 1901.
Last night I filled the book to which these sheets belong. Some time ago I tore them out – now I'll fill them and put them in again.

Now for the rest of my recitals. N[audé] makes a splendid officer. He is tall, fair and rather slender with a pair of brave blue eyes, fair moustache and beautiful teeth. He was clean shaven and looked an English officer, every inch of him, that is to say as long as he kept his mouth closed – his English is very bad.

Now let me tell you how he was dressed – too interesting for anything. He had on the uniform of Col Ferrol[234] who was killed at Bethal! Revolvers, whistle, leggings, helmet etc all complete, even the colonel's crowns and stars on his shoulders! The suit had <u>six</u> bullet holes and many blood stains just as N[audé] had taken it from the body of the Col after that terrible battle at Bethal. He himself took Col Benson's papers from him as he lay mortally wounded. He was surrounded by doctors and high men – who at first refused to let N[audé] touch them, but he ordered them all aside and gently took every scrap of papers out of his pockets. He also took his two crowns and has promised to bring them to me when he comes again. When Benson was dead someone else took all his clothing

Naudé in a British officer's uniform

and covered his body with a blanket or something. Why not? The Boers are badly off for clothing and the living go before the dead. As long as the dead are treated with respect I see no harm in taking their clothes. Benson had no important documents on him – only private papers, which N[audé] returned of course. They say there has seldom been a battle like this during the war. About 12 Boers were killed at once, two or three died afterwards and about 30 were wounded – all in all nearly 50 casualties. English officers 10 dead, 3 or 4 died of wounds and about 15 more wounded.[235] Men over 400 on the battle field but of these figures they

---

234 No reference to a Colonel Ferrol could be found. In her book *The Petticoat Commando*, p 306, the diarist records that the uniform belonged to a Colonel Thorold who was killed in action in the Battle of Bakenlaagte. She probably means Captain Frederick Temple Thorold of the 2nd Yorkshire Light Infantry who was killed in action at Bakenlaagte on 1901-10-31 – See http://redcoat.future.easyspace.com/BoerT.htm, accessed on 2003-07-04.

235 This was the battle of Bakenlaagte (see diary entry on 1901-11-04).

are not quite sure. With the storming of the cannon Boers and English were so close together that the one could hear what the other said. Venter saw a poor Tommy fall back mortally wounded and heard him gasp out with his dying breath, "Oh, dear Mother." God of pity! Who will tell that bereaved parent that her son's last thoughts and words were for her alone? V[enter] says it was awful to hear the wounded and dying calling on their God – here a Boer cried to God in Dutch, there, quite near him, an Englishman prayed for help or committed his soul in the Hands of the Maker. Nationality, enmity, hatred were forgotten – side by side those mortal foes prepared to meet their God – one God! What is so terrible is when they implore for help or pray for one drop of water and there is no one to help and not a drop of water to give them in their dying agonies. The Boers took the two cannon and afterwards destroyed one – the other they are using now. N[audé] was with Botha three weeks ago and heard from him of a very narrow escape he had had. He was completely surrounded and barely escaped with his life – even his hat was left behind and his Bible and hymn books. Kitchener with due courtesy and a touch of humour sent him the books afterwards with a boy's hat which was found on the field, thinking that the latter was the property of Botha's little son, who goes through everything with him, but Botha returned the hat to Lord K[itchener] with a message that it was not his son's but had belonged to his "achter-rijer",[236] and thanking him very much for the books. It is too lovely for anything! Botha's own hat was never heard of again. Our brave general is fit and brown and well. After the victory at Bethal he spoke a few touching words to his men, thanking them for their courage and congratulating them on the success of their enterprise. Since then he has not addressed them publicly, so it is not true that he is continually making speeches to keep the men in the field. They need no encouragement.

Let me try and remember some of N[audé]'s adventures. They were once pursued for four hours by about 1 000 English (28 Boers) and the bullets hailed round them. N[audé] has a saddle that he is keeping as a curiosity, because of the bullet hole in it and once a bullet passed between his coat and shirt along his stomach. The shock took his breath away and he thought he was mortally wounded. Once they came upon a kraal containing the bodies of over 500 sheep in an advanced stage of decomposition – with their skulls all cleft in two by swords or their throats cut. Does it not seem horrible that the English slaughter innocent

---

[236]   "attendant on horseback".

creatures for the mere pleasure of destroying? With our women and children dying of starvation it seems such a wicked waste to kill animals and leave them to rot. But it does not matter – it only makes the Boers more furious. We asked N[audé] what the Boers thought of the extermination of their families – whether it would have any effect on the war and his answer was an emphatic "No". It would only prolong the war for it has made the men perfectly reckless. They all say "We must do our duty, we are not responsible for the death of our dear ones. Even if our wives and children are all exterminated our duty is to fight to the end." N[audé] himself has a wife and two little children in a camp in Natal and Mrs M[alan] brought him some photos – snapshots taken in the camp. Poor fellow! he gazed on them for a long time and then muttered under his breath "Hiervoor moet die Engelschman bars!"[237] Afterwards he told us that he had not recognised his wife – she looked like an old, old woman and he would not even take the photos with him. After seeing them he was quiet and moody and I could see how disagreeably he had been impressed. I really felt awfully sorry for him and regretted that he had seen them at all.

I feel more than ever convinced that the Boers will never give in. They want their independence and nothing less and while there are a 1 000 men in the field the war will go on. N[audé] says there are more men than we imagine and in some marvellous way their numbers seem to increase instead of diminishing. What troubles us very much indeed is that they complain of sore gums. V[enter] asked me to get something from a doctor as he had promised lots of his friends that he would bring them medicine, but Mama told him no medicine in the world could cure that. What they wanted was a change of diet – fresh vegetables and fruit, lime juice etc. They get it from living on meat and mealies and it is a bad sign because it is the beginning of scurvy. It makes me awfully miserable but what can we do? It was no use sending them any lime juice – what would that be but a drop in an ocean, certainly not worth the trouble of carrying under such difficult and dangerous circumstances. They have to creep through a network of barbed wire near the railway bridge about as wide as our dining room is long 20 f[ee]t[238] and first they have to throw their parcels across! I cannot understand how they do it. N[audé] says he never clips the wires round a town because then the English know at once that spies have been in – he creeps through, even if it takes him

---

237 "For this the English will suffer".
238 About 6 metres.

<u>hours</u> – but in the veld they cut every wire they come across. I hope they won't forget to take out the bottles of French brandy before they throw Venter's bag across – fine smell of drink there would be – enough to attract all the Tommies in the neighbourhood. N[audé] will never be taken alive. He is armed to the teeth and will sell his life dearly for is there not a heavy price on his head? He says some time ago the English sent out a few men to bring in, dead or alive, the six leaders, Botha, de Wet, Meers,[239] N[audé] and two others – £2 000 reward! They were warned and never heard or saw anything of the traitors (for they were Boers).

Naudé (sitting at the right) and his spy corps

N[audé] says when the Boers come upon a deserted camp they are covered in vermin in a few minutes and the Tommies' clothes <u>swarm</u> with l[ic]e and have to be <u>boiled</u> before they can be worn. And then the English talk of "dirty Boers!" He says the hardest thing for him is to have a handsupper shot or a traitor or an armed Kaffir. The latter are shot without mercy. He told us how it is done, how he informs the doomed man of his fate, how he pleads for mercy and offers to join the Boers, how he prays when he sees there is no hope for him, how he folds his arms or covers his face and how the shots ring out and he falls down dead. N[audé] has a very tender, pitiful heart but when his duty must be done he is immovable as a rock. He shows no

---

239   Probably Commandant Walter Mears, who was initially a member of the Theron Scout Corps, but in the latter phases of the war joined General C. de Wet's forces. See C.R. de Wet, *Die stryd tussen Boer en Brit. Die herinneringe van die Boere-generaal C.R. de Wet,* p 270n.

mercy to traitors but he has them taken away, he does not witness their death himself.

– I was his secretary here and yesterday's mail took a despatch from me to Dr L[eyds]. Somewhere else I have it to refer to. If people only knew what I carelessly threw into the post! A white envelope addressed to a certain Mrs Fredericson[240] in Holland – containing a simple New Year's card – but on the inside of the envelope, closely written in lemon juice, a full report of the condition of our commandos. The poor censor would get a fit if he knew what information he is passing to head quarters. We asked Dr L[eyds] some questions and N[audé] is coming back to Pretoria for the answer after 8 weeks – but he may come in before that time with something very important for the consuls from Botha. Good heavens! I must be careful. There are some things I may not even put down in white on white – it is so dangerous, even in this way. Christmas! if Tommy gets hold of these papers! my very hair rises at the thought.

We have just got a bit of fright. The sergeant major is standing talking with a man who looks a little like a private detective. They are pointing this way and gesticulating and I have just made up my mind to take away every paper this afternoon. H[241] will stow them away for me, I know. Now I must finish writing about N[audé] and make away with all these dangerous things.

Poor B[242] had a terrible time here. His people live in a small house and are surrounded by khakis and handsuppers. Some of them know this boy quite well so he had to be hidden away so well that no one could catch a glimpse of him. The poor boy was stowed away for three days and two nights in a tiny attic hardly large enough to hold a man, just under a zinc roof. No one can imagine what the poor boy had to endure in the suffocating heat of those endless days. He was bathed in perspiration from morning till night and lay there gasping for breath. I don't think he will come to Pretoria again in a hurry.

We told N[audé] all about the camps – all my experiences there and how the people are persecuted and bullied by the commandant. N[audé] got pale with rage when I told him of Esselen's treatment of the women and children and then and there made a plan to go and murder him. I had to describe the position of the camp, where the hospital is and the dispensary and stores but I could not tell him whereabouts the

---

240   Not identified. Probably a pseudonym.
241   Not identified.
242   Probably Brinckmann.

Com[mandant]'s house is. He fully intends riding in one night as officer, with ten armed boers in khaki, stab Esselen and ride out again. We encouraged him in it because it will be a splendid example for the other commandants. They are nearly all renegades, cowardly brutes, who have been expressly chosen because they will torture the people. I call myself a Christian, dear diary, and yet I will thank God when I hear that Esselen and Scholtz have been murdered.

Now I must take this away. Goodbye, dear little sheets of white paper. You look so innocent I am sure you will never betray me.

J[ohanna] v[an] W[armelo].

[Thus ends the last entry in the "Secret diary"]

Christmas Eve [1901]. Tuesday.

This is our third Xmas under Martial Law and I shall not say anything about it – it is too utterly, hopelessly sad. Last year we thought we were miserable, but this year! Our land is just one great blackened wilderness. Yesterday I was told that Ermelo no longer exists – it has been wiped clean off the face of the earth, partly by the Boers, chiefly by Khaki. A German doctor, Dr Albrecht[243] or some such name, has come in from the Boer commandos where he has been working since the beginning of the war. He is on his way home now – comes straight from Botha – and brings rather encouraging reports. He told Baron P[litner] that clothing was scarce, and ammunition, but otherwise everything is plentiful. His opinion is that about 20 000 men are still in the field, Colonials and all, and they can hold out indefinitely – years perhaps. Very little sickness on commando. I should love to get hold of a man like that to ask him a thousand and one questions. How much he could tell us that we are longing to know! Anna F[lockens] had news of her husband through him. Botha is somewhere near Middelburg and can have 6 000 men round him at a moment's notice. He says the Boers were so sorry when Benson fell. They all had the greatest respect for him and admired his courage and daring, and they only meant to catch him, so they were very sad when he was mortally wounded. – I hear that Kritzinger has died of his wounds. I hope it is true for anything would be preferable to being hanged or shot. He was not a rebel – was born

---

243   Not identified.

in the Free State – but he was condemned to death for shooting armed natives.[244] Our generals do not all court martial the natives – Botha does not – at least not yet; but he is "deliberating" and I am sure he will in the end. They <u>must</u> do it. This evil will spread if not put a stop to immediately and heaven only knows what the consequences will be. If one general does it they ought all to do it otherwise it seems as if they have not the sanction or approval of the Com[mandant] Gen[eral]. A good many prisoners have been brought in again and Capt Pretorius[245] has also been captured – they all get sent away almost immediately and <u>no one</u> is allowed to see them in the Rest Camp. Formerly almost anyone could get permits to see prisoners but now the watch kept over them is much stricter. I suppose they brought in too much news.

Tomorrow we are going to have dinner with the Maré's – that will be our way of celebrating Christmas.

December 28th [1901]. Saturday.

A lot of fighting has been taking place all over the country, according to Dame Rumour. In the Free State and near Standerton where the English are said to have had a disaster even greater than Benson's and another colonel, Spence[246] or something, is reported killed or mortally wounded. The Boers are supposed to be concentrating in large numbers and the general opinion is that they want to strike big blows when parliament is sitting. I am really quite afraid to make <u>any</u> statements because I generally have to contradict them again. Now I hear for a fact that Kritzinger is <u>not</u> dead.

Esselen has left Irene and another com[mandant] has been put in his place. May the change be for the better!

---

244   Kritzinger was born in the Port Elizabeth district of the Cape Colony but moved to the Orange Free State with his parents when he was only 12 years old. He was a citizen of that Republic. He was severely wounded on 16 December 1901 and fell in British hands. He recovered and was accused of serious offences in a British military court, but was acquitted. See D.W. Krüger, Kritzinger, Pieter Hendrik, in *DSAB* III, pp 496–497.

245   Captain J.L. Pretorius of the Transvaal State Artillery was indeed captured at the end of 1901 and went to St Helena as a prisoner-of-war. See J.P. Brits, Pretorius, Johannes Lodewicus (Lood), in *DSAB* III, pp 693–694.

246   Not identified.

J. Westmaas[247] told me yesterday that when her brother was a prisoner in the rest camp, she went to see him and he told her how the "Judas Boers" make the struggle a thousand times more difficult for our gallant fighting men. He was sent to "*brand-wacht*"[248] with a cartload of provisions and came suddenly upon a lot of these Judas Boers as we call them. They fired on him, killing one of his mules, and he surrendered and found himself in the hands of men whose faces he knew quite well – Pretoria men. He and his friend Gregan were brought here and when he was sent away Gregan had to remain behind because it was not quite decided what would be his fate for breaking the oath of neutrality. Frans cried like a baby thinkink [sic] that Gregan would be shot. Poor boy, he is barely sixteen and J [Westmaas] says that when she went to the station to see him off she saw quite a lot of boys playing marbles. These children were the mighty England's prisoners of war!

– Lord K[itchener] is now living in Johannesburg – I don't know if he intends coming back here.

Last night during a great thunder storm there was a terrific crash – so near that I made sure it must be in the garden and this morning Jim came to call us to see where a bolt had struck. The large willow near the fowl-run was furrowed from top to bottom and had the bark cleft in two and scorched like paper. Jim was much concerned because his little kitchen is just under the tree and now he is afraid to use it. He said "The ole baas was very cross last night, little missie, an' when he cross nothing can stop him. Jim won't use kitchen again – Jim want to live a little longer". The poor fowls must have had an awful shock and I am thankful my dear little kittens were not in their snug home in the trunk of the tree, where they were born. Poor orphans! Their mother was caught in the Tommies' trap and killed last week and now I have to feed and care for the poor little things.

Old Year 1901.

For the last time I write 1901. It is 10.30 a.m. and another two hours and a half will see the death of this wonderful, eventful, sad old year,

---

247 J. Westmaas was the sister of Frans Westmaas mentioned in the diary for the first time on 1901-12-08.

248 Guard duty.

and the birth of the new one, with its clean white pages, its hidden mysteries, and unknown joys and sorrows. Oh, I wonder what it will bring me. Taken as a whole I think 1901 has been the most eventful year of my life – my Irene experiences, my engagement and ever so many thrilling adventures have been crowded into it and I have suffered – God only knows how I have suffered. The joy of my betrothal has been so mixed with sorrow that it can hardly be called a joy at all, but perhaps that is still in store for me – who know what happiness will be mine in 1902. Let us hope so. We live on hope during these dark days. I can hardly believe that this is the dawning of the <u>third</u> new year during the war – how have we managed to live through such a terrible time? And not only <u>lived</u> but been hopeful and courageous under it all. I very seldom yielded to feelings of despondency and no matter how bad things are I hope I never shall. We are closing the old year well. Someone told us news this afternoon that has made our hearts very glad. de Wet gave the English such paddywhacks in the Free State that they don't know what to do with themselves – took 250 000 rounds of ammunition (hip!) 400 prisoners (hip!!) and a whole convoy (hooray!!!). Five officers were killed and I don't know how many wounded and the poor Tommies lost heavily.[249] I do not rejoice over the casualties, Oh God, no! When one thinks that every man has someone waiting for him, a mother or sister or sweetheart, and that many lives are shadowed and many hearts broken each time there is a fight, one would be a fiend indeed to <u>rejoice</u> – and yet I know the salvation of my land and people rests on the number of disasters the English have, especially now, when Parliament is sitting.

I may not forget that I am a woman and yet I must pray fervently to God that the Boers may strike <u>heavy</u> blows next month. Our all depends upon it and I think they know it and the Lord will be with them and help them. We <u>are</u> glad about that convoy and ammunition. Now de Wet can at least have a happy new year, with something better to eat

---

[249] On Christmas Day 1901 De Wet and his burghers overpowered a British unit on Groenkop (Green Hill) in the eastern Orange Free State. The British losses were at least 57 dead, 84 wounded and another about 120 captured. Casualties on the Boer side were 14 men dead and about 30 wounded. The Boers captured large stocks of ammunition and war supplies. See P.G. Cloete, *The Anglo-Boer War a chronology*, p 287.

than mealie porridge. Near Bronkhorstspruit Botha had a great victory, but we know no details. – We are going to bed now to sleep over the critical midnight hours – not like olden days when we all sat up and congratulated one another – Good night, old year; Goodbye. –

Part 5

"[W]e expect startling events soon" – Pretoria, 3 January to 30 April 1902

January 3rd 1902. Friday.

The new year is three days old already and this is my first entry in my diary – not a very good beginning, but what would you when there is nothing to tell? We spent New Year's Day with the aunts and uncles and cousins – a regular family party but first I attended the 9 o'clock service in the morning. There was a fairly good attendance and the sermon was very appropriate, but a military band crossed the square and made such a noise and oh, it was more bitter than death to me to hear the enemy making merry outside while we were sitting inside with aching hearts and tearful eyes. I believe they purposely disturb us at our devotions, at least it is a thing that happens far too often.

A dear stupid old Englishman told Mama mournfully today that the British had had "four hard knocks" lately and when she said "indeed!" with well-assumed surprise, he went into detail and told her all we had heard before and a good deal that was news to us. Things are going very fine and we are full of new hope and courage.

January 5th [1902]. Sunday.

I went to Church this morning feeling very cheerful and light-hearted. It was such a radiant Sabbath morn and I was full of joy at the remembrance of all the good things I had received by yesterday's mail – Lou's first letter as an accepted man, his mother's and Emilia's[1] congratulations and a great many other tokens of love and friendship. His mother's welcome to me is very warm and she is so sweet and sympathetic and opens her heart and home to me with the greatest readiness and cordial-

---

[1] Probably Emelia Frijlinck, the future wife of the diarist's brother Willem. See footnote 285 p 172.

ity. It was *"avondmaal"*[2] this morning and I partook of it with feelings of deep thankfulness, but alas, there was trouble in store for me when I left the church – bad news of a friend who had got into great trouble through helping us. There are too many complications in the matter – I cannot mention them here, but we are sad and troubled tonight and we want all our strength of mind to bear up bravely under the many cares and burdens that oppress us. I have a great physical weakness against which I am powerless – all mental suffering causes vomiting and I have been deadly sick the whole afternoon, but now I feel better and inclined to confide my woes to this silent friend – hence this out pouring! [sic] But after all this is not much of a friend in war time [sic], for one has to be so careful in making confidences. There is always a chance that this book may fall into the hands of the enemy, but all they will find is my very candid opinion of them and their abominable actions, and a few confessions of love for my far-away lover, which I would certainly not like anyone to read. This thought is making me very cautious and takes away half the pleasure of keeping a diary. Never mind *"alles zal reg kom!"*[3]

January 10th [1902]. Friday.

My poor old diary! I begin to foresee that it is by degrees going to die a natural death – simply because I am tired of recording lies and rumours. I am now busy preparing for a little trip to Johannesburg, but oh dear, the difficulty one has to get permits! The English have never been so strict before. Major H[oskins] sent me to the Commissioner of Police, there I was asked to produce a note or recommendation from my ward officer and when I asked in bewilderment who and what that may be, was sent to B Ward, far away from any other office. I had to wait quite half an hour and was then shown into the presence of an officer who was very courteous, but refused to give me a permit without a medical certificate that I required a change but when I told him I knew Gen M[axwell] very well and that I would go to him for a permit he said that made all the difference. He wrote down my name and then asked the address of the people I was going to. I told him I could give their box number but did not know where they lived. No, that would not

---

2   Holy Communion.
3   "Everything will turn out all right!"

do I would have to give the name of the street and the number of the house! Well, then I had to go home without that permit. Next morning I trotted to B Ward again with Pauline's[4] address in my pocket and after a lot of fuss and waiting I got a letter to the Com[missioner] of P[olice] but there I was informed that enquiries would have to be made the permit would have to go through two or three offices and then come back again to be signed by the Com[missioner] of Police. Would I call again on Monday? That was Thursday so you see what a fuss they make and how difficult it is to get away from this place. Now I do not even know whether it will please their lordships to issue a permit to me on Monday – I begin to doubt it very much. The same difficulties are placed in our way when we want to visit the camps, or send things to our people. I went to the Burger Camp Department to get permission to take some groceries and clothing to Irene, or have it sent, but was refused. They went over my list of things and scratched out everything except salmon and vinegar – the other things, milk, jam, vegetables, soap, candles, oatmeal, etc they get "more than they can use". More than they can use! O God, my heart nearly broke when I heard those lying, pitiless words and realized my utter helplessness. I had to get up and go away without uttering the words that were ready to burst from my lips. What it is to us to listen to such things no one can conceive – knowing that thousands upon thousands of women and children are slowly succumbing to the effects of privation and semi-starvation and to be absolutely powerless to help them – and the men who know the horrible truth of these death camps calmly inform us that we shall not be allowed to send even the necessaries of life because the people get more than they can use. Naked and starving as I know them to be – is it any wonder I felt inclined to lay my head on that man's desk and sob my heart out in my helplessness and misery. When I asked permission to go to the camp myself he said that the new Commandant was a very "firm" man and would not allow people to walk in and out of his camp.[5] This made my heart sink again because if the new man is "firmer" than his brutal predecessors, Scholtz and Esselen, what is to become of the people?

4   Pauline Ramme. See J. Brandt, *Die Kappiekommando of Boerevroue in geheime dienst,* p 151.

5   The new Commandant was Lieutenant L.M. Bruce of the Royal Army Medical Corps. See J.L. Hattingh, *Die Irenekonsentrasiekamp,* p 104.

But we have had a bit of silver lining for which we are very thankful. I went to the Provost Marshal again and at last got the promise that Dietlof will have an officer's privileges again in future. They were very reluctant at first but I stood there and looked so imploring that there was no refusing me. Hurrah! now my poor old brother will at least be as comfortable as a man in exile can be. It is a great comfort to us. This morning we heard heavy firing in the direction of Skinner's Court. The Italian gardeners say the fight began at about 4 o'clock in the morning but we heard it first just before breakfast and it was at its very worst between 11 and 12. I have never heard anything like it. There were no heavy guns but the rattle of maxims and pom-poms never broke off. At about 12 firing ceased. B[6] told me he saw a whole Red Cross train at the station that the Boers had simply shot to fragments, because they found cannon, arms, ammunition and troops in it. Of course we know the English are constantly doing that sort of thing and we are always very glad to hear that the Boers have punished them. There is no end to their atrocities. Mr A[7] told me that 8 Boer prisoners were sent to a town under an armed <u>native</u> escort (this is an everyday occurrence – many of our friends have <u>seen</u> prisoners brought into town by Kaffirs) and the Kaffirs assaulted the men, slashed their bodies with knives and put out their eyes. Beyers heard of it and in his fury attacked the tribe to which they belonged, with about 35 men but he was beaten back, and afterwards he was joined by de la Rey's whole commando and they exterminated the whole tribe. Mr A says in Zoutpansberg a volley was fired into a small "lager" of women and children and soon afterwards some English officers rode up, followed by a whole regiment of armed Kaffirs. They did no more mischief but took away the men who were there to protect the women and children. One child of three years was killed, and one of eight, and another one was shot through the knee.

January 13th [1902] Monday.

Tomorrow night I hope to be in Johannesburg and I am very busy getting ready for the morrow's journey. Got my permit this morning with-

---

6   Not identified.

7   Perhaps Mr Aubert, the French Consul in Pretoria. These rumours were false.

out further trouble. I shall take this valuable book with me and make notes of anything worth recording. Goodbye Harmony.

Johannesburg. January 14ᵗʰ [1902]. Tuesday.

This is just to say that I am here, but too sleepy and tired to write. Will tell my experiences tomorrow.

Armagh Villa No. 2. Johannesburg. January 15ᵗʰ [1902].

What a sell! When I went to bed last night I arranged with Pauline that I would sleep late this morning. After a lovely night's rest I woke, bright and early – the sun shining and sounds of life all over the house. I sprang up, dressed in a great hurry and found no one astir except the boy who pointed in some surprise at the clock. Quarter past six. So here I am upstairs again in my own room, which I have tidied. Nearly two hours before breakfast! Well, I can have a nice quiet read and write to the mother when I have finished my dairy. Fortunately I have my fountain pen and all other necessary writing materials with me. The journey passed off without any adventures and I was met at the station by Pauline and her husband and their lovely big dog, Nero.

They are living in a house about as big as a matchbox, but spotlessly clean and so bright and cheerful. And they are so happy! Next month the small family will be enriched by a bran [sic] new little inmate and then I do believe there will be nothing more on earth that my friend can desire. She is looking wonderfully well and it is a pleasure to see husband and wife together. They evidently adore one another. Of course I have seen nothing of Johannesburg yet but the air is perfect, so pure and fresh and invigorating – I feel better already.

Along the line yesterday I saw many ruined homesteads and deserted farms and a few block houses at the different stations. Everywhere there were signs of the war, Red Cross trains, field hospitals, troops and two or three trains (trucks) laden with women and children. That devilish work is pursuing its course relentlessly.

January 19ᵗʰ [1902]. Sunday.

My stay here is drawing to a close and I have been making no entries – simply because there have been no entries to make. Pauline and I sit sewing and talking nearly the whole day. On Friday aft[ernoon] A[8] took me to the Gordons[9] who were not at home, so we wandered about the streets and then drank tea at the Anglo-Austrian. It has been raining ever since – yesterday a perfect deluge and today a damp drizzle that keeps one in doors [sic] and interferes with all my lovely plans. We were going to Sans-souci this morning and yesterday AB[10] was going to take me for a long drive and K[arel de Kok][11] is coming this afternoon to take me for a drive if only the weather would clear up a little. I was much agitated yesterday by K[arel]'s unexpected visit but he was very nice and congratulated me on my engagement and asked if we could be friends now as if there had been no past. I am afraid we can never be friends but I am only too glad to forget the past and be able to meet him without any pain in the future. He is looking very well and, to use his own words, "is simply coining money". Unhappy man! When I think of the price he has had to pay for that prosperity I have nothing but compassion in my heart for him. He is a Rand Rifleman, a traitor to land and people and "is simply coining money" while he ought to be in the field where my own dear brother is. I pity him with his worldly successes, with a pity that has no little contempt in it, but because of the past I ignore these things when we are together and absolutely refuse to discuss them with him. I want to forget all that now and only think of the revelation that A[ndrew] B[rown] has been to me. I have looked deep into his soul, he has made a friend, a confidante of me and I feel sure our relationship will stand for ever, [sic] after the confidences, the intimate conversation of yesterday afternoon. One thing is certain, Lou must know of this deep and rare friendship and he must approve of a future correspondence.

I can trust myself and A[ndrew] B[rown] well enough – there will be no sentimentality, nothing that a husband could object to and if Lou

---

8   Probably Aling Tulleken.
9   US Consul in Johannesburg.
10   Andrew Brown. In a brief, undated letter written on "Friday afternoon", Andrew Brown wrote to the diarist: "I shall take it for granted that I shall have the pleasure of taking you for a drive tomorrow afternoon." See Archives of the *Nederduitsch Hervormde Kerk van Afrika*, Pretoria, L.E. Brandt Collection, LIX/165, file 1, *Briewe aan Ds en Mev L.E. Brandt 1892–1911*, unsorted.
11   The diarist's former fiancé.

does not trust me sufficiently for that, then it is a bad look-out for our future. I feel the distance between us now more than ever. How do I know what his ideas are on this subject? We are all but strangers to one another and though I have given myself to him heart and soul I do not know whether he thinks with me on things that are of vital importance to me, and letters are of very little use in these cases. I often wish he were a better correspondent – I shall never get to know him through his letters as anyone might learn to know me through mine.

Harmony. January 22nd [1902]. Wednesday.

Came home last night and found everything in perfect order. Received a post-card from the mother just before I left Johannesburg that our house had been searched! On Sunday morning when she was still asleep Jim knocked at her window and said the police wanted to see her. She dressed in a hurry and on going out found an officer, who informed her that he had been ordered by the Commissioner of Police to search her house. Armed men were standing about – one at the front door and one under the mulberry tree near the kitchen door. The officer was very courteous and just glanced through all the rooms, looked under beds, behind screens, and opened wardrobes. When the house had been thoroughly examined they went through the outside rooms but found nothing of course. They were looking "for men", if you please!

Now there is only one kind of man that one looks for under beds etc now-a-days and it is a perfect mystery to me how the English got such ideas of us into their heads. We are actually suspected of having harboured spies! What a lark! I can't help laughing at the idea of my proper old mother being in such a predicament, and that while I was away from home! It is very strange that they should have waited until I was safely out of the way, what difference could my presence here make? And I am more than sorry at having missed the excitement – My stay at J[o]h[anne]sburg was clouded by two stormy interviews with K[arel]. Poor fellow! he wants me to take him back again – evidently the sight of me and the thought of my engagement were too much for him. I shall never forget what passed between us – our last meetings, I hope.

January 26th Sunday [1902].

I saw a man yesterday who had been in that same morning's railway accident. It must have been a terrible smash. The passenger train, coming to Pretoria, was run into by a truck laden with rails, that had broken away at one of the steep places between Irene and Pretoria. The driver saw this awful thing bearing down on him with terrific speed and promptly reversed the engine but there was not much time and the truck caught the train unfortunately in the deep cutting, so that there was no chance of escape. The driver and stoker were killed at once and the rails flew from the truck with such force that they went right through the boiler, so that the passengers found themselves in a hot bath. They were all bruised and many of them senseless but no one else was killed. I cannot help being thankful that it did not happen to my train.

– We are having such funny weather, rainy and cloudy, and I don't think I have seen the sun three times since I came home five days ago. We have had no visitors except the Rev le Pla[12] from Cape Town. People are avoiding us a good deal on account of the suspicion we are under – but what do I care? If we come through the ordeal with half a dozen friends I shall be quite satisfied. I don't care a rap about those who have proved to be fair-weather friends and yet one cannot help feeling rather disappointed in them. I am learning to do without "people" – I have my flowers, books and music, my cats and dogs and household duties, and best of all, my thoughts and love-letters. The war drags on week after week and no one can see the end of it. Yesterday I saw a train come in on the Eastern line – first an engine, then two trucks laden with women and children, then another engine and after that goods and a van. Of course the women and children are put in such a dangerous position to be blown up if anything happened and as a sort of protection to the engines. Everyone knows that in these times the safest part of the train is

---

[12]   On 5 January 1902 Hilda Buyskes, of Queen Victoria Street (probably in Cape Town) wrote to the diarist that she requested the Reverend James le Pla to visit them in Pretoria. According to the letter Le Pla was for several years the pastor of the Congregation Church in Caledon Square and was "going to Pretoria to see what prospects there are of establishing a church of the same denomination there." Archives of the *Nederduitsch Hervormde Kerk van Afrika*, Pretoria, L.E. Brandt Collection, IX/165, file 1, *Briewe aan Ds en Mev L.E. Brandt 1892–1911*, unsorted.

as far as possible from the engines and when I went to J[o]h[anne]sburg, Major H[oskins] and the Provost Marshal and other high officials travelled in reserved compartments right at the end of the train and we, ordinary passengers, were right in front. God only knows how inhuman their every action is. To put women and tender little children in open trucks between two engines seems to me the height of barbarism.

There is war news. Pietersburg has been taken by the Boers, with all the stores and ammunition they found in it. This is splendid. Then there is a rumour of many cannon having been captured by de Wet, but that is only a rumour as far as I know. Scheepers has been shot[13] and Kritzinger is now being tried – a mock trial – for everyone knows beforehand what his fate will be. These men are not rebels, mind you – they are simply being condemned to death for wrecking trains and shooting armed natives – to which they have every right as the whole world knows. Of course nothing can be better for our cause than this attitude on the part of the English – it is only making the Boers more desperate and determined. Krause[14] has been sentenced to two years' hard labour. – [British] Parliament was opened last Monday but we know nothing of the proceedings except that everyone says "the Boers must not be left one shred of independence" – evidently all are determined on that point. Well, man proposes but England must not forget that God disposes and we have yet to learn what His plans are concerning our two republics. I have no doubt that right will triumph over might in the end.

In lighter vein. I always forget to tell you, dear diary, of a certain important little member of our household. It is called Flippie and is a little Boer boy, thirteen years old – our "tiger", our boy of all trades, our torment and our joy. Flippie came here more than three months ago and asked for "work". The mother looked him up and down and said she did not farm with children. F[lippie] looked straight in front of him and said never a word until two great tears rolled down his cheeks. This touched me and I asked where his mother was. "Dead". "Father?" "Fighting with five sons". Then I felt inclined to take Flippie in my arms and give him a kiss for his dead mother and brave father and

---

[13]   See diary entry on 1901-10-16, p 374.
[14]   See diary entry on 1901-09-09, p 341.

brothers. Well, the mother decided to try him and offered him £1 a month for running on errands and doing all sorts of light work about the house and garden, and now we simply can't do without him. He is a perfect "boy" of business, as sharp as sharp can be – goes to market every morning, washes dishes, rubs floors and gardens, but some (I mean he does gardening, he does not rub gardens) but some days he is lazy and irritating. Then one can do nothing with him and we usually leave him severely alone until his sunny temperament asserts itself. He is the merriest little soul one can come across and he has an infectious, ringing laugh that is a positive pleasure to listen to. He is ambitious and enterprising. Mama gave him a bit of ground to plant vegetables on for himself and now he spends every spare moment in this garden of his. I hope to be his first customer although he protests vehemently against the idea of selling things for me. That Flippie is destined for the gallows I have not a shadow of doubt – he can tell lies and deceive with the most angelic face and can melt into tears on the least provocation. His head is one of the most remarkable I have ever come across and the first time I noticed his profile I asked him to let me make a sketch of it – but it was a failure – only the hand of an artist could reproduce <u>that</u> face. His forehead recedes and recedes until there is nothing left of it but a great bump at the back of his head, and his little nose tilts up at you in a most impertinent manner, which is given the lie to by the drooping corners of his sensitive mouth. He is either going to be a genius or a criminal – time will show. What I admire in him is his loyalty. He is as true as steel and I would feel quite safe in confiding an important secret to him, child as he is. While I was away he slept in the back passage – guarding the mother![15]

There is one drawback to having him here and that is his dreadful old grandmother.[16] She visits us all hours of the day – came before 6 a.m. several times until we protested – and is quite dumb, so that entertaining her is a difficult and tiring task. We call her "Um-Ah" because that is all she ever says and it means yes and no and everything else. She is a sharp old woman and can understand all one says to her but her

---

[15]   According to the diarist Flippie did end up in prison eventually, and died there. See her own preface to the second edition of *Die Kappie Kommando,* p ix. No further information on Flippie could be found.

[16]   Not identified.

tongue and right hand have been paralysed by a stroke she had twenty
years ago, after having given birth to a child. Poor old soul! I am so sorry
for her but really she is a great affliction to us. She is so inquisitive and
meddlesome – wants to know all about everything, the price of what
I have on, who wrote that letter and where does it come from, who is
that visitor and why does he speak English, what does he say, why does
he laugh, etc and as it all goes by signs a lot of time is lost in trying to
understand what she wants. She comes here and eats and drinks everything we set before her and has an inconvenient habit of dropping in
just at meal times. I have to peel her fruit and cut her meat and butter
her bread – she is quite helpless. One day she stretched herself on the
sofa after dinner and slept till five o'clock. I could not resist the temptation of taking a few visitors into the dining-room to have a stealthy peep
at her. She was lying on her back with her mouth wide open and her
knees drawn up high in front of her – too funny for anything. She takes
the whole of Flippie's salary and refuses to give him so much as a sixpence to buy sweets with – greedy old thing. Mama has been obliged to
give him an extra half crown monthly, without Um-Ah's knowledge, to
keep his heart in the work, because it must be very disheartening to the
little chap to work for *Ouma*,[17] and yet the other day he bought some
gingerbeer for her with a stray sixpence he had. He is so generous and
always wants to give me the chocolates and things he gets from the kind-
hearted Tommies next-door.

What a writing fit I have on me this morning! Ten pages on one
day. It is quite surprising and will have to last me for the rest of this
week perhaps. Jim has gone to Town for the mail and I am looking out
eagerly for a letter from Lou – his last was so loving and sweet and oh, I
am longing so much for him.

January 27th Monday [1902].

There is news today, a mixture of good and bad. De Wet has taken ten
cannon in the Free State and completely annihilated the Imperial Light
Horse. General Bruce-Hamilton [sic] seriously wounded.[18] There has

17   Grandmother.
18   General Bruce Hamilton was never wounded during the Anglo-Boer War
      of 1899–1902. See B.J.T. Leverton, Hamilton, Sir Bruce Meade, in *DSAB*
      III, p 379.

been fighting the last three days with Botha, near Middelburg. The bad news is the capture of Ben Viljoen.[19] He was riding ahead of his commando with forty men when the enemy surprised him and took him with two adjutants – I believe the others escaped. This is a very sad business for us but de Wet's great victory ought to make up for it.

C[onnie] M[innaar] went to Lady Maxwell's ball. Oh, Connie, is the loss of your good name, as one of the few loyal "Boer" girls, worth that bit of pleasure? I can no longer know you and can no longer visit your house – you, too must pass out of my life like everyone else who deserts his or her post at a time like this. To go to a ball at all when our land is so desolate is bad enough, but to go to a khaki ball and to dance with the enemy when our women and children are dying in thousands, is <u>terrible</u>. This is what I call her first "downward step" – goodness only knows what it will lead to. There is no one left for me to trust – wherever I turn I see treachery, deceit, weakness, and it makes one's heart very sore.

Sunday morning under the trees. Feb[ruary] 2nd [1902].

I am much, much too happy to go to church this morning. Does not this sound wicked? And yet I mean it. I'd rather a thousand times sit here amid all this radiant beauty, absorbed in my own sweet thoughts than be listening to the ramblings of those dear, dreadful old German pastors, who always seem to be our fate lately. The Sunnyside church is being treated shamefully – anything seems good enough for it and we have had to listen to some fearful and wonderful discour[s]es. Sometimes Mr Bosman preaches and then the building is crowded but I did not know whose turn it was today, so, as I said before, I decided that I was far too happy and good and excited for anything but a morning under Harmony's trees. I simply don't know myself now-a-days.

Dear diary, I have told you very little about my great love and newly-found happiness but that was because I was afraid you would fall into wrong hands, but how I have nearly done with you, and as soon as the few following blank pages have been filled, you are going away to your other comrades for safety's sake, and so I feel this glorious Sabbath morn as if I <u>must</u> tell you all about it. You are my only confidant, though

---

19   General Viljoen was captured by the British on 25 January 1902. See J.W.
      Meijer, *Generaal Ben Viljoen 1868–1917*, p 234.

other people know I am happy. The smile when they look at my face, which must be a reflection of some wonderful thought within. I am so happy, so happy – in our desolate, lonely home, surrounded by misery, sin and suffering with my loved ones far, far away, some in banishment, some in captivity, some in deadly peril night and day, in a country laid waste by the enemy's ruthless hand – I can still say with truth, "I am happier than I have ever been before".

Dear Love, this is the greatest tribute I can pay you. You have glorified my dreary life, you have triumphed over the degrading influences that have been struggling for the mastery over me, you have soothed, comforted, strengthened me and I thank you a thousand times for it. Now I can only repay you by a few miserable censored letters, but the day will come that I can repay you with my love and life. Oh Beloved, when shall we be together? I may not let you know of my yearnings because you have your own to fight against. Do I not detect them in every line of your guarded letters? I love you all the more for them but they make the path of duty harder for me. My own intense longings are often more than I can bear and I can only lift my heart in fervent prayers to the Father of Love. When, oh when will He hear us? I know that you are praying daily, hourly, that we are often together in prayer and the thought helps me, but it only makes my longings more intense. If you were with me at this moment I could die of content in your arms, Beloved. Do you know that for many months I have been fighting against this growing love, simply because I thought it must be an idea, that a woman can't really love a man passionately until he has kissed her and wooed her ardently, that she must first be with him for some time to learn to know him, but it seems I was mistaken. I don't know why I love him – I only know I love him and that I am a new being. And why am I so particularly joyful today? Well, yesterday's mail brought me letters from some of his dear ones and now that other people tell me how happy he is and how he loves me, I seem to realize it as I never did before. I lay awake last night, still as a mouse, thinking, thinking until my brain reeled with its load of bliss. Such a white, white night! I shall never forget it. None but the most sacred thought entered my mind and for that time at least I was pure as an infant. After a dreamless, refreshing slumber I woke this morning to find the world beautiful beyond description.

The glamour of the night is still upon me and I feel this morning as if the thought of Lou will <u>always</u> keep me good and why not?

I have had my worries and vexations as usual today but I have been able to face them with unruffled good-nature; I have heard war news and been filled with bitterness towards our cruel enemy and yet it has not poisoned the serenity of my mind. As I write the Pom-poms are firing from our fort,[20] reminding me of the destruction and death that fills our mourning land and yet I can look up to the Father of us all, and leave all in His hands with unshaken faith in His mercy and goodness. Dear Love, it was not always so with me. I have so often been crushed, despairing, rebellious and oh, I have suffered so that sometimes there seemed to be nothing in me but pain, but that is past for ever, I hope.

Pom-pom-pom from the fort, ceaselessly. What can it mean? Are the Boers so near the Town as to be within reach of the guns on the fort? That must be it, for they would not have gun practice on Sunday surely. Those shots ringing out in the stillness of this fair and perfect day of "rest" – what do they not remind me of? But no, not one word on that subject this morning of all mornings.

I cannot imagine anything more exquisite than Harmony as it is just this minute with its hundreds of shades of green, its glowing, crimson fruit and great clusters of purple grapes, its flowers, birds and bees and the faint ripple of water that reaches my ears – only those pom-poms!! Carlo is lying in the grass in lazy contentment, looking affectionately at me out of the corner of one eye every time I move or turn over a page. He seems to understand me well enough. You know why I am beaming all over, don't you, Carlo old man? You are more to me than almost any human being in Pretoria, you dear faithful adoring old animal. Sometimes he sits straight up and looks at me without a word – lost in admiration! and when he has had his fill he lies down again but never sleeps so soundly that my lightest movement escapes him. Flippie is at the top of an apple tree with a long rake, and has just brought me some of his spoil. <u>He</u> seems to be enjoying his Sunday morning. What a lovely breath of air! My poor Love is not having such a good time I am sure. Snow, ice, rain, fog – those are the things he has to endure now, while I am under a canopy of sapphire blue – sun-lit, cloudless, radiant. It is just about twelve o'clock and I must really make an effort to tear

---

20   Probably Fort Schanskop.

myself away from this intoxicating scene. One must eat, I suppose, no matter <u>how</u> happy one is.

Harmony

Harmony's fruit trees

Fancy, yesterday's mail brought me a letter from Lou, cruelly entreated by the censor. Something in it was evidently displeasing to his highness so he just brushed over the offending passages with what seems to me a sort of boot polish – oily, inky stuff that has made havoc of every line it touched. We rubbed some of it off with a damp cloth and now I can read parts of it – it appears to be about blockhouses and soldiers and English newspapers. Lou must really be more careful. I suppose I ought to be thankful to have got the mutilated remains of this letter, which might just as well have been consigned whole to the waste paper basket.

February 4th. Tuesday [1902].

This extraordinary state of blissfulness has "come to stay" it seems. I told the mother last night in a burst of confidence that I was so "smoor verliefd"[21] that I did not know what to do with myself. She laughed as if it amused her very much and then she said gravely that if it was so with me I had better make up my mind to go to Holland in May or June – she would let Harmony and go and live at the sea-side, somewhere near Line. Since then I am like one intoxicated with joy and love and anticipation. As a rule I don't dream about Lou but last night he was with me so vividly that even now it appears to have been reality and not merely a vision of the night. I dreamt that we had been engaged a long time and we were always together, but we never did more than shake hands and he never touched me as lovers do, and I was quite satisfied. We did not seem to want more, until one day it came over me with a great rush, an overwhelming yearning "I wish he would kiss me". We were in a crowded assembly and I looked across at him and found him gazing at me with the same thought, the same passionate yearning in his eyes, in answer to mine as it were. Spell-bound we looked and looked into each other's eyes until the assembly faded away and we found ourselves alone, and then I stretched out my arms to him and found myself pressed closely to his heart, while the burning kisses rained on my face. The rapture and content of that moment were unlike anything I have ever experienced in real life – even now the recollection of it makes my brain reel. Will our meeting be anything like that, I wonder. Oh, it

---

21   Hopelessly in love.

would be too much, too much, after these long, weary months of separation and unfulfilled desire.

– I am a mystery to myself now. That feeling of utter unworthiness has fallen from me like a cloak and has been replaced by the conviction that a love as great as mine is ennobling and purifying enough to make any woman worthy of the best of men. With every love-laden hour I feel more incapable of doing an unworthy action or thinking an unworthy thought and if this goes on I shall become a perfect "angel without wings". My one desire now is to write and write to him, to pour out my whole heart to him, to tell him all these wonderful thoughts and feelings, but that is impossible. I cannot do otherwise than write guardedly while my letters have to pass through the censor's hands, but I can unburden myself to my diary as I am doing now. It does me a lot of good and I must just hide my diary in some safe place. I think I'll write the next in the form of a letter to him – that will be an "agreeable" way.

They say the woman in the camps get such good rations now – frozen meat and 4 ozs.[22] butter weekly, and every child under 2 y[ea]rs gets two bottle of milk daily. It seems almost too good to be true. Bruce Hamilton is said to have died of his wounds. de Wet is also reported dead but I don't see how the immortal Christian can be touched by a bullet.

February 5th Wednesday [1902].

Not feeling so very well today and consequently rather depressed, although the feeling of exultation comes over me with a rush every now and then. Have been alone all day sewing and keeping very quiet. Mama was in town all morning, just came home for dinner and went to *oom*[23] Paul this afternoon. The sun is just going down and it is a most divinely beautiful evening – peaceful beyond description. Oh, my Love, it is my longing for you that is making me ill. I am looking ghostly today. The strain is too much for me, dear. One moment I am radiant with happiness, the next I am overwhelmed with depression and melancholy and the misery of this long, awful separation.

The shades of night are falling fast and I can barely see to write – I am sitting under the trees as usual. Beloved, where are you now? Are

---

22   Ounces. Four ounces = 113 grams.
23   Uncle.

you thinking of your lonely little girl, are you praying for her? Oh, she needs all your thoughts and prayers and love to help her through these weary days - - - to be continued in better light.

Sunday. Feb[ruary] 9th [1902].

Pouring with rain so that I can't go to church. This bewildered little girl must try to collect her senses sufficiently to make a few entries - bewildered. I should think so, dearest, as you would be if you saw what the mail brought me yesterday - piles of letters in writings strange and familiar, from loved ones and relatives and friends and casual acquaintances and total strangers. Lou's was very sweet, and longer than the last - but that is not saying very much, for my best beloved is my Worst Correspondent, bless his dear heart! - but there was a nice one from Daisy[24] and two from his, Lou's, parents to Mama, and to me from the aunts and cousins, Albert Schilthuis, Kees B.[25] Mrs Ameshoff[26] etc etc in dozens.[27] This week my dear diary will have to be sorely neglected for I shall have to write and write until all these good wishes and congratulations have been thanked for. Lou says he heard from Oom Paul[28] and Dr Leyds and all my aunts and "things". He says "I am sending you two good photos" but never a photo did I get, which disturbed me so much that I dreamt all night that I was hunting for them in the post office. The officials helped me and we unpacked one case after the other, containing parcels addressed to me, hats, dresses, great bales of silk, music, books, boxes of sweets and chocolates until the whole post office was cram full of brown paper parcels but nowhere could we find my belov-

---

24   Daisy Brandt, a sister of Louis Brandt. See B. du Toit, *Die verhaal van Johanna Brandt*, p 47.

25   Not identified.

26   Probably Ernestina Hendrika Ignatia Ameshoff, baroness of Ittersum, the wife of H.A. Ameshoff, who was a criminal judge in the supreme court of the Transvaal and lived in Pretoria before the war, but returned to the Netherlands when the hostilities began. See V.G. Hiemstra, Ameshoff, Herman Arnold, in *DSAB* III, pp 20–21.

27   The L.E. Brandt Collection in the Archives of the *Nederduitsch Hervormde Kerk van Afrika,* Pretoria, contains a whole file filled with letters and cards of congratulations that the diarist received around this time. See Brandt Collection, LIX/15, 1902, *Briewe met verlowing* [Letters on engagement], unsorted.

28   President Paul Kruger.

ed's photos. Disconsolately I asked of the officials " *Wat baat mij al deze heerlijkheden als ik zijn portret niet heb?*"[29] but no one could help me and my slumbers were one hideous nightmare. Poor me! I have not the least objection to dreaming about Lou when he appears to me as he did on the night of the 3rd inst[ant] but he must please not come and torment me with such mad freaks as last night's were.

Sunday <u>afternoon</u>: My morning was broken up by a long visit from A[rchie] T[ruter], when the weather cleared a little – and now we are expecting our usual Sun[day] aft[ernoon] visitors. The day is perfect after the rain – there is the first batch of visitors.

Sunday <u>evening</u>. You see I am determined to write today. It is 9 o'clock and I am sure no one will disturb me now so I can write some more about Lou. I am anxious to get this book filled and out of the way. There are only a few pages left and I have such an idea that before they are full, our friend the enemy will come and search our house for documents and then they will carry away this chronicle of my griefs and woes and – joys, lately. What agonies I would endure if this book were to fall into strange hands! – We had a lot of visitors today – people who are not afraid of coming under suspicion by being seen in our company. De la Rey's daughter, Mrs B[rugman] was here with her husband, and she told me that she hears that a sister of hers, who has all along been in the neighbourhood of her father's commando, was married some months ago to young Ferreira,[30] one of Fritz's fellow students in the Inner Temple. It appears that the General always sends word to the little "*vrouwen-kamp*"[31] which way they must flee, whenever there is danger and Mrs B[rugman] thinks her sister must have had so many escapes and queer adventures with her lover, that her father thought it would be better for them to be man and wife under the unusual circumstances, so he had them married. If that is not romantic, I don't know what is.

The wind is wailing round the house and my Mammie is fast asleep on the sofa. She gets up so early that by about 9 o'clock she can no

---

29   "What is the use of the delicasies if I do not have his photograph?"

30   De la Rey's second daughter, Adriana (Ada) indeed married Advocate Ignatius Ferreira, who was the General's private secretary, but the wedding took place after the war. See J. Meintjies, *De la Rey – Lion of the West. A biography*, pp 68, 271–274.

31   women's camp.

longer keep her eyes open. My thoughts travel fast and far on a night like this and they all collect and centre on a certain solitary individual in a lonely parsonage right up in the north of Holland. My poor Love, if you long for me as I do for you, you must be a sad and lonely man this night. I wish I could see my way clear to leaving home, but do what I will there seems to be nothing before me but a very thorny path of duty, and I am so much afraid that Lou will think I do not care as much as I ought. I care so much that my resolution often wavers and I lie awake at night thinking, thinking of some way of joining my beloved before long, but as yet there is not one ray of light.

February 18th [1902]. Tuesday.

More than a week since my last entry but the last mail brought me another enormous batch of letters and I have been busy answering them. There are still <u>dozens</u> to answer and my poor bewildered brain is beginning to turn under the strain. Lou's photos arrived too – splendid ones. The eyes are a little bit staring as one often sees them on a photo but on the whole they are very fine and I show them to everyone, as proud as proud can be.

What war news have I heard lately? The immortal de Wet seems to have been doing no end of mischief again but no one knows how and when and where. He was "completely shut in" – "absolutely no chance for him this time, you know" and yet when you hear of him again he is scouring the country. I want to kiss his hand still one of these fine days. We hear that a big convoy was taken near Fraserburg Road – deep in the Colony, and the Boers have taken a lot of ammunition again[32] (Bother! I have been interrupted about seven times while writing the above.) No, it is not use attempting to relate war news – we have no <u>facts</u>.

Yesterday I put on my best frock and went to the Mil[itary] Gov[ernor]'s office to see him about the camps and to ask what was being done for the approaching winter. At first he was a bit short with me

---

[32]   On 5 February 1902 a Boer commando under Fighting General Wynand Malan defeated a British force at Uitspanningsfontein near Fraserburg. As a result they captured a convoy of between 60 and 70 donkey wagons, without the loss of any casualties, while the British loss was 13 killed, 41 wounded and more than 250 prisoners of war. See H.J.C. Pieterse, *Oorlogsavonture van genl. Wynand Malan*, pp 284–288; P.G. Cloete, *The Anglo-Boer War a chronology*, p 300.

and told me not to "Jash"[33] myself, but when I said "But I do, and <u>will</u> as long as there is a camp in S[outh] A[frica]" he laughed a little and began telling me all their plans. Huts are being built in all the coldest camps – of bricks, with iron roofs, and the men have been commandeered to make wooden bed-steads, and hundreds and thousands of blankets are coming out. He showed me a plan of the huts and then a list of statistics. The mortality just now is wonderfully small. He promised to send me a full list of the rations they are getting now and put himself to no end of trouble to convince me that the people are in clover and have nothing to complain of now. I had a nice chat with him – asked him to make an end to the war soon because I want to go to Holland to get married – then he asked in some surprise if my fiancé was not still in the field – he thought he was.

Just as I was going away I reproached him laughingly with allowing his men to treat us so badly – searching our house and terrifying my Mammie while I was in J[o]h[anne]sburg. He wanted to know what I meant and said he knew absolutely nothing about it and would never have allowed such a thing – made notes of the date and how it was done and told me he was positive it was <u>not</u> by the order of the Commissioner of Police, he would make enquiries at once, etc. Evidently he really does not know anything about it and suggested that probably some enemy of ours had informed the police that there was a lot of ammunition hidden in our house, and looked more astonished than ever when I said "No, they were looking for <u>spies</u>". I could not help laughing and thanking him again sarcastically when he said we had behaved on the whole "fairly well" and he did not think we deserved such treatment. I wonder now where the suspicion came from – it is a mystery to me.

I am "*toch*"[34] so happy. The mother insists on my going to my beloved in May or June and I feel as if I cannot fight against everybody any longer. <u>Everyone</u> urges me to go and the general opinion is that the war is going to drag on for the next year of two. The preparations in the camps show that England herself does not hope for an early settlement, so why should I wait on here? I feel I <u>must</u> go to Lou and we must be married soon I can't live without him any longer and intend asking him to let us be united in holy wedlock in September at the very

---

33   Can be "task" or "fash".
34   Altogether.

latest, brazen-faced creature that I am. But he won't mind, I can stake my life on that.

Now in a few days I shall write again and then take this book away to some place of safety.

Feb[ruary] 23rd [1902] Sunday.

This is to be goodbye. I have been feeling very ill and stayed in bed the greater part of the day – but it was nothing unusual and this evening I am much brighter, but rather shaky.

Last night we had a visitor – an Englishman with very pro-Boer sympathies. We had a long and very interesting conversation about the war and I was delighted at his fair-mindedness. He has got permits to visit the Irene and Krugersdorp camps and tried hard to get a permit for me to accompany him, but every argument he used was in vain. All answer he got was "Not Miss v[an] W[armelo]" and when he asked for a satisfactory reason, Mr M[35] said "Well, you know she is such a propagandist". This is my newest name and delights everyone so much that I am sure it is going to stick to me. Mr LP[36] is so determined to have my company that he is going to try Gen Maxwell tomorrow but I am afraid it's no good. I am a black sheep – branded for life!

We talked last night of the shameful way the English make use of Boers against Boers and Mr LP condemned the policy utterly – not only on account of its baseness and immorality but because of the intense hatred and bitterness it is arousing amongst our own people – a hatred that will last for years and out live [sic] all the other evil passions excited by this cruel war. He says it is "Kitchener's pet scheme", he has done if before in previous campaigns and always with success, and every imaginable thing is being done here, to induce the Boers to take up arms against their brethern [sic]. All Superintendents of camps have orders to leave no argument untried and to bring the utmost pressure to bear upon their unhappy prisoners. Mr L[37] the superintendent of Krugersdorp camp is so much against it that he does not do it himself but leaves it to the officials under him. They say the turn-coats are over

---

35   Not identified.
36   Not identified.
37   Not identified.

2 000 strong and increase daily. In a letter from Bermuda a man tells his wife that now that "the agents" have gone they have some rest – they had no rest night or day and every mortal thing was done to induce the men to come out and fight. These sentences must have escaped the censor's notice, for we are made to believe that the men are clamouring in thousands to come out. From the depths of my heart I pity the unhappy wretches, who sell their souls – their honour, for money! They lose all self-respect with that first fatal downward step and then they go from bad to worse. I pity them, my heart is filled with deep compassion for them and yet – I loathe and despise them for their weakness. God knows that many of them are tempted almost beyond human endurance, but what of that? If a man cannot stand when such great issues are at stake, he deserves all the contempt he gets. Oh, in all this bitter war nothing has been so tragic as this proof of human weakness. And where is it going to? Our heroes in the field cannot stand against their own people – they are being captured in hundreds by these "National Corps", that have all the principal scouting to do, and if this goes on much longer we shall really find ourselves in a "guerrilla war" against a "few marauding bands" as the English have called it for more than a year.

And now, my own dear Love, I am going to send you this book. If you are disappointed that it contains so little about you and our love, remember that I was always afraid it would fall into English hands and wrote as guardedly as possible on that account. In this book you will find much to interest you but as a personal narrative it must be a disappointment to you. Needless to say, it is for your eyes only and you must believe me when I tell you that originally I did not even intend you to read any of my diaries. When I wrote them I could not have believed that I would ever let anyone else set eyes on them, but since I learnt to love you and especially since that Sunday morning (see Feb[ruary] 2nd) I have known that it would be impossible to keep anything from you, and in future I will write my diary for you.

I date our engagement from the 10th Nov[ember] for on that date I received the letter in which you say "I love you" and the same night I wrote to you, promising to be your wife, but real love only came to me in Feb[ruary] – this blessed month. Goodbye, beloved.

[Continue in Script VI again, after the entry on 1901-09-08]

Harmony. Pretoria. March 16th 1902.

I made away with this book in September last year and got it back yesterday, so I shall just fill up the remaining blank pages, for Harmony is quite safe for the present and I am not afraid of a second visit from the Khakis. I am very thankful I had no diaries here when our house was searched two months ago. Much has happened since I saw this book last but to me the most important event has been my sudden resolve to leave "*land en volk*"[38] for the man I have promised to marry. Elsewhere will be found all the reasons for this sudden plan – There is lots of news. Methuen's disaster seems to have been a second Magersfontein. 52 officers were killed, over 1 200 prisoners captured and an enormous convoy taken.[39] Lord Methuen was so badly wounded that the Boers gave him back to the English, but they are keeping his staff. General de la Rey gave him a "*schaap-bout*",[40] a few loaves of bread and a "*Jakals vel baatje*"[41] beautifully lined, which he values above everything. His leg has to be amputated, poor man, so he will never be on active service again and I hear that Gen Maxwell is going to take his place. I don't feel inclined to write any more this evening so goodnight.

March 18th [1902].

Mama is ill and we are "miserable" all around. That poor sister of mine is also having no end of trouble – servants etc and seems to be very melancholy. Henry[42] is against her coming to us and does everything to dissuade her, but she is determined to come if only her permit is granted, which I very much doubt it will be if it is true that Gen Maxwell has gone "to the front". – I have had to do everything today and feel very tired. I had to go and sing with Riek[H] this afternoon at Dr B[rugman]'s – a long walk and though I sang very well and enjoyed the

---

38   country and people
39   In the Battle of Tweebosch of 1902-03-07, General Koos de la Rey's commando inflicted a heavy defeat on the British forces of General Lord Methuen. The latter was himself wounded and captured. See J. Meintjies, *De la Rey – Lion of the West*, pp 235–237, 239–241.
40   Leg of mutton. Mrs Nonnie de la Rey wrote in her memoirs that she cooked him a chicken dinner. See J.E. de la Rey, *Mijne Omzwervingen en Beproevingen gedurende den Oorlog*, p 60.
41   A jacket made from jackal hides/skin.
42   Henry Cloete – husband of the diarist's sister Deliana (Line).

music immensely, I was too worried and tired and longed to get home. I was really in splendid voice. Yesterday Mrs Brugman had a wire from her father (Gen de la Rey) through Lord Kitchener, to say that he and "mother and the children" were well. It is said that Kitchener took the wire to B[rugman] himself! de la Rey treated Lord Methuen so well that the English want to do anything for him, but it won't keep them from catching him if they get the chance. They are after him now with 30 000 men.

March 25th [1902] .Tuesday.

General Koos de la Rey

It is exactly a week since I made my last entry and what a lot has happened since! Mama has been very ill again and I have had no end of cooking and nursing and housework to do, in fact, I am so worn out with want of rest that I can hardly hold my pen – Just look at this scrawl. I have never in my life been so worried and anxious. On Sunday night we got a few lines from Deliana to say that she has her permit and she is leaving Cape Town on Thursday. I was mad with excitement but the mother was too ill to rejoice. I am now busy cleaning up the house so as to be free when she comes. I have a woman to help me every morning and together we polish and rub and scour the whole day long – it is a terrible piece of work. Everything has been so long neglected that there is no end of cleaning to be done but I want the whole house to be spick and span when my beloved sister comes.

I have actually received my first wedding present – a beautiful little gold watch from an old friend. Mama is giving me her diamond brooch and set of garnets, so I am feeling quite rich already.

There was intense excitement in Town on Saturday. Six of our men, Schalk Burger, Reitz, Louis Jacobsz, Krogh, Lucas Meyer and vd Velde came to Pretoria under an armed escort to "negotiate" with Kitchener. I believe they spent the night here and went out the following day. They have gone to Kroonstad now to discuss matters with de Wet and Steyn.[43]

43   S.W. Burger was at that time the acting president, F.W. Reitz the state sec-

Many people say "peace is at our door" but I have not a grain of faith in these negotiations as long as the British refuse our independence.

March 30th [1902]. Sunday.

I must make an effort to write in my diary, though how that is to happen, with my beloved sister, large as life, sitting opposite me, I don't know. It is a blissful fact that she arrived last night. I met her at the Station but over that meeting we shall draw a veil, dear diary. She is looking too splendid, for anything – the picture of health and as sweet and good and beautiful as ever. I simply can't take my eyes off her and sit gazing at her in dumb admiration. And the way we talk! But I can't write about it – she wants me to go and sing and play to her. I shall never forget the week that is past. Mama was very ill all the time and I had to make all the preparations for receiving Line, in addition to the cooking, nursing etc. I got no sleep at night and no rest by day and was thoroughly knocked up, but today I took things easy and do nothing but talk and gaze at the vision of loveliness before me. Yesterday was one of the happiest in my life, crowned in the evening by a sweet and loving letter from my Lou.

April 6th [1902]. Sunday.

I am neglecting this book but never mind! There are other things to interest me now. But we have heard wonderful news and I must make a few entries. I think it was on Thursday that T.L.[44] told us in great confidence what the peace proposals are. There are five points:

1. The return of all our prisoners and free pardon for all rebels.
2. Full compensation for all the damage done.
3. The existence of the two republics under a united English and

---

retary, L.J. Jacobsz the assistant state attorney, J.C. Krogh and L.J. Meyer members of the executive council and D.E. van Velden the secretary of the executive council. These six members of the Transvaal government were in Pretoria on 22 March, but only spent an hour in the city on their way to Kroonstad. Peace negotiations were indeed beginning. See J.D. Kestell & D.E. van Velden, *De Vredesonderhandelingen tusschen de Regeering der twee Zuid-Afrikaansche Republieken en de Vertegenwoordigers der Britsche Regeering*, pp 12–13.

44   Not identified.

Boer flag – the Vierkleur and the Union Jack, and the Free State flag and the Union Jack.

4. That all burgers[45] who become subjects of the new Government may carry arms – no one else.

5. That the people choose a governor with the approval of the English Government.

If all this is true I am almost sure the Boers will accept and we shall have peace this month! but I have given up hoping for peace and just wait patiently for events to develope [sic] themselves. I am afraid to think of things being settled before I leave my beloved country – it would be too lovely for words. What a glorious meeting I would have with Lou and how absolutely perfect our honey-moon [sic] would be!!! Talking of honey-moons [sic] reminds me that my beloved's letter yesterday was so excited and happy at the prospect of seeing me so soon and Daisy [Brandt] writes also how glad they all are. I had a lovely mail. Oh, we are so happy lately that I am sure most of our troubles are over and nothing but joy is in store for us.

– Now let's think of news. The peace delegates after seeking vainly for Steyn and de Wet in the Free State are now waiting for them in Bloemfontein, where they are to be met by the six English delegates who have come out with Lord Wolseley to "confab" with our generals. Steyn and de Wet have been with de la Rey and are now supposed to be in Krugersdorp, from where they are going to join the others in Bloemfontein.[46] It is said that Louis Botha passed through Pretoria yesterday on his way to the conference, and we expect startling events soon. – General Maxwell is very badly wounded in the leg and is lying in the Klerksdorp hospital. The disaster to von Dunop's was on Feb[ruary] 24[th47] and since then we have had one victory after the other.

---

45 Citizens of the Republics.
46 These were false rumours.
47 On 25 February 1902 General Koos de la Rey's commandoes defeated a British unit under Lieutenant-Colonel S.P. von Donop at Yzerspruit in the Western Transvaal. As a result the Boers captured 127 wagons, two guns and large quantities of munitions. See J.C.G. Kemp, *Vir vryheid en vir reg*, pp 448–450.

Mrs Adriana de la Rey, mother of
General Koos de la Rey

April 12th [1902]. Saturday.
We are all in a great state of
excitement. This morning our
"peace" delegates arrived in Pretoria and are all here this very
minute, Botha, Steyn, de la Rey,
de Wet, Reitz and ever so many
others, and we think the conference will begin on Monday.
J.B.[48] came flying on his bicycle
this morning to tell us the news
and asked us to come over this
afternoon, as it is de la Rey's old
mother's[49] birthday, a *dapper*[50]
old lady of 84 years, but just as
we were getting dressed after dinner he came to tell us that they all
had permission to go and see the
general from 4 to 6, so we would
not find them at home now we
are dying to know how the event-
ful visit passed off and more than all we wonder what changes the next
few days will bring. We must just possess our souls in patience.

Now, dear diary, I want to tell you of a wonderful experience I had
last night. Deliana is a medium and goes in for spiritualism and last night
we had a séance – the first in my life and the most astonishing thing I
have ever come across. We were restless and miserable and longed to
know something definite about the future so we two decided to ask the
spirits some questions. Mama was asleep and we went quietly to the
drawing-room, where we arranged the letters of the alphabet in a circle
on a round table and placed a tumbler upside-down in the centre. We
sat opposite one another and touched the glass lightly with our four fingers (fore) and Deliana asked the first questions. "Is there a spirit in this

---

48   Probably Jacobus Brugman, General de la Rey's son-in-law.
49   Adriana Wilhelmina de la Rey (born Van Rooyen).
50   Gutsy.

room?" The glass did not move and she had to repeat it over and over again. At last I felt it stirring slightly and then the glass glided slowly from one letter to the other, Y E S, stopping a second before each letter and going back to the middle of the table when the word was spelt. "Whose spirit is it?" "Kanfoohoo" the answer was and Deliana told me that that was her spirit, the one who always answered her questions. "When shall we have peace?" In April. This year? Yes. Shall we have absolute independence? No. Peace with honour? Yes. Will the English be masters here? No. Have the powers intervened? No. Have you a message for us? Go to Colony. Why? English will be angry. Will they find out anything about us? Yes. (Then a dialogue followed that I cannot repeat here, but it was too marvellous for anything. We then asked: –) Is Fritz safe and well? Yes. Where? Colony. What part of the Colony? Jansenville. How is Dietlof? Well. – Then I asked the name of <u>my</u> spirit and it spelt

a long and curious name beginning with a Y. When shall I go
to Europe? In May, (but the first
time I asked this question the answer was "Brandt" and I believe
I must have <u>thought</u> "Whom
shall I marry?" so that the spirit
did not know which to answer)
When shall I be married? In
September. – We asked a great
many questions after that and
had some strange answers but
some things the spirit persistently
refused to answer and just spelt a
lot of meaningless words instead.
Once we asked again "Have you
a message for us?" and the answer was "Kanfoohoo" as much
as to say "I have told you once
what to do, and that is enough".
I was awfully excited but not
nervous and I felt as if it were all

President M.T. Steyn

quite natural but Deliana was tingling all over and streams of electricity were coursing through her veins and she did not sleep all night after it. It always takes it out of her terribly so she does it very seldom. Now we shall see how much truth there is in these answers.

April 22nd [1902]. Tuesday.

We have had no end of excitement since last I wrote. While our generals were here we were unfit for anything and just wanted to live on the streets in order to catch glimpses of them. We were unusually fortunate and were greeted several times by Steyn and de Wet, and once Gen Botha took off his hat to us from his balcony and kissed both hands to us. We were simply crazy with delight and it is astonishing the way a salute from a "Boar" can effect the patriotic mind. The house they were living in (Rood's)[51] was well guarded by armed Tommies who ordered us to "move on" whenever we stopped a moment to wave our handkerchiefs.

Parkzicht, the home of Karel Rood, where the Boer delegates stayed in April 1902

---

51   Parkzicht, in Maré Street (today Jacob Maré Street).

450

A great many ladies had permission to visit our dear generals, but most of them were related to them – there were only a few exceptions. We tried hard to be exceptions too, but it was no use and our permits were obstinately refused by that beautiful Provost Marshall, who seems to have some special spite against me! I detest the man, especially when he is sarcastically friendly and funny as he was the last time I had the misfortune to interview him. A few days ago I sent him a letter asking for my permit to leave S[outh] Africa, and last night his answer came .... "the present regulations do not allow burgers or their families to leave South Africa for the present."[52] I was amazed, but saw through it at once, a mean, sneaky bit of bullying and bravado, for no such regulations exist as Major Peters[53] told me himself this afternoon I went to him and he has promised to see Colonel Poore tomorrow morning and let me know. I am not a burger, neither am I the family of a burger, so I don't see how I can be kept in S[outh] A[frica] against my wish. For years we were afraid the British would send us out of the country and now that I want to go my permit is refused. Well, well, this is a beautiful state of affairs, and there my poor Lou is waiting and longing for me and blessing every hour that passes. – Henry [Cloete] writes that I must let him know at once whether he must book my passage by the "Galicia", which sails on the 14ᵗʰ May, or by the "Aberdeen", sailing on the 20ᵗʰ. I have decided for the latter, as it gives me more time, and it strikes me I shall require plenty of time if they are going to make such a fuss about my permit.

Line and I are going to visit Irene on Friday – There is quite a history attached to the way we got those permits but I have no time to go

---

52 On 21 April 1902 Poore wrote the following official letter to the diarist: "Your letter of the 18ᵗʰ April to hand. I shall be very glad to know if you have a permit to proceed to Europe. The present regulations do not allow burghers or their families to go out of South Africa for the present." (Archives of the *Nederduitsch Hervormde Kerk van Afrika,* Pretoria, L.E. Brandt Collection, LIX/163, file titled *Korrespondensie met vriende en kennisse, 1897–1900,* unsorted, R.M. Poore, Lt Col – Miss J. van Warmelo, 21 April 1902.)

53 Either Major C.W. Peters, who was the Assistant to the Military Governor, Pretoria (See National Archives, Pretoria, TAB, T115, Inventory to the Papers of the Military Governor Pretoria, p vii), or P.M. Peters, who was appointed (as a Captain) as a staff member of the Commissioner of Police in Pretoria in June 1900. See Transvaal *Government Gazette Extraordinary,* 1/2, 16 June 1900, p 9.

into details – we are frightfully busy now, for of course I am just going on with my packing and goodbye visits.

No one knows what the result is of the Peace Conference. Our generals went back to their commandos on the 18th or 19th, to lay the terms before the burgers who have to decide whether they can be accepted or not. We don't know yet <u>what</u> the terms are.

A[ndrew] B[rown] came over from Johannesburg to pay me a goodbye visit. He stayed from Sat[urday] till Monday afternoon and I saw him <u>six</u> times! What will my Lou say, I wonder? But it is all right, my own dear Love, you need'nt [sic] be at all anxious about my friendship with AB. We had several long and intimate conversations and got to know one another far better than before and I think ever so much more highly of him now. He is a splendid man and an ideal friend. We had a little séance one evening just to show him, because he was so much interested in the subject, but we only asked a few questions, and "Father" answered. When we asked if it were right to communicate with spirits, the answer was "Spiritualism is God's message on earth". The[n] Andrew asked what the work of the guardian angels is and the answer was, "To rescue".

Once we had a séance with Oom Paul, who was simply amazed at the answers. "Father" answered then and said my guardian angel is "Zoroaster" – Line's, "Queen Yolande", Mama's, "Anne of York" and Oom Paul's, "Kuyper"! (Andrew's was Bruno, to our amusement.) The strange part of it was that Oom Paul told us long ago that a medium once said to him, "Mr Maré, whenever I see you I see a man beside you – a tall Dutchman, in a reddish brown moleskin suit, with a scar on his forehead". Oom Paul thought about it and then said that exactly described a man he knew in Zoutpansberg long ago – a big Hollander, who shot himself through the head. He wore a suit of that description. We were astonished when he told us this but our amazement knew no bounds when the glass deliberately spelt the word "Kuyper". That day we had some more strange answers. Oom Paul had to "leave Pretoria" and we were again advised most urgently to "prepare leave soon"[.] When Mama asked for advice she got this, "Boni (the Italian)[54] must get garden" and then she asked to whom the house must be let and the

---

54   Not identified.

answer was "James le Pla". The strange thing about it is that Mr le Pla wishes to come and live here and has asked us to let him have the house if Mama thinks of going away. The spirits told us for the third time that Fritz was in Jansenville and under "General Maritz"[55] we were informed last time. – Spiritualism is a most wonderful thing.

April 27th [1902]. Sunday.

It is very sad that my heart should be so heavy and troubled on a divinely beautiful morning like this, and yet, so it is. The last thing in the world that I expected has befallen me, viz. refusal on the part of the English to grant my permit to leave South Africa. They say it is against present regulations, but my opinion is that it is a bit of personal spite on Col Poore's part, and they are afraid I will make use of what I know of the camps. My preparations are at a standstill now and I am at my wit's end. I have written to Lord Kitchener myself and am looking out eagerly for his answer – if he condescends to answer, which I am inclined to doubt. Yesterday's mail took the sad news to my Lou, but I have decided to cable to him as soon as I know definitely what my fate is going to be.

Deliana and I went to Irene Camp on Friday and had a delightful day. It rained heavily the night before and we were afraid we would have to swim to the Station, but when the sun rose the clouds dispersed and the air became clear and fresh and a high wind blew all day, so that we were cool all the time and had no dust at all. We could not possibly have had finer weather, in fact everything was in our favour that day. We reached the Station ¾ h[ou]rs too soon, through a misunderstanding but we were thankful afterwards, for we found a whole truck full of women and children, waiting to be sent to Natal. There were five families in one open truck and they had been all night in the rain, tiny babies and little children. We stood talking to them quite a long time and they told us they were brought from their farms in the north of Zoutpansberg, where they had been living in peace and comfort all the time. Their homes were destroyed, so it is a lie when the British assert that the work of devastation has long since ceased, and they were

---

55   The only General Maritz in the Republican forces was S.G. (Manie) Maritz, who was active in the Northwestern Cape at that time and was never even close to Jansenville, which is in the Eastern Cape. See S.B. Spies, Maritz, Salomon Gerhardus (Manie), in *DSAB* I, p 513.

brought to Pretoria without food or clothing. I fortunately had some money with me and gave them about £10. We had £50 to distribute at Irene – money that was sent to us from Switzerland – and I had the bag and a note-book and believe me, I made many sad hearts happy that day. We came home without a penny and I could easily have given out £1 000, there was so much want – but only in the way of clothing, for the rations they get now are excellent and more than enough.

April 30th [1902]. Wednesday.

I was too lazy last Sunday to finish about Irene and now I am too nervous and unstrung. I have had a dreadful experience – but more of this presently. Let me first finish with Irene. We found the camp shifted to a new situation and tremendously improved in every respect. There are 2 300 children under 16 y[ea]rs and they look brown and healthy and happy, in fact, I noticed the same air of contentment and prosperity all over the camp. I found a great many of my old friends and I was made more than happy by what they told me of their present treatment, and we had a fine dinner in one of the tents – good meat, stewed with potatoes, carrots, rice with raisins, beetroot salad, bread and coffee. They have had plenty of vegetables the whole summer and get milk and syrup, good flour and plenty of frozen meat, so they have nothing to complain of in that respect. The children get a mug of good broth once a day and more "Ideal Milk" than they can use. All we have to complain of now, is the clothing, which is very scanty and threadbare, and the tents. The latter are getting woefully ragged with the long exposure to the elements, and with the winter on us, this is certainly a matter of serious importance. After dinner there was an opening service held in the new building which has been erected, a huge place with an iron roof resting on rafters, and strong canvas sides. The service was conducted by Rev Bosman and we attended – sat in seats of honour on his right hand, facing the densely packed congregation. I think there must have been quite 1 500 people and it was a most impressive ceremony which I would not have missed for anything.

The 'hall' in the Irene Concentration Camp

After the service Mr Bosman addressed a few words of thanks and appreciation to the Superintendent, Mr Bruce, in the name of all the people, who seem to adore him. Mr Bruce answered most feelingly and then Mr Bosman announced to the people that they had in their midst the two daughters of their most honoured and beloved "leeraar,[56] Ds van Warmelo", whose services etc etc. Both daughters work and live only for one thing, "the cause", and the elder was here on a visit from the Colony, while the younger hoped soon to depart for Holland, where she intended entering into holy ... etc etc and may all good wishes follow her!!! We were quite overcome by this unexpected publicity and just looked straight before us with crimson cheeks and big lumps in our throats. I always get like that when my father's name is mentioned. Afterwards we asked to be introduced to Mr Bruce and he was charming to us, drove us all about the camp in his dog-cart, showed us the hospital with its latest improvements and did everything in his power to make our visit enjoyable. I have no time now to say more but we came home quite happy and satisfied and no detail of that eventful day will escape our memory.

I have not heard from Lord K[itchener] yet so my fate is still undecided and in consequence my health is giving way. I have borne many

---

[56]   Minister.

things patiently and have suffered long but this is the climax, and now I don't know what to do or how to endure it. Since that first refusal I have had a wonderful throbbing in my throat, every time I think or speak about my permit my throat begins to throb and I feel as if I want to laugh and cry and scream. I told the mother and she looked serious and said it was a sort of hysteria, so I must keep myself calm and well-controlled, but last night at supper we had an argument and they contradicted me and I flew into a rage – insulted the mother and Line, sprang up, sent my cup and saucer crashing to the floor, rushed about the room uttering shriek after shriek and pummelling the sofa and cushions. It must have been something terrific, but I know nothing about it until I found myself pinioned in Line's arms and my face and head dashed with cold water. When I saw the ruins about me and heard my own mad yells I thought I had lost my reason and that made me worse again. Even now I hear myself shrieking "Ma, Ma, Line, ik is gek geworden!"[57] It was too horrible, but I became calm afterwards and lay on the sofa thoroughly exhausted. I had a bad night after it and feel nervous and restless now. I am horrified at myself and wonder how I could have lost my self control so completely, but it only shows how I am run down by all we have suffered. Now that I am prepared for it I do not think such a thing will occur again. – We spent this afternoon with Mrs Brugman and had the pleasure of meeting her grannie, [sic] our general de la Rey's mother, a dear, *dapper* old lady of 84 years – but more about her some other time, I am too tired now.

The end of my war-diary: –
"I am too tired now"

Johannesburg, June 23 [year not mentioned]

---

[57] "Mother, Mother, Line, I am going mad!"

Bibliography

(The acronym *DSAB* stands for
Dictionary of South African Biography.
For archival sources see footnotes.)

Amery, L.S., *The Times history of the war in South Africa, 1899–1902.*
7 volumes. London, 1900–1909.

Anon, Beyers, Christiaan Frederik, in *DSAB* III, pp 64–67.

Anon, *Mrs Grundy,* http://en.wikipedia.org/wiki/Mrs_Grundy, accessed 24
July 2007.

Anon, *Officers died: South Africa 1899 – 1902,* http://redcoat.future.
easyspace.com/BoerP.html, accessed 25 April 2003.

Anon, *Boer War Services of Military Officers of the British and Colonial
Armies Imperial Yeomanry Infantry Local Units & cc 1899 – 1902
including Earlier Services.* Savannah Publications, 1999.

Anon, Steyn, Marthinus Theunis, in *DSAB* II, pp 707–715.

Anon, *The 1892 Double Shafted pound that nearly brought down the Kruger
Government,* http://www.tokencoins.com/zar03.htm, accessed 2 June
2006.

Augustus, D.S., Maxwell, Sir John Grenfell, in *DSAB* V, pp 496–497.

Batts, H.J., *Pretoria from within during the War 1899-1900.* London, 1901.

Brandt, J., *The Petticoat Commando, or Boer Women in Secret
Service,* 1913. Translated into Dutch as *Die Kappie Kommando of
Boerevrouwen in Geheime Dienst,* Kaapstad, Hollandsch-Afrikaansche
Uitgevers-Maatschappij, 1915 (Second printing).

Brandt-van Warmelo, J., *Het Concentratie-kamp van Iréne.* Amsterdam,
Cape Town, 1905.

Botha, J.P., *Die beleg van Mafeking tydens die Anglo-Boereoorlog.*
Unpublished thesis, University of South Africa, 1967.

Breytenbach, J.H., *Die Geskiedenis van die Tweede Vryheidsoorlog in
Suid-Afrika, 1899–1902.* 6 volumes. Pretoria, Government Printer,
1969–1983.

Brits, J.P. Botha, Philip Rudolph, in *DSAB* IV, pp 51–52.

Brits, J.P., Naudé, Jacobus Johannes, in *DSAB* III, p 652.

Brits, J.P., Pretorius, Johannes Lodewicus (Lood), in *DSAB* III,
pp 693–694.

Changuion, L., *Silence of the guns. The history of the Long Toms of the Anglo-Boer War.* Pretoria, Protea Book House, 2001.

Changuion, L., *Uncle Sam, Oom Paul en John Bull: Amerika en die Anglo-Boereoorlog, 1899 – 1902.* Pretoria, Protea Boekhuis, 2001.

Cloete, P.G., *The Anglo-Boer War a chronology.* Pretoria, J.P. van der Walt, 2000.

Davenport, T.R.H., *South Africa. A modern history.* Fourth Edition, London, 1991.

Davey, A.M. (ed.), *Breaker Morant and the Bushveldt Carbineers.* Van Riebeeck Society Second Series No. 18, Cape Town, 1987.

Dekker, G., Van Wouw, Anton, in *DSAB* I, pp 841–844.

De Kock, W.J., *Die Krügerhuis Pretoria. 'n Aandenkingsbrosjure.* Pretoria, 1949.

De la Rey, J.E., *Mijne Omzwervingen en Beproevingen gedurende den Oorlog.* Amsterdam, Hoveker & Wormser, 1903.

De Villiers, D.W., Ackermann, Daniël Petrus, in *DSAB* V, p 2.

De Wet, C.R., *Die Stryd tussen Boer en Brit. Die Herinneringe van die Boere-Generaal C.R. de Wet,* translated into Afrikaans and annotated by M.C.E. van Schoor, Kaapstad, Tafelberg, 1999.

Donaldson & Hill's Transvaal and Rhodesia Directory 1899. Johannesburg, 1899.

Dreyer, P.S., Brandt, Louis Ernst, in *DSAB* II, p 84.

Du Plessis, J.S., De la Rey, Jacobus Hercules, in *DSAB* I, pp 214–218.

Du Plessis, J.S. Joubert, Petrus Jacobus, in *DSAB* I, pp 412–417.

Du Preez, S., *Vredespogings gedurende die Anglo-Boereoorlog tot Maart 1901.* Unpublished MA dissertation, University of Pretoria, 1976.

Du Toit, B., *Die verhaal van Johanna Brandt.* Protea Boekhuis, Pretoria, 1999.

Du Toit, F.G.M., Brandt, Johanna, in *DSAB* IV, p 55.

Du Toit, F.G.M., Bosman, Hermanus Stephanus, in *DSAB* I, pp 104–105.

Engelenburg, F.V. & Preller, G.S., *Onze Krijgs-Officieren. Album van portretten met levens-schetsen der Transvaalse Generaals en Kommandanten e.a.* Pretoria, Uitgegeven ten "Volksstem" kantore, 1904.

Ferreira, O.J.O. (ed.), *Geschiedenis Werken en Streven van S.P.E. Trichard, Luitenant Kolonel der vroegere Staats-artillerie ZAR door hemzelve beschreven.* Human Sciences Research Council, Pretoria, 1975.

Ferreira, O.J.O., Hart (later Hart-Synnot), Arthur Fitzroy, in *DSAB* III, pp 374–375.

Ferreira, O.J.O. (ed.), *Krijgsgevangenschap van L.C. Ruijssenaers 1899 – 1902.* Human Sciences Research Council, Pretoria, 1977.

Fourie, L.M., *Die militêre loopbaan van Manie Maritz tot aan die einde van die Anglo-Boereoorlog.* MA dissertation, Potchefstroom University, 1975.

Garson, N.G., Rhodes, Cecil John, in *DSAB* III, pp 704–715.

Government Gazette / Government Gazette Extraordinary (Transvaal), Pretoria, 1900–1902.

Greyling, P.J., *Pretoria and the Anglo-Boer War.* Pretoria, 2000.

Grobler, J.E.H., *Die Eerste Vryheidsoorlog 1880–1881, 'n militêr-historiese benadering.* Unpublished D.Phil thesis, Pretoria, University of Pretoria, 1980.

Grundlingh, A.M., *Die "hendsoppers" en "joiners". Die rasionaal en verskynsel van verraad.* Protea Boekhuis, Pretoria, 1999.

Harington, A.L. Lyttelton, Sir Neville Gerald, in *DSAB* IV, p 334.

Harington, A.L., Milner, Alfred, First Viscount, in *DSAB* III, pp 613–617.

Harington, A.L., Victoria (Alexandrina Victoria), in *DSAB* V, pp 841–842.

Harvey, P. (ed), *The Oxford Companion to English Literature.* Fourth, Revised Edition, Oxford, Clarendon Press, 1973.

Hattingh, J.L., *Die Irenekonsentrasiekamp,* Archives Year Book of South African History 30(1), Johannesburg, 1967.

Henning, C.G., Ten Brink, Jan Hendrik, in *DSAB* IV, pp 643–644.

Hind, R.J., Labouchere, Henry Du Pré, in *DSAB* III, pp 492–493.

Hiemstra, V.G., Ameshoff, Herman Arnold, in *DSAB* III, pp 20–21.

Kemp, J.C.G., *Vir vryheid en vir reg.* Kaapstad, Bloemfontein & Port Elizabeth, Nasionale Pers Beperk, 1941.

Kempff, K., Oerder, Frans David, in *DSAB* IV, pp 418–420.

Kepper, G.L., *De Zuid-Afrikaansche Oorlog. Historisch Gedenkboek.* Leiden, c1900.

Kestell, J.D. & D.E. van Velden, *De Vredesonderhandelingen tusschen de Regeering der twee Zuid-Afrikaansche Republieken en de Vertegenwoordigers der Britsche Regeering, welke uitliepen op den Vrede, op 31 Mei 1902 te Vereeniging gesloten.* Pretoria – Amsterdam, J.H. de Bussy, 1909.

Krüger, D.W., Botha, Louis, in *DSAB* IV, pp 41–51.

Krüger, D.W., Du Toit, Heinrich Sebastian Davel, in *DSAB* III, p 253.

Krüger, D.W., Hofmeyr, Adriaan Jacobus Louw, in *DSAB* III, pp 401–402.

Krüger, D.W., Kritzinger, Pieter Hendrik, in *DSAB* III, p 693–694.

Krüger, D.W., Kruger, Stephanus Johannes Paulus, in *DSAB* I, pp 444–455.

Krüger, D.W., Leyds, Willem Johannes, in *DSAB* III, pp 516–520.

Krüger, D.W., Stead, William Thomas, in *DSAB* II, pp 704–705.

Krüger, D.W., Viljoen, Benjamin Johannes, in *DSAB* IV, pp 740–742.

Kruger, R., *Good-Bye Dolly Gray. A history of the Boer War.* London, 1967.

Leverton, B.J.T., Graaff, Sir David Pieter de Villiers, in *DSAB* II, pp 267–269.

Leverton, B.J.T., Hamilton, Sir Bruce Meade, in *DSAB* III, p 379.

Leverton, B.J.T., Sanford, Paul, third Baron Methuen of Corsham, in *DSAB* II, pp 616–617.

Lombard, R.T.J., Maré, Dietlof Siegfried, in *DSAB* II, p 446.

Lombard, R.T.J., Maré, Tobias Johannes Albertus, in *DSAB* III, p 581.

Longland's Pretoria Dictionary for 1899. Johannesburg, 1899.

Meijer, J.W., *Generaal Ben Viljoen 1868–1917.* Pretoria, Protea Boekhuis, 2000.

Meintjies, J, *De la Rey – Lion of the West. A biography.* Johannesburg, Hugh Keartland, 1966.

Methuen, A.M.S., *Peace or war in South Africa.* London, 1901.

Mouton, J.A., *Genl Piet Joubert in die Transvaalse Geskiedenis.* Archives Year Book of South African history 20(1), Cape Town, Government Printer, 1957.

Musiker, R. and N., Franks, Sir Kendal Matthew St John, in *DSAB* V, pp 277–278.

Natal Witness, Durban, 1901.

Naudé, J.F., *Vechten en vluchten van Beyers en Kemp "bokant" De Wet.* Rotterdam, 1903.

Oberholster, A.G. (ed.), *Oorlogsdagboek van Jan F.E. Celliers 1899–1902.* Human Sciences Research Council, Pretoria, 1978.

Ould, C.R., Poutsma, Hessel Jacob, in *DSAB* I, pp 672–673.

Otto, J.C., *Die konsentrasiekampe.* Cape Town et al, 1954.

Pakenham, T., *The Boer War.* New York, Random House, 1979.

Pereira, E., Baden-Powell, Robert Stephenson Smyth, in *DSAB* I, pp 33–34.

Pienaar, T.C., Armstrong, Henriette Ester Carolina, in *DSAB* III, pp 30–31.

Pienaar, T.C., Botha, Annie Frances Bland, in *DSAB* III, p 89.

Pieterse, H.J.C., *Oorlogsavonture van genl. Wynand Malan.* Cape Town et al, Nasionale Pers Beperk, 1946 (second printing).

Ploeger, J., Coster, Hermanus (Herman) Jacob, in *DSAB* II, pp 148–149.

Ploeger, J., De Wildt, Mauritz Edgar, in *DSAB* V, pp 196–197.

Ploeger, J., Fockens, Willem Jacobus, in *DSAB* III, pp 300–301.

Ploeger, J., Höhls, Johann Otto, in *DSAB* III, p 408.

Ploeger, J., *Nederlanders in Transvaal 1850–1950.* Pretoria, J.L. van Schaik, 1994.

Ploeger, J., Van Alphen, Isaac Nicolaas, in *DSAB* V, pp 788–789.

Ploeger, J., Wilhelmina (Helena Paulin Maria), *DSAB* IV, pp 780–781.

Ploeger, J., Wolmarans, Jan Francois, in *DSAB* III, p 852.

Pont, A.D., Goddefroy, Marius Joseph, in *DSAB* III, p 329.

Pont, A.D., *Nicolaas Jacobus van Warmelo 1835–1892.* Utrecht, Drukkerij en Uitgevers-Maatschappij v/h Kemink & Zoon NV, 1955.

Pont, A.D., Van Warmelo, Nicolaas Jacobus, in *DSAB* I, pp 840–841.

Preller, G.S. (ed.), *Scheepers se dagboek en die stryd in Kaapland (1 Okt. 1901 – 18 Jan. 1902).* Kaapstad, Bloemfontein en Port Elizabeth, Nasionale Pers Bpk., 1938.

Preller, J.F., Erasmus, Daniël Jacobus Elardus, in *DSAB* II, pp 219–220.

Reitz, F.W., *Oorlogs en andere gedichten.* Potchefstroom, Unie Lees- en Studie-Bibliotheek, 1910.

Roberts, B., *Those Bloody Women. Three Heroines of the Boer War.* London, John Murray, 1991.

Scheepers Strydom, C.J., *Kaapland en die Tweede Vryheidsoorlog.* Nasionale Pers, Kaapstad, Bloemfontein & Port Elizabeth, 1943 (Second printing).

Schoeman, J., *Generaal Hendrik Schoeman – was hy 'n verraaier?* Pretoria, 1950.

Schoeman, J.M., Burger, Schalk Willem, in *DSAB* II, pp 106–108.

Schoeman, J.M., Kock (Kok), Johannes Hermanus Michiel, in *DSAB* II, pp 370–371.

Schoeman, J.M., Meyer (Meijer), Lukas (Lucas) Johannes, in *DSAB* III, pp 607–608.

Scholes, P.A. (ed.), *The Oxford Companion to Music.* Tenth edition, London, 1974.

Scholtz, G.D., *Europa en die Tweede Vryheidsoorlog 1899–1902.* Johannesburg & Pretoria, Voortrekkerpers Beperk, 1939.

Scholtz, G.D., *Generaal Christiaan Frederik Beyers 1869–1914.* Johannesburg et al., Voortrekkerpers Beperk, 1941.

Scholtz, G.D., *In Doodsgevaar. Die Oorlogservarings van Kapt. J.J. Naudé tydens die Tweede Vryheidsoorlog 1899–1902.* Johannesburg, Voortrekkerpers Beperk, 1940.

Smith, I.R., *The Origins of the South African War, 1899–1902.* London & New York, Longman, 1996.

Spies, F.J. du T., Middelberg, Gerrit Adriaan Arnold, in *DSAB* II, pp 473–474.

Spies, F.J. du T., Wierda, Sytze Wopke(s), in *DSAB* III, pp 842–843.

Spies, S.B., Buller, Sir Redvers Henry, in *DSAB* II, pp 99–101.

Spies, S.B., Churchill, Sir Winston Leonard Spencer, in *DSAB* V, pp 126–129.

Spies, S.B., French, John Denton Pinkstone, in *DSAB* II, pp 242–243.

Spies, S.B., Kekewich, Robert George, in *DSAB* II, pp 360–361.

Spies, S.B., Kemp, Jan Christoffel Greyling, in *DSAB* I, pp 420–421.

Spies, S.B., Kitchener, Horatio Herbert, in *DSAB* II, pp 365–368.

Spies, S.B., Maritz, Salomon Gerhardus (Manie), in *DSAB* I, pp 513–515.

Spies, S.B., Roberts, Frederick Sleigh, in *DSAB* II, pp 598–602.

Spies, S.B., Schoeman, Hendrik Jacobus, in *DSAB* II, pp 633–634.

Spies, S.B., *Methods of Barbarism? Roberts and Kitchener and Civilians in the Boer Republics January 1900 – May 1902.* Cape Town & Pretoria, Human & Rousseau, 1978.

Smit, A.P. & L. Maré (ed.), *Die beleg van Mafeking. Dagboek van Abraham Stafleu.* Pretoria, Human Sciences Research Council, 1985.

Theron, B. (ed.), *Dear Sue. The letters of Bessie Collins from Pretoria during the Anglo-Boer War.* Pretoria, Protea Boekhuis, 2000.

Theron, B., *Pretoria at war 1899–1900.* Pretoria, Protea Book House, 2000.

Thompson, D. (ed.) *The Concise Oxford Dictionary of Current English.* Ninth Edition. Oxford, Oxford University Press, 1995.

Van Dalsen, J., *Die Hollander Korps tydens die Tweede Vryheidsoorlog.* Unpublished MA dissertation, University of Pretoria, 1942.

Van den Bergh, G., *24 Veldslae en Slagvelde van die Noordwes Provinsie.* Potchefstroom, 1996.

Van den Bergh, G.N., Van Dam, Gerard Marie Johan, in *DSAB* II, pp 764–765.

Van den Hoek, A., Lötter, Johannes Cornelius, in *DSAB* V, pp 462–463.

Van der Merwe, M.E., *Johanna Brandt en die kritieke jare in Transvaal, 1899 – 1908.* Unpublished MA dissertation, Pretoria, University of Pretoria, 1989.

Van der Merwe, N.J., *Marthinus Theunis Steyn, 'n lewensbeskrywing,* II. Kaapstad, 1921.

Van der Poel, J. & S.I.M. du Plessis, Smuts, Jan Christiaan (Christian), in *DSAB* I, pp 737–758.

Van der Walt, H.R., Greene, Sir William Conyngham, in *DSAB* III, pp 346–347.

Van Dyk, J.H., Eloff, Sarel Johannes, in *DSAB* III, pp 270–271.

Van Oudsthoorn, W.P. van R., Delfos, Cornelis Frederik, in *DSAB* II, pp 170–171.

Van Reenen, R. (ed.), *Emily Hobhouse. Boer War letters.* Human & Rousseau, Cape Town & Pretoria, 1984.

Van Rensburg, T. (ed.), *Camp diary of Henrietta E.C. Armstrong: Experiences of a Boer nurse in the Irene concentration camp, 6 April – 11 October 1901.* Pretoria, Human Sciences Research Council, 1980.

Van Rensburg, T. (ed.), *Vir vaderland, vryheid en eer. Oorlogsherinneringe van Wilhelm Mangold 1899–1902.* Pretoria, Human Sciences Research Council, 1988.

Van Rhyn, J.N.R., Krause, Frederick (Fritz) Edward Traugott, in *DSAB* III, pp 479–480.

Van Schoor, M.C.E., *'n Bittereinder aan die woord, Marthinus Theunis Steyn.* Bloemfontein, Oorlogsmuseum van die Boererepublieke, 1997.

Van Warmelo, D.S., *Mijn commando en guerilla commando-leven.* Amsterdam, A. Versluys, 1901.

Van Warmelo, J., War diary (7 volumes, unpublished), Archives of the *Nederduitsch Hervormde Kerk,* Pretoria.

Van Warmelo, P., Kock, Antonie (Antonius, Antoine) Francois, in *DSAB* IV, p 283.

Van Zyl, M.C., Schiel, Adolf Friedrich, in *DSAB* II, pp 628–629.

Volkstem, De. Pretoria, 1899.

Wasserman, J. & B. Kearney (eds), *A warrior's gateway. Durban and the Anglo-Boer War 1899–1902.* Pretoria, 2002.

Webster, N., *Webster's Comprehensive Reference Dictionary and Encyclopaedia.* The World Publishing Company, 1951.

Webster, N. & F.J. Meine, *The Consolidated Webster encyclopaedic dictionary; a library of essential knowledge.* Chicago, 1947.

Wessels, A., *Die Anglo-Boereoorlog 1899–1902, 'n oorsig van die militêre verloop van die stryd.* Bloemfontein, Oorlogsmuseum van Boererepublieke, 1991.

Witton, G.R., *Scapegoats of the Empire. The story of the Bushveldt Carbineers.* Melbourne, 1907.

Index